THE ROSE AND GERYON

THE ROSE AND GERYON

The Poetics of Fraud and Violence in Jean de Meun and Dante

Gabriella I. Baika

The Catholic University of America Press
Washington, D.C.

The paper used in this publication meets the minimum requirements of American National Standards for Information Science—Permanence of Paper for Printed Library Materials, ANSI Z39.48-1984.
∞

LIBRARY OF CONGRESS
CATALOGING-IN-PUBLICATION DATA

Baika, Gabriella I.
The rose and geryon : the poetics of fraud and violence in Jean de Meun and Dante / Gabriella I. Baika.
pages cm
Includes bibliographical references and index.
ISBN 978-0-8132-2609-5 (cloth : alk. paper)
1. Guillaume, de Lorris, active 1230. Roman de la rose. 2. Jean, de Meun, approximately 1240–approximately 1305—Ethics. 3. Dante Alighieri, 1265–1321. Divina commedia. 4. Dante Alighieri, 1265–1321—Ethics. 5. Literature, Medieval—History and criticism. 6. Rhetoric, Medieval. 7. Language and languages in literature. 8. Vices in literature. 9. Ethics in literature. I. Title.
PQ1528.B25 2014
841'.1—dc23 2013050344

To Ioan ("Jean") and Virginia Baciu,
and Marian Papahagi,
in piam memoriam

As modern readers we shall stand helpless before the *Roman* and a great deal else in medieval literature unless we are willing to assess the implications of the profound and essential differences between the foundations of medieval thought and those of our own—which is easy enough to say, but laborious to try to carry out. The exercise of the historical imagination requires both hard work and creative insight; it can promise at best only partial success, and it often fails totally. Yet the game is worth the candle.

{John V. Fleming, *The "Roman de la Rose"* 204}

Contents

Acknowledgments

When I began writing my PhD dissertation under the direction of Marian Papahagi, a renowned scholar of Romance languages, I could not foresee that I would eventually finish my dissertation, but not the same one, and not with the same director. The premature death of Marian Papahagi put an end to my dream of becoming a Romance philologist but, at the same time, opened for me venues that I had never envisioned before. The intellectual addiction to old literary texts that he had instilled in me, along with my personal interest in religious studies due to my Christian upbringing, led me to another PhD program, at the University of Pittsburgh. The present book is a distant relative of the dissertation on transgressive speech in the *Romance of the Rose* and the *Divine Comedy* that I wrote and defended at Pitt under the direction of two of the finest medievalists there are: Renate Blumenfeld-Kosinski and Dennis Looney. They are part of a small but extraordinary department that keeps fighting worldly adversities to ensure the prestigious Romance cultures the exalted station they deserve. Their exceptional expertise in their professional field is paralleled only by their outstanding human qualities.

I am equally indebted to Yves Citton, this formidable *éminence grise* of my professional decisions, who has supported my work with interest and heart-warming enthusiasm. Diana Mériz, my favorite scholar of Old Provençal, and colleagues from the department of Humanities and Communication at Florida Institute of Technology, Anna Montoya and Robert Shearer in particular, have kindly read, and commented on, sections of this book. I am also grateful to my Italian colleagues, Simone Tarud Bettini from the University of Bologna, and Mauro Zanchetta from the University of Padua, who for the last year have kept me updated on the research on Domenico Cavalca in Italy and have clarified some of my questions. Over the course of the last three years, Christopher Kleinhenz has generously accepted excerpts from this project as paper presentations in the Dante sessions at the International Congress on Medieval Studies at Kalamazoo. Reinhold Glei, editor in chief of *Medievalia et Humanistica,* and Gianni Cicali, editor in chief of *Quaderni d'italianistica,* have kindly allowed me to incorporate into this book my essays on Faus Semblant and Ulysses, respectively. Thus, the section on "Bilinguium" appeared in a slighly different version in *Medievalia et Humanistica* 35 (2009): 15–32, and the section on "Evil counselors in the *Inferno*" was published in an earlier version in *Quaderni di italianistica*, no. 2 (2011): 5–26.

My humblest thanks go to Trevor Lipscombe, director of the Catholic University of America Press, whose editorial flair, availability, and effectiveness have made possible the publication of my manuscript and, thereby, the fulfillment of a dream. I owe to Carol A. Kennedy an attentive and meticulous copyediting of my manuscript.

Last but not least, I thank my family, my daughter especially, who has grown up with this project (and many times fiercely competed with it), and who represents my constantly renewed source of energy, hope, and love.

THE ROSE AND GERYON

Introduction

As early as the fifteenth century, readers of Jean de Meun's *Romance of the Rose* and Dante's *Divine Comedy* compared the two poetic narratives, discovering striking resemblances between them and highlighting a common concern with human vices as the primary link between the two poems. Christine de Pizan (1365–ca. 1434) and Laurent de Premierfait (ca. 1380–1418) were the first to comment on the two works from a comparative perspective, thus pioneering a critical practice of collating the *Rose* and the *Comedy* from various viewpoints in order to illustrate aspects of the medieval civilization.[1] The year 1878 marked a turning point in this comparative approach with the discovery of the *Fiore* and the *Detto d'Amore,* two thirteenth-century Italian translations of the *Romance of the Rose.* Based on a textual analysis of these findings, Gianfranco Contini and Luigi Vanossi have credited Dante Alighieri with penning the *Fiore,* an authorship that would represent the irrefutable piece of evidence for both Dante's familiar-

1. For the full text of Laurent's and Christine's comparisons between the *Rose* and the *Comedy,* see Christine McWebb, ed., *Debating the "Roman de la Rose": A Critical Anthology* (New York: Routledge, 2007), 176, 422. Sylvia Huot offers insightful comments on Christine de Pizan's assessment of Jean and Dante, in "Seduction and Sublimation: Christine de Pizan, Jean de Meun, and Dante," *Romance Notes* 25 (1985): 361–73.

ity with the *Rose* and the influence of the French narrative on the *Comedy.*[2]

In modern times, various literary critics have discussed compelling aspects shared by the two literary masterworks, aspects related to astronomy, mythology, poetics, and Scholastic philosophy.[3] It is surprising, however, that the common concern with vices noted by Christine de Pizan and Laurent de Premierfait has not yet been investigated by literary critics. We lack today a comparative examination of the two allegorical poems from the viewpoint of moral philosophy, a branch of thought that both Jean and Dante consistently cultivated. Although critics readily apply the denomination "medieval summa" to both the *Rose* and the *Comedy,* they tend to use this categorization loosely. The term *summa* had a rather broad spectrum of meanings; the works of Vincent of Beauvais, who practiced this genre from multiple perspectives, best exemplify this polysemy. Depending on the field of knowledge envisioned, a *summa*—Latin for the more modern coinage "encyclopedia"—could be *naturale* (when it dealt with natural sciences), *historiale* (when it investigated the past), *doctrinale* (when it considered the corpus of theological doctrines), and finally *morale* (when it focused on vices and virtues).

Following up on Christine de Pizan's and Laurent de Premierfait's remarks about Jean and Dante's common preoccupation with ethics, I suggest that the *Romance of the Rose* and the *Divine Comedy* should be considered first and foremost in their intersection as *moral summae.* The ideological focus on vices and virtues represents the main meeting point between the two literary masterpieces; it is here that one needs to look for affinities, before any other considerations related to the narrative form, to the recycling of myths ... or to the moon spots.[4] While there are studies treating

2. For Contini, see "Un nodo della cultura medievale: La serie *Roman de la Rose-Fiore-Divina Commedia,*" *Lettere italiane* 25 (1973): 162–89, and for Vanossi, *Dante e il "Roman de la Rose: Saggio sul "Fiore"* (Florence: Olschski, 1979). A useful study of the *Fiore* in its historical context has also been offered by Zygmunt G. Barański and Patrick Boyde, *The "Fiore" in Context: Dante, France and Tuscany* (Notre Dame, Ind.: Notre Dame University Press, 1997). The most recent findings and standpoints with respect to the *Fiore* as a work attributable to Dante have been reunited by Johannes Bartuschat and Luciano Rossi, *Studi sul canone letterario del Trecento: Per Michelangelo Picone* (Ravenna: Longo, 2003).

3. For an outline of the history of these comparative attempts, see Earl J. Richards, *Dante and the "Roman de la Rose": An Investigation into the Vernacular Narrative Context of the "Commedia"* (Tübingen: Niemeyer, 1981), 71–81.

4. The latter are often evoked in literary criticism to prove the influence of the *Rose* on the *Comedy.*

the *Comedy* from the viewpoint either of its genre as a moral summa or of its virtual connections with the Latin treatises on vices, we lack such fundamental studies in *Rose* criticism. To my knowledge, no scholar has yet systematically responded to the provocative challenge voiced by Jean de Meun, who invites his readers to discover and count the vices he has scattered throughout his poem (ll. 19870–87). In an attempt to identify the sources on which Jean has drawn for his handling of ethical notions, I undertake to gently lift up the gauntlet the poet threw at the face of his so-often scandalized readers and to look more closely at a class of sin highly debated by the moral authors from the High Middle Ages—the *peccata linguae,* "sins of the tongue."

Between 1190 and 1260, lingual transgressions mobilized the attention of an impressive number of clerical writers, who, starting from St. James's description of the tongue as an untamable and socially destructive fire, set out to identify instances of sinful speech and to classify them within ethical systems. In this period of time, transgressions such as blasphemy, flattery, lying, or slander were typically viewed as different from murder, adultery, or theft, in that they were committed with the aid of the tongue, the organ responsible for speech. At the same time, however, *peccata linguae* gradually came to be considered as grievous as these sins of deeds (with which they were often compared) and occasionally deemed mortal trespasses.

In the early twelfth century, Hugh of St. Victor recycled the notion of *disciplina in locutione* ("discipline in speech") from Roman rhetoric and applied it to the rules of monastic life. Alain of Lille defined several verbal transgressions in his theological glossary and virulently denounced them in his allegorical poems. The Franciscan master Radulfus Ardens devoted a voluminous section of his *Speculum universale* to speech acts, a section titled "De moribus linguae" (On the mores of the tongue), in which he defined wicked speaking habits in relationship to various socio-professional classes. During the first decades of the thirteenth century, William Peraldus wrote *Summa vitiorum* (Summa of vices), in which to the seven chapters corresponding to the seven deadly sins he added an eighth, called "De peccato linguae" (On the sin of the tongue), where he grouped twenty-four manifestations of this sin. Peraldus no longer took verbal trespasses for "daughters" of the seven deadly sins, as Cassian or Gregory had done before him, but gave them an autonomous status as sins committed through the medium of speech. Moreover, the great number of linguistic trespasses Peraldus united under the caption "De peccato linguae" far exceeded the number of verbal sins scattered as progeny of the capital vices in Cassian's and Gregory's systems.

After Peraldus, in the age of great Scholasticism, the preoccupation with the sins of the tongue became so acute that it ended up permeating the major theological treatises of the time; Alexander of Hales, Vincent of Beauvais, and Thomas Aquinas devoted a privileged space to the discussion of sinful speech in their summae. This abundance of texts promoting an ethics of language use has prompted Silvana Vecchio and Carla Casagrande to brand the timeframe between 1190 and 1260 as the great age of the sins of the tongue.[5] Two major phenomena were responsible for this explosion of treatises: on the one hand, the rise of new models of lay piety triggered by the intense activity of the Franciscan and the Dominican orders, and on the other hand, the development of new forms of expression in vernacular languages. The Fourth Lateran Council from 1215, which imposed the obligation of confession on all Christians, also had an important role to play in the heightened sensitivity to verbal transgressions. For in order for penitent Christians to confess their trespasses, they needed to be educated on how to recognize and avoid moral errors, including the ones made in speaking.[6] Although Casagrande and Vecchio note that the medieval preoccupation with verbal sins extends beyond the golden period of seventy years, they focus mostly on this period and deal only with its major religious representatives, ranging from preachers and confessors to canonists and Scholastic theologians.[7] Understandably, the consid-

5. Carla Casagrande and Silvana Vecchio, *I peccati della lingua: Disciplina ed etica della parola nella cultura medievale* (Rome: Istituto della Enciclopedia Italiana, 1987), 6.

6. Convoked by Pope Innocent III, the Fourth Lateran Council committed to setting up a program of reforms and to training preachers in advocating these reforms to the laity by means of sermons against sins. Along these lines, Canon 21 of the Council, "Omnis utriusque sexus," decreed annual confession and communion obligatory for all adult Christians. This canon, which was actually merely confirming and reinforcing earlier legislation and custom had a stronger effect this time, as it produced a remarkable explosion of pastoral texts all across Western Europe. Encouraged by Canon 21, the reformers and their followers created a vast amount of user-friendly homiletic tools designed to instruct and help preachers in their pastoral efforts, tools ranging from manuals of preaching and treatises on sin to confession handbooks. The classifications of sins and the confession guidebooks aided parish priests in interrogating rapidly and completely penitent sinners, while the preaching manuals provided these priests with various collections of sermons on different moral topics. For a thorough overview of this type of penitential literature, see Pierre Michaud-Quantin, *Sommes de casuistique et manuels de confession au Moyen Âge (XII–XVI siècles)* (Louvain: Nauwelaerts, 1962).

7. The two authors have examined dozens of primary texts (some of them never edited), ranging from short sermons to vast moral and theological encyclopedias.

eration of the literary works of the period would have exceeded the scope of such an extensive review.

My study on transgressive speech in the *Romance of the Rose* and the *Divine Comedy* has been inspired by the findings of Carla Casagrande and Silvana Vecchio. The two masterpieces of medieval poetry in France and Italy, one of which (the *Rose*) is allegedly a model for the other one (the *Comedy*), testify to the same preoccupation with the evils of speech that Casagrande and Vecchio document in *I peccati della lingua.* The dates at which these two literary works were written (1269–1278, Jean's *Rose,* and 1306–1320, the *Comedy*) situate them in the immediate temporal proximity of the golden age of the sins of the tongue. Both Jean and Dante reserve an impressive amount of space for the transgressions of speech: in the *Rose,* every major protagonist discusses uses and abuses of language, whereas Dante punishes several sins of the tongue in *Inferno* and often alludes to them in *Purgatorio* and *Paradiso.*

The examination of the myriad ways in which two iconic writers of medieval France and Italy absorbed the tradition of *peccata linguae* has offered me the key argument for this study: the preoccupation with transgressive speech was not the exclusive sphere of ecclesiastical writers; secular poetry in the vernacular enriched in original ways the debate on verbal vices. The dialogue that the two allegorical poems sustained with the cultural context of the *lingua*-texts was channeled through two ethical and psychological notions: fraud and violence.[8] It is in these vast and dark domains of the human psyche that Jean and Dante saw the greatest potentiality for sin through language, and it is here that we need to look for affiliations with the texts on verbal sins. In the fictive worlds of the *Rose* and the *Comedy,* speech acts rooted in fraud or violence are so abundant that they promote these moral concepts as two of the most important emblems of the poems. The Rose (a symbol of the chaste young lady pursued by the Lover) is conquered only through ruse and rape, whereas Geryon, the monster with a human face in Dante's text, symbolizes and foreshadows the mortal sins of fraud punished in Malebolge ("Evil pouches"). The study of the interactive verbal deceit and violence practiced by Jean's and Dante's characters will allow me to weave the poets' moral messages into the concert of medieval authorities deploring the abuse of the divine gift of speech by humans.

8. I borrow the term "*lingua*-text" from Ralf G. Bogner (*Die Bezahmung der Zunge: Literatur und Disziplinierung der Alltagskommunikation in der fruhen Neuzeit* [Tübingen: Niemeyer, 1997]), who uses it to describe the medieval productions concerned with verbal sins.

Since identifying the connections that the two poems establish with the tracts on transgressive speech is a fundamental task of my book, in the first chapter I trace the evolution of the concept of verbal sin from its first elaboration in the works of Hugh of St. Victor to its fullest expression in Thomas Aquinas's thought. In this historical excursus I devote special attention to William Peraldus, whose "De peccato linguae" was a seminal text not only in France but also in Italy, and which seems to have left indelible marks on the poems under consideration. For, although neither Jean nor Dante names Peraldus in his work, numerous textual indications suggest that the two poets were acquainted with his thought on verbal sin. These indications have not eluded major literary critics. In the late 1960s, for instance, two *Rose* scholars, Lionel Friedman and John V. Fleming, posited Peraldus's *Summa vitiorum* as a possible source of inspiration for Jean de Meun. In more recent Dante studies, Siegfried Wenzel, Carlo Delcorno, and Franco Mancini, to name just a few, have adduced strong arguments for Dante's familiarity with Peraldus's work. Zygmunt G. Barański has analyzed Canto 18 of the *Inferno* specifically from the angle of the pastoral discourse on *peccata linguae*.[9]

Two of Peraldus's transmitters, Laurent of Orléans and Domenico Cavalca, help me answer another important question related to my critical inquiry: what was the status of the moral lexicon of speech in the Romance vernaculars? Jean and Dante wrote at a time when the main vehicle of ethical writings was Latin. To what degree did they absorb and contribute to this lexicon in their vernacular works? These are essential questions whose answers I suggest by discussing Laurent of Orléans's *Somme le Roi* (Summa for the king), and Domenico Cavalca's *Pungilingua* (The wounding tongue). Since the former translated "De peccato linguae" into French in 1280 and the latter into Italian in 1340, their vocabulary offers me functional hermeneutic keys for the notions describing acts of speech in the *Rose* and the *Comedy*. Thomas Aquinas, a native Italian teaching at the University of Paris during the time of Jean and Dante, is another great participant in the ecclesiastic debate on sinful speech. Aquinas contributed significant aspects to the discussion by establishing degrees of comparison among (verbal) vices and by promoting the human will as the main agent in the commission

9. Zygmunt G. Barański, "Scatology and Obscenity in Dante," in *Dante for the New Millennium,* edited by Teodolinda Barolini and H. Wayne Storey (New York: Fordham University Press, 2003), 259–72.

of trespasses. I share Earl Jeffrey Richards's amazement and disappointment that there is no scholarship on the possible influence of Aquinas on Jean de Meun, when it is well known that the former was very active and influential in the intellectual orbit of the University of Paris during Jean's youth.[10]

Thus, a closer look at the cultural context reveals that the greatest authorities on deviant speech were directly connected to Jean and Dante either chronologically or geographically. Such connections highlight the two poets' exposure to the pastoral discourse on transgressive speech. In addition to these extratextual links, there are also many textual clues that indicate a dialogue between vernacular poetry, as represented by Jean de Meun and Dante, and the Latin golden age of *peccata linguae.* The analysis and synthesis of these textual indications occupy the remainder of my study. My interpretive method combines historical reading with instances of textual analysis; I begin the discussion of each verbal sin on which I focus with a short history of it, as established by the ethicists of speech above mentioned; then I use key concepts from their theories to shed light on the treatment of that specific sin in the two poetic works.

The second chapter of my book draws the contours of a moral theory of speech in Jean and Dante and proposes itself as a necessary propedeutics for an investigation of the lingual transgressions rooted in fraud and violence that are discussed in the poems. For the *Rose,* I examine three main aspects of Jean's view of linguistic morality, aspects related to the use of obscene speech, the will as the chief agent in verbal sins, and the criticism of female verbosity. For Dante, I first consider three early works: *De vulgari eloquentia* (On the vernacular eloquence), *De monarchia* (On the monarchy), and *Convivio* (The banquet), and then *Purgatorio* and *Paradiso.* This corpus of texts frames and at the same time enlightens Dante's treatment of verbal sins in the *Inferno.*

10. Earl J. Richards, "*Les contraires choses:* Irony in Jean de Meun's Part of the *Roman de la Rose* and the Problem of Truth and Intelligibility in Thomas Aquinas," in *Nouvelles de la Rose: Actualité et perspectives du Roman de la Rose,* edited by Dulce Maria González-Doreste and Maria del Pilar Mendoza-Ramos (La Laguna: Universidad de La Laguna, 2011), 388. In this very recent essay, Richards argues that several features of Jean's manipulation of irony as a rhetorical device are borrowings from Aquinas. For instance, the question of the intelligibility of the world that lies at the heart of the *Rose* echoes the Thomistic position from *De veritate,* and Jean's famous formulation *Ainsinc va des contraires choses, / Les unes sont des aultres gloses* (ll. 21543–45) is a translation of the Thomistic principle of *differentia contraria* (Richards, "*Les contraires choses,*" 388–89).

Jean's *Rose* is a philosophical poem about love and human nature, written with wit and cynicism. The work is organized around the discourses of several allegorical characters, such as Dame Raison (Lady Reason), Amant (Lover), Nature, Genius, Ami (Friend), La Vieille (the Old Woman), Le Mari Jaloux (the Jealous Husband), and Faus Semblant (False Seeming). All these characters convey two major ideas: love is nothing more than carnal gratification, and human nature is fraught with vices. Thus, Raison denounces fraudulent behavior practices in which speech plays a pivotal role, while Nature bitterly complains about the human appetite for slander, lying, perjury, and boastfulness. The discourses of Ami, La Vieille, and Faus Semblant overtly advocate the use of false promises, lies, flattery, perjury, and double talk in interpersonal relationships. Jean also gives substance to an allegorical character named Malebouche (Evil Mouth), who embodies all the possible deviations from virtuous language.

Jean's authorial agency poses several problems related to the polyphonic nature of the poem, for the writer speaks "in characters," and these discursive characters are so numerous. Because what they say is often conflictive (they often contradict each other, and, paradoxically, they also contradict themselves), it is a daunting task to detect Jean's own voice, his genuine standpoint with respect to the above-mentioned abuses of speech. Is Jean really criticizing wicked verbal habits through the voices of Amant, Nature, and Genius, or rather recommending hypocrisy, false promises, lying, and evil counseling, through Ami, La Vieille, and Faus Semblant? Which personage best represents the original thought of Jean de Meun? Is he, as a writer, able to stand outside the material that he seems to criticize?

Comparing the French poet with Dante, I note that Jean's approach to verbal behavior is very flexible. His concern is not to devise a new moral system as Dante will do; rather, his goal is to provide a global vision of the degeneracy of human language and to exemplify as many negative verbal practices as possible. The second salient difference is that Jean does not imagine a hellish world where the negligent speaker can end up for a verbal trespass, whereas Dante meticulously designs infernal places where souls are punished for having abused language in the form of blasphemy, seduction, flattery, fraudulent counsel, sowing of discord, and falsifying of words. The creation of a gigantic universe with infernal mechanisms of torture is the hallmark of Dante's treatment of sins.

A few words should be said here about the structure of Hell, as it is relevant to the questions that my study proposes to answer.[11] Whereas for most medieval Christians, hell was an undifferentiated place full of fire, smoke, and pitch, for Dante it was an incredibly precise world, with a well-determined geography, finely divided into specific areas. The underworld is imagined as an extremely deep structure, articulated in nine different floors populated by souls. Each of the nine "floors," or circles, corresponds to a specific major sin and each subdivision of the circle to a subclass of that sin. The area of violence, for instance, is divided into three zones, punishing the violent against God (the blasphemers), the violent against others (the murderers), and the violent against oneself (the suicides). Malebolge, the area hosting the sins of fraud, is even more minutely divided into ten different zones, punishing, in an apparently random order, panderers and seducers (in one zone), flatterers, simoniacs, diviners, barrators, hypocrites, thieves, fraudulent counselors, sowers of discord, and falsifiers.

The order of the sins in Malebolge, as in the entirety of Hell, is only apparently random. In fact, by imagining a multilevel construction, Dante establishes a detailed hierarchy of sins, taking their degree of gravity as a criterion: the "lighter" sins are assigned to the upper part of Hell, whereas the more serious go to the lower part. At the root of the funnel lies the most grievous sin of all—betrayal, exemplified by Lucifer, Judas, and Brutus. Dante's vision of moral errors as a hierarchy based on their seriousness is an extraordinary contribution to the medieval theories of sins, just as the geography of his underworld is a rich gift to the medieval literary patrimony. For no moralist before Dante has gone so far as to place the major transgressions of humankind in a precise, mathematical order, and no poetic fantasy has ever imagined in what ways the forces of evil can become instruments of divine justice. When Dante establishes an architectonics of human trespasses, by embedding sins of speech among sins of deed, he implicitly achieves a hierarchy of verbal transgressions as well. Several questions arise at this point. Why out of twenty-four sins of the tongue, as organized by Peraldus for instance, does Dante choose only a few, specific ones? What organizing principles account for the embedding of these verbal sins among sins of deed, in a particular order? Why does Dante, a devout Christian, deem flattery more reprehensible than blasphemy? Why are evil counseling and sowing of discord more heinous than flattery? In

11. All throughout my study, I make a distinction between "hell" as a general theological concept and "Hell" as Dante's underworld.

other words, what criteria are prevalent when he judges some verbal abuses more abominable than others?

Over the course of time several attempts have been made at explaining the structure of Hell. William H. Reade, Francesco Mazzoni, and more recently Patrick Boyde and Marc Cogan, have undertaken to explain the reasons why Dante borrowed elements from the Gregorian system of the seven deadly sins and grafted them on the Aristotelian theory of the soul's three dispositions to evil (incontinence, violence, and fraud). The abovementioned critical endeavors are remarkable interpretations of the structure of Hell from different standpoints. Understandably, as these interpretations are concerned with the overall structure of the underworld, they do not reserve much room for a discussion of the sins of the tongue. These sins deserve, however, a special treatment inasmuch as, being committed through the medium of language, they stand apart from lust, theft, barratry, and the like. On account of their relationship to speech, blasphemy, flattery, sowing of discord, and falsifying of words ought to be treated as a separate thematic block. In the division of Hell, blasphemy is the only lingual transgression rooted in violence and directed against the divinity; all the other abuses of speech spring from a common stem of ruse, a perversion of reason directed against other human beings. Violence and fraud are thus the main ethical levels on which Dante builds his scaffolding of lingual trespasses, a micro-construction that he artfully welds into his macrosystem of deadly sins.

In chapter 3, I group several verbal transgressions (flattery, evil counsel, double talk, sowing of discord, and falsifying of words) under the heading *Lingua dolosa,* "The Guileful Tongue," since both Jean and Dante are particularly concerned about these forms of deceit taking place in language. The sin of *adulatio,* "flattery," obsessively recurs in the polyphonic fabric of the *Rose,* and in the *Inferno* the flatterers are mercilessly punished as deceitful speakers by immersion in feces. *Pravum consilium,* "evil counsel," also has representatives in both literary works: La Vieille and Ami, two main discursive figures in the *Rose,* strongly advocate the use of guile in amorous liaisons, while Ulysses, Diomedes, and Guido da Montefeltro are punished by Dante in Malebolge as fraudulent counselors. Faus Semblant, the remarkable chameleonic figure of the *Rose* who embodies the habits of double talk and sowing of discord, is one of the main sites in which Jean places his treatment of interactive fraud and socially destructive violence.

Sowing of discord and falsifying of words are also two classes of sins well represented in Dante's underworld, where they are assigned to two of the deepest areas of Malebolge. Mythology and history govern Jean's and Dante's choices of the characters and examples meant to illustrate the powerful negative impact of the vices of speech in the evolution of humankind. But more importantly for my line of argument, all the verbal deviations the poets choose to discuss or represent in their fictive universes constitute well-defined notions in the contemporary ethical tracts, where they have technical denominations (*bilinguium,* "double talk"; *seminantium discordiae,* "sowing of discord"; *turpiloquium,* "obscene speech"; etc.), or where they are analyzed for the first time in the history of sin.

What renders the assimilation of the clerical discourse on speech problematic in Jean and Dante is the specificity of their literary métier. Both authors emphasize the notion that writing is a daunting task, Jean by stressing how difficult it is to write things down (ll. 15181–96; l. 19916), and Dante by mentioning the ascetic constraints to which his poem has forced him (*Paradiso* 25.1–3). As practitioners of an art based on written words, the poets are doubly more sensitive to, and responsible for, what they say (i.e., cast on paper) than an ordinary speaker. Horace, one of the medieval moralists' favorite sources, had urged his contemporaries to speak carefully, for once a word was uttered, it could not be taken back. Jean is echoing this dictum in French vernacular: "Mais parole une fois volee / Ne peut puis estre rapelee" ("But once a speech has taken wing it cannot be called back"; ll. 16548–50).[12] The situation is all the more dramatic when one entrusts a message to a written medium with the hope that such a vehicle will reach a wider audience and will be preserved for future generations; "verba volant, scripta manent" ("spoken words fly away, written words remain"), goes one of the most popular proverbs of Roman antiquity.

Jean's and Dante's moral dilemmas are further compounded by the fact that they write from the position of Catholic thinkers, at a time when poetry was required to convey the truths of theology and to be an expressive vehicle for faith and moral values.[13] Moreover, they write at a time when

12. The English version of the *Rose* I use is by Charles Dahlberg: Guillaume de Lorris and Jean de Meun, *The Romance of the Rose,* 3rd ed., translated by Charles Dahlberg (Princeton, N.J.: Princeton University Press, 1995).

13. For the inextricable link between poetry and ethics in medieval times, see Judson Boyce Allen, *The Ethical Poetic of the Later Middle Ages: A Decorum of Convenient Distinctions* (Toronto: University of Toronto Press, 1982), in which the author also devotes a few pages to Dante.

the vernacular languages were opening up to the formation or reception of new words, some of them unacceptable by the norms of written language.[14] In this framework, the two poets are concerned not only with other people's verbal transgressions but also with their own potential sins as writers. This issue is the focus of my last chapter, devoted to blasphemy and to the relationship between violence and poetics.

In the *Rose,* with the exception of Raison and Faus Semblant, who mention blasphemy in passing, the characters do not discuss this verbal deviation. Jean de Meun himself, however, is concerned about this sin and alludes to it in lines 15139–306, in reference to his own person. This is the so-called apologetic segment of the *Rose,* where, for the first and only time in the poem, Jean assumes his own, authorial voice. The motive for this exceptional gesture is the poet's wish to confess, and apologize for, his transgressive artistic diction. He admits to having written too daringly, used many forbidden words, and expressed many unorthodox ideas. He explicitly directs this apology to his readership and, very significantly, to the Catholic Church.

Jean's confession of verbal sins is a very important piece of evidence linking the obscene and garrulous vernacular poet to the stern ecclesiastic debate on immoral speech. What is also special about this moment is that it generates one of the most fascinating facts in the history of French literary culture. The charge of sinful language that Jean feared from his readership would eventually be actualized by Jean Gerson, a great theologian involved in the *Querelle de la Rose,* an admirer of William Peraldus and a moralist of speech himself. About one hundred years after the composition of Jean's *Rose,* Gerson harshly denounces both the ideological content and the literary style of the poem, and, finding it full of blasphemies and heresies, he asks of readers to burn it at the stake. I thus reopen the discussion of the transgressive authorial agency of Jean de Meun from the perspective of Gerson's role in the *Querelle,* and more importantly, from that of the Gersonian texts on blasphemy, which so far have remained unexplored in *Rose* studies.

With his apologies, Jean de Meun intended to avoid the potential charge of blasphemy hovering over his scandalous poem and to ensure a safe circulation of it. Since he was fashioning his work at a time when the Catholic

14. In "Au XIIIe siècle: Une parole nouvelle," Jacques Le Goff and Jean-Claude Schmitt offer a review of the main changes that vernacular languages underwent in this time period ("Au XIIIe siècle: Une parole nouvelle," in *Histoire vécue du peuple chrétien,* 257–79 [Toulouse: Privat, 1979]).

Church was taking great measures to police the use of language, his decision to anticipate a possible negative reaction from ecclesiastical authorities by incorporating a confession of sins in the very text of his poetic work was a very shrewd strategy meant to keep censors at bay. It is both ironic and fascinating that, although Jean's poem was produced during the great medieval discourse on deviant speech, it would eventually be judged as a transgressive literary work by a world-renowned Churchman, but ... one century later (or too late!).

Whether Dante would have punished Jean de Meun as a violent and blasphemous speaker is a question that can only put a smile on the readers' faces. The fact remains, however, that the Italian poet places blasphemy in Hell as a sin of violence and handles it in idiosyncratic ways. In the medieval tradition of the *lingua*-texts, blasphemy was considered the most grievous verbal transgression. Dante reverses this taxonomy and, by placing blasphemers in the upper part of Hell, devises an original hierarchy of verbal trespasses within which blasphemy (a sin of violence) is outweighed in seriousness by sins of fraud such as flattery, fraudulent counsel, sowing of discord, and falsifying of words. The reasons for this reversal of terms seem to lie in the social and political consequences triggered by the sins of fraud, consequences that prevailed for Dante as a politically engaged citizen. On the other hand, if we place ourselves outside the universe of fiction and inside the poet's writing workshop, we have to consider that Dante was keenly aware of the potentiality for sin of his own art and often expressed fear that his poem might be misinterpreted by inept readers. Consequently, as Giuseppe Mazzotta and Teodolinda Barolini have demonstrated, the poet took constant care throughout the *Comedy* to secure his theological and moral messages as conveyers of truth.[15]

In the metalanguage I adopt to discuss instances of immoral speech, I would like to draw attention to two terminological distinctions. The synecdoche *lingua indisciplinata,* "unruly tongue," which I sometimes use, belongs to Hugh of St. Victor and refers to the speaker who breaks the rules of orderly speech, rules imposed by the moral imperatives of self-control and discernment. My other favorite term, "transgressive," has a patristic

15. For Mazzotta, see *Dante, Poet of the Desert: History and Allegory in the "Divine Comedy"* (Princeton, N.J.: Princeton University Press, 1979); for Barolini, *Dante's Poets: Textuality and Truth in the "Divine Comedy"* (Princeton, N.J.: Princeton University Press, 1984), and *The Undivine Comedy* (Princeton, N.J.: Princeton University Press, 1992).

overtone and centers on the same idea of words violating unseen spiritual boundaries. Thomas Aquinas constructed his theory of sinful language on the Augustinian definition of words as signs. The implication is that there is a moral borderline within the use of language, a borderline beyond which one cannot pass without incurring the fatal risk of losing one's soul. Transgressive speech is an ethical *trapassar del segno* ("trespassing of the sign") by human beings, of which Dante's Ulysses is the perfect paradigm. It is a way of speaking based on deceit and aggression, as is seen in Cavalca's *Pungilingua,* where perjury is defined as a *trapassar,* "trespassing," of the licit and truthful oath. Transgressive speech is ultimately the opposite of Dante's imparadised language in the third *cantica* of the *Divine Comedy,* a verbal and moral level that the poet was able to attain only by the extraordinary experience of his *trasumanar,* "going beyond the human state."

In concluding my analysis of the contributions Jean and Dante make to the prolific debate on abusive speech, I highlight the remarkable balancing act performed by the two poets, who respond to this debate in ways that reflect their life experiences, their artistic tempers, and their moral agendas. Jean is writing from the comfort of his Parisian home located on Rue St. Jacques, which was also the street of the major Dominican convent where Peraldus and Aquinas were read and highly prized. But he does not love Dominicans, in general, and when he builds the character of Faus Semblant into his poem, he seeks to represent them and to harshly lampoon their vices. Jean is a satirist, who likes to poke fun at people's moral errors, including the verbal ones; his weapons are biting irony, sardonic laughter, and paradox. Dante, on the other hand, writes under the bitter and dramatic circumstances of his exile. For him, transgressions in deed or in word are a matter of life and death, since they determine one's personal salvation. His distinctive artistic instrument is the solemn—sometimes outraged but always pained—tone of the Christian moralist, who sets out to correct people's ways by admonishing them and by showing them in detail the three realms in which their souls may end up after death.

There can be no greater balancing act, or contrast, than the one achieved by these two modes of treating morality and language, but it is precisely this stark contrast that constitutes the richness and depth of the response given by vernacular poetry to the otherwise too rigid nature of the Latin tracts on vices and virtues, tracts that functioned as pillars of Christian ethics in the Middle Ages.

ONE

The Verbal Sin as a Cultural Construct

Sin, then, is any transgression in deed, or word, or desire, of the eternal law.
{St. Augustine, *Against Faustus* 22.27}

The notion of an indissoluble relationship between language and divinity is as ancient as the Old Testament, according to which the universe began as a response to God's verbal command. Language thus was as miraculous as Creation itself. The Christian doctrine of the Incarnation further elaborated this idea and posited the notion of Christ as the embodied Word. Since ordinary humans were endowed with the gift of speech as well, for Christians human language became the most direct connection between the secular world, corrupt and corruptible, and the transcendental world, perfect and eternal. As early as the fourth century AD, Augustine of Hippo, the first philosopher of Christianity, wrote at length on the specular relationship between human words and the Word—*verbum Dei*—and drew attention to a major split within language. According to St. Augustine, people use two different types of speech: an outer one, consisting of the vocal expression of concepts and ideas, and an inner one—*verbum cordis* (or *mentis*), "the word of the heart" (or "of the mind"), which is the true language reflecting God's Word (*On the Trinity,* Book 15).[1] In moral terms, the closer people's outer words are to their inner, mental words, the closer people are to transcendental standards of speech. When there is a discrepancy between what one says and what one actually thinks, human communication becomes tarnished with the sins of lying and double talk. Augustine's doctrine of interiority, his philosophy of language, as well as his ethical concepts, represented a fundamental cultural legacy for medieval Christians, who paid particular attention to the sins committed through the medium of speech. Combining major Augustinian themes with other strands of thought (classical or patristic), medieval thinkers enriched the debate on verbal sin with their own speculative and moral insights.

The first sign of this increased sensitivity to the dangerous potential of spoken words appeared at the dawn of the twelfth century in the works of the influential writer Hugh of St. Victor. As a Parisian master in theology operating at the Augustinian monastery of St. Victor, Hugh concentrated his religious efforts on the elaboration of a moral reform designed to help the "outer man" (an Augustinian concept) reach a state of perfection close to divine bliss. This state of felicity could be reached only by way of a rigorously disciplined behavior, including gestures, attitudes, and use of language. This whole complex of behavioral attitudes belonged to the *scientia recte vivendi* ("art of proper living"), which Hugh elaborated in *De institutione novitiorum* (On the instruction of novices), a moral tract written before 1125 and designed for aspiring monks. In Hugh's view, speech ought not to be a spontaneous and arbitrary flow of words but a phenomenon controllable by means of knowledge and method. In order to shape all human utterances, a specific science provided norms for disciplined speech. More specifically, Hugh's notion of *disciplina in locutione* involved the observance of a set of rules meant to regulate the production of words, a set that he borrowed from classical rhetoric and reworked in a Christian context. These rules gravitated around the six factors a speaker had to consider before uttering words: in what capacity he was speaking, what he had to say, to whom, how, when, and where. Such factors, which in pagan rhetoric had been the parameters for forging a convincing political/public argu-

1. For an analysis of Augustine's theory of inner speech, see Claude Panaccio, "Augustin, le verbe mental e l'amour," in *Les philosophies morales et politiques au Moyen Âge: Proceedings of the 9th International Congress of Medieval Philosophy,* edited by B. Carlos Bazán et al. (New York: Legas, 1995), 777–85.

mentation, became norms tailored for the virtuous speech of Christians. Each of these circumstances enabled a pious individual to achieve *discretio loquendi,* "discernment/prudence in speaking." The language user who failed to observe these linguistic-moral norms was an "indiscreet" (i.e., imprudent) speaker, and the tongue with which he uttered the indiscriminate words, a *lingua indisciplinata.* Thus, Hugh's contribution to the medieval ethics of eloquence is also remarkable for the creation of a metalinguistic vocabulary, that is, of a lexicon employed to describe the workings of language.[2] The label "discreet" that Hugh applies to morally correct speaking will echo in the most prominent moralists of the thirteenth and fourteenth centuries: Radulfus Ardens, William Peraldus, Thomas Aquinas, Brunetto Latini, and Dante.

A few decades after the redaction of *De institutione novitiorum,* the Franciscan master Radulfus Ardens elaborated a vast ethical work titled *Speculum universale* (ca. 1193–1200), which advanced high standards for virtuous speech. In the seventy-two chapters of "De moribus linguae" (Book 13 of the *Speculum*), he first expounds norms for morally proper speech and then discusses deviances from them. At the beginning of the book, he posits five moral criteria indispensable to the production of good discourse: truth, usefulness, propriety, discernment, and orientation (13.1).[3] All of these criteria must act simultaneously in the act of speech, because when just one of them is transgressed, words fail to be morally perfect, and *mala locutio,* "evil speech," occurs. For instance, when the moral criterion of truth is violated, speech falls prey to sins such as lying, perjury, false promise, and false doctrine. When the criterion of usefulness is violated, words became idle, frivolous, and mocking, or they take the shape of evil counsels. When the imperative of propriety is ignored, the sin of obscenity is committed, whereas when the quality of discernment is transgressed, several verbal sins,

2. For more on Hugh's contributions to the development of a moral and theological lexicon, see Roger Baron, "Hugues de St. Victor lexicographe," *Cultura Neolatina* 16 (1956). 109–45.

3. The manuscript I use for Radulfus Ardens is *Speculum universale IX–XIV,* MS Lat. 3240 (Paris: BnF). My main sources for the life and work of this author are Johannes Gründel ("L'Œuvre encyclopédique de Raoul Ardent: Le *Speculum Universale,*" *Cahiers d'histoire mondiale* 9 [1966]: 553–70, and *Die Lehre des Radulfus Ardens von den Verstandestugenden auf dem Hintergrund seiner Seelenlehre* [Munich: Schoning, 1976]) and Carla Casagrande and Silvana Vecchio (*I peccati della lingua: Disciplina ed etica della parola nella cultura medievale* [Rome: Istituto della Enciclopedia Italiana, 1987]).

such as foolish talk, disclosing of secrets, and the like, occur.[4] Unlike Hugh's theory of disciplined speech from *De institutione novitiorum,* which has focused exclusively on the verbal behavior of aspiring monks, "De moribus linguae" offers a wider analytical angle for the verbal habits of society, as it studies several socio-professional classes. Aside from the linguistic conduct of ecclesiastics, the tract also considers the speech of laymen in all aspects of their everyday lives (political, commercial, or family communications). Like Hugh, but on a much larger scale, Radulfus is concerned to establish norms for an impeccable use of speech and to inveigh against the violations of these norms. All these transgressions are as many sins of the tongue that can harm God, oneself, or others. Johannes Gründel, who has extensively analyzed *Speculum universale,* considers it a masterpiece of ethics in twelfth-century Europe.[5]

Contemporary with Radulfus Ardens and preoccupied with the same problematic of sinful speech was Alain of Lille, a leading figure of French culture, who had a strong influence on both the theology and the poetry of the West European Middle Ages. The concern with the harms one can do in speaking is a constant of Alain's ethical meditations, being present in virtually all of his writings. The *Tractus* on virtues and vices devotes lengthy paragraphs to lying, false testimony, and perjury, whereas the *Liber,* the vast glossary of theological terms, defines several terms pertaining to evil speech. Alain's famous corpus of sermons associates sins of the tongue with various social and professional categories (merchants, lawyers, monks, etc.) and condemns the dissolute words triggered by drunkenness or lust, the verbal offenses caused by anger, and the verbosity prompted by pride. Evil silence and pompousness are criticized in the *Plaint of Nature,* which also violently inveighs against the sins of flattery and slander as progeny of the capital sin of envy. In his moral discourse, Alain adopts as a starter the Gregorian framework of the seven capital vices, but because he perceives it as too schematic or obsolete, he adds new categories of verbal sin (he distinguishes between injurious speech and offensive speech as different daughters of the sin of wrath, for instance) and introduces a more precise philo-

4. As to the criterion of *discretio,* Radulfus faithfully follows Hugh of St. Victor and maintains the same rigorous scheme of the circumstances of speech. If only one of the circumstances is not observed, the entire discourse is considered failed, for, just as virtuous speech springs from intellect and deliberation, so in turn imprudent speech is born out of numbness of mind and lack of forethought (*Speculum* XIII.12, f. 164v).

5. Gründel, *Die Lehre des Radulfus Ardens.*

sophical and linguistic terminology (he no longer speaks of concatenated vices in terms of progeny or fruits, but of *species* of capital vices). As Alain was one of Jean de Meun's and Dante's acknowledged intellectual models, I will often invoke his stance on sin to provide a larger historical context for my discussion.[6]

PERALDUS'S EIGHTH "CAPITAL" VICE

The efforts made by the twelfth-century French churchmen to provide rules for morally correct speech and to sensitize Christians to the harm caused by transgressions of these rules bore remarkable fruits in the thirteenth century. About 1236, William Peraldus (ca. 1200–1271) was the first great theologian to imply that abusive speech was such a widespread and dangerous social epidemic that it should be considered an eighth class of capital sin.[7] Born about 1200 in Peyraud, in the department of Ardèche, Peraldus was a Dominican friar whose intense religious activity was concentrated in Lyon (where about 1260 he was a prior of the Dominican convent) and in Vienna. Several contemporary testimonies portray him as a man of exceptional erudition, endowed with great intellectual and rhetorical abilities matched only by his outstanding human qualities. According to some medieval sources, even at an old age, Peraldus was climbing the hard slopes of the Alps in order to reach the most isolated settlements of Christians in need of spiritual

6. For Jean de Meun's debt to Alain in the field of allegorical poetry, see Ernest Langlois, *Origines et sources;* Guy Raynaud de Lage, *Alain de Lille, poète du XIIe siècle* (Montréal: Institut d'Etudes Médiévales, 1951); Alan Gunn, *The Mirror of Love: A Reinterpretation of the "Romance of the Rose"* (Lubbock: Texas Tech Press, 1952); Pierre-Yves Badel, *Le "Roman de la Rose" au XIVème siècle: Etude de la réception de l'œuvre* (Geneva: Droz, 1980); Daniel Poirion, "Alain de Lille et Jean de Meun," in *Alain de Lille, Gautier de Chatillon, Jakemart Giélée et leur temps,* 35–51 (Lille: Presses Universitaires, 1980), and Barbara Newman, *God and the Goddesses: Vision, Poetry, and Belief in the Middle Ages* (Philadelphia: University of Pennsylvania Press, 2003). For Dante's relationship to Alain, see Peter Dronke, "Boethius, Alanus and Dante," *Romanische Forschungen* 78 (1966): 119–25, and Andrea Ciotti, "Alano e Dante," *Convivium* 28 (1960): 257–88.

7. In Cassian's eightfold system, lust gives rise to obscenity, scurrility, and idle talk; avarice generates lying, perjury, and false testimony; sloth engenders verbosity. Vanity gives rise to discord and boasting, whereas pride to blasphemy, murmur, and slander. Gregory's sevenfold scheme establishes the following relationships: vainglory causes boasting, quarrel, and discord; envy lies at the root of whispering and slander; wrath is responsible for strife, insult, contradiction, and blasphemy. In its turn, avarice engenders deceit and perjury, while gluttony leads to lewd language and loquacity.

assistance. His preaching skills and sermons had made him so famous in Europe that two intellectuals of the time, Fra Adam Salimbene and Gérard de Frachet, noted down the impressions left by their encounters with him, recording highly praiseworthy words about his personality and service.[8]

Among the five main works attributed to Peraldus, the great *Summa vitiorum et virtutibus* (*SVV*) is by far the most celebrated. Written in its entirety before 1250, it is a work of moral theology with a bipolar structure: its first part deals with the capital vices and its second one with the cardinal and theological virtues, as well as with the beatitudes.[9] What is remarkable about Peraldus is that, out of modesty and humility, he never signed any of his texts with his name but only with the appellation "ego minimus de ordine fratrum predicatorum" ("I, the smallest one of the order of the preaching friars"). The earliest manuscripts of *SVV* preserved this anonymity, and only at the end of the thirteenth century did copyists begin affixing Peraldus's name to his ethical work. It seems that the thirteenth century favored the first part of *SVV,* the one on vices, since there are more than twice as many copies of the *Summa vitiorum* as of the *Summa virtutibus* dating from that period. This disproportion is due not only to the temporal anteriority of *Summa vitiorum* but also to its greater utilitarian nature, for the tract on vices was very useful to preachers who needed to instruct their audience on how to identify and avoid evil. Many manuscripts of this tract would bear the phrases "perutilis ad predicationem" ("useful to preaching") and "perutilis valde ad peccatorum detestationem" ("very useful to the detestation of sins").

Summa vitiorum (*SV*) adopts but at the same time alters the traditional Gregorian scheme of the deadly sins. The French Dominican writes a chapter on each of the seven evil inclinations postulated by Gregory the Great, but he also adds an eighth sin, examined in a distinct chapter titled "De peccato linguae."[10] Peraldus scholars agree that by adding this "new" trespass to the conventional seven, the author assigns to wicked speech

8. Dondaine, "Guillaume Peyraut," 181–82.

9. The first half of the work circulated under two names—*Summa de vitiis* and *Summa vitiorum.* Based on Ms. 591 (Combray 1277), this first part dates from as early as 1236; the *Summa de virtutibus* was written a few years later, in about 1248, but both works were in circulation in 1250. Dondaine ("Guillaume Peyraut") adds that when medieval copyists reunited these two texts under one heading—*Summa de vitiis* (or *vitiorum*) *et virtutibus*—they kept the division into two volumes but sometimes inverted the right order of the texts by beginning with the tract on virtues. It is the case, for example, of the edition that I use, whose title is *Summa virtutum ac vitiorum.*

10. Wenzel correctly points out that the addition of a new category of vice is not the only

the status of an eighth *capital* sin. The implication of this addition is that the harm people commit in word is as serious as the harm they commit in deed. According to the same interpreters (Casagrande, Vecchio, Wenzel, and Craun), the inclusion of an eighth deadly sin, the one "of the tongue," represents the hallmark of Peraldus's moral system.

Under the generic heading "De peccato linguae," the medieval moralist discusses twenty-four classes of verbal sin, treated in twenty-four separate subchapters:

1. *blasphemia* (blasphemy)
2. *murmur* (murmuring, or tale-bearing)
3. *peccati defensio* (excusing one's sin)
4. *periurium* (perjury)
5. *mendacium* and *falsum testimonium* (lying and false testimony)
6. *detractio* (slander)
7. *adulatio* (flattery)
8. *maledictio* (cursing)
9. *convitium* (insult)
10. *contentio* (quarreling)
11. *derisio* (derision)
12. *pravum consilium* (evil counsel)
13. *seminantium discordiae* (sowing of discord)
14. *bilinguium* (double talk)
15. *rumor amantium* (rumor mongering)
16. *iactantia* (boasting)
17. *secretorum revelatio* (ferreting of secrets)
18. *indiscreta comminatio* (blunt threats)
19. *indiscreta promissio* (imprudent promise)
20. *verbum otiosum* (idle talk)
21. *multiloquium* (loquacity)
22. *turpiloquium* (lewd talk)
23. *scurrilitas* (scurrility)
24. *indiscreta taciturnitas* (imprudent taciturnity, or sullenness)

---

liberty Peraldus takes with respect to the Gregorian system. He also changes the order of the vices within the system, establishing the arrangement gluttony, lechery, avarice, sullenness, pride, envy, and wrath, which reverses the Gregorian order that begins with pride and ends with lechery ("The Continuing Life," 137).

The rationale for the inclusion of an eighth sin in a work structured on a sevenfold system is given in the first lines of the tract, where Peraldus obliquely complains about the insufficiency of the Gregorian scheme, unable to encompass the multifarious manifestations of sinful speech, this so widely diffused social phenomenon: "Ultimo inter peccata dicendum est de peccato linguae quia istud peccatum remanet post alia peccata" ("lastly among the sins we must speak of the sin of the tongue, because this sin remains after the other sins").[11] To this argument bearing on the structure of his work, he adds another complaint, prompted by a compelling moral reality: even among people truly regretful of their sins, few are aware of the evils they commit when they speak, and so they fail to confess their verbal transgressions to the priest. Since Christians are not knowledgeable about all the ways in which their words may harm others, they do not work on shunning or redeeming their oral transgressions. Peraldus's objective is thus to warn his auditors/readers about the great destructive potentiality of speech and to instruct them how to adjust their verbal behavior according to moral standards.

As far as the structure of "De peccato linguae" is concerned, the author maintains the tripartite pattern of treatment he has hitherto applied to the other capital vices: *detestatio* (a list of reasons why Christians should abhor a specific vice), *species* (subclasses of each chief vice), and *remedia* (practical solutions for fighting evil inclinations). The introductory part of the tractate discusses the theme of *custodia linguae,* "guard of the tongue." Taking up Hugh's theory of disciplined speech, just as Radulfus Ardens has done before him, Peraldus lodges the evils of speech in the tongue, an organ that, through its anatomic mobility, is naturally prone to moral deviance. It is on account of this great ambivalence of the tongue, an instrument that can be used for verbalizing both good and evil, that people are inclined to gossip, quarrel, slander, and so on. Thus, the first imperative in combating social conflicts generated by verbal misbehavior is a good government of one's tongue. The careful and detailed way in which Peraldus builds his argumentation for *custodia linguae* shows at work a highly analytical moralist of speech, who leaves no stone unturned in forging a list of eighteen (!) reasons why people should watch their mouths. I will sum up here only a few representative ones.

11. Peraldus, *SV,* 19. Peraldus uses the terms "vice" and "sin" interchangeably, as synonyms. The technical distinction between vice, as a steady moral disposition toward evil, and sin, the actual accomplishment of the disposition, will be made only later on, by Thomas Aquinas.

The first of these motives highlights the unique gift God made to man by giving him the power to speak; the great benefit of such a gift is obvious when a man loses his ability to speak, for he would rather get it back than gain a large amount of money. It is therefore a great misfortune that man uses specifically the tongue, this *membrum,* "limb," in which God honored him, to offend the divinity. Secondly, we should consider that the tongue is reason's instrument; therefore, we should speak according only to reason, not to the senses. Being such a noble organ, the tongue ought to be used only in speech acts like praying, praising, thanking God, confessing, getting the Eucharist, and preaching. It should never be used to vituperate against God or human beings. Another reason regards the intimate connection between heart and language; since spoken words express thoughts or feelings, the better one controls one's speech, the better one will be able to dominate one's feelings, and therefore a better person (read Christian) one will be. Unfortunately, Peraldus says, since the tongue is located in the mouth, a very humid place, it is naturally prone to many verbal abuses. Indicative of the tongue's natural disposition toward sin is the fact that it is the only limb imprisoned or hidden in the body by physical barriers like the lips and the teeth; all the other bodily limbs are visible. Peraldus reiterates St. James's notion that every animal nature, bird, beast, or serpent, can be tamed, but nobody can tame the human tongue. When the Holy Spirit descended upon the Apostles, he chose to manifest himself as a fiery tongue, because it was necessary that the evils of the human tongue be redeemed and purified by a transcendental one. On account of the same need for purification, the Holy Church decreed that at baptism one grain of salt be placed into the mouths of those to be baptized. Peraldus goes on to explain that if St. James chose fire to metaphorically illustrate the activity of the tongue, it is because fire is the most dangerous of all the natural elements, able to cause the greatest devastation in the shortest time. In the same way, spiritually and socially, the harm produced by the tongue is the most rapid and the most destructive of all.

Another consideration that should motivate us to rein in our tongues is that in hell, the sinners painfully bite their tongues; at work is the divine law according to which the sinner is punished in the limb with which he has sinned. As an example, Peraldus invokes the scriptural story of the rich man who, in hell, begged Abraham to send down Lazarus to put a cool finger on his inflamed tongue (this story will become a frequent *exemplum* in the *lingua*-texts). Under the same consideration, Peraldus takes up the doctrine of verbal *discretio,* "discernment," and lists the two main circumstances that a speaker (here a preacher) should consider before opening his mouth: to whom he addresses his sermon and whether the moment is well chosen. Other considerations that should make people bridle their tongues are the exhortations of the scriptures and the example of the saints, who all used their spiritual gift of speech in positive and virtuous ways. Finally, what should move us to watch our mouths is that, as the Gospel says, our language reveals not only our ethnicity but also our membership in a nation of good or evil people.[12]

When Peraldus proceeds to analyze the twenty-four lingual sins, he considers that the first four (blasphemy, murmur, excusing one's sin, and perjury) offend God directly, while all the other ones offend man directly and God indirectly. He deems blasphemy the gravest trespass of all but makes no other attempt at classifying sins according to their degrees of gravity; his tract lacks explicit references to a hierarchy of the verbal sins that he examines. We can get a sense, however, of the varying levels of seriousness of these sins if we consider the different spans of attention he pays to them. Thus, if the sins of blasphemy, murmuring, slander, perjury, and lying, for instance, are discussed at length and with wealth of details, the sins of derision, rumor mongering, ferreting secrets, lewd talk, and blunt threats are devoted only a few sentences each. Most of the twenty-four sections of "De peccato linguae" provide definitions of the verbal vices they present, but some of these definitions are sketchy, very concise, and sometimes are lacking entirely (see rumor mongering, for instance). The moralist is more interested in the phenomenology of the sin and most often characterizes a trespass only obliquely, by analyzing the specific behavior of the sinner. A keen observer of the contemporary social scene, Peraldus frequently associates verbal sins with specific segments of society, tying, for instance, murmur and rumor to monks, lying to merchants, scurrility to minstrels, quarreling to women, and blasphemy to drunkards. To reinforce his ethical message, he draws extensively from scriptural and patristic authorities, which he intersperses with quotes from classical writers.[13] Due

12. The scriptural saying that Peraldus quotes here—"Vere tu ex illis es, nam et loquela tua manifestum te fecit" ("Surely though also art one of them; for thy speech bewrayeth thee"; Matt. 26:73)—will be reiterated in *Inferno* 10.25, in the context of Farinata's recognizing Dante as a Tuscan by his dialect: "La tua loquela ti fa manifesto" ("Your speech makes you manifest").

13. Peraldus quotes from Terence, Juvenal, Seneca, Cicero, Quintilian (among the classics)

to the heavy influence of the scriptures, his stylistic treatment of vices is eminently metaphorical, and the obsessive insistence with which certain motives recur is the arsenal of the skilled Christian orator concerned with persuading sinners to avoid immoral behavior. The last part of "De peccato linguae" provides a list of eight remedies against verbal transgressions, which are in fact repressive attitudes against sinful tendencies of the tongue (among them some are more theoretical: considering the dangers inherent in speaking, or how noble and useful the tongue is; some others are more practical: speaking rarely or little, taking time to think before speaking, or avoiding the persons who may cause someone to sin in words).[14]

In the late Middle Ages and the early Renaissance, Peraldus's *SVV* enjoyed an exceptional fortune; more than three hundred manuscripts are known from the thirteenth to the fifteenth century. In the fourteenth and fifteenth centuries both the tract on vices and the one on virtues could be found in all major libraries across Europe, whether monastic or secular, often even in multiple copies.[15] Of the medieval manuscripts of the text, Craun counts thirty-three copies in England alone.[16] Jean Gerson, the highly respected chancellor of the University of Paris, mentions Peraldus's *SVV* in his 1423 tract, *De examinatione doctrinarum* (On the examination of doctrines). It seems that the esteem in which Gerson held the Peraldian work was high; the chancellor allegedly said that if it happened that all the books in the world suddenly vanished and only Peraldus's great work survived, the loss would be tolerable.[17] In the sixteenth century, three editions of *SVV* were printed in 1571 alone, and in the seventeenth century, four different editions were printed in the same year—1668. This extraordinary success can be accounted for by the eminently practical nature of

and frequently from St. Augustine, Gregory the Great, and St. Bernard (among the Fathers). He rarely mentions Aristotle in *SV*, but we have to take into account that at that time, the moral thought of the Greek philosopher was not yet an essential part of Western culture. In Paris, the *Nicomachean Ethics* was known in full translation only in 1245.

14. For a discussion of Peraldus's system of verbal sins, see also Casagrande and Vecchio, *I peccati della lingua*, 103–40, and, more recently, Edwin Craun, *Lies, Slander and Obscenity in Medieval English Literature* (Cambridge: Cambridge University Press, 1997), 14–17.

15. Siegfried Wenzel, "The Continuing Life of William Peraldus's *Summa vitiorum*," in *Ad litteram: Authoritative Texts and Their Medieval Readers* (Notre Dame, Ind.: University of Notre Dame Press, 1992), 136.

16. Craun, *Lies, Slander and Obscenity*, 16.

17. Quoted in Siegfried Wenzel, "Dante's Rationale for the Seven Deadly Sins (*Purgatorio* XVII)," *Modern Language Review* 60 (1965): 529–33, at 531.

Peraldus's ethical system, which answered a catechetical need to which the speculative theologians of the day were less sensitive. After the seventeenth century, however, the remarkable popularity of *SVV* began to decline. In his 1948 study on Peraldus, Antoine Dondaine bitterly noted the fact that this outstanding medieval work had in modern times slipped into oblivion along with the name of its author. Peraldus should be granted a place of honor in the doctrinal history of the Middle Ages, for his *SVV* was the exceptional product of a type of Christian ethics essentially traditional and Latin, very different from the Greco-Arab wisdom that began to infiltrate medieval Christian thought.[18]

The last three to four decades have brought a marked change in the attitude of medieval scholarship toward Peraldus. Siegfried Wenzel, Richard Newhauser, Edwin Craun, and Bridget Balint are preparing a new edition of Peraldus's *Summa de vitiis* (*SV*).[19] Casagrande and Vecchio's book has also contributed a great deal to the revival of interest in the figure and works of the medieval moralist. Modern scholarship on Peraldus has amply proven *SV*'s influence on subsequent Western European moral thought, an influence that took various shapes, ranging from expansions of the work to abbreviations of it, adaptations, or simple quotes. In his 1992 study, Wenzel thoroughly examined and detected Peraldus's presence in works such as: *Erchantnuzz der Sund* (Knowledge of sin, fourteenth century, Vienna), *De lingua* (On the tongue, fourteenth century, Oxford), *Summa iusticie* (Summa of justice, beginning of the fourteenth century, England), Alexander Carpenter's *Destructiorum vitiorum* (On the destruction of vices, fifteenth century, England), and some others. Casagrande and Vecchio have also adduced strong arguments for Peraldus's influence on Vincent of Beauvais, Bartholomew of San Concord, John of Friburgh, Steven of Bourbon, Servasanto da Faenza, Laurent of Orléans, and Domenico Cavalca.

In this series of names it is worth highlighting Servasanto da Faenza, a Florentine Franciscan friar, who wrote *Liber de virtutibus et vitiis* (The book of virtues and vices, 1277–1285), a Latin adaptation of Peraldus's foundational work. In the section "De vitio lingue et eius multiplici specie" (On the vices of the tongue and its multiple species), Servasanto offers a summary of the Peraldian chapter on verbal sin but takes up only a few classes,

18. Dondaine, "Guillaume Peyraut," 162, 189.

19. A part of their work, including the full text of "De peccato linguae," can be consulted at http://www. english.unc.edu/swenzel/peraldus.html.

such as blasphemy, murmur, slander, flattery, sowing of discord, and double talk. As Dante's biography attests that he had a strong sympathy for the Franciscan order, Servasanto's activity in Florence during the years preceding Dante's exile increases the probability of the poet's familiarity with Peraldus. To my knowledge, Casagrande and Vecchio's mention of Servasanto da Faenza has not yet been connected with Dante.[20] Another name with a strong resonance in Dante's biography might have been the intermediary between Peraldus and Dante. According to Jean-Thiébaut Welter, Brunetto Latini undoubtedly drew on *SV* in his *Book of Treasure* (ca. 1266), a work reputedly known to Dante. Dondaine and Bettina Lindorfer adhere to Welter's assertion.[21]

Two studies dealing with Dante's relationship to Peraldus strongly argue for the Italian poet's familiarity with *SV*. In "Un' *Auctoritas* di Dante," Franco Mancini contends that Peraldus's work is one of the models that Dante visited most frequently as a reader. Noting first Peraldus's stamp on Iacopone da Todi and Brunetto Latini, Mancini signals the presence of many copies of *SV* in Dante's time in cities such as Pisa, Assisi, and Perugia. He then compares lines from the *Comedy* with passages from *SV*, drawing an impressive list of similarities between the two works. Although some of these analogies are problematic (like the comparison of Ulysses's *orazion picciola* with Peraldus's words on *superbia*), other similarities Mancini has highlighted are too striking to be dismissed.[22] I will mention here Dante's *contrapasso* for usurers, identical with Peraldus's description of this type of sinners, and the representation of Cayaphas in *Inferno* 23, echoing an eerily

20. To document that the Franciscans held Peraldus in high esteem, Wenzel adduces two cases: 1. Adam Salimbene, a Franciscan chronicler, who commended Peraldus and his *SV* in 1248; and 2. the anonymous Franciscan *Liber exemplorum* (*The Book of Examples*, 1275–1279), which was molded after *SV* (Wenzel, "The Continuing Life," 156). I feel compelled to add that these facts speak again in favor of Dante's possible familiarity with Peraldus's moral work.

21. Jean-Thiébaut Welter, *L'exemplum dans la littérature religieuse et didactique du Moyen Âge* (Paris: Occitania, 1927), 168; Dondaine, "Guillaume Peyraut," 191; Bettina Lindorfer, "*Peccatum linguae* and the Punishment of Speech Violations in the Middle Ages and Early Modern Times," in *Speaking in the Medieval World*, edited by Jean E. Godsall-Myers (Leiden: Brill, 2003), 27.

22. In his definition of *superbia*, Peraldus exclaims: "[Indocti] miseri sunt in vita ista. Quodammodo enim brutis inferiores sunt" ("The unlearned are unhappy in this life. They are even inferior to beasts"). The problem is that in this very passage, Peraldus reinforces his claim with a kindred quote from Boethius, an author whose influence on the *Comedy* Dante himself acknowledges. Ulysses's *orazion picciola* may thus have been shaped by Boethius through a direct influence, not necessarily through Peraldus's intermediary.

similar description in *SV.* According to Mancini, the portrayal of the Man of Crete should also be related to Peraldus, just as dozens of other images or metaphors that the critic generously selects from the three *canticas* of the *Comedy* and painstakingly compares with quotes from *SV.* The evidence Mancini gathers to substantiate his claim is indeed overwhelming; in addition, he does not confine himself to the *Comedy* but suggests that *Convivio* bears Peraldian marks as well. One idea seems to me particularly tantalizing in his study: that Dante's relationship to Peraldus did not take the shape of slavish imitation. *SV* represented an inexhaustible source of inspiration from which Dante gleaned scraps of information, concepts, and metaphorical images that he used in idiosyncratic ways in his vernacular poem; thus, Dante would be a *traduttore-traditore* of Peraldus. My analysis of the infernal circles punishing verbal sinners will add more affinities between *SV* and the *Comedy* to the already long list drawn up by Mancini.

Although focusing on just one aspect of the connection between the two works, Wenzel's study on Dante's rationale for the seven deadly sins in *Purgatorio* brings more compelling evidence for Dante's reliance on Peraldus. The seven forms of evil love according to which Dante disposes the terraces of the mount Purgatory correspond to the manifestations of *amor inordinatus,* "disorderly love," that Peraldus ascribes to the concept of sin. More precisely, the theory that serves Virgil to explain the structure of the purgatorial realm reproduces Peraldus's doctrine of sin from the chapter "De superbia" (On pride) of his *SV.* In Wenzel's opinion, since this approach to sin is unique in the moral theology of the Middle Ages, Dante could have taken it only from Peraldus. More recently, Carlo Delcorno, Bruno Porcelli, and Richard A. Shoaf have contributed further textual evidence in favor of a connection between Dante and Peraldus.[23] In light of all these historical and textual findings, the examination of the Peraldian treatment of the sins of the tongue in connection to the *Comedy* seems to me unavoidable and common sense. I will thus point to possible affinities between Dante's poem and "De peccato linguae" every time these similarities stand out. As to the ways in which Dante may have become familiar with Peraldus work, I adhere to Wenzel's conclusion:

23. Carlo Delcorno, "Dante e Peraldo," in *Exemplum e letteratura: Tra Medioevo e Rinascimento* (Bologna: Il Mulino, 1989), 195–227; Bruno Porcelli, "*Peccatum linguae,* modello mosaico, climax narrativo nel canto di Ulisse," *Critica letteraria* 19, no. 72 (1991): 423–43; Richard A. Shoaf, "Dante and Peraldus: The 'acqua falsa' of Maestro Adamo (A Note on *Inferno* 30, 64–69)," *Quaderni d'italianistica* 10 (1989): 311–13.

> Whether or not Dante knew Peraldus' *Summa* directly is hard to say. The material which Peraldus had collected was soon used and propagated by authors of Latin and vernacular manuals on sins and on confession. Hence it is possible that Dante became acquainted with our passage second hand, although the rationale [for the seven deadly sins] itself is usually not found in the less speculative, more popular handbooks of the time. On the other hand, Dante may have seen the *Summa* during his contacts with Dominican friars at Santa Maria Novella in Florence or at the Sorbonne.[24]

I feel compelled to mention that there is, however, no biographical evidence to support the hypothesis of Dante's trip to Paris. Based on Welter's study mentioned above, we should rather add Brunetto Latini to the list of possible intermediaries between Dante's and Peraldus's works, just as, based on Casagrande and Vecchio's findings, we should also add Servasanto da Faenza's name.

As far as Jean de Meun is concerned, he not only wrote his sequel to the *Rose* during the years when Peraldus's major work was very popular, but he also wrote it on Rue St. Jacques, the nucleus of the Dominican activity in Paris, where Peraldus's book of ethics was certainly very well known (Laurent of Orléans, a prior of the convent at that time, was translating sections of *SV*). We also have to remember that Jean was a great reader of, and translator from, Latin. In both Jean's and Dante's cases, the question "why do they not mention Peraldus's name in their works?" can be answered at least in one very simple way: humble Peraldus never signed his writings with his real name. As we have seen, for many decades his texts first circulated under the anonymous authorial signature "I, the smallest one of the order of the preaching friars." In the context of *Rose* criticism, it is worth mentioning that in the late 1960s, Lionel Friedman and John V. Fleming posited *SV* as a likely source of inspiration for Jean.[25] To my knowledge, distinct studies on the relationship between Jean and Peraldus do not exist, as they do for Dante and Peraldus. This fact is deplorable and highlights the stringent necessity of a closer look at Jean's debt to one of the most famous French pastoral writers of his time. If many Dante scholars convincingly speak of Peraldus's influence on the Italian poet, it is appropriate to believe that Jean de Meun, a Frenchman living and writing a poem on vices in the near vi-

24. Wenzel, "Dante's Rationale," 533.

25. Lionel Friedman, "Jean de Meun and Ethelred of Rievaulx," *L'esprit créateur* 2, no. 3 (1962): 135–41, at 18, and John V. Fleming, *The "Roman de la Rose": A Study in Allegory and Iconography* (Princeton, N.J.: Princeton University Press, 1969), 172.

cinity of a strong Dominican center of activity at the time when *SV* was already circulating intensely, had some knowledge of Peraldus's work. Likewise, if Edwin Craun, in analyzing four of the major medieval writers in English, argues for Peraldus's influence on them (and, tellingly, one of these writers is Chaucer, a translator of the *Rose*), we have even more reasons to look for Peraldian traces in Jean's own poem. Ernest Langlois makes a very important point about Jean's manipulation of sources: the poet promptly and excessively names the ancients every time he borrows from them directly or indirectly, but he takes care to conceal the more important debts he has toward the moderns.[26]

The most challenging question in the discussion of Jean's and Dante's relationships to Peraldus is not whether they are indebted to him or not, but whether they knew his *SV* directly, in its original Latin text, or indirectly, through the intermediary of its numerous Latin adaptations and/or vernacular translations analyzed by Wenzel, Casagrande, and Vecchio. But this is a question that, in the absence of historical documents and explicit textual references, even the most arduous historicists in Jean de Meun and Dante studies can answer only by focusing exclusively on it and by volunteering hypotheses based on speculations or personal intuitions. In my critical investigation, it is more important to situate the *Rose* and the *Inferno* in the general framework of the pastoral debate on verbal sins, to explore how Jean and Dante absorbed this debate in their poems and how they contributed to it from an ideological perspective and from the viewpoint of the moral terminology in the vernacular.

Since in French culture, Jean's efforts at the vernacularization of the ethical lexicon of speech are contemporary with Laurent of Orléans's translation of Peraldus's "De peccato linguae," a brief look at Laurent's *Somme le Roi* (1279–1280) seems adequate to me. In Italian culture, Dante's *Inferno* shortly precedes Cavalca's *Pungilingua* (1330–1342), the vast and exceptional reworking of "De peccato linguae." It is true that, just as we cannot consider *Somme le Roi* as a textual source for Jean's *Rose,* in the same way, we cannot posit *Pungilingua* as a source for the *Inferno;* but it is significant that in Italian culture, too, we have an exceptionally talented poet, who writes a *Comedy* on vices and virtues, and at about the same time, we have Cavalca, a prominent pastoral personality, who writes moral tracts in

26. Ernest Langlois, *Origines et sources du "Roman de la Rose"* (Paris: E. Thorin, 1890), 173.

the vernacular. *Inferno* and *Pungilingua* were written a few decades apart, but they do meet on the common ground of their authors' obsession with language and vernacularization of ethics. As a continuator of Peraldus, Cavalca is essential to my investigation for two reasons: he clarifies technical terms that in Peraldus are rather obscure (for they are not explained in enough detail but described metaphorically), and his *Pungilingua,* having come down to us in the Florentine dialect, offers me a very effective hermeneutic instrument for the interpretation of the speech abuses punished in the *Inferno,* a moral-allegorical poem written in the same idiom.

LAURENT OF ORLÉANS AND THE *PECHIES DE LA LANGUE* ("SINS OF THE TONGUE")

Somme le Roi, also known as *Somme Lorens* (Laurent's *Summa*) or even *Li livres royaux des vices et des vertus* (The royal books of vices and virtues), is a moral encyclopedia that, according to several of its interpreters, bears the irrefutable imprint of Peraldus's *SVV.*[27] As a Dominican friar confessor to Philip III, Laurent wrote this work at the request of the king, who wanted to have and to offer his court a major book of moral instruction drafted in the living, everyday language of lay people. In Charles Langlois's view, a great part of the immediate success of the *Somme* must be attributed to the fact that, being a book commissioned by the king himself, it easily aroused the curiosity of the aristocratic circles of the time.[28] The book is structured in six major tracts, with several chapters each: 1. the Ten Commandments; 2. the twelve articles of faith; 3. the seven deadly sins; 4. the virtues; 5. the commentary on the *Pater noster;* and 6. the seven gifts of the Holy Spirit.[29]

27. The earliest assertion in this sense belongs to R. Elfreda Fowler, who in 1905 argued that both Gower (in *Mirour de l'Omme* and *Confessio Amantis*) and Laurent of Orléans (in *Somme le Roi*) drew extensively on Peraldus's *SVV.* Welter also asserts that the *Somme* contains vast borrowings from the Peraldian work (*L'exemplum dans la littérature,* 169). (It is worth mentioning that in Welter's list of writers influenced by Peraldus, *Somme le Roi* immediately follows Brunetto Latini's *Book of Treasure.*) According to Casagrande and Vecchio (*I peccati della lingua*), one of the places where Peraldus's influence on Laurent of Orléans is more easily recognizable is the chapter on the "pechies de la langue" from *Somme le Roi* (132–33).

28. Charles V. Langlois, *La Vie en France au Moyen Âge de la fin du XIIe au milieu du XIVe siècle,* 2nd ed., 2 vols. (Paris: Slatkine, 1984), 123.

29. In Ms. 2071 (Arsenal Library) that I follow, the seven deadly sins are placed at the very beginning, in order to emphasize the importance of the ethical component of the work. The manuscript ends with the Ten Commandments, while the part devoted to the seven gifts of the

None of these tracts is original; they are all translations or adaptations of extraneous writings, mostly Latin. Langlois notes that the entire work, generally "un livre mal fait" ("a badly conceived book"), is a shorter version of another moral tractate, titled *Miroir* (Mirror). Even when *Somme* deviates from *Miroir* (the chapter on the sins of the tongue and the tract on the gifts of the Holy Spirit, for instance, do not exist in the latter), it is still not original, because these two sections are borrowings from Peraldus. The great eclecticism on account of which Langlois passed his severe judgment on the originality of *Somme* does not weigh negatively in my consideration of Laurent of Orléans.[30] My purpose is precisely to examine the way in which a moral theologian writing in French vernacular adapted Peraldus's Latin tract on verbal sins. What matters for me is Laurent's work as a translator, the terms and notions he uses to describe verbal transgressions.

In *Somme,* the discussion on the sins of the tongue is imbedded into the larger category of "pechies de la gueule" ("sins of the mouth"), which occupy the seventh position within the scheme of the capital sins. Here, Laurent adopts an allegorical framework based on St. John's apocalyptic vision of the seven-headed beast; within this scheme, the seven capital sins correspond to the seven heads of the beast, and the ten horns of it are *trespassemens,* "trespasses," of the ten commandments. This parallel makes sense if we consider the etymology of the adjective in "*capital* sins" (from Lat. *capus,* "head," from which the offspring derive). Unfortunately, however, when Laurent moves on to treating the subdivisions of the seven sins, he quits the allegory of the seven-headed beast and, all of a sudden, starts speaking of the branches and twigs of the tree of evil.[31] (This structural in-

Holy Spirit is missing. There are several other French manuscripts of *Somme* beginning with the seven deadly sins instead of the Ten Commandments (Ms. 409 and 2932, two of the oldest ones, and the Alençon Ms.).

30. Despite his negative assessment of Laurent as a writer, Langlois is quick to evoke the great and long success of *Somme,* a work preserved in nearly one hundred manuscripts and translated early on into several European languages (Italian, Spanish, Provençal, English, and Flemish). For the English adaptations of *Somme,* see Leo Carruthers, *La "Somme le Roi" de Lorens d'Orléans et ses traductions anglaises : Etude comparée* (Paris: Association des médiévistes anglicistes de l'enseignement supérieur, 1986). One of the English versions of the work is available in a modern edition: Laurent of Orléans, *The Book of Vices and Virtues: A Fourteenth-Century English Translation of the "Somme le Roi" of Lorens d'Orléans,* edited by N. Francis (London: Oxford University Press, 1942.

31. The allegory of the trees of good and evil was the general framework in which *Miroir* had treated virtues and vices. Thus, although Laurent replaced the image of the tree of evil

consistency is one of the main charges critics address to Laurent.) The seventh head of the apocalyptic beast is represented by the sins of the mouth, but this "head" is further subdivided into ... the tree of gluttony and the tree of verbal transgressions.[32] The examination of the sins of the tongue flows quite naturally from a virulent condemnation of drunkenness, as a manifestation of the sin of gluttony. Since drunkards have the bad habit of frequenting taverns, it is here, in this "ecole et chapelle du diable" ("school and chapel of the devil") that people lose their self-control and commit very many verbal offenses.

This is the springboard from which Laurent launches his disquisition on the sins of the tongue. If we collate this section with "De peccato linguae," one major difference stands out: out of the twenty-four verbal transgressions identified by Peraldus, Laurent retains only ten, justifying his reduction with the help of another biblical analogy. *La male langue* ("the evil tongue") is the dry tree Jesus cursed on his way to Jerusalem because it was bearing no fruits. Counting the ways in which the *male langue* manifests itself would be as difficult and daunting as counting the leaves of a tree. What can be counted more easily, though, are the branches of the tree, and Laurent identifies ten such ramifications: *oiseuse,* "idle talk"; *vantise,* "boasting"; *losenge/losengerie,* "flattery"; *detraction,* "slander"; *mensonge* (or *fallace*), "lying/fallacy"; *perjure* (or *faus serment*), "perjury/false oath"; *contenz,* "contention"; *murmure,* "murmur"; *rebellion,* "rebellion"; and *blaspheme,* "blasphemy." In the category of idle talk, Laurent ranges: vain words, peddlers' words, storytelling, and jokes. Taking up an Augustinian idea via Peraldus, he asserts that those who give in to idle speech waste not only time but also their inner self: "ils vuident le tresor du Coeur" ("they empty the treasure of the heart"). Boasting is another form of transgressive speech, for he who boasts acts like a "voleur de Dieu" ("thief who steals from God"), who credits himself with what is in fact God's work. For the sin of flattery, the third branch of the tree of the evil tongue, Laurent uses three terms: *adulateur,* reminiscent of Peraldus's *adulator,* and more often, *losengeur,* "singer of praises," or *flateur,* "flatterer," which were more common in everyday language. (We will

---

with that of the apocalyptic beast, he was unable to move further within this framework and switched back to the tree, which could lend itself more easily to divisions and ramifications.

32. Although in *SV,* Peraldus had not discussed the sins of the tongue along with the sins of *gula,* the association between gluttony and verbal sin was a traditional coupling in the moral tracts of the period (Casagrande and Vecchio, *I peccati della lingua,* 141–68).

encounter all these vernacular terms in the *Rose,* when the habit of flattery is discussed.) Peraldus's *detractio* is translated as *detraction,* but the perpetrator of this sin is called less often a *detracteur,* "detractor," as in Peraldus, and more often a *medisans* (which etymologically means "evil speaker"). The technical terms from "De peccato linguae" are thus not only gallicized (as in the couple *detractio-detraction*) but also replaced with terms from the living language, which the laymen were able to understand. The sin of *mendacium,* translated as *mensonge,* is described along Peraldian lines as a falsification of reality. Lying, Laurent says, falsifies man as one falsifies the royal seal or money; therefore, the liar will be judged at the Last Judgment as a falsifier.

From lying, Laurent moves on, just like Peraldus, to perjury, defined as a trespassing of the truthful oath. The next category, quarreling, is Peraldus's former *contentio,* but here again new moral terms are introduced, as this sin is further subdivided into seven twigs: *estriver,* "contradicting"; *tencier,* "quarreling"; *ledengier,* "name calling"/"insulting"; *mal dire,* "cursing"; *remponer,* "admonishing"; *menassier,* "menacing"; *descorde sosciter,* "sowing of discord." Among these seven divisions of quarreling (several of which Peraldus had treated as autonomous categories unrelated to *contentio*), Laurent establishes a vague hierarchy, asserting that the most dangerous is the sin of sowing of discord, because it disrupts the civic order and social harmony. He discusses the sin of murmur after that of quarreling, for the reason that those who do not dare argue loudly still contend in a low voice. This class of verbal sin is further divided into murmuring against man (like the servants against their masters, or the poor against the rich, etc.) and murmuring against God. The next verbal sin, rebellion, is closely related to, and deemed more grievous than, murmuring, given that, if protesting in a low voice is a bad thing, it is even worse to rebel, Laurent explains. In order to impose their will on others, rebels do not heed other people's orders or recommendations but scornfully disobey them. In Laurent's view, rebellion has an obvious verbal root, for if rebels are chided, they defend themselves verbally and protest against laws and scriptural warnings.

It is worth adding that rebellion was not among the twenty-four classes of *peccata linguae* established by Peraldus; it is Laurent's own contribution, likely made to please the king, who had commissioned the book. No other virtue could please the ruler of a country more than submission, the opposite of rebellion, a sin to be inveighed against virulently, as Laurent does. Blasphemy, the last sin on Laurent's list, is treated differently from Peraldus's line of thinking. In "De peccato linguae," blasphemy was the most grievous form of sinful speech and was consequently discussed at length at the very beginning of the chapter. Although the reasons driving people to insult God or the saints are reiterated in *Somme,* the harsh tone of Peraldus's condemnation of blasphemy does not persist in Laurent. Again, the reason for this depreciation of the gravity of blasphemy might lie in the addressee of the book. As a king, Philip was more concerned with political and worldly matters than with religious ones, and Laurent was undoubtedly well aware thereof. Gaston Paris remarks in this respect the mild tone of Laurent's work and assumes that the author did not want to "turn the world into a cloister."[33] Charles Langlois even ventures to speak of the embarrassment the humble Laurent may have felt in writing a book of moral instruction for his majesty, the king.[34]

All these factors may account for the major differences between Peraldus's "De peccato linguae" and Laurent's chapter on the sins of the tongue. As the latter author manipulates a moral lexicon in French at about the same time that Jean de Meun was writing his allegorical poem, a reading of *Somme,* even a perfunctory one as I have provided here, may cast light on the verbal habits that Jean's characters debate with great passion.

DOMENICO CAVALCA

Like Peraldus and Laurent, Domenico Cavalca was a Dominican friar, one of the most prolific writers of his order. Born about 1270 in Vicopisano near Pisa, he was educated at the ecclesiastic school of St. Catherine of Alexandria in Pisa. According to the *Chronicles* and the *Annals* of the Dominican priory in Pisa, the sources that document his life and career, Cavalca did not hold an academic degree but was extremely active as a preacher and ecclesiastic reformer. His constant support for the poor and the sick in hospitals and prisons earned him the nickname *Dominicus hospedalarius.* He died in 1342, holding the reputation of a holy man.[35]

33. Gaston Paris, *La Littérature française au Moyen Âge* (Paris: Hachette, 1914), 157.

34. Charles Langlois, *La Vie en France,* 140.

35. The *Annals* report that the entire city took part in the funeral, especially the underprivileged, who deeply mourned the loss of their protector. The *Chronicles* mention the reputation of holiness he deservedly enjoyed upon his death (both sources are quoted in Benedict M. Ashley, *Dominic Cavalca and the Spirituality of the Word,* Web, 3 March 2004, http:/www.op.org/domcentral/study/Ashley/Cavalca.html). For more on Cavalca's life and works, see Carmelina

All throughout his life, Cavalca alternated his charitable works with studying and writing. His religious texts are numerous and variegated and have proven very influential in Dominican circles.[36] An important part of these writings is represented by the so-called *volgarizzamenti,* "vulgarizations," such as: *Atti degli Apostoli* (Acts of the Apostles), *Dialogo di san Gregorio* (Dialogue of St. Gregory the Great), *Vite dei Santi Padri* (Lives of the Holy Fathers), *Lo specchio de' peccati* (Mirror of sins), *Medicina del cuore ovvero trattato della Patientia* (Medicine of the heart or Treatise on patience), *Pungilingua* (The wounding tongue), and *Epistola a Eustochio* (Epistle to

Naselli, *Domenico Cavalca* (Città di Castello: Il Solco, 1925), and Telio Taddei, "La Vita del Cavalca dai suoi scritti," *Memorie domenicane* 1 (1942). For the complete list of critical studies on Cavalca in the nineteenth century, see *Dizionario critico della letteratura italiana* (Turin: Unione Tipografica-Editrice Torinese, 1986).

36. The last few decades have witnessed a renewal of the critical and philological research on Domenico Cavalca, research channeled mainly in two directions: an investigation of the sources of Cavalca's writings, in order to establish the extent of the author's originality, and a study of the rich manuscript tradition, with the purpose of assessing Cavalca's popularity and sphere of influence as a vernacular writer. The former trend of investigation is represented by: Olga A. Rossi, "Questione del Cavalca: Further Findings," *PMLA* (1949): 829–63; Renzo Lotti, *Contributi su Domenico Cavalca (c. 1270–1342)* (Amsterdam: Kaal Boek, 1987); and Mauro Zanchetta, "Il 'Pungilingua' di Domenico Cavalca (Edizione)" (PhD diss., University of Studies of Padua, 2011), who propose textual readings of *Pungilingua* (Rossi and Zanchetta) and of *Frutti della Lingua* (Lotti), in comparison with Peraldus's *Summa.* For the study of the manuscript tradition, see Carlo Delcorno, *La Tradizione delle Vite dei Santi Padri* (Venice: Istituto Veneto di Scienze, Lettere ed Arti, 2000); Marcello Ciccuto, "Tradizione delle opere di Domenico Cavalca: Gli esempi dei trattati morali," *Italianistica* 19, no. 1 (1990): 39–67; Alfredo Troiano, "Un contributo alla tradizione manoscritta dello *Specchio di Croce* di Domenico Cavalca: il ms. 129 della Newberry Library di Chicago," *Lettere italiane* 2 (April–June 2008): 226–35; and again Zanchetta. More recently, Edoardo Barbieri has offered a synopsis of the life and works of Domenico Cavalca ("Domenico Cavalca volgarizzatore degli *Actus Apostolorum,*" in *La Bibbia in Italiano tra Medioevo e Rinascimento: Atti del Convegno Internazionale, Firenze, Certosa del Galluzzo, November 8–9 1996,* edited by Lino Leonardi [Florence: SISMEL, 1998], 291–328). A note on Domenico Cavalca by Steven Botterill has also been included in *Medieval Italy: An Encyclopedia* ("Cavalca, Domenico" in *Medieval Italy: An Encyclopedia,* edited by Christopher Kleinhenz et al. [New York: Routledge, 2004], 1:197–98), whereas the prestigious series *Patrimoine littéraire européen* has devoted several pages to the literary activity of the Italian moralist and included nineteenth-century French translations of two of his works (Jean Claude Polet et al., eds., *Patrimoine littéraire européen,* vol. 5: *Premières mutations: de Petrarque à Chaucer (1304–1400)* (Paris: Boeck University, 1995), 5:198–205). Manu Radhakrishnan has devoted his doctoral dissertation to an analysis of Cavalca's skills as a translator ("Domenico Cavalca and the "Liber Vitaspatrum": Vernacular Hagiography in Late Medieval and Early Modern Italy" [PhD diss., Princeton University, 2012], http://arks.princeton.edu/ark:/88435/dsp01sb397828g.

Eustochio), translations highly valued by both Cavalca's contemporaries and modern critics.[37] The last three texts are compilations of materials drawn from Peraldus's works; *Lo specchio de' peccati* is a synopsis of *SV*, *Medicina del cuore* is a lengthy reworking of Peraldus's chapter on anger, and *Pungilingua* is an extended rewrite of "De peccato linguae."

Another substantial part of Cavalca's output is a series of more original writings, such as *Specchio di croce* (Mirror of the cross), *Frutti della Lingua* (The fruits of the tongue), *Disciplina degli spirituali* (The discipline of spiritual persons), and *Trattato delle trenta stoltitie* (Tractate on the thirty follies). Although these texts still draw on external sources (Western and Eastern patristic writings or more contemporary authors, such as the Victorines and Peraldus, in particular), they reveal more of the creative side of Cavalca.[38] What is common to these works (original or translations) is the moral obligation the author feels toward the unlearned Christians unable to understand Latin. In the prologue to *Specchio di croce,* he confesses: "I have

37. In *Dizionario critico,* Sebastiano Bastianetto notes that typically, Cavalca contributes so much to the spirit of the text he vernacularizes that he seems to write an original text ("Cavalca, Domenico," in *Dizionario critico della letteratura italiana* [Turin: Unione Tipografica-Editrice Torinese, 1986], 562). In his turn, Ashley notes that along with Cassian's *Conferences* (a text dear to St. Dominic, the founder of the Dominican order), Cavalca's Italian version of the *Lives* contributed to the transmission of the important legacy of Byzantine spirituality to the Latin West. Analyzing the manuscript tradition of the *Lives,* Carlo Delcorno proves that Cavalca wrote this work in the dialect of Pisa, but since it was almost immediately "modernized" and rewritten in Florentine, it was in the latter idiom that Cavalca's *Lives* were ever printed and circulated, becoming models of language for centuries to come (Domenico Cavalca, *Vite dei santi Padri,* edited by Carlo Delcorno [Florence: Galluzzo, 2009], 1:xi–xiv). Although Delcorno does not make specific reference to *Pungilingua,* this translation from Peraldus may have undergone the same treatment. The tract has come down to us in Florentine. For the latest report on the manuscript tradition of *Pungilingua,* see Zanchetta, "Il 'Pungilingua,'" who in his doctoral dissertation also provides a new, critical edition of the text.

38. *Specchio di croce* is an original meditation on the Passion, the first text of this type in the Dominican culture, whereas *Trattato delle trenta stoltitie* analyses the spiritual abuses made by those engaged in a combat against the world and its evils (among such abuses or "follies" are: practicing penances in excess, hoping to win the battle without God's help, getting discouraged after the first defeat, etc.). In the manuscripts, *Trattato* often joins *Disciplina degli spirituali,* a text dealing with the defects of the pious (lukewarmness, self-righteousness, depression, etc.) and bearing the imprint of Peraldus's thought. The tract *Frutti della lingua* is an optimistic response to Peraldus's chapter on verbal sins and a sequel to Cavalca's own popularization of it, the *Pungilingua.* In *Frutti,* Cavalca develops the Peraldian insights on the benefits of speech and structures his material in three main parts: one on prayer, one on preaching, and the last one on confession.

thought that, although I am not very skilled, with the scanty knowledge I have, I can at least write a work; not a subtle one, nor in Latin, but in the vernacular, so that some devout laymen, who are unlearned and very busy, may find in it an incentive to devotion."[39] Cavalca's concern with offering lay people moral instruction in their own, living language is similar to the goal of Dante's *Convivio,* another vernacular work that aims at sharing the light of knowledge with those who find themselves in spiritual darkness.

One of the most notable features of Cavalca's output, a feature highlighted by practically all the secondary sources I have consulted, is his writing style, characterized by simplicity of syntax and clarity, qualities that established him as an artistic model for subsequent centuries. It is relevant in this sense that the Italian purists considered Cavalca's language and style examples of perfection characteristic of "the golden Trecento."[40] Thus, speaking of the cultural osmosis proper to the thirteenth and fourteenth centuries, an age in which many efforts were directed to the creation of a vernacular literary language faithful to the spirit of Latin works but comprehensible even by the unlearned, Sebastiano Bastianetto considers Cavalca a leading exponent of this process, a "pioneer of language and spirituality."[41]

Pungilingua (The Wounding Tongue)

The modern reader who would undertake to read *Pungilingua* after "De peccato linguae" might have the uncanny feeling that Cavalca is Peraldus himself speaking an Italian dialect, so well the former adheres to the ethical message of the latter. If we consider the two authors in their historical contexts, it is not difficult to understand why Peraldus exerted such a powerful influence on Cavalca. Born just one generation after Peraldus and belonging to the same fraternal order, with which he shared the preoccupations

39. Quoted in Carlo Delcorno, "Cavalca, Domenico," in *Dizionario biografico degli italiani* (Rome: Istituto della Cultura Italiana, 1979), 22:561. Since there is no English version of Cavalca's works, the translation of the passages I cite is mine.

40. Cavalca's texts became very popular again in the eighteenth and nineteenth centuries, when they were reprinted and widely circulated. Delcorno explains this revival by the interest of the eighteenth-century religious culture in the devotional works of the friar, which are now presented to the public as models of both spiritual and linguistic value. In the age of the *purismo,* the Italian philologists promote Cavalca as the perfect representative of the pure language of Trecento ("Cavalca, Domenico," 585).

41. Bastianetto, "Cavalca, Domenico," 562.

with preaching and moral reformation, Cavalca could not remain insensitive to the pastoral output of the French master from Lyon. By the time Cavalca began his writing activity in Pisa, *SVV* was, as we have seen, already present in several places in Italy. His decision to translate Peraldus's moral texts testifies to the great authority the French Dominican had in Italy in the first decades of the fourteenth century, when Dante was still alive. "De peccato linguae" must have impressed Cavalca in a special way, since he decided to translate it as an autonomous book and under a new title. It is highly likely that one of the reasons why he was so attentive to this class of sins was his catechetical agenda. Preaching, the main apostolic activity of the Dominican Order, was intimately related to a good control of spoken words. Another plausible reason for Cavalca's idiosyncratic treatment of "De peccato linguae" is that this chapter was one of Peraldus's most original developments in *SV*. And finally, we have to consider that, besides being a moralist and a preacher, Cavalca was also an experienced translator. Reproducing a Latin tract on verbal sins in the vernacular must have seemed a very appealing undertaking to him, since it provided him with the opportunity to verify how Peraldian moral-linguistic theories would hold in the vulgar language. Would the spirit of vernacular Italian fit into the mold of Peraldus's Latin discourse and examples?

Cavalca's *Pungilingua* is more than a slavish reproduction of "De peccato linguae." While the Italian writer follows the general pattern of the Peraldian approach (the division into twenty-four sins, for example), he also takes many liberties with respect to it in the form of developments of old ideas or deviations from them. This ambivalent attitude toward the original—fidelity and distance—is programmatically expressed in the prologue, where Cavalca gives the rationale for his writing *Pungilingua.* Here, he introduces himself as a humble compiler of Peraldus, whose devotion and wisdom in writing on the "twenty-four *mortal* sins proceeding from the tongue" he deeply admires and acknowledges.[42] It is important to note that Peraldus had never called *peccata linguae* "mortal" (although the eightfold structure of his ethics suggests that he implied this). Cavalca, however, takes Peraldus's approach one step further, as he explicitly and boldly assigns to the manifestations of evil speech the status of mortal sins. The Italian translator also forewarns readers about his personal contribution to the Peraldian tract: he confesses to hav-

42. Domenico Cavalca, *Il Pungilingua,* edited by Giorgio Bottari (Milan, 1837), xvi; emphasis mine.

ing added new ideas to it and enriched it with new examples. Aware of his originality, Cavalca contrives a title for this new product—*Pungilingua,* a pun articulated on the twofold ability of the tongue, that of harming and of being harmed. The tongue, as a vehicle for sin, will be wounded by this educational tract in the vernacular, which aims at repressing the tongue's proneness to evil. Cavalca's self-awareness as a writer is paralleled by his concern as an ecclesiastic author of *vernacular* works; he justifies his linguistic choice by the universality of the verbal sin, which can affect both the educated and the unlearned. His pastoral care thus addresses a category of Christians unable to read Peraldus's tract in the original: the uninstructed laity, barred from access to Latin. The laymen, too, had to be sensitized to the destructive power of imprudent speech, and in this process of spiritual education, the vernacular, in its most quotidian and accessible aspect, was the perfect linguistic tool.

Unlike Peraldus's "De peccato linguae," which was divided into twenty-four chapters according to the twenty-four sins of the tongue identified, Cavalca's book is structured in thirty chapters, because some of the sins are paid more attention to than others and treated in more than one chapter. The list of the sins is as follows:

1. *bestemmiare Dio* (cursing God)
2. *mormorare* (murmuring; four distinct chapters)
3. *difendere e scusare il peccato suo o altrui* (defending and excusing the sin of oneself or of another)
4. *spergiuro, e male giudicare* (perjury and bad judgment)
5. *bugiare* (lying)
6. *detrazione* (slander; three chapters)
7. *peccato degli adulatori* (sin of flatterers, accompanied, in the same chapter, by the kindred sin of those who listen to flatterers)
8. *maladire e bestemmiare* (cursing and blaspheming)
9. *convizio* (insult)
10. *contenzione e garrire* (contention and scolding)
11. *derisione* (derision; two chapters)
12. *peccato de' mali consiglieri e confortatori al male* (sin of evil counselors and instigators to evil)
13. *peccato dei renunziatori e seminatori di discordie* (sin of informers and sowers of discord)
14. *peccato dei bilingui e novellieri* (sin of double talkers and peddlers)
15. *peccato della jattanza* (sin of boasting)

16. *peccato del rivelare i secreti* (sin of ferreting secrets)

17. *peccato dello stolto promettere e minaciare altrui* (sin of foolish promise and threatening another)

18. *peccato del parlare ozioso e multiloquio* (sin of idle and excessive speech)

19. *peccato del parlare disonesto e giullaresco* (sin of dishonest and jocular speech)

20. *peccato di varj e dissoluti balli e canti* (sin of various dances and songs; two chapters)

21. *peccato degl' indovini ed incantatrici e malefici* (sin of diviners and magicians and evil spirits)[43]

If we compare this list with Peraldus's, we will notice a few structural changes. Cavalca conflates two formerly distinct sins (murmur with rumor), adds a new category of verbal sinners (the *novellieri,* "peddlers," whose analysis he includes in the chapter devoted to double talkers), and pairs up the sins of foolish promise and menace in another chapter. He does the same with idle talk and loquacity. He then further divides the Peraldian *scurrilitas* into the sins of dissolute songs . . . and dance, of which the French Dominican had not spoken. The last sin on Peraldus's list, *indiscreta taciturnitas,* is replaced in *Pungilingua* by the sins of the diviners and magicians, who misuse their verbal gifts to predict future events or to drive people to idolatry. Cavalca does acknowledge the existence of a transgression such as *mal tacere,* "evil silence," but he counts it as a twenty-fifth sin (Peraldus had spoken only of twenty-four) and promises to deal with it at length in a separate tract, given that this type of transgression is too serious to be debated in just one chapter. The idea of such a new project might also explain the most striking omission with respect to Peraldus's system: the absence of the list of remedies for verbal sins with which the French ecclesiastic had concluded his "De peccato linguae."[44]

Like Peraldus, Cavalca defines the sin through the behavior of the sinner. Sometimes, the Italian moralist does not even use the technical name of the sin (*adulatio,* or *pravum consilium,* for instance, as Peraldus had done at the beginning of each subchapter), but introduces it indirectly: "the sin of flatterers," "the sin of evil counselors," to give just two examples. A new as-

43. All the quotes from *Pungilingua* I give throughout this book come from the Bottari edition.

44. For a chapter-by-chapter account of the differences between Peraldus's text and Cavalca's, see Zanchetta, "Il 'Pungilingua,'" 435–443.

pect in *Pungilingua,* an aspect that is to be accounted for by Cavalca's skills as a translator, is the constant care he takes to explain the ethical terms he uses. When he introduces notions such as *convizio, adulatori,* or *derisione,* for instance, he immediately specifies the meanings of the words: "del convizio, cioè di villaneggiare e vituperare il prossimo con parole d'obbrobrio" ("of insult, that is, of vilifying and vituperating against one's neighbor with words of opprobrium"), or: "del peccato degli adulatori ciòe dei lusinghieri" ("of the sin of adulators, that is to say flatterers"), or again: "della derisione, cioè di fare beffe d'altrui" ("of derision, that is to say, of mocking another"). Thanks to Cavalca's efforts at proper and subtle translation, many lexical resources of the vernacular were exploited and fixed in a written form, maybe for the first time in the history of the language. His contribution to the creation, enrichment, or consolidation of a moral lexicon in the vernacular deserves a much deeper consideration than I can offer here. As far as my critical endeavor is concerned, however, Cavalca's work as a moralist of speech, albeit briefly underscored, is fundamental. The lengthy explanations that he furnishes to the great variety of verbal sins Peraldus had briefly discussed in Latin, just as the wealth of exemplary stories with which Cavalca illustrates these sins, can constitute a major key in understanding Dante's metalanguage and view of sinful speech.

THOMAS AQUINAS AND THE *PECCATA VERBI* ("SINS OF WORD")

Written between 1266 and 1274, more than two decades after Peraldus's *SVV, Summa theologica* (or *theologiae*) is the fruit of one of the finest Dominican thinkers of the Middle Ages. *Doctor Angelicus,* as Thomas Aquinas was surnamed, would be elevated to the rank of saint by the Catholic Church, which would adopt his theological views as the official doctrine of Catholicism. His short but very intense life deeply marked the cultural climate of both France and Italy at the time when Jean and Dante were establishing themselves as writers. Aquinas was a student in Paris from 1245 to 1247, when he decided to follow his master, Albert the Great, to his newly founded *Studium generale* in Cologne. In 1252, Aquinas returned to the University of Paris to complete his training; then he taught there from 1256 to 1259, when he left for Italy. He returned to Paris in 1269 and continued his teaching at the University of Paris until 1272. In 1272–1273 he was a regent-master at Naples. He died in 1274, at the age of forty-nine.[45] His major work, *Summa theologica* (*ST*), includes important sections on moral questions, both in *Prima secundae* and in the celebrated *Secunda secundae*.[46] Although built on Aristotelian premises, Aquinas's moral system absorbs in idiosyncratic ways the most significant aspects of previous Christian ethical theories and raises them to the heights of Scholastic philosophy. *ST* is very different from the Peraldian work in its approach to vices. Peraldus aimed at giving his readers practical knowledge of evil and at teaching them how to avoid the various forms of temptation. It was a rhetorical work designed (and immediately used) as homiletic material in which a preacher could find a vast array of discussions on vices, viewpoints endorsed by Roman moralists or patristic sources and illustrated by exemplary anecdotes. The discourse on vices in *ST,* on the other hand, is eminently speculative, aiming at doctrinal clarification and taxonomy. Aristotle's *Ethics* plays a fundamental role in helping Aquinas establish the nature of sins, the difference between a sin and a vice, and the various subspecies of each chief transgression. The discussion of sins is structured on the pattern of *questions* composed of several *articles* each; in a typically Scholastic fashion, all articles begin with possible objections to the problem posed, objections followed by Aquinas's detailed refutation and brilliantly developed arguments. Reason and strict logical analysis replace the gripping anecdotes and emotional tone of outraged Peraldus. The ethical vocabulary also becomes more stable and precise. *ST* was and remains a masterpiece of philosophical analysis and synthesis, a monument of human thought. Its debt to and difference from Peraldus's *Summa* are yet to be investigated.

For Aquinas, morality is a movement of the rational creature toward God, an aspiration achieved by means of human actions. The philosopher investigates these actions from the perspective of the *liber arbitrium,* "free will," which, like reason and language, represents a divine gift bestowed exclusively on man. Were it not for man's free will, the punishments or rewards, the commandments, or the laws could not find a justification. Depending on whether the choice turns toward good or evil, a human action

45. For more information about his life and activity, see Jean-Pierre Torrell, *Saint Thomas Aquinas,* vol. 1: *The Person and His Work,* translated by Robert Royal, rev. ed. (Washington D.C.: The Catholic University of America Press, 2005), and the *Cambridge Companion to Aquinas* (12–196).

46. Hereafter *ST* Ia-IIae and *ST* IIa-IIae.

is qualified as moral or immoral. In the process of examining whether an action is moral or not, the most important role is played by the object and end of that particular human act, by its finality.[47] Since etymologically *arbitrium* means "judgment," Aquinas defines the notion of free will in intellectual terms, as an active entity operating through choices. As he makes it explicit in Ia IIae Q. 74.1, sin originates in the power of free choice: "Sin is an act.... Now since it is proper to moral acts that they are voluntary, it follows that the will, which is the principle of all voluntary acts, both of good acts, and of evil acts or sins, is the principle of sins." This postulate of the will as the cause of evil actions will have a major bearing on Aquinas's conception of the sins of word, as well.

In human operations, the will as the main moral mover works in tandem with the faculty of deliberation (judgment), for the operating subject must be aware of his goal and means. Thus, an involuntary action of violence, committed out of anger, is pardonable, since the willful movement of the soul was affected by a disorderly state of mind. When, however, the will of an individual is not affected by impulses, weakness, or carelessness, but exerts itself with deliberation and in all awareness, the individual is fully responsible for his evil act and has no palliative excuses for it. Starting from the premise, "it is a heretic error to consider all sins to be equal and that all the pains of hell are equal," the theologian compares sins of deed with sins of word and of thought, establishing precise degrees of seriousness for each individual trespass in respect to the others.[48] He argues that verbal trespasses are of a less grievous nature than the ones of deed: "Sins of word have a certain levity, in so far as they are apt to occur through a slip of the tongue, and

47. *ST* IIa-IIae Q. 110.1. For important overviews of Thomas Aquinas's ethical doctrines, see: Etienne Gilson, *Moral Values and the Moral Life: The Ethical Theory of St. Thomas Aquinas* (Hamden, Conn.: Shoe String Press, 1961); G. Simon Harak, ed., *Aquinas and Empowerment: Classical Ethics for Ordinary Lives* (Washington, D.C.: Washington University Press, 1996); and the *Cambridge Companion to Aquinas* (196–216). More recently, Peter Karl Koritanksy, who has written a book on Aquinas's punitive theory, situates the theologian's moral system in his philosophy of natural law, defined as that part of divine law that applies to human beings. Koritansky highlights that in Aquinas's view, human beings have the principles of the eternal law instilled in their minds by means of an intellectual habit called "synderesis." This is defined as a natural knowledge that all individuals have, and on account of which they can discern the basic moral laws of their human nature (the fact, for instance, that adultery is morally wrong and contrary to human nature (*Thomas Aquinas and the Philosophy of Punishment,* [Washington, D.C.: The Catholic University of America Press, 2012], 80–81).

48. *ST* Ia-IIae QQ. 72–73.

without much forethought."[49] Occasionally, however, he does not hesitate to put sins of word on the same par with sins of deeds and concedes that in certain circumstances (for instance, when a verbal abuse is committed deliberately, with premeditation), this verbal sin becomes mortal: "an idle word, which is generally speaking, venial, may even be a mortal sin."[50]

Aquinas states that assessing deeds, words, or thoughts as specific human acts is not an easy task for a moralist, for he has to analyze every act from all angles and to consider all the circumstances under which a specific deed, word, or thought has occurred. Weighing these circumstances is of utmost importance because the circumstantial situation may decide whether a particular error is mortal or venial, and whether the soul will end up in hell or not. Thus, salvation or damnation is often a matter of conjunctural framework. For, if the origin of a sin depends on its inclination to an end (i.e., on the thing toward which the sin turns), the gravity of a sin, which determines the fate of the soul after death, depends on what it turns away from. Question 73.3 of IIa IIae represents the crux of Aquinas's thought on the various degrees of seriousness in moral errors. Here, he postulates that sins are different from one another in the same way as sicknesses diverge from one another; just as a physical condition affecting the body can be more or less serious than others, in the same way sins have various degrees of gravity.

The theologian weighs the sins committed against one's neighbor by the injury they inflict on him, and, starting from the principle that man's goods are of three kinds (ranged in the descending order of their intrinsic value: soul, body, and external things), he draws the conclusion that the greater the good taken away, the greater the injury. The soul, the highest human good, can be taken away only by fraudulent means (an evil persuasion, for instance), whereas bodily lives and external things can be taken away through violence. This hierarchical scheme enables Aquinas to rank murder as the most grievous of the sins committed against one's neighbor, a sin closely followed by adultery, which is contrary to the laws of human generation. Among external things, the theologian deems a man's reputation more valuable than his wealth, because a good name is of a more spiritual nature. Consequently, the sin of backbiting is more grievous than theft but less grievous than murder or adultery. Aggravating or extenuating circumstances, however, can alter this order, and occasionally a backbiter is as

49. *ST* IIa-IIae Q. 73.3.

50. *ST* Ia-IIae Q. 72.6.

guilty as a murderer, since his words may cause someone else to hate or despise his neighbor.[51] Aquinas's notion of a hierarchy of sins based on their varying degree of gravity underpins his belief in the necessity of a ranking of (canonical or legal) punishments, which are defined as medicine intended to keep man away from sin, and which ought to be tailored according to the degrees of seriousness of sins.[52]

But what place did Aquinas reserve for the sins committed through the medium of speech? The question is extremely important, as he marks a great departure from the line of thinking of previous ethicists. In his theory, since all moral acts originate in the will, verbal sins are no longer the results of the wild and mobile nature of the tongue. On account of the Augustinian tripartition of moral errors with which Aquinas operates throughout his ethics, the phrase *peccata verbi* comes to refer to what in Peraldus's *SV* was considered (and called) *peccata linguae*. More importantly, the transgressions committed by means of words are no longer a separate, eighth capital vice, but, along with the sins of deeds and of thoughts, they constitute subspecies (or degrees) of immorality. In order to prove this notion, the author takes up the illustrative Aristotelian metaphor of the house and compares sins of thought with the foundation of the house, those of word with its walls, and those of deed with its roof. He specifies, however, that these three classes are not autonomous species but degrees of evil spirituality proceeding from the same motive. More precisely, a sin typically begins in thought, then it continues as a verbal declaration, and it consummates itself in the deed. He exemplifies this theory with the case of an angry man who, wishing to avenge an offense, is at first disturbed in his thoughts, then bursts out into abusive words, and eventually commits criminal acts. Aquinas concludes that mental and verbal sins are not distinct from sins of deed when they are stages of the same process, but only when each is found by itself, just as one phase of a movement is not different from the whole movement when this is continuous, but only when there is an interruption in it.[53]

What allows Aquinas to compare sins of word with sins of deed is the

51. Aquinas's postulate of friendship as the most valuable of man's external things leads him to establish degrees of comparisons among verbal sins such as backbiting, tale-bearing, and reviling: "Again, a man's good name whereof backbiting deprives him is most necessary to him that he may be fitted for friendship. Therefore tale-bearing is a greater sin than backbiting or even reviling, because a friend is better than honor, and to be loved is better than to be honored, according to the Philosopher" (IIa-IIae Q. 74. 2).

52. *ST* IIa-IIae Q. 39.2.

53. *ST* Ia-IIae Q. 72.7.

similar way in which they manifest themselves; for example, unlike transgressions of thought, which are committed secretly, transgressions both of word and of deed are committed openly.[54] In assessing words, Aquinas, like Augustine, makes the distinction between their mere phonic aspect (their signifier, in more modern terms), and their referents.[55] The ability of a word to do harm (the *potestas nocendi* of which Peraldus was speaking but in reference to the tongue) derives for Aquinas from the signified of the words, which ultimately depends on the intention of the one who utters them: "Sins of word should be weighed chiefly by the intention of the speaker, wherefore these sins are differentiated according to the various intentions of those who speak against another."[56]

Following this principle of differentiation, Aquinas identifies eighteen verbal sins, which he defines as transgressions of the cardinal and theological virtues. Within this framework, the sin of blasphemy is opposed to the theological virtue of faith, contention to charity, perjury to justice (in its subclass religion); reviling, slander, tale-bearing, derision, and cursing are also opposed to justice (but in the subclass of piety). Lying, boasting, and irony (the latter taken in its medieval meaning, that of dissimulating one's own qualities or strengths) are opposed to truth, another subspecies of justice, whereas flattery and quarreling contravene friendship, yet another subclass of justice. The remaining sins of word (scurrility, loquacity, obscene talk, wanton words, and foolish talk) trespass the rules of temperance in various subcategories of this virtue. Thus, scurrility and loquacity are transgressions of abstinence, while obscene talk, wanton words, and foolish talk

54. As far as verbal abuses are concerned, Aquinas defines them in a very simple way: "sins of word consist in speaking evil" (IIa-IIae Q. 74.2). In referring to these abuses, the theologian employs two phrases: *peccata oris* "sins of the mouth," used rarely, and *peccata verbi/verborum,* a phrase that I have found translated either as "sins of word(s)" or "sin(s) of speech." The translation of the Dominican Fathers I use privileges the variant "sin(s) of word" even where Aquinas says *peccata oris.* This variant seems acceptable to me in light of Casagrande and Vecchio's remark that in the Thomistic system, the agent responsible for trespasses is no longer the tongue but the will (*I peccati della lingua,* 175–203).

55. *ST* IIa-IIae Q. 72. The foundation of the Thomistic treatment of verbal sins is Augustine's theory of words as signs, a theory that Aquinas quotes several times throughout his ethics. One of these times occurs in the major section devoted to lying (IIa-IIae Q. 110.1–3), which was to be expected if we consider that Augustine was the foremost authority on which the medieval theorists on *peccata linguae* relied for their view of mendacity. For an excellent reading of Aquinas's semiotic theory and its relationship to Augustine, see Marcia L. Colish, *The Mirror of Language: A Study in the Medieval Theory of Knowledge* (Lincoln: Nebraska University Press, 1983), 111–50.

56. *ST* IIa-IIae Q. 75.1.

violate chastity. Three of the eighteen sins of word belong to more than one category. Blasphemy, for instance, as a manifestation of anger, is opposed not only to faith but also to temperance. Quarreling violates not only justice but also temperance as another symptom of wrath. Finally, boasting, as a manifestation of pride, opposes both justice (in its subclass truth) and temperance (in its subclass humility). It is, however, interesting that Aquinas debates these verbal sins preferentially, without explaining his motives. While he devotes entire *questions,* with several articles each, to sins such as blasphemy, contention, derision, lying, reviling, slander, tale-bearing, cursing, flattery, and quarreling, he mentions others only in passing (scurrility, obscene speech, loquacity, and wanton speech, for example). The criterion for such discrimination must certainly lie in the varying degree of gravity Aquinas implicitly attached to these sins.

Echoes of the Scholastic thought on verbal sins and on the pivotal role played by the will resonate in the *Romance of the Rose.* Here, through the highly theological discourse of Dame Nature, Jean makes authoritative statements about the critical intervention of free will in speech acts. As to the *Divine Comedy,* both the hierarchy of sins and its immediate corollary, that of the varying scale/nature of divine punishments, are visibly at work in the overall system of Hell. In regard to the verbal sins, we will see that the way in which Dante embeds them into the structure of the Inferno presents not only affinities with Aquinas's theories of immoral speech but also significant deviations from it.[57]

57. On Dante's relationship to Aquinas, fundamental studies have been written first in Europe, by Pierre Mandonnet (*Dante le théologien* [Paris: Desclée de Brouwert, 1935]), Etienne Gilson (*Moral Values and the Moral Life: The Ethical Theory of St. Thomas Aquinas* [Hamden, Conn.: Shoe String Press, 1961]), and Bruno Nardi. For the latter, see especially *Saggi di filosofia dantesca* (Florence: La Nuova Italia Editrice, 1967), 341–81, where, engaged in a virulent polemic with Busnelli, Nardi reaches the conclusion that Dante is as much a *Tomista* as he is a *non-Tomista.* In the United States, the absorption of Aquinas's ethical views by Dante has thoroughly been studied by Philip H. Wicksteed, *Dante and Aquinas* (New York: E. P. Dutton, 1913), and William H. V. Reade, *The Moral System of Dante's "Inferno,"* 2nd ed. (Port Washington, N.Y.: Kennikat Press, 1969). Reade, however, does not investigate Dante's relationship to Aquinas in the field of verbal sins. More recently, Marc Cogan has undertaken a systematic reading of the three canticles of the *Comedy* in light of the Aristotelian-Thomistic doctrine of the three appetites: concupiscible, irascible, and of the will (*Design in the Wax: The Structure of the "Divine Comedy" and Its Meaning* [Notre Dame, Ind.: Notre Dame University Press, 1999]). One of the conclusions Cogan draws with regard to the structure of the Inferno—that the Malebolge correspond to the inner disposition of the will—offers additional support to my notion that Dante's approach to the sins of the tongue is fundamentally Scholastic.

TWO

From Jean De Meun's Multidiscursive Dispersal to Dante's System of Sins

Car li clers voit en escripture / Avoec les sciences prouvees, / Raisonnables et demoustrees, / Touz maus dont l'en se doit retraire / Et touz les biens que l'en puet faire. / Les choses voit dou monde escriptes / Si comme el sont faites et dites; / Il voit es anciennes vies / De touz vilains les vilanies / Et touz les faiz des cortois hommes / Et des cortoisies les sommes.

{*Romance of the Rose* 18644–54}

The epigraph reads: "In the things that are written, clerks see, with proved, reasonable and demonstrated information, all the evil from which one should withdraw and all the good things that one can do. He sees all things of the world written down, just as they are done and said. In the lives of the ancients he sees the villainies of the villains, all the deeds of the courteous men, the summae of all courtesies." This passage is inserted in Nature's discourse on the nobility proper to philosophers and aristocrats, nobility that should also characterize clerks, who deserve honor if they follow the path of virtue described in the books they read.

The value of this opening quote lies in Jean's outline of a clerk's relationship to his sources, a description that indirectly applies to him as well, and that we can also extend to Dante. In learning (or teaching others) about the evils to be shunned and the good deeds to be done, a clerk's first impulse and duty is to turn to books. Not to the world out there, built on deceptive perceptions and misleading appearances, but to books. The *saeculum* is better understood when it has already been described, analyzed, and explained in written texts, which have the merit of offering (and preserving) proofs, rational arguments, and verified information about society. There is nothing in the secular world that is not recorded by writers (historians? theologians? moralists? poets? translators?—these categorizations lack here), who note down not only how things happen but also how they are said. Both history and orality are subsumed and, at the same time, transcended by the act of writing; they are only the raw materials of it, serving one, overarching purpose: that of instructing potential/future readers. The word "all," occurring four times in this short quote, emphasizes the reliability of the written sources wherein information and examples of good and evil seem to have the value of rules carved in stone. The act of (clerkly) reading logically postdates the one of historical or moral writing, but although the passage implicitly refers to the past, it does not contain a single verb in the past. This strange collapsing of the temporal distance can be an indication of Jean's own participation in the present of writing—he reads but at the same time also writes moral texts. More likely, however, this avoidance of the past tense portrays him as reading moral texts that had been written or were still being written during his own time. Either way, what is undisputable is that the entire discussion about a clerk's necessary manipulation of written sources gravitates around the two poles of ethics: good and evil. In learning and teaching about morality, Jean indirectly depicts himself as supremely addicted to (near) past and contemporary ethical texts.

The word *sommes* is also intriguing, since semantically it points in two different directions: to bookish *summaries* of noble deeds from the past, but also to the cultural context contemporary with Jean. Dahlberg's translation of the word as "summae" endorses the latter interpretation, which I myself favor because it testifies to Jean's familiarity with this fundamental conceptual construction of morality that was the summa of vices and virtues. Another important indication is the one regarding the use of ancient lives that can serve as behavioral examples for readers. I know of no other vernacular text written before Jean's *Rose* that spells out the procedure of didactic writing so clearly. This description bespeaks the poet's acquaintance with the methodology of the texts on vices and virtues, a methodology that he himself (and then Dante) will follow, for what Jean is actually giving us here is a sketch of his *techné* as a moral writer, as an educator. He observes the world and human nature, but before writing about them to instruct others, he first edifies himself by looking for answers to his questions in the historical and moral texts of the past or present. As he sifts through these texts, he sorts out "old lives" (from myth? history?—again these categorizations are not made) that he can further use as exempla in his own writings to educate his readers.

Sin is a central concern in the thought and works of the two Romance poets under consideration. The *Rose* is the ironic chronicle of a lover whose course of action is "the typical path of sin as described by innumerable medieval psychologists,"[1] and the *Comedy*'s architectonics are built on a foundational study of man's sinful inclinations. These major poems, along with the other works by Jean and Dante, provide countless moral judgments of verbal habits, and if we take a closer look at these instances, we can outline a theory of speech ethics for each author. For the French poet, it has long been noted that since he speaks in so many characters, it is hard to detect his genuine voice. However, three of the discursive characters in the *Rose* express standpoints with respect to verbal sins that I consider representative of Jean as a satirical moralist. Dame Raison speaks at length about linguistic obscenity, Dame Nature about the will as the first mover in speech acts, and Genius about wicked female speech. Since these notions are three constants of the poem, and since for two of them (obscenity and misogyny) Jean himself apologizes in the text (ll. 15139–306), they propose themselves as hallmarks of the poet's ethics of speech. Jean de Meun's *Testament* also criticizes forms of deviant verbal communication and situates its brief exposition on the seven deadly sins in the context of a discourse on prayer.

Dante did not leave us a unique text dealing with his view of humans' use of language, but he made references to this topic in virtually all his works. *De vulgari eloquentia,* a work of linguistic and literary theory, undertakes to assess the status of the Italian dialects and their expressive capabilities. Even in such a technical treatise, Dante cannot obliterate his ethi-

1. Fleming, *The "Roman de la Rose,"* 50.

cal concerns but makes constant connections between language and sin. *De monarchia* places the use of speech in a political perspective and argues that verbal transgressions may lead to divisions of the body politic. Book 4 of *Convivio* has all the characteristics of a moral tract and contains many discussions about the vices and virtues of verbal communication. The linguistic and moral notions from these three tracts converge into a unique, coherent perspective that can help us grasp Dante's handling of the verbal sins in the complex construction of Hell. In addition, the occasional references to sinful speech the poet makes in *Purgatorio* and *Paradiso* can also illuminate our understanding of the verbal transgressions punished in *Inferno.*

ORIGIN, FUNCTIONS, AND SINS OF SPEECH IN THE *ROMANCE OF THE ROSE*

Dame Raison on Human Abuses of Speech

In the *Rose,* the secular world is often described in apocalyptic terms. Long before Faus Semblant's self-introduction as an Antichrist, Dame Raison, the first allegorical character to emerge in Jean's poem, presents the contemporary scene in very dark colors. Baraz (Fraud) has taken possession of the whole world and corrupted all good mores and honest practices. The virtues that had hitherto dominated society have all vanished under the terror of Malice, this "mother of all kingdoms" (l. 5561), who brought along only evils and sins. Merchants, lawyers, and medicine men practice their crafts not out of passion but for money and privileges. Even preachers speak the words of the gospel not for the sake of evangelization but to acquire riches and social power. Judges no longer defend the innocent but accept false testimonies, manipulate trials, and make unjust decisions for the sake of money (ll. 5067–84). It becomes apparent that in the fallen world depicted by Raison, language itself has become corrupted with sin.[2] All of the major interpreters of the poem have meditated on this complex allegorical personage, and of the two books Fleming has written on the *Rose,*

2. John M. Fyler offers an in-depth analysis of Jean's view of "fallen language" in relationship to the myth of the Golden Age, as recounted by Raison, Ami, La Vieille, and Genius. Fyler correctly points out that the poet grafted the history of language, as drawn by biblical commentaries, on the classical myth (*Language and the Declining World in Chaucer, Dante, and Jean de Meun* [Cambridge: Cambridge University Press, 2007], 81–87).

one is devoted specifically to this female character and Amant (Lover), her interlocutor.

Spanning about three thousand lines, Raison's discourse is the longest in Jean's poem; it represents one fifth of it (ll. 4225–7186). Her teachings are so deeply rooted in an analysis of human mores that it forms a "nearly autonomous moral tractate" that attaches to the main story line with "loose ties."[3] From a generic point of view, it is designed as a protreptic discourse, an exhortation to a life of philosophy and moral virtue.[4] It is also a professed Christianized version of protreptic literature, since both Amant and Raison herself brand this exhortation a "sermon" (l. 4656, ll. 4671–72). It tackles problems related to good and evil—malice, fraud, injustice—and, more specifically, fraudulent behavioral practices in which speech plays a pivotal role. The springboard from which this allegorical character launches her long disquisition is a detailed analysis of love. *Amors* is a polysemous word in French, denoting several types of feelings. There is first erotic love, a catastrophic disorder of the senses, from which Amant is suffering. In the same category of unhealthy attachments lies the love of riches. Opposed to these two types of nocuous affections, there is a positive and noble love, governed by the rules of friendship and charity. Finally, the noblest form of love is the attachment to reason, the highest human faculty. Obviously, Dame Raison embodies the latter kind of affection, and as such, she offers herself as an alternative to Amant's cupidinous feelings for the Rose. In her attempt to convince Amant to follow her, Raison launches a virulent campaign of denigration of carnal love, a campaign verbalized in a long oxymoronic series designed to depict this feeling as full of contradictions and dangers (a heinous peace and a lovely hatred, a healthy languishing and a feverish health, a sweet evil and an unpleasant sweetness, etc.; ll. 4290–326).[5] One expression will be striking in this fastidious list of metaphors and oxymora describing how the erotic confusion of senses affects the spiri-

3. Strubel, note to *Le Roman de la Rose,* 299.

4. It is Fleming who situates the dialogue between Raison and Amant in the protreptic tradition of Cicero's *Hortensius,* a literary exhortation to philosophy. As to Raison's cultural lineage, Fleming adduces strong arguments to prove that her direct ancestress is the allegorical character Ratio from St. Augustine's *Soliloquia.* This lineage helps the critic interpret Jean's Raison as Christian Wisdom, the "sapiential Christ in man," and as a mistress of moral life (*Reason and the Lover,* [Princeton, N.J.: Princeton University Press, 1984], 30–63, 133).

5. For an analysis of this extended oxymoronic series and its relationship to its source (Alain of Lille's *Plaint of Nature*), see Newman, *God and the Goddesses,* 100.

tual balance of a human being: "entechiez de pardon pechiez, / De pechiez pardon entechiez" (ll. 4312–13; "a sin stained with forgiveness, a pardon stained with sin"). Carnal love is thus introduced from the outset through a severe ethical term condemning it as a sinful feeling, an immoral attitude that humans need to shun at all cost. Although Raison does not go so far as to use a more technical term such as *luxure* (lechery), one of the seven deadly sins, this what she is talking about.

In these positions vis-à-vis the world and erotic love lies the essence of the extremely long discourse of Dame Raison. Shored up by numerous quotations from Roman authors, it is a disquisition built upon the values of classical rationalism but framed within the conceptual context of Christianity. (When she invokes Suetonius, she calls him a *desloial homme,* "man of no faith," noting with outrage that he had considered the Christian religion false, uncanny, and dangerous; ll. 6454–58). Raison's entire approach to the complex problematic of human behavior bears the marks of this amalgam of pagan ethics and Christian theories about virtues and vices. Not surprisingly, the eclectic fabric of her discourse is typical of the medieval tracts on sin, which were built on both Greco-Roman moral philosophy and Christian texts (biblical and patristic); William Peraldus's *Summa* is a splendid example of this eclecticism.[6] By the same token, Raison's numerous references to deceitful verbal practices will rest on both pagan sources and Christian authorities. These references occur early on in her discourse, when she starts complaining about the decay of courtly love. We remember that in Guillaume de Lorris's section of the poem, *fin'amors* entailed a specific set of behavioral norms, one of which was a most polite and reverent way of speaking. Amant himself, at the beginning of his conversation with Raison in Jean's *Rose,* recalls that he had three faithful companions: Doux Penser (Sweet Thought), Doux Parler (Sweet Talk), and Doux Regard (Sweet Glance), which have all abandoned him. He now has to face several fierce enemies alone: Dangier (Resistance), Peur (Fear), Honte (Shame), and Malebouche. Doux Parler and Malebouche are "survivors" of the linguistic universe of courtly love; the latter will remain in the *Rose* until the meeting with Faus Semblant, who will kill him. But at this point

6. Alastair Minnis casts Jean in the tradition of the followers of Bernard de Cluny, who promoted the symbiosis between the pagan criticism of vices and the Christian contempt of the world (*Magister amoris: The "Romance of the Rose" and Vernacular Hermeneutics* [Oxford: Oxford University Press, 2001], 96).

of the narrative, Dame Raison is concerned with lovers for whom "sweet talk" no longer corresponds to the inner voice of the heart but becomes a deliberate method of seducing women: "Toutevois fins amans se faignent, / Mais par amours amer ne daignent / Et se gabent ainsi des dames / Et lor promettent cors et ames, / Et jurent mensonges et fables / A ceuls qu'il tiennent decevables, / Tant qu'il ont leur delit eü" (ll. 4387–93; "They always pretend to be pure lovers and do not deign to love par amour; thus, they deceive ladies by promising them their hearts and souls and by swearing lies and fables to those whom they find gullible, until they have taken their pleasure with them").[7] *Se faindre,* "to pretend," *se gaber,* "to fool," and *decevable,* "gullible," belong to a lexicon of deception that is placed in immediate relationship with acts of speech: lies, oaths, and false promises. With these verbal practices, lovers leave the refined space of *fin'amors* and enter the world of fraud.

Further evil verbal habits are condemned in the framework of the discussion of friendship. Within the series of good and bad loves on Raison's list, one form of attachment that should definitely be cultivated is friendship, a feeling built on spiritual brotherhood, which, unlike carnal love, may lead the soul on the path of virtue. Unmindful attitudes, however, can undermine this noble feeling, and one may easily lose a friend not only through attitudes of pride or anger but also by use of words in an inadequate way: "Len le pert par orgueill, par ire, / Par reprouche, par reveler / Les secrez qui font a celer, / Et par la plaie doulereuse / De detracion venimeuse" (ll. 4930–35; "love [of friends] may be lost through pride, wrath, and reproach; by revealing secrets which should be kept hidden; and by the woeful complaints of venomous detraction"). Lionel Friedman has proven that this passage is a verbatim reproduction of the list of "five dissolvants of friendship" posited by Ethelred of Rievaulx, whose *De amicitia spirituali* (On spiritual friendship) Jean had translated.[8] The fact that the poet chose to insert this passage in the very text of the *Rose* not only bespeaks his sen-

7. The passage is to be read in opposition to a remark about the use of speech Raison makes in another place in the poem: "Car volentiers recorde bouche / Chose qui pres dou cuer li touche" ("For the mouth willingly utters what touches one near the heart"; ll. 6863–64). Typically, the words that form in one's mouth (should) reflect what is in one's heart. By the same token, the words that are not in a specular relationship to the inner language of feelings constitute acts of deception and thereby transgressions.

8. Lionel J. Friedman, "Jean de Meun and Ethelred of Rievaulx," *L'esprit créateur* 2, no. 3 (1962): 140–41.

sitivity to the effects of malicious verbal acts but also shows him mining old texts for quotes that can buttress his characters' (or his own) views of the usage of speech in interpersonal communication. The three linguistic habits above mentioned—reproaches, ferreting secrets, and slander—are implicitly raised to the rank of capital vices, since they are enumerated next to pride and anger. This approach to verbal abuses is typical of Peraldus's ethics, where manifestations of deviant speech constitute an eighth class of capital sin. Slander and ferreting secrets (*detractio* and *secretorum revelatio*) are among Peraldus's twenty-four subclasses of verbal sin, and they are treated specifically in relationship to friendship. At this point, we can wonder if *De amicitia spirituali* was not one of the sources of inspiration for Peraldus himself. In any case, Ethelred's list of five destructive agents of social brotherhood (two of which are verbal acts) was a good match for the cultural climate of the time, which considered the sins of the tongue as serious as the seven deadly sins.

Raison goes on to say that at the polar opposite of the man who discloses his friends' secrets stands the true friend, who will never betray his companion and will never reproach him with anything: "Quant son secré dit li avra, / Jamais li tierz ne le savra; / Ne de reprouche n'a il garde, / Car sages hons sa langue garde. / Ce ne savroit mie fous faire: / Nus fous ne set sa langue taire" (ll. 4726–30; "When one has told a secret to him, no third person will ever know it; nor will the teller fear any reproach, for a wise man keeps watch over his tongue, a thing no fool could do, for a fool doesn't know how to keep his tongue still"). The theme of *custodia linguae* is also a product of the cultural period in which Jean lived; we have seen it amply developed by William Peraldus. Following up on Greco-Roman moralists and the scriptures (Solomon especially, with his numerous references to undisciplined speech), Peraldus insistently underlines the necessity to rein in one's tongue and to carefully choose the proper time to speak and the words to utter. As I highlighted in chapter 1, "De peccato linguae" is divided into three main parts, the first of which is entirely devoted to the question of *custodia linguae.*

Dame Raison is obsessed with her obligation to impart to Amant the lesson of disciplined speech. She posits herself as a linguistic model by teaching him that *tenciers,* "quarrel," and *mesdire,* "detraction," are two great misdeeds that she has never practiced (ll. 7001–5). (Let us note in passing that both sins are on Peraldus's and Laurent's lists; actually, Laurent uses exactly the terms *tenciers* and *mesdire* to translate Peraldus's *contentio* and *detractio*). If Amant errs in words or deeds, she will correct him with her own actions or words, but in so doing, she will never appeal to blame or denigration. Raison adds that her speech is always good and truthful, and whenever she chastises people, she takes extreme care not to utter anything foolish or harm them with her words. She also argues that when it comes to friendships, speech makes the difference between the wise and the foolish, and later on, she develops this notion with a great wealth of details and bookish references:

Si rest taire vertu petite, / Mais dire les choses a taire / C'est trop grant dyablie a faire. / Langue doit estre refrenee, / Car nous lisons de Tholomee / Une parole mout honneste / Au commencement de l'Almageste: / Que sages est cil qui met paine / A ce que sa langue refraine, / Fors sanz plus quant de dieu parole / La n'a on pas trop de parole / Car nus ne puet dieu trop loer.… Chatons meïsmes s'i acorde, / S'il est qui son livre recorde. / La puez en escrit trouver tu / Que la premeraine vertu / C'est de mettre a sa langue frain: / Donte donc la toe et refrain / De folie dire et d'outrages, / Si feras que preuz et que sages, / Qu'il fait bon croire les paiens / Com de leur diz granz biens aiens. (7030–58)

To keep silent remains a small virtue; but to speak the things to be kept silent is to commit a diabolical deed. The tongue should be held in check. We read a very honest saying of Ptolemy at the beginning of the Almagest: he who takes trouble over what restrains his tongue is a wise man, except when he speaks of God and nothing more. On that subject one does not speak too much, for no man can praise God too much.… Cato himself agrees, if there is anyone who recalls his book, where you may find in writing that the first virtue is to put a bridle on one's tongue. Subdue yours then, and refrain from saying foolish and wild things; then you will do only what is worthy and wise. It is good to believe the pagans, for we may gain great benefit from their sayings.

Important notions related to the ethics of speech permeate this segment of Dame Raison's discourse. In examining Jean's sources for them, we have to consider the long-standing tradition of philosophical sayings in which he places himself. In this specific quote, he mentions Ptolemy and Cato, but these authors (like all the other Greco-Roman moralists for which speech was a constant theme of reflection) were one of the main source-strains in the pastoral discourse on sinful speech contemporary with Jean (the other two are the scriptures and patristic writings). The two classical quotes Jean provides here are common places in the *lingua*-texts, which feature a great array of similar maxims. Cato, Cicero, Seneca, Horace, to name just a few, are writers from which the medieval moralists drew extensively to legitimize their own theories about virtuous versus transgressive language. It would be therefore difficult to determine whether Jean knew these quotes directly from the authors he mentions, or he borrowed them from the contemporary pastoral writers on sin, who were recycling them. The notion of the great spiritual danger inherent in one's inability to keep silent at the right time is, however, a clear Christian development, since loquacity and betrayal are presented as springing directly from the devil. It is worth adding that in "De peccato linguae," both *multiloquium* (loquacity) and *secretorum revelatio* are descried as devilish sins. The by now traditional appeal to *custodia linguae* occurs twice in this relatively short passage, translating an obsession worthy of the ethicists of speech. Even the notion that the only good case of loquacity is when one praises God is a common denominator of the above-mentioned *lingua*-tracts. This eclecticism of sources in Raison's pronouncements validates Fleming's point that this character has a meaningful habit of citing classical philosophers in their Christian redactions.[9]

However, not even in this passage fraught with references to the sinfulness of speech do we encounter yet the word "sin." Surprisingly, this emerges when Dame Raison sets out to assess the quality of her own verbal habits. One of the most controversial and debated moments in the narrative of the poem occurs when Raison recounts the castration of Saturn by his son Jupiter and she refers to Saturn's genitalia as *viz,* "prick," and *coilles,* "testicles." Her lexical choices prompt the outraged reaction of Amant, who qualifies Raison's speech as *parleüre baude,* "bawdy speech," and expresses his attachment to good linguistic manners, which he has learned from the god of love. It is true, Amant says, that God created man and the male genitalia directly, but he did not create the words people use to name them, which are full of obscenities. The reproaches Amant levels at Raison belong, first, to the courtly literary tradition, which imposes the use of euphemisms as a norm for language, and then to a popular, commonsensical strain, which requires even uneducated women to use a circumlocutory manner of speech in reference to intimate body parts. It is worth noting that in this reproach, Amant himself reiterates the exact word he said he would never

9. Fleming, *Reason and the Lover,* 98, 118.

use: "Si ne vous tieng pas a cortoise / Quant vous m'avez coilles nommées" (ll. 6924–25;"I do not consider you courteous when just now you named the testicles to me"). This subtly ironical detail is symbolic of Jean's satirical technique, whereby he manages to dismantle a character from within, by having him/her say things that eventually turn against him/her. What is most important in Amant's reaction to Raison's improper language is that it causes her to take a stand with respect to her own choice of words and to defend herself:

Biaus ami, je puis bien nommer / Sanz moi faire mal renommer / Apertement par propre non / Chose qui n'est se bonne non. / Voire, dou mal seürement / Puis je bien parler proprement, / Car de riens nulle je n'ai honte / S'el n'est tels que *a pechié monte. / Mais riens ou pechié se meïst / N'est nus qui faire me feïst, / N'ainc en ma vie ne pechié / N'encor ne faz je pas pechié / Se je nomme les nobles choses / Par plain texte sanz mettre gloses,* / Que mes peres en paradis / Fist de ses propres mains jadis, / Et tous les autres estrumenz /Qui sont piliers et argumenz / A soustenir nature humaine. /Qui sanz euls fust or casse et vaine. (6941–60; emphasis added)[10]

Fair friend, I can very well, without creating a bad reputation for myself, name openly and by its own name a thing which is nothing if not good. In truth, I can safely speak properly of evil, for I have no shame about anything *if it is not such that it may be sinful. But a thing in which sin lay could make no difference to me, for I never sinned in my life; if I name noble things in plain text, without gloss, I still commit no sin*, since my father in Paradise made them formerly with his own hands, along with all the other instruments that are the pillars and arguments for sustaining human nature, which, without them, would now be destroyed and empty.

This passage has given rise to an extraordinary critical response over the course of time.[11] The interpretations have mainly revolved around the no-

10. Minnis links this passage with Jean's antipathy for integumental discourse, given that, although the poet constantly promises to provide gloss on some of his most cryptic definitions, a coherent integumental program does not exist in the *Rose* (*Magister amoris,* 136). Pierre Yves Badel also alludes to Jean's reluctance to the practice of *integumentum* and explains it through the poet's determination to denunciate the Joachimist deviation of exegesis (*Le "Roman de la Rose,"* 15).

11. In David Hult's view, this surge of interest is due to the modern development of semiotics and hermeneutics ("Language and Dismemberment: Abélard, Origen, and the *Romance of the Rose,*" in *Rethinking the "Romance of the Rose: Text, Image, Reception,"* edited by Kevin Brownlee and Sylvia Huot [Philadelphia: University of Pennsylvania Press, 1992], 109). Over the course of time, remarkable studies of Jean's view of language have also been written by: Daniel Poirion, Fleming, Marc-René Jung, Gustav Ineichen, Maureen Quilligan, and, more recently, Fyler.

tion that here, Jean explicitly airs his adherence to the nominalist position with respect to language (the mouthpiece for this critical trend is Daniel Poirion). Raison's stand can be summed up as follows: she praises the gift of speech granted her by God and invokes Plato, according to whom speech is given for expressing feelings, for teaching, and for learning.[12] God, the source of all courtesy, allows Raison to speak any way she wants, so it is her wont to speak literally about things, whenever she likes to, without wishing to gloss them. She is the maker of words, and since she considers male genitalia beautiful, any word she would use to name them would be beautiful. But discussions about Jean's philosophy of language from a Platonic position do not exhaust the overall significance of this celebrated fragment of the *Rose,* for the dispute between Raison and Amant may primarily arise not from the choice of words but from a difference in the perception of the private parts. These are base for Amant (at least this is what he says), whereas for Raison they are as beautiful as any other thing made directly by her divine father. How could she not name God's works by their own names, she is asking rhetorically.

With this argument, the question of a verbal sin is raised for the first time in the poem and, at the same time, adamantly rejected. Charles Muscatine, who places this concern about linguistic obscenity in direct relationship with the notion of courtliness, notes that a strong sensitivity to dirty language had already developed by the early thirteenth century.[13] Since Muscatine does not make the connection between this enhanced sensitivity and the *lingua*-texts of the period, I feel compelled to add that in the ethical tracts I presented in chapter 1, obscene talk represents a major topic of conversation. The first theologian to make a significant and detailed contribution to the discussion of *turpiloquium* (lewd talk) is

12. Fleming has textually proven that the purposes of language enumerated by Raison correspond to those listed by Adeodatus in Augustine's *On the Teacher,* a text that lays the foundation for the major linguistic theory from *On the Christian Doctrine.* The notion that Reason is the inventress of human language is also of Augustinian origin, since it was first expressed in *On Order* 2.12 (*Reason and the Lover,* 37 and 100). Fyler, however, analyzes Raison's theory of naming to prove that Jean uses this character ironically, in order to show how much language has deteriorated since the Fall. In Fyler's view, Raison's discourse is self-destructive, in that the issues it tackles (euphemism, integument, metaphor, and translation) are all linguistic symptoms of the fallen world (*Language and the Declining World,* 93–98).

13. Charles Muscatine, "The Fabliaux, Courtly Literature, and the (Re)Invention of Vulgarity," in *Obscenity: Social Control and Artistic Creation in the European Middle Ages,* edited by Jan M. Ziolkowski (Boston: Brill, 1998), 284.

Radulfus Ardens, who defines it as a morally unhealthy linguistic habit, which affects both the speaker and the listener and which has two subspecies: speaking about base things performed according to the laws of nature and speaking of base things committed against nature. The latter type is exemplified by the speech describing sodomy, incest, or sexual intercourse between men and animals, and is considered the most grievous. The former type is represented by the speech depicting human genitalia or natural physiological processes, such as heterosexual intercourse or elimination of bodily fluids in men and women. This type of obscene talk is less shameful and serious, but it is still transgressive, in that it describes things or acts that even nature chooses to hide. When speaking about these natural but intimate things/acts, extreme care should be taken to describe them; the euphemism is the only solution recommended.[14] If proper linguistic care is not taken, obscene words sully the one who utters them and, at the same time, corrupt the mores of the one who listens to them, because lewd language often arouses carnal desires. In his turn, Peraldus also strongly condemns this sin, and, quoting St. Paul and Seneca in the same paragraph, he qualifies speaking about dirty things and fornication as a highly indecent form of "turpitudo in ore."[15] The repulsion Peraldus feels toward indecent speech is so strong that he actually includes it among his eighteen reasons for *custodia linguae.*

What is a repulsive sin of the tongue for him and Radulfus is mere lexical convention and necessity for Dame Raison, in her role of divinely appointed linguist. She has nothing against women who use euphemisms by prudery, but she reserves for herself the right to use the proper, nonfigurative terms when she wants to speak clearly. In the war between speculative linguistics and speech ethics, for her the former prevails. Raison in

14. "Que [turpitudines] si quando necesse est significari honestioribus verbis sunt significanda et occultanda, sicut occultat ea et ipsa natura. Nonne vides quomodo horum inhonestatem honestioribus verbis significant sacra scriptura" ("If vile things must be expressed, these things must be coached or concealed in honest words, as nature herself conceals them. Can you not see how, in the Sacred Scripture, the dishonesty of those men is expressed through more honest words?"; Radulfus Ardens, *Speculum universale,* XIII, f. 164r; translation mine). When Radulfus speaks of nature's concealing vile things, he alludes to the medieval belief according to which, at God's command, nature chose to hide the shameful parts of the body, by placing them in the lower part of it.

15. "Depravity in the mouth"; Guglielmo Peraldo [William Peraldus, Guillaume Peyraut], *Summa virtutum ac vitiorum,* edited by Gulielmum Rovilium [Guillaume Rouillé] (Lyon, 1585?), 2:415.

fact touches upon a limit of language, in that she considers the euphemism a source of referential ambiguity, intimately related to verbal hypocrisy, a practice that she overtly criticizes as fraudulent. Here, the question of verbal sin resurfaces, but in a different guise. Even if women called the male genitalia unashamedly, with their proper names, they would still commit no sin, for it is more appalling to use prudish words for the organs of reproduction than to actually name them (ll. 7137–38). Using euphemisms for genitalia is an utterly dishonest practice, a concealed lie. It is interesting that Amant, who, from his stance as a courtly lover, is accusing Raison of being a foolish and rude speaker, never qualifies obscene language as sin; the term *peche,* "sin," appears, significantly, only in Raison's vocabulary. She is the one who identifies her verbal boldness and outspokenness as a transgression. (Amant has not read the *lingua*-texts; Raison has!) I have mentioned that her discourse is a mixed formula of Christian theories grafted on the classical tradition of ethical texts. But the pagan authors she quotes, who had drawn attention to various abuses of language, had never qualified obscenity as a "sin." The notion of sin, in the meaning we assign it today, is a Christian development, and the qualification of *turpiloquium* as a class of verbal sin is a contribution of the medieval pastoral discourse on *peccata linguae.* Thus, by using the term *peche* in reference to her linguistic crudity, Raison marks her membership in the clerkly debate on transgressive speech.

But why is she so determined to refute the potential sinfulness that hovers above her words? To answer this question we have to relate Dame Raison's discourse to Jean's apologies that come later on in the poem. The only instance in the *Rose* in which the author removes the masks of the characters he impersonates and speaks in his own voice is when he apologizes to the audience and to the Catholic Church for the verbal transgressions he may have committed while writing his poem.

Si vous pri, seigneurs amoreus, / Par les geus d'amours savoreus, / Que se vous i trouvez paroles / Semblanz trop baudes ou trop foles, / Par quoi saillent li mesdisant / Qui de nous aillent mesdisant / Des choses a dire ou dites, / Que cortoisement les desdites. (15163–71)

Therefore I beg you, amorous lords, by the delicious games of love, if you find here any speeches that are too bawdy or silly and that might make slanderous critics who go around speaking ill of us rise up over things that I have said or will say, that you will courteously oppose them.

What is striking in this passage is the coincidence between Amant's assessment of Raison's language as bawdy and foolish and Jean's personal apologies for the same kinds of words. This textual overlapping reveals that Dame Raison's concerns about her deviations of language translate, in fact, the authorial awareness of transgressive speech. Raison's sin of *turpiloquium* is Jean's own. If she refutes Amant's accusation by obliquely invoking the Platonic theory of naming, it is because Jean himself is constantly conscious of the accusation of obscene (written) speech he may face. Whether they are ironic or not, his apologies to the reader and to the Church are evidence. The problem is all the more serious when the moralists I have quoted argue that *turpiloquium* constitutes a real moral danger for listeners/readers, since it can cause them to sin. As chapter 4 explains, both Christine de Pizan and Jean Gerson will accuse Jean de Meun of lewd language conducive to sin and of nocuous influence on readers.

Dame Nature on the (Verbal) Vices of Man

On the level of the plot in the *Rose,* a combat takes place (ll. 15307–630), which opposes Amant's supporters—Franchise (Openness), Pitié (Pity), Bien Cacher (Skillful Concealment), Courage (Boldness), and Plaisir (Delight)—to the defendants of the castle where Bel Accueil (Fair Welcome) is imprisoned: Dangier, Honte (Shame), and Peur (Fear). What is important in this parodic imitation of Prudentius's *Psychomachia* is that the weaponry some of these allegorical characters display bears symbolic representations of speech acts. The tip of Franchise's lance is made of sweet prayers; her shield consists of supplications and is bordered with promises, agreements, oaths, and engagements. Pitié's shield is made of relief and bordered by sighs and laments. Engaged in close combat with Dangier, Pitié wins only when she starts crying. Her tears, notes the narrator, hurt the enemy more than any possible deed or word, a brief remark bespeaking again Jean's awareness of the psychological detriment speech can cause. Honte's targe has a name, like the swords of the famous knights from the Arthurian romances. It is called "Doute de male renomee" ("Fear of a bad reputation") and has several tongues painted on it. Bien Cacher has a silent sword, comparable to a *langue coupée,* "cut off tongue" (l. 15494). The figure Courage is introduced as "aperz par faiz et par diz" ("honest in deeds and words"; l. 15540). After a tough fight, the two armies reach an armistice, but this does not last long. The one who breaks it is Venus's son, Cupid, who, the narrator warns, has never kept any engagement, promise, or word. When the fight resumes even more intensely than before, the characters shoot at each other arrows feathered with large promises (either of services or gifts); the tips of these arrows are covered with the iron of oaths and assurances (ll. 15819–22).

The whole picture seems to represent not a physical combat but a verbal one. We witness a huge allegorical clash between vices and virtues in which the acts of speech are prevalent; the shields are painted with tongues or made out of human utterances, the swords look like tongues, too, whereas the arrows consist entirely of various forms of verbal commitment. What is most worrying about this allegorical fight is that the moral worth of the intense verbal activity it represents seems to be nil. If we were to "translate" this allegory, an allegory of human speech, we could read the multitude of utterances it conveys as a flamboyant rhetorical display that is void of substance. People are quick to say numerous words to each other and to commit to each other through various linguistic acts; human lives bubble with oaths of all kinds, but the truth—and the danger—is that this whole intense and noisy activity is lacking essence. As the combat takes place under the patronage of Cupid, a god famous for his lack of constancy and seriousness, for his failure to keep his word, Jean is suggesting that love is a sum of promissory words that are meaningless most of the time, because they are not corroborated by deeds.

On a discursive level, before we know what the outcome of the psychomachic clash is, we have to follow two more long disquisitions—Nature's and Genius's. When the fight reaches an impasse, we see Cupid asking for his mother's help and then swearing along with her to help Amant and the laws of Nature. At hearing them, the divine Dame Nature, who was forging human beings in her workshop, leaves her activity for a while, and, thanking Venus and Cupid for their help, begins to talk about some problems of her own.[16] Her intercession starts as a painful lament on the issue of male

16. The entire Nature-Genius segment spans five thousand verses. Although Jean borrows Dame Nature from Alain of Lille's *Plaint of Nature,* he alters her fundamentally. George Economou remarks in this respect that in Alain, the goddess *Natura* represented not only man's sensitive nature but also the functions of human reason, whereas in Jean, Raison and Nature are two distinct characters, each with a specific role. Economou also points out that, whereas Alain posited a clear contrast between (immoral) Venus and (moral) Nature, in Jean, both Nature

homosexuality but soon branches off into a dizzying array of highly philosophical themes, beginning with divine foreknowledge, predestination, and free will. These themes are well known to Jean from Boethius's *Consolation of Philosophy,* but a closer look at the French poem reveals important departures from the Boethian text.

In the *Rose,* the discussion of predestination stems from a description of the heavenly bodies and their influence on human lives, a theme that the *Consolation* does not debate. Although Dame Nature does not deny that these bodies exert a certain control on the sublunary world and on humans, she rejects the idea of their absolute influence. Following almost *ad litteram* Augustine's theory of stellar determinism from Book 5.1–9 of *The City of God,* she admits that the spheres can affect human characters, in the sense that they instill certain attributes in individuals—the so-called predispositions; but at the same time she asserts that people can oppose these innate inclinations through their power of choice.[17] Through education, proper nourishment, good company, use of reason, and even medical remedies, people can obtain great results in their lives, if they apply themselves to bridling their natural ways. From this point on, Nature sets out to solve another Augustinian theme: the apparent conflict between predestination (and divine foreknowledge) on the one hand, and the individual free will, on the other (the theme becomes a Boethian obsession in Book 4, Prose 4, of the *Consolation*). This conflict is not easy to explain to the laity, warns Nature. How, despite all appearances, free will accommodates predestination is a difficult concept for laymen, who have a hard time understanding it even if they are offered all the answers to all the possible objections. But the temptation to undertake such a challenging theological task as that of clarifying this false conflict is too great for Dame Nature, so she succumbs to it and begins a long disquisition on this topic (815 lines, 17063–878).[18] Not only

and Genius are enlisted in the service of Venus and her son, Cupid (*The Goddess Natura in Medieval Literature* [Cambridge, Mass.: Harvard University Press, 1972],120).

17. The high Scholasticism contemporary with Jean took up Augustine's resolution. In Ia-IIae Q. 9.5 ("Whether the Will Is Moved by a Heavenly Body"), Aquinas reaches the conclusion that a star can affect the will only indirectly (by influencing the sensitive appetite; for instance, when a person is cold, his will wishes for a warm coat). But there can be no direct influence of a heavenly body on the human will, since the former is material and the latter immaterial.

18. All these technical terms appear grouped in three lines that serve Jean to express his regret for not being able to develop this theme even further (a rhetorical excuse, since the whole

the themes that the female character debates but also the terms she uses (*espondre,* "expound"; *opposer,* "to oppose"; *respondre,* "to respond") are distinctive features of the dialectical method that characterizes classic Scholastic discourse. Gerard Paré proved long ago that, although the chief source for Nature's discussion of the dynamics between free will and divine determinism was Boethius's *Consolation,* these notions were reprised and hotly debated by the great Scholastics contemporary with Jean.[19] By speaking like a knowledgeable "Schoolwoman," Nature marks a great departure from the homonymous character of Alain of Lille's work, on whom she is modeled, and reflects the concerns of her new textual father, Jean de Meun, who is fascinated by the philosophical discourse on sin from his time period.

Dame Nature argues that the predestination instilled by the celestial influences cannot overcome man's reason and free will.[20] (The phrases Jean uses in translating *liber arbitrium* are no fewer than four: *frans voloirs, pooir d'eslection, franche volonté,* and *franc voloir d'ellire,* a lexical wealth testifying to the poet's outstanding skills as a translator).[21] If free will were less important than innate dispositions, there would be no vices or virtues, and consequently there would be no rewards for good works and no punishments for felonies. The argument of those who sustain the prevalence of predestination is completely false, since virtues and vices do exist, and divine justice exerts itself in accordance to them. At the same time, there can be no conflict between divine foreknowledge and the power of choice, for God knows

sequence dedicated to predestination and free will spans no fewer than 667 lines, from 17063 to 17730).

19. The two Scholastic authors whom Gérard Paré quotes are Albert the Great and his pupil Thomas Aquinas. In analyzing the rich syncretism of Jean's poem, Paré argues that among the many influences that shaped the text (Ovid, Alain, Boethius), the one that exerted the strongest control was the Aristotelianism cultivated at the University of Paris in the thirteenth century. A great deal of Paré's attention is directed to the deterministic theses of Etienne Tempier (1270, 1277), which Paré identifies in Nature's disquisition (*Les idées et les lettres au XIIIe siècle. Le "Roman de la Rose"* [Montréal: Centre de Psychologie et de Pédagogie, 1947]), 232. In 1969, however, Fleming adamantly rejected this identification as erroneous (*The "Roman de la Rose,"* 214–18).

20. The relationship she establishes between reason and free will (i.e., the latter has to appeal to the former in order to be able to exert itself virtuously; ll. 17715–18) is also present in Aquinas (see Ia-IIae Q. 13.1, "Whether Choice Is an Act of Will or of Reason").

21. For a modern edition of Jean's translation of *De consolatione,* see V. L. Dedeck-Héry, "Boethius' *De Consolatione* by Jean de Meun," *Mediaeval Studies* 14 (1952): 165–275. As to the way in which the poet assimilates Scholastic vocabulary in his works, see Gisela Hilder, *Der scholastiche Wortschatz bei Jean de Meun: Die Artes Liberales* (Tübingen: Max Niemeyer, 1972).

all the actions a man can take and the results to which each of these actions may lead, but the eventual course of action is decided by man himself, not by God (ll. 17372–75). Destiny is not fixed to such a point, Jean says, that individuals cannot make decisions for themselves, an Augustinian-Boethian conclusion taken up by Aquinas's philosophy.[22] In Dame Nature's scheme of things, it is false to believe that everything people do, say, or think is predestined. Those who believe this actually try to excuse themselves for their wrongdoings, by claiming that they could not have done otherwise. Jean phrases the defective thinking of these individuals as follows: "Donc couvient il par vive force, / Quant voloir d'omme a riens s'efforce, / De quanqu'il fait, k'ainsi le face, / Pense, *die*, vueille ou porchace: / Donc est ce chose destinee / Qui ne puet estre detornee" (ll. 17151–56, emphasis added; "Hence, when man's will exerts itself in any direction, he must perforce, in whatever he does, perform it, think, *say,* wish or obtain it in just that way. Then the thing that cannot be defected is destined"). This kind of argumentation is unacceptable, Jean maintains, because it basically leaves no room for man's free choice.

The textual reproduction of the erroneous reasoning of those who oppose the pivotal role of free will is important for my discussion, for it obliquely conveys the poet's notion that the deeds, words, and wishes of people depend entirely on their intentions, not on predestination. A person is fully responsible for the consequences of his/her deeds or sayings. With this theory, speech is from the outset assigned to the sphere of interiority, as a human act grounded in individual intention. This principle is reiterated when Jean adduces a new possible objection to the idea of free will. Those who oppose the importance of free choice maintain that if a possible thing happens, if someone had foreseen this thing and said, "This will unavoidably happen," he would have told the truth. And since truth and necessity are interchangeable, it results that the thing that happened was necessary, that is, predetermined. This argumentation, Jean says again, is not worth a penny, since in such a case we would be dealing with conditional necessity, not with absolute necessity.[23] Were the adversaries of free

22. "God moves man's will, as the Universal Mover, to the universal object of the will, which is good.... But man determines himself by his reason to will this or that, which is true or apparent good" (*ST* Ia-IIae Q. 9.6).

23. The notions of the possible, the necessary, and the truth do not exist in Boethius's *Consolation,* Armand Strubel tells us (*Romance of the Rose,* 901n1), but the assertion is inaccurate.

will right, men would not feel the urge to work or seek advice in various circumstances of life. If things were divinely preordained, all human advice would be futile and all undertaking vain. By the same token, the notions of more or less, better or worse, could not apply to our thoughts, deeds, or words (ll. 17243–56). This section of Nature's speech seems to echo Aquinas's Ia-IIae Q. 83.2 ("Of Free Will"): "Man has free will: otherwise counsels, exhortations, commands, prohibitions, rewards and punishments would be in vain."[24] As voiced by Dame Nature, Jean's subliminal message is that we should be mature enough to assume the consequences and the responsibility for our actions and speeches. We should not blame the divinity for whatever we do or undertake as individual human beings. The decision to translate an idea into action, to say something, or to keep quiet lies entirely in the sphere of man's personal choices. Deeds or words do not happen by necessity; humans are the only ones to choose what to do or what to say. Examples of free will applied to the use of speech come in the text when Nature evokes another sample of defective thinking:

Qu'il meïsmes seult souvent dire / Qu'il n'a pas franc voloir d'ellire, / Car Dieus par sa prevision / Si le tient en subjection, / Qui tout par destinee maine, / Et l'oeuvre et la pensee humaine, / Si que s'il veult a vertu traire, / Ce li fait Dieus a force faire / Et s'il de mal faire s'efforce, / Ce li refait Dieus faire a force, / Qui mieus le tient que par le doit, / Si qu'il fait ce que faire doit / De tout pechié, de toute aumosne, / *De biau parler et de ramprosne, / De los et de detraction,* / de larrecin, d'occision / Et de pais et de mariage, / Soit par raison, soit par outrage: / "Ainsi, fait-il, couvient il estre." (17749–67; emphasis added)

He himself is accustomed to say often that he does not have the free will to choose, because God, with his foresight, holds him in such subjection that he directs every human thought and deed by destiny. Thus if he wants to draw toward virtue, God

---

These notions are specifically the three conceptual pillars around which Boethius develops his theory (see Book V, Prose 3, 4 and 6). The two types of necessity Jean evokes here are also borrowed from the *Consolation* (Book V, Prose 6). Echoes of the dynamic possible-necessary-true also resonate in *ST* Ia-Iae Q. 14.3, where Aquinas is debating "Whether the Knowledge of God Is of Future Contingent Things."

24. In commenting on this section of Nature's *lectio,* Strubel notes that the insistence with which Jean argues for the necessity of free will in the domain of sin is to be accounted for by the interest that his epoch had in confession and in the just retribution for moral errors (*Romance of the Rose,* 893n3). As I have pointed out, the theory of the will as the main agent in the commission of sin is a fundamental Thomistic development, taken up by Aquinas's followers, and eventually adopted as official doctrine by the Catholic Church.

makes him do so by force, and if he strives to do evil, it is again God who forces him to do it. God does more than hold him by the finger, so that he does whatever he must—sinning, almsgiving, *speaking well or cuttingly, giving praise or detraction*, thieving, killing, making peace or marriage—either reasonably or foolishly. "Thus," he says, "it must be."[25]

In this passage, Nature/Jean continues to ridicule the philosophy according to which human actions are independent from men's power of will, being entirely dictated by divine providence. The representatives of this flawed line of thinking mistakenly attribute even their ways of speaking to a superior force. From Nature's adamant rebuttal of such a notion, we can again get a sense of Jean's view of the workings of speech. Insolence, which is opposed to reverent words, and slander, which is opposed to giving praise, both depend on man's individual choice; attributing these verbal attitudes to God is a preposterous idea. Reason and speech are divine gifts of which humans should be proud, and which they should use properly, because it is these gifts that distinguish us from animals.

The Augustinian theory that people were given the ability to speak for mutual comprehension and instruction could not lack in a text as obsessed with speech as Jean's. This notion surfaces within the comparison the poet draws between dumb animals, by nature incapable of knowing, understanding, or speaking, and people. In Jean's view, if animals were endowed with speech and reason with which to understand and instruct each another, they would take over the planet to the destruction of mankind (ll. 17797–803). The poet further imagines an apocalyptic world, in which animals can think and speak. Within this scenario, domestic animals would never serve man and obey his orders, and wild animals would all want to strangle him.[26] Birds would pull out his eyes when he would sleep. Man

25. This passage also resonates with strong Thomistic echoes, if we peruse *ST* Ia-IIae Q. 19.10 ("Whether It Is Necessary for the Human Will, in Order to Be Good, to Be Conformed to the Divine Will, as Regards the Thing Willed") and Ia-IIae Q. 79.1 ("Whether God Is a Cause of Sin").

26. Jean may have taken his cue for this scenario from Book 22, chapter 22, of the *City of God,* where Augustine lists the many reasons why human beings cannot attain happiness in their earthly lives. On this lengthy list there are also the fears of calamities triggered by nonhuman sources: "the terror of being crushed by falling buildings, of attacks by animals, in panic or in malice; of the bites of wild beasts, which may only be painful, but may sometimes be fatal, as in the rabies which is caught from an infected dog, so that an animal normally tame and affectionate to its master sometimes causes more panic and terror than a lion or poisonous snake,

would not be in any way superior to animals, since they would know how to make pieces of weaponry and clothes. As far as the use of speech is concerned, beasts would make such a skillful use of it that they "porroient estre escrivains" ("could be writers"; l. 17839). The passage describing this apocalyptic world is much longer and detailed than the description I have just provided. Although the whole discussion about what animals could do had they reason may seem a new extended parenthesis in Jean's text, it is actually not out of place, for it leads to a specific point the author wants to make: it is not human nature per se that is defective; it is people's use of free will that is so.

I have evoked this fragment of the *Rose* for two reasons: for the manner in which it presents the act of writing as the utmost form of expression a creature endowed with reason can practice, and for the conclusion to which it leads and which justifies this otherwise unexpected deviation. Animals' actual ignorance comes from their nature; in the same way, the intellectual capacities of humans (or angels) come from the nature God gave them. But if man, as a reasonable creature, refuses to use these divine gifts properly, this is a defect stemming from his own vice that confuses his senses (ll. 17866–70). The decision to sin is alone responsible for man's straying from the right path, because naturally he is endowed with reason and the ability to make right choices. This argument should put an end to the foolish discussions of those who claim that man is not responsible for his actions: "Et pour ce tant dit vous en ai / Et tels raisons vous amenai / Que leur jangles vueill estanchier, / Car nus ne s'en puet revanchier (ll. 17875–78; "It is for this reason that I have said so much to you about it and brought up arguments to quell men's gossip on the subject, for nothing can defend them against it"). This final remark is important not only because it justifies Nature's disquisition on the rebellion of animals, but also because it gives us a measure of the obsession that Jean's contemporaries had with free will.

In debating ethical issues, Dame Nature achieves a splendid connection with the ideology of Dame Raison, to whom she is traditionally opposed in *Rose* criticism. Thus, I do not share Winthrop Wetherbee's opinion that for Jean, "the ideal cooperation of Nature and Raison has become impos-

and the effect on anyone who happens to be infected by its bite is to make him the object of greater dread to parents, wife or children than any wild beast" (Augustine of Hippo, *Concerning the City of God against the Pagans,* translated by Henry Bettenson [New York: Penguin Books, 2003], 1066–67).

sible."[27] It is here, in the discussion of man's free choices, that the discourses of Jean's two divine ladies converge, thus realizing a concatenation of ideas that grants cohesion to this highly polyphonic literary work. As Boethius in *Consolation* and Aquinas in *Secunda Secundae,* Jean posits that human deeds and words are not dictated by necessity or providence, but performed by virtue of individual, free choices. There is no good excuse for an evil action or a wicked word; the blame for them should be fully assumed on a personal basis. (This philosophy, patterned on the Scholastic view of morality as a sum of actions rooted in individual intentions, will resonate in Dante's works as well.) In the *Rose,* Jean gives specific examples of the kinds of (verbal) sins to which man is prone. The mouthpiece through which he exemplifies human sinfulness is again Nature. Toward the end of her discourse, the allegorical character expresses her regret for having made man and gives as reasons for her lament a comprehensive list of man's chief sins. She further excuses herself for spelling out this list by invoking her typically feminine loquacity—"Fame sui, si ne me puis taire" ("I am a woman and cannot keep silent"; l. 19222)—loquacity that allows her to tell the whole, unaltered truth about human deviations. Thus, although at first glance the association of femininity with garrulity seems another of Jean's jibes at women's discursive appetite, here, garrulousness is mandatory and positive, because it serves the moral obligation of saying the truth. Nature has to speak much because the list of human vices she has to draw is so long (twenty-six vices in all):

Orgueilleus est, murtriers et lerres, / Fel, couvoiteus, avers, trichierres, / Desesperez et *mesdisanz* / Et haïnneus et despisanz, / Mescreanz, envieus, *mentierres, / Parjurs, faussaires*, foz, *vantierres*, / Glouz, Inconstanz et foloiables, / Ydolastres, *desagreables*, / Traïstre et faus ypocrites / Et pareceus et sodomites. / Briement, tant est chaitis et nices / Qu'il est sers a trestouz les vices / Et trestouz en soi les heberge. (19229–41; emphasis added)

He is a proud, murderous thief, cruel, covetous, miserly, and treacherous. He is desperate, greedy, *slanderous*, hateful, and spiteful; unfaithful and envious, he *lies*, *perjures* himself, and *falsifies*; he is foolish, *boastful*, inconstant, and senseless; he is a *quarrelsome* idolatror, a traitorous, *false hypocrite*, and a lazy sodomite; in short he is such a stupid wretch that he is slave to all the vices, and harbors them all within himself.[28]

27. Winthrop Wetherbee, *Platonism and Poetry in the Twelfth Century: The Literary Influence of the School of Chartres* (Princeton, N.J.: Princeton University Press, 1972), 263.

28. Since Dahlberg's translation was not based on the French edition I use, his list of vices does not correspond entirely with the one in this French quote.

Fleming points out that this list echoes the one drawn by St. Paul in his Epistle to the Romans (1:29–31).[29] The Pauline roster contains four social evils directly associated with speech (strife, whispering, slander, boastfulness) and three that have an indirect relationship to language: guile, covenant-breaking, and insolence. However, the three other sins Nature mentions—lying, perjury, and hypocrisy—are not on St. Paul's list. Like a fine moralist, in her virulent criticism of man's sinfulness, Nature paves the ground for psychological analysis and gives us an important indication of Jean's general conception of vice. Her list, which is a *summa vitiorum* in a nutshell, is as important for the economy of the *Rose* as is *Inferno* 11 (where Virgil explains the structure of Hell) for Dante's *Comedy.* For Nature's discourse is the only site in the poem where Jean takes the time to draw a detailed tally of sinful inclinations. The fundamental difference, however, with respect to *Inferno* 11 is the lack of a rigorous system, the absence of order and classification. Dame Nature extensively enumerates vices, but she does it in a random fashion, with no regard for a coherent organization or relationship among sins. She/Jean is a moralist, but an unconventional one, since he rarely names vices as such; Nature's roster is one of these rare occurrences. It is also worth noting that in this long record of moral errors, all the verbal abuses are categories amply described by Peraldus and his followers. Moreover, in Jean's text, the label *faussaire,* "falsifier," immediately follows lying and perjury, vices of the tongue that Peraldus defined in terms of falsity. (In chapter 3, we will see that Dante is also sensitive to the alignment of speech with falsehood and groups liars and perjurers with other types of falsifiers in the Malebolge.)

After Dame Nature delivers her summa of vices, she also evokes a series of horrendous punishments that await in hell those who give in to these vices. By implication, even those who commit the sins of speech above mentioned will end up in the underworld. No sinner will be able to escape the infernal punishments, because there is a supreme, transcendental authority who judges all the errors people have committed in deeds or words (l. 19320). This scriptural notion is again essential for Jean's ethical project because it establishes a relationship of equivalence between deeds and words: what is weighed at the eternal judgment is not only what people have done in their earthly lives but also what they have said. The biblical

29. Fleming, *The "Roman de la Rose,"* 121.

quote recycled here gives us another index of Jean's preoccupation with the (mis)uses of language.

Critics who have collated Jean's poem with Alain's *Plaint of Nature* have highlighted the distance that Jean's Nature takes with respect to her homonymous ancestress. Indeed, Dame Nature is no longer Alain's *Natura,* since she speaks in a scholastic fashion and has a great theological mind (meaningfully, when Jean introduces her in the poem, he describes her as "thinking about things"). Jean is obviously fascinated by the doctrine of free will and sin, which he considers an essential part of ethics; otherwise he would not have gone through the trouble of reproducing it and explaining it in such great detail and with so much passion (after he has warned us how hard it would be to do so).[30] I cannot agree with Denise Baker's assertion that "morality is clearly beyond her [Nature's] ken."[31] Paradoxically, Jean's Nature delivers one of the most important discourses on human morality in the *Romance of the Rose.* I say paradoxically because the highly philosophical themes she debates seem at odds with one of her main allegorical functions, that of assuring the perpetuation of species (and for humans she allows the sin of lechery as an effective agent). When she speaks about the prevalence of volition in the commission of sins, she presents the Scholastic doctrine of reason and free will with such expertise that we wonder why Jean did not place this presentation in Dame Raison's speech. I believe that, specifically because Nature's Scholastic doctrine is so contrary to her allegorical mission (the one consecrated by Alain of Lille) and so much more appropriate to Jean's own educational mission, her stance in the discourse on free will expresses that of the poet himself.

On the other hand, Jean's paradoxes can best be solved by applying the historical method of interpretation. If we take a final look at Aquinas's *ST,* we will see that actually Jean made no mistake in placing the debate on free will as the agent of sin in Nature's speech. In Ia-IIae Q. 10.1 ("Whether the Will Is Moved to Anything Naturally"), Aquinas speaks at length on the theme of "nature," listing the multiple meanings of this word (material form,

30. Strubel points out that the highly philosophical content of Nature's speech is not due entirely to Jean's pedantry. The poet is writing at the time of the triumph of great Scholasticism, when the gap between literature and sciences becomes deeper, but he sees no conflict between the two. Rather, in his view, establishing a harmonious relationship between poetry and philosophy is the very nature of his mission as a clerk (*Romance of the Rose,* 907n1).

31. Denise N. Baker, "The Priesthood of Genius," *Speculum* 51 (1976): 277–91, at 285.

substance, being) and highlighting the relationship between nature and will: "But since the will is founded on some nature, it is necessary that the movement proper to nature be shared by the will, to some extent: just as what belongs to a previous cause is shared by a subsequent cause. Because in every thing, being itself, which is from nature, precedes volition, which is from the will. And hence it is that the will wills something naturally." Later on, Aquinas defines vices specifically as inclinations against nature.[32] This moral philosophy, which defines not only homosexuality but ALL vices as unnatural tendencies, justifies Dame Nature's complaint against the vices of man and her regret of having made him. All these pieces of extratextual information convey that in the *Rose,* Nature was the character best suited to deliver a scholastic *lectio* on the relationship between free will and immorality. At the same time, on a metalinguistic level, we have to be aware that her systematic exposition of the (moral) world represents "one of the earliest instances of the use of a vernacular in the treatment of philosophical ideas."[33]

Genius's Grievances against Feminine Speech

Nature's long and eclectic disquisition is bracketed by two segments of Genius's discourse (ll. 16299–710, the first one, and ll. 19509–671, the second one). Jean borrows this character from Alain's *Plaint of Nature* but ends up reinventing him along satirical lines. Genius is introduced as Dame Nature's priest, a *bien enpallez,* "good speaker" (l. 19339) and is the recipient of her confession.[34] We have seen Nature invoking her femininity as an excuse

32. *ST* Ia-IIae Q. 71.3, "Whether Vice Is Contrary to Nature."

33. Economou, *The Goddess Natura,* 108.

34. The studies on Genius as a figure in both classical and medieval works are numerous. Jane Chance Nitzsche investigates his twofold role (god of procreation and moral guide) throughout literary history, and George Economou (1970) draws a detailed parallel between the roles played by Genius in the two French poets (Alain and Jean) and Gower, their English admirer. Focusing on Genius's capacity as a priest, Denise Baker relates him first to his classical sources (Bernardus Silvestris, Apuleius, and Martianus Capella) then to Alain's text. In analyzing the same character in Gower, she concludes that the dual priesthood of Gower's Genius "testifies to the English poet's awareness of the difference between this character's tutelary role in *The Plaint of Nature* and in the *Roman de la Rose*" ("The Priesthood of Genius," 287). A. J. Minnis (1983), Winthrop Wetherbee, and Edwin Craun (1997) further study the role played by Genius in English literature. Among them, very important in my critical investigation is Craun, who argues that Genius's sermon in *Confessio Amantis* is highly indebted to the medieval pastoral discourse on abusive speech (*Lies, Slander and Obscenity,* 113–57).

for speaking her mind, for not hiding things. But if in that self-defensive statement, her typically feminine loquaciousness had a positive function—revealing things that needed to be known by the audience—in other places, she expresses strongly negative views of women's verbosity. When Genius says, for instance, that nothing swears and lies more boldly than a woman (l. 18132), Dame Nature concedes that women swear and lie more frequently than men (ll. 18140–41). Interesting in this reply, however, is that she obliquely reminds her priest that men lie, too. Later on, she makes another comment offensive to women: "Bon fait prolexité foïr. / Si sont fames mout ennuieuses / Et de parler contrarieuses" (ll. 18302–4; "It is a good thing to flee prolixity. Women are very troublesome and contrary about talking"). She makes this assertion to justify her own prolixity (here, the lengthy speech on mirrors), but behind this move lies Jean himself, who misses no occasion to lacerate ladies for their verbal appetite.

Studying various attitudes toward feminine rhetoric in medieval England, Sandy Bardsley notes that in the late Middle Ages the view of women's eloquence underwent a radical change caused by the pastoral discourse on sinful language.[35] Bardsley argues that in this pastoral tradition, the notion of morally deviant speech was increasingly feminized, since female speech was often ridiculed by an eminently patriarchal society, and a woman who dared speak her mind was considered a threat to family and society. Feminine rhetoric was often associated with, and held responsible for, crimes such as sexual disorder, assault, and eavesdropping. In an attempt to control female "disruptive" speech, the British legal system even devised the category of "scolding woman." Among medieval writers with negative attitudes toward feminine voices, Bardsley also mentions Chaucer, the English translator of the *Rose,* who was greatly influenced by Jean.

Genius's discourse in the *Rose* could make a case for Bardsley's theory. His satire against women spans four hundred verses and is, as Ernest Langlois reminds us, "completely disconnected from the topic" of the poem.[36] This discursive deviation from the storyline reinforces my sense that Genius, the parodic priest, is one of the channels through which Jean conveys his own criticism of women's mores. When Dame Nature starts weeping and apologizes for this female weakness, Genius immediately seizes the

35. Sandy Bardsley, *Venomous Tongues: Speech and Gender in Late Medieval England* (Philadelphia: University of Pennsylvania Press, 2006), 2.

36. Ernest Langlois, *Origines et sources,* 149.

moment and launches a virulent critique of women's temper and (evil) eloquence.[37] Woman, says Genius in a phrase that has now become legendary in criticism of the *Rose,* is a very irritable animal (l. 16333). She is not only prone to wrath but also harbors a great predisposition to sinfulness, for she is full of malice and has perverse habits. Of all the vices of women, the one that mostly upsets Genius is their extraordinary propensity to talking, their inability to keep the secrets their husbands reveal to them.[38] In his view, sharing one's feelings and thoughts with one's wife is a major mistake, because soon those intimate things will become public knowledge, and the social image of the husband will be damaged irremediably (ll. 16351–72). On the other hand, the man who hits his wife as a punishment for her loquacity incurs the risk of being publicly exposed by her, so there is really no solution to this problem. In general, he who trusts a woman is a great fool who is risking his own life, for if he dares criticize her, or reproach her with anything, she will have him killed by her friends. Genius pushes the theme of women's control over their husbands to a ridiculous extreme and gives the example of a couple in which the man has something on his conscience. This foolish husband who committed (or plans to commit) a crime for which he could pay with his life is in great danger in the bed, next to his wife, and because of her. Although he wants to keep quiet about what lies on his conscience, at night, if she sees him worried, she will draw him to her with sexually charged gestures and will manipulate him with her smooth talk until he starts disclosing all of his secrets.

Here Genius adopts a female voice and reproduces at length the manipulative speech the woman gives in the conjugal bed. She first reassures her husband that there is no one around, that their room is safely isolated from the rest of the house. Then she reminds him how much she loves him

37. Wetherbee, who is impressed by Nature's "larger-than-life-femininity," considers her polemic with Genius the most brilliant subversion of Alain's allegory in the *Plaint of Nature.* With the help of Nature and Genius, Jean demolishes Alain's allegorical world in order to build his own world "out of the actual facts of experience" (*Platonism and Poetry,* 264–65).

38. According to Lee Patterson, the theme of the wicked delight a woman takes in ferreting out masculine secrets is a common denominator of the medieval misogynistic literature (see "Feminine Rhetoric and the Politics of Subjectivity: The Old Woman and the Wife of Bath," in *Rethinking the "Romance of the Rose: Text, Image, Reception,"* edited by Kevin Brownlee and Sylvia Huot [Philadelphia: University of Pennsylvania Press, 1992]). He exemplifies this theme with two texts: Chaucer's *Wife of Bath* and the *Sermon Joyeux de la patience des femmes obstineées contre leur maris* (Joyful sermon on the patience of women obstinate against their husbands).

and how faithful she is to him. She invokes Jesus' name and the sacred oath of matrimony to convince him that they form a sacred union, and therefore she is entitled to know everything about him. She gives him the example of other married couples, in which at night, in the safety of their beds, the men tell their wives all their secrets and ask for advice. These men confess themselves to their wives more often than to the priest, Genius adds in a slightly scandalized tone. The reproduced discourse of the curious wife becomes ironical when she admits that she knows about what happens in other people's beds ... from the wives themselves—her female friends who report to her everything they had discussed with their husbands. Unlike these other wives, however, she says that she dislikes talking too much, gossiping, or quarrelling. Again, she invokes God's name to make her husband open up to her, and she emotionally blackmails him by telling him that she will die if he does not talk to her. At this point of the poem, the direct discourse of the inquisitive wife ceases, and Genius intervenes with a cynical comment assuring the audience that, after delivering her devilishly skillful speech, the wife will start caressing her spouse and covering him with hypocritical kisses and tears until he gives up and reveals his secrets, "hanging himself with his words" (ll. 16545–60).

Knowledge is power, and Genius draws attention to the fact that from the moment a wife knows the secrets of her man, she will have a very strong means to hold him under her control. He will no longer afford to get mad at her or mistreat her, for she now has absolute power over him. In the best-case scenario, she might remain faithful to him and not reveal his secrets until they break up, but not even this is sure, so great is the female urge to speak. Chances are that she will share her husband's secrets with somebody else even before she breaks up with him. Genius's belief in women's malice is so firm that he exhorts his followers to preach themselves the mistrust of women, so that every man will know how to protect himself against this terrible enemy. Genius warns that he who will sermonize against women might anger them, for they have wicked tongues (l. 16579), but he is confident that that speaker will at least have told the truth. Then he dramatically urges all men to flee women or at least to guard themselves against them in conversations (ll. 16581–89).

Genius is, however, like all the other counselors in the poem, a contradictory character. His discourse is highly inconsistent, since immediately after urging men to avoid the "female beast," he reframes his position, and advises men to respect, love, and cultivate women. Men should cherish women, dress them well, overwhelm them with their attention, and serve them properly, so that the human race will be perpetuated (ll. 16621–30). Then, again, Genius jumps to the opposite extreme and warns men about the harm women can do to them if they know too many things about them. The greatest danger that might arise within a couple lies in the bed; it is where women seduce men with their sexuality that the latter are most prone to talk. Speaking in bed is a foolish mistake on the part of a man, says the god of procreation, for sex is good but should never be mixed up with self-revelations: "Mais se preuz estes et senez / Quant entre vos bras les tenez / Et les acollez et baisiez, / Taisiez, taisiez, taisiez, taisiez! / Pensez de vos langues tenir, / Car riens n'en puet a chief venir / Quant des secrez sont parçonierres, / Tant sont orgueilleuses et fieres / Et tant ont les langues cuisanz, / Et venimeuses et nuisanz (ll. 16662–72; "But if you are wise and intelligent you will keep quiet when you hold them in your arms and hug them and kiss them. Keep quiet, quiet, quiet, quiet.[39] Think about holding your tongue, for nothing can come to any conclusion when they share secrets, so proud and haughty are they, with such corrosive, venomous and harmful tongues"). To reinforce the truth of his message, Genius adduces the *exemplum* of Delilah, who first seduced Samson with her flattering words, then made him open up to her and reveal his deepest secrets. Thereafter, she cut off Samson's hair while he was sleeping and deprived him of his magical powers. Although Genius considers that this cautionary tale is amply sufficient to illustrate female malice, he still finds it useful to reinforce his mistrust of women with a Sapiential quote: Solomon, who was well aware of the great harm a woman may cause to a man if he tells her too many things, explicitly warned men to guard the gates of their mouths against the women they love (ll. 16698–700).[40]

39. Dahlberg translates this verse as "Stay still, still, still," which does not accurately reflect the original "taisez, taisez, taisez, taisez."

40. Heather Arden explains Genius's misogynistic views by his reducing women to their procreative function (*The Romance of the Rose* [Boston: Twayne Publishers, 1987], 64). In my opinion, Genius's misogyny is more subtle, since in fact, he has a high opinion about women as participants in the act of procreation, a natural good; this is why he concedes that men should cultivate their friendship and worship them. Rather, Genius's main problem with women is that that *they do not let themselves* be limited to their procreative role. Ladies have their own intelligence, their own ways, and especially their own voices. Genius maligns women only insofar as they do not always submit to male desires and control. This is why he vituperates against fe-

The first part of Genius's sermon ends with these cautionary words; the second part follows Dame Nature's confession and addresses the god of love and his barons. Genius promises that the gates of paradise will be open to all men who work hard toward procreation, regardless of the settings of their sexual encounters—within the marriage or outside of it (this is a great difference with respect to Alain's Genius, who had insisted that the only licit context of erotic love was the marital institution). He harshly condemns the practices of abstinence and chastity, and his unorthodox theological views also allow him to air an extremist idea: that all sins of men will be forgiven, if, and only if, men work to fulfill Nature's greatest commandment—procreation.

As Dame Nature's priest, Genius seems highly concerned about vices and exhorts his listeners to fight against them, but instead of broaching an actual sermon on this topic, he asks his listeners to refer back to the discourse of his goddess, who has enumerated twenty-six vices (and if we check Nature's tally, we will see that Genius's number is correct). The "lovely *Romance of the Rose*," he goes on to say, explains these vices quite briefly, so he invites his audience to find out more about them from her speech, in order to guard themselves better against moral errors (ll. 19870–75). Genius's invitation is of vital importance in the economy of the poem. First, because his referring back with such accuracy to Nature's *summa vitiorum* ensures once again the cohesion of this highly multidiscursive text that is the *Rose*. Second and most importantly, because it shows us how careful the author behind Genius's voice is in handling the ethical material and concepts he presents. Genius's injunction is a special moment in the evolution of the text in that it offers us the accurate, distinct timbre of Jean's own voice. For here, it is not the parodic priest who speaks anymore; it is the writer himself, who for a split second steps out of his fictive world to do some publicity for his work. In the advertisement he is airing, Jean invites his audience to read his "lovely" book not for entertainment but for learning how to shield themselves against temptations and deviant habits.

In the world of fiction, Genius avoids reiterating the vices listed by Dame Nature and confines his teachings to just a few words exhorting Christians to serve her laws, to return what they have stolen, to stay away from murder, to be loyal, thoughtful of others, and also to keep their hands

male fickleness and above all, female eloquence. Women's temper and rhetoric are two domains men have difficulty controlling.

and mouths clean (ll. 20640–50). The fact that even in such a condensed homily there is still room for a reference to the use of speech is significant, despite the sense we may have that this reference is just another stereotypical (and ironic) homiletic closure. This new call to disciplined speech highlights *custodia linguae* as an overarching theme of the poem; we have seen it first in Dame Raison's disquisition, then in Dame Nature's speech, and now, we encounter it in Genius's mock sermon. We will find it mentioned again in the brief intervention of Contrainte Astinence (Constraint Abstinence), a Beguine sister, who explains to Malebouche why he deserves to die. This passage compels attention, because, on the one hand, it casts the topic of the guarded tongue in terms reminiscent of Peraldus's prologue to "De peccato linguae," and, on the other hand, the sister will in effect assist her lover, Faus Semblant, in slaying the rumor monger:

> Sire, la vertu premeraine, / La plus grant, la plus souveraine / Que nus hom mortieus puisse avoir / Par science ne par avoir, / C'est de la langue refrener: / A ce se doit chascuns pener, / K'ades vient mieus que l'en se taise / Que dire parole mauvaise; / Et cil qui volentiers l'escoute / N'est pas preudons ne dieu ne doute. / Sire, seur touz autres pechiez, / De cestui estes entechiez! (ll. 12183–94)

> Sir, the chief virtue, the greatest and most sovereign that any mortal man may have, through knowledge or possession, is to bridle his tongue. Everyone should take the trouble to do so, since it is always better to keep silent than to utter a wicked thing, while he who listens to it willingly is neither worthy nor God fearing. Sir, you are stained with this sin above all others.

Once we overcome the shock of seeing Contrainte Astinence, an allegorical character, become an accessory to the murder of Malebouche, another allegorical character, we are left with the mission of solving this new semiotic conundrum. What is the meaning of the confrontation between Contrainte Astinence, who preaches virtues and abstinence but is fake to the core, pregnant, and capable of murder, and Malebouche, another highly corrupt figure, who has allegedly destroyed many lives with his wicked tongue? To answer this question, we have to remember that Contrainte Astinence is not only an allegory whose behavior compromises the values of Christian asceticism, but she is also a walking concept that "materializes" itself as a Beguine, a religious figure grounded in contemporary history. She is therefore a (mock) theological allegory well equipped ideologically to deliver a micro-sermon on sin and to communicate a death sentence based on a major crime: undisciplined speech. Contrainte Astinence is the only character in the *Rose* who uses the word "sin" to refer to manifestations of evil speech that in the pastoral tradition were grouped under the catch-all term *lingua indisciplinata,* a transgressive notion (Dame Raison had branded only obscene speech as a sin). In his turn, Malebouche is a walking-talking embodiment of this very transgressive concept, as he comes from the world of the courtly scandalmongers. Although he is eventually slain, the verbal evils associated with him will not cease on the stage of the narrative; Faus Semblant will refine Malebouche's linguistic techniques and will use them in the service of the devil, undercutting thus Contrainte Astinence's lesson on *custodia linguae.*

This failure of the pastoral discourse on transgressive speech is not unique in the economy of the *Rose,* nor is it the most serious. In a way, it prefigures a more dramatic "shipwreck"—that of the authorial agency in relationship to its own poetic diction. For outside the world of fiction and inside the writer's workshop, Jean himself, as a user of language, systematically and vigorously tramples underfoot all the good advice about the virtuous use of speech that Raison, Nature, Genius, and Contrainte Astinence generously offer. In a sense, Jean is himself a Malebouche, a foul speaker who in writing poetry transgresses all the rules of clean language posited by the pastoral discourse that he seems to know so well. He is also a Faus Semblant, a writer who is not what he seems to be. Often times, Jean speaks more like the women whose sinuous, deceptive, and dirty talk he virulently criticizes. His writerly discourse confirms Lee Patterson's sense that in medieval poetry "the voice of the poet is inescapably aligned with that of women."[41] As we shall see in chapter 4 through the lenses of the fifteenth-century debate on the *Romance of the Rose,* keeping one's mouth clean is a beautiful moral precept that Jean seems unable to follow.

Le Testament Maistre Jehan de Meun (The Testament of Master Jean de Meun) (1291–1292)

In chapter 1, I pointed out that Peraldus's *SV* was already very popular when Jean was writing his poem. Laurent, who translated large sections of

41. Patterson, "Feminine Rhetoric," 319. Patterson gives Matheolus's *Lamentations* as an example of how the poetic function becomes associated with feminine speaking: "in complaining about her [his wife's] endless nagging, Matheolus repeats himself verbatim and at length, just like a woman" (Patterson, "Feminine Rhetoric," 321).

SV into the vernacular, was also contemporary with Jean; in addition, he was a prior of the Dominican convent on Rue St. Jacques, in Paris. Also significant is the activity developed by Thomas Aquinas at the University of Paris during the time Jean was composing the *Rose.* What I feel compelled to add, starting from the premise that Jean's authorship of the *Testament* is indisputable, is that the poet's fascination with the tracts on the deadly sins does not end with his allegorical poem; on the contrary, it is enhanced in the later work, which provides a delightful summa on vices, worth analyzing here in some detail.[42] I say delightful because although Jean is not terribly original in his exposition on sin, the poetic way in which he speaks of it gives freshness and persuasive force to his message in the vernacular.

Aimée Bourneuf's 1956 edition of the *Testament* repairs in a PhD dissertation an unjust process of cultural neglect, as she peruses several manuscripts of the text, offers an Old French version of it based on the Vatican MS 367, and eventually, supported by the overwhelming textual and contextual evidence that presents itself to her, reassigns the authorship of the poem to Jean de Meun. I say reassign because in the early and mid-1990s a few French scholars branded Jean's authorship of the *Testament* as uncertain, a situation similar to the questioning of Dante's authorship of the

42. Bourneuf's research and 1956 edition of the *Testament* leave no doubt that this poem was written by Jean de Meun; Fleming (*The "Roman de la Rose,"* 46–47) and Jillian M. L. Hill (*The Medieval Debate on Jean de Meung's "Roman de la Rose": Morality Versus Art* [Lewiston, N.Y.: Edwin Mellen, 1991], 45–51) endorse her findings. In favor of Jean's authorship of the *Testament* speak several contextual facts: 1. in manuscripts of the *Rose,* it regularly followed the allegorical love poem; 2. in three separate manuscripts, it was attached to Jean's translations of Boethius and Vegetius; 3. in seven different codices, it accompanied two poems attributed to Jean; 4. at least on one occasion it was coupled with Honoré Bouvet's *Apparicion maistre Jehan de Meun* (The apparition of Master Jean de Meun); 5. the participants in the *Querelle de la Rose* treated the *Testament* as another of Jean's works (more on this in chapter 4). There are also many internal textual correspondences linking the content of the *Testament* with that of the *Rose;* one good example is that four passages of the *Testament* contain notions borrowed from Boethius's *Consolation,* notions that also appear in the *Rose.* It is also worth adding that several moral questions raised in the love poem are answered in the *Testament.* For a more detailed account of the coincidences between the two original works by Jean, see Buzzetti Gallaratti, *Le Testament Maistre Jehan de Meun: Un caso letterario* (Turin: Edizioni dell'Orso, 1989), 7–111. Apart from the *Rose* and the *Testament,* Jean authored no other original text; his other works are translations from Latin: Boethius's *Consolation,* Ethelred's *On Spiritual Friendship,* Vegetius's military tract, and the letters of Abélard and Héloïse. For Jean's own outline of his "record of publications," see the introduction he wrote to Boethius (Dedeck-Héry, "Boethius' *De Consolatione,*" 168).

Fiore, in the Italian context. In the field of French studies, the root of this critical reluctance lies in the fact that it is the fourteenth-century copyists of the *Testament* who first attributed it to Jean; the poet never inserted his name in the text, as he had done it in the *Rose.* Jean's avoidance of an internal signature, however, is implicitly justified in the text by the poet himself. In the opening lines of the *Testament,* he establishes a marked distance between his youthful works, written *par vanité,* "out of vanity," and this new product of his old age, which he is writing *par charité et humilité,* "out of charity and humility," and with the purpose of mending the authorial sins committed in the *Rose,* a highly controversial moral poem. As an analogy with Jean's self-imposed anonymity and humbleness toward the text he is writing, I can adduce William Peraldus, who never signed his works with his own name, but only with the humble self-designation "ego, miminus de ordine fratrem predicatorum." But Jean's avoidance of an internal signature is itself a controversial notion, if we consider that D. M. Méon, the first modern editor of the *Testament,* found manuscripts of it ending with the lines: "Ci finiray mon dit, *je Jehan de Mehun,* / Que je por Testament laiz à tout le commun" ("Here ends my speech that *I, Jean de Meun,* leave as a *Testament* to everyone"; translation and emphasis mine).[43]

Aimée Bourneuf's philological work on the *Testament* is deep and detailed, and her introduction and notes thoroughly researched. The glossary she attaches to her study is also of great help to the reader who dares approach this medieval literary work. One can only wonder why such a PhD dissertation has never been published as a book. It is important, however, that her doctoral work faced a panel of experts at Fordham University who ultimately endorsed her project.

More recently, an Italian Scholar, Silvia Buzzetti Gallarati, has reopened the discussion around Jean's *Testament,* first in 1978 with a substantive study on the manuscript tradition of the text, and then in 1989 with the publication of a new Old French version of the *Testament,* based on MS 178 of the Public Library of Geneva. Buzzetti Gallarati undertakes a thorough structural analysis of the poem, pointing to rhetorical patterns typical of high Scholasticism and to social and moral themes of topical relevance. She does not draw a parallel with Dante's *Comedy,* focused as she is on highlighting

43. Quoted by Winthrop Huntington Rice, *The European Ancestry of Villon's Satirical Testaments* (New York: Corporate Press, 1941), 152. Rice notes that the doubt cast on the authorship of the *Testament* does not seem to be justified (151n14).

similarities between the *Testament* and the *Romance of the Rose,* similarities that serve her to prove that both poems were penned by Jean de Meun. Since the textual and historical evidence presented by Buzzetti Gallarati is irrefutable, I will widen the research on the *Testament* by placing it into a cross-cultural perspective and by seeking to determine to what degree it might have served as a source of poetic inspiration for Dante's *Comedy.*

It is well known that the first and strongest link between Jean de Meun and Dante is the *Fiore,* the Italian translation of the *Romance of the Rose* that many modern scholars attribute to Dante. Thus, in his seminal study "Un nodo della cultura medievale," Gianfranco Contini speaks of a "continuità culturale" between the *Rose* and the *Comedy* through the mediation of the *Fiore.*[44] I dare suggest that a closer look at Jean's later work reveals that the cultural continuity between Jean and Dante is even more marked in the case of the *Testament,* for the similarities between this text and the *Comedy* are even more salient and striking than the ones between the *Rose* and the *Comedy.*

Dated 1291–1292, the fictional *Testament* of Maistre Jean de Meun is a poem of 2,120 lines, written in monorhyme alexàndrine quatrains, the typical stanza of thirteenth-century *dits* and moral poetic compositions. As a literary genre with ancestry in classical antiquity, the testament offers Jean the authenticating framework of a written document in which, typically, a testator establishes his last will and legacy to future generations of readers.[45] For Jean, this legacy consists of moral and religious instruction, sometimes heightened by mild satire, as the author criticizes the mendicants' efforts to gain temporal power by means of the confessional and their assistance in the drawing up of wills. Thematically, the *Testament* is a very complex poem that treats several major topics, such as the opposition between young age and old age, the theme of *memento mori,* the nobility of the soul, the relationship between the dying and their heirs, the current state of the Church and the education of its members, women's mores, the seven deadly sins, and the spiritual benefits of prayer.[46]

44. Contini, "Un nodo della cultura medievale," 162.

45. For an outline of the genealogy and evolution of the testament as a legal and literary genre, see Rice, who also takes into discussion François Villon's debts to Jean de Meun's *Testament* (*The European Ancestry;* see in particular chapter 5, "The French Vernacular Wills," 141–224).

46. For the Old French edition of the *Testament* I rely on Buzzetti Gallarati. Due to the absence of an English version of it, the translations from this text are mine.

The *Testament* begins by defining sin as the greatest human evil, for it crucifies God, our heavenly Father, who created us not for his own benefit, since he is self-sufficient, but for our own sake. Out of gratitude, we should not do anything that might displease and anger him, because for the person who dies in sin there is no longer any help or hope of salvation. It is preferable to be cut into pieces rather than to upset God; therefore, we should not wait until we are old to start doing good deeds, since old age brings along physical handicaps and even senility. The first part of the work deplores several linguistic immoral practices related to social life: rhetoric not corroborated by deeds, adulation, and contention. Moral instruction is absolutely necessary in society, Jean stresses, and it is the clerics' duty to perform it both in deed and in word (l. 690). Without clerical instruction, Christians are in spiritual danger, because they cannot prevent the pus oozing from the rotten tree that shoots forth vices. Whoever intends to blame someone needs to be himself without stain, because speaking well without doing good deeds is just light smoke in the air (ll. 689–96). Jean has problems, however, with the doubtful moral quality of the religious entities of the day; he mistrusts the secular clergy because they practice simony, and the friars because, although they do have superior education, they are deeply corrupt and amass fortunes at the expense of the sick and of the dying.[47] The mendicants lead a happy social life, enjoying the flatteries they are told and skillfully practicing themselves the art of flattery (ll. 741–856). Jean opposes them to the Cistercian and Cluniac monks, who do not exploit the human weaknesses of those still alive but pray for the dead, give alms to the poor, and host strangers. These monks are very humble and poor, and in terms of education, they can make such progress that within ten years they will count many intellectual members among their ranks, Jean adds. Education is worthless if it leads to the sins of pride and contention (ll. 977–1032).[48]

47. Jean is referring to the fact that the mendicant orders were constantly assisting in the making of wills, as they had made a practice of hearing confessions especially at deathbeds. This practice allowed the mendicants to build fortunes, powers, and reputation. Bishops and regular pastors fiercely opposed the friars' confession privileges, but in 1281, Pope Martin IV issued the bull *Ad fructus uberes,* which allowed the Franciscans and Dominicans to preach and hear confessions wherever they liked, without the permissions of bishops or regular pastors (Aimé Céleste Bourneuf, "The 'Testament' of Jean de Meun: Vatican MS 367 [1291–1292]" [PhD diss., Fordham University, New York, 1956], xxi).

48. These lines refer again to the heated quarrels over the privileges of the mendicants to

The author spends a great deal of time criticizing the friars, whom he portrays as greedy for riches, deceptive, and publicly dangerous. He mentions that they like the company of widows, whom they can fool and exploit more easily than widowers. Women themselves are depicted as shallow, lustful, and vain, mourning the death of their husbands for show, and thereafter putting on beautiful clothes and jewels to seduce other men. Jean concedes, however, that some of the prayers widows say in church on behalf of their late husbands might be sincere, and this remark opens a lengthy disquisition on the therapeutic and salvific value of prayer. It is then within the context of this tractate on prayer (ll. 1329–2116) that the exposition on the seven deadly sins is situated (ll. 1673–796).

Jean states that only the souls in purgatory can benefit from the supplications said by the living, but since we do not know who is where after death, we need to pray for all the dead. Three prerequisites must be met for a prayer to be answered: the petitioner needs to be in a state of grace, has to place a reasonable request, and finally, has to formulate the petition in a courteous linguistic manner. The greatest obstacle in the way of our prayers being answered is sin. One can acquire vices very easily, and these in turn spread like weeds in society and lead to deadly sins. One mortal sin can kill the soul, by devastating what is good in us. The author incriminates himself for his past mistakes and regrets having begun to do good rather late in life. This personal remark then gives him the occasion to introduce the traditional scheme of the three agents of sin (the world, the flesh, and the devil) and to emphasize that the greatest source of evil lies within ourselves (another comment hinting at a process of self-examination?). In this spiritually dangerous framework, prayer is an absolute necessity, because a repenting, praying heart opens a direct channel of communication with God, the source of all good, who can save our souls. There is one condition, however, that must be fulfilled for this communication to take place—our words must agree with our thoughts, since God always knows what we "say, think, or do" (l. 1353).

The notion of the equivalence between thought and speech seems to be of paramount importance for the author, since he develops it in no fewer than seven stanzas (ll. 1445–72). He begins by arguing that it is of little

hear confessions. For a detailed account of this controversy that spans one third of the *Testament,* see ibid., xx–xxxiv.

profit to oneself and of little honor to God if one says one thing and thinks another. Some have their tongues in heaven but their hearts drag on earth, and it is not at all morally suitable for a heart to be steeped in venom, when the tongue speaks words infused with honey. When your speech is clean (in the text "white") and your thought is tawny, you fly into darkness like a bat. Such clean words are worthless, Jean argues, for it is out of the heart that what saves us or damns us must come. Of what profit is it to you to move your lips toward God, when your heart only thinks of earthly possessions? Your tongue is not healthy if your heart is in fever, and the Lord sees both afflictions. After admonishing his readers through this merciless diatribe, Jean enjoins them to place their "sayings, deeds, and thoughts" not in vanity, but in the Creator, this bird who only preys on human hearts, in which he takes comfort and joy (ll. 1473–76). Augustine's theories of interiority and of the specular relationship between the language of the mouth and that of the mind are at the core of Jean's treatise on prayer, just as these theories are dramatized throughout Faus Semblant's speech in the *Rose.* I return to this issue in chapter 3 to emphasize that the violation of the Augustinian principle of harmony between the two languages of man (outer and inner) can only lead to linguistic fraud.

The *Testament* devotes a great amount of poetic material to an analysis of the heart (*cuer,* in the text) as a cardinal moral concept. This is also an interesting lexical choice, in that it is different from *âme,* "soul," rarely used in the text. The prevalence of the word "heart" might suggest Jean's intention to emphasize the notion of affection, of vulnerability, less apparent in the highly philosophical concept of "soul." Since in the person of Jesus, God was incarnate as a man to win hearts on earth, Jean reminds us, let us keep ours clean and ready to receive him as our only inner guest, for it is from the heart that the Lord is loved, believed, served, praised, and known. The heart (singular!) governs bodies and renders souls to God (a puzzling formulation!); it records and reports to him all of our quarrels. God has no use for a heart that is cold, pale, and rotten, because a dead thing cannot contain him. Ultimately, if the heart is bodily, God is spiritual; if the heart is mendacious, God is very truthful. Within this scheme of things, we humans need to hate what he hates most: sin, which is not his creation, but nothingness (*neant*). In this Augustinian framework, he who lives in sin takes repose in nothingness, specifies Jean, who adds that in people of weak characters sin disguises itself under the appearance of good. We have to be aware, however, that sin is only a deceptive good, which brings along a great deal of suffering and causes the worm of conscience to torment us for the rest of our lives (the theme of conscience as a guard of the heart and instrument of God is also remarkably developed and deserves more consideration than I can give it here).

Jean goes on to say that sin puts the devil in our hearts, and we can chase him out only with God's help, which we need to ask in our prayers. Concomitantly, we can also help ourselves by saying "I don't like it at all!" or "I won't!" to such sins as laziness, pride, lust, and envy. I find this mention very significant since it implicitly underlines the participation of the will in the commission of, or the refraining from, sins. Yes, temptations will always exist, Jean is suggesting; the world is there to offer them to us, our flesh has needs, and our hearts are weak. But to overcome these obstacles we always have the magic powers of prayer, and we can mobilize our volition to resist sinful temptations. The devil is trying to seduce and conquer us by means of the seven deadly sins, which Jean enumerates in this order: pride, wrath, lust, sloth, avarice, envy, and gluttony (ll. 1673–74). The remainder of the *Testament* is occupied by this micro-tract on the deadly sins, which concludes with a vivid depiction of paradise and hell, a depiction professedly achieved for instructive purposes. Interesting in Jean's treatment of the deadly sins is the concatenation he establishes among them at the very beginning of his micro-tract, as he considers that one deadly sin automatically leads to another. The interconnectivity of sins was an essential part of the ethical treatises of the time, and Jean's mention of it adds further proof to his acquaintance with the procedures of contemporary moral theology. More interesting, however, and here we can sense the author of the *Rose,* is that in the *Testament*'s disquisition on sins, the one of lust is described as the most widespread and nocuous, because it overcomes all senses and everyone, even great spirits such as David, Solomon, Virgil, and Aristotle. Jean's obsession with the sin of lechery explains why, at the level of the text, all the other sins are discussed in a few lines, whereas the analysis (and virulent criticism) of lust not only spans sixteen stanzas in its initial formulation but is obsessively reiterated throughout the remainder of the work.

Toward the end of the *Testament,* the author provides a poetic account of two otherworldly realms: Heaven (ll. 1831–904) and Hell (ll. 1905–2044). To sum up this account here would greatly detract from the art of the poet; a personal reading of the text is the best way to taste the savor of Old French as it tries to capture the essence of the two realms. For once again, in this description Jean seems to be echoing commonplace theological notions, but the language and style in which he does it are unparalleled in the French literature of the period. I will mention only a few, relevant aspects. In Heaven we can enter only if we have lived lives characterized by virtues, out of which the most essential is charity, the only *monnaie,* "coin," that circulates in this kingdom (l. 1882). Dante will also use this monetary image in reference to faith in *Paradiso* 24.83–87.

In Jean's Heaven, where the great mysteries of hope and faith will be revealed, one cannot fake charity anymore, but loves with a burning, unstoppable, eternal passion. Here, our "eye" (singular!) shall see the form of all sacraments in God, a beautiful Neoplatonic idea, likely filtered through St. Augustine. In Paradise, we shall see God, his Son, his Mother, the guardian angels, along with all the souls we have saved through our prayers. The topos of the inability of language as a system of reference to capture the supernatural beauty of the transcendental world could not lack in such a long, poetic description. "Langue ne pourroit dire" ("the tongue could not say"; l. 1859) how beautiful, pure, luminous, and glorious the heavenly creatures are. Faced with this drama of linguistic referentiality (which will haunt Dante as well), Jean eventually invites his readers to picture for themselves all this wonderful universe, to take delight in thinking of it, and to strive to get there through a life of virtue. If we allow ourselves to presume that Dante read Jean's *Testament* and thus this invitation, we now know that at least one of Jean's readers not only took this invitation very seriously but also raised the depiction of heaven to a sublime poetic peak.

In contrast to the saved souls, who enjoy eternal happiness in paradise, the souls of the damned will always be sad, as they will be tortured not only by the worm of conscience, but also by countless physical punishments, ranging from extreme heat to extreme cold, strong winds, thunder, tempests, hailstorms, ice, unbearable stench, visions of devils, and pains of all sorts (both common and specific). As a result, the tormented souls will endlessly moan, scream, cry, and lament. The devils will subject them to such an *aspre hachie,* "tough axe" that all the sinners will curse their creator. The damned souls cannot die, and therefore they hate their new life; moreover, they cannot want not to exist (l. 1979–80). Let us mention parenthetically that this theological notion of the souls who in hell are deprived of their will to die is also emphasized in *Inferno* 3, where the neutrals are described as unable to hope for death (l. 46), and where the souls about to cross the Acheron see their fear to enter Hell turned into desire (l. 126). Like in Dante's underworld, in Jean's view, *all* sinful souls will end up in Hell, regardless of their social status on earth: popes, kings, knights, false laymen, false clerics, false regular clergy, false religious, and false secular clergy (ll. 1937–39), an emphatic enumeration conveying Jean's critical view of the powerful of the day and his profound dislike of moral fraud. Special attention is paid here to lustful souls, whose description I am going to quote because it is similar in the smallest detail to Dante's *contrapasso* in *Inferno* 5:

S'aucuns par fole amour se sont entredampné, / Il seront mis ensemble, conjoint et enchainné, / Batu et derompu, froissié et enchanné, / Et maudiront le jour qu'il furent d'Adam né. / Or ont pour leur amour perpetüel haÿne, / Pour leur joye tristesce, pour leur pais ataÿne, / Et pour leur faux deliz tres destraingnant gehine; / Perilleuse est amour qui tel queue traÿne. (1945–52)

Those who by foolish love damned each other / Will be brought together, conjoined and chained, / Beaten and torn apart, tossed and chained, / And will curse the day they were born of Adam. / Now they have perpetual hate for their love, / For their joy sadness, for their peace war, / And for their false delights very destructive inferno. / Perilous is the love that drags such tail.

The notion that those who caused each other's damnation by their love (read lust) will be together in hell and will share the same pain seems to be Jean's own, as he carefully introduces it as *m'opiniön*, "my opinion" (l. 1961). The most fascinating aspect of this imaginary fate reserved for lustful lovers (fate that seems to solve the moral question raised by the foolish love described in the *Rose*) is that its minute details will be present in the *contrapasso* Dante reserves for his foolish lovers from the circle of the lustful. As a consequence of their lecherous love that led to adultery, Paolo and Francesca suffer together, tossed by the wind, and belong to a block of souls that curse God's power (I revert to this description in chapter 4, in my discussion of the sin of blasphemy).

Another intriguing aspect of the *Testament* worth mentioning here is an unexpected, long (ten stanzas), and moving prayer to the Virgin that Jean composes toward the end of the text (ll. 2057–96), from which I will quote only a small excerpt:

Vierge, qui du corps Dieu ton fil t'enceinturas, / Qui le doux fruit de vie en tes flans meüras, / Dont toute l'amertume du monde assavouras, / Ne nous oublies mie, la cure de nous as. / Dame de Paradis, roÿne courronee, / Tresoriere de grace avant sainte que nee, / De la grant sapïence de Dieu predestinee, / Benoitte soit l'eure que tu fus engendree. / Dame en la qui biauté tout paradis se mire, / Dame la qui bonté nuls homs ne puet descrire; / Tant a de biens en toy que nulz ne puet souffire; / Tu es mere de Dieu: Nuns ne te puet miex dire. (ll. 2065–76)

Virgin, who in the flesh became pregnant with the Son of God, / Who in your womb held the sweet fruit of life, / Who tasted the whole bitterness of the world, / Do not ever forget us, watch over us. / Lady of Paradise, crowned queen, / Treasurer of grace holy before being born, / Predestined by the great wisdom of God, / Blessed be the hour when you were born. / Lady in whose beauty the whole of heaven contemplates itself, / Lady whose goodness no man can describe, / So many blessings are in you that nothing compares to them; / You are the mother of God: No one can describe you better. (translation mine)

St. Bernard's prayer to the Virgin in *Paradiso* 33 (especially lines 1–21) is very similar in imagery and poetic tone to Jean's prayer. I will quote again only a few lines as an example:

Vergine madre, figlia del tuo Figlio / umile e alta più che creatura, / termine fisso d'etterno consiglio: / tu se' colei che l'umana natura nobilitasti / sì che'l suo fattore non disdegnò di farsi sua fattura. / Nel ventre tuo si riaccese l'Amore / per lo cui caldo nell'etterna pace / così e germinato questo fiore. (ll. 1–9)

Virgin mother, daughter of your son, humble / and exalted more than any other creature, fixed / term of eternal counsel: / you are she who ennobled human nature so / much that its Maker did not disdain to make / himself his own creature. / Within your womb that Love kindled itself / against whose warmth, in the eternal peace, has / caused the germinating of this flower.[49]

To conclude, Jean's overall account of the two realms is to be placed in relationship not only with the earlier one from the *Rose* (ll. 19935–20034, for heaven, and ll. 19267–326, 19809–68, for hell), but also with the *Comedy,* in search for textual affinities that can further validate Dante's familiarity with the works of Jean de Meun. Let us recall in passing that in 1409, Laurent de Premierfait bluntly stated that Dante modeled his great poem after Jean's *Rose,* which had succinctly depicted "le paradis des bons et

49. Luigi Gambero has compiled a complex anthology of medieval texts devoted to the Virgin Mary, in which he also makes a reference to Dante's prayer from *Paradiso* 33, without actually including it in the collection. Jean's prayer from the *Testament* is not mentioned at all.

l'enfer des mauvais" ("the heaven of the good people and the hell of the evil people").[50] But since in the *Rose* we only have a few lines of text devoted to this topic, whereas in the *Testament* we have numerous stanzas, I believe that not only the *Rose* but also the *Testament* served Dante in the conception of his great poem. If Dante is indeed the author of the *Fiore,* as the overwhelming modern evidence suggests, it is highly likely that the Italian poet was interested in, and read, not only Jean's *Rose* but his *Testament* as well.

In support of my argument, I would like to recall a few historical facts discovered by Luciano Rossi while he was working in the archives of Bologna. According to Rossi, Jean de Meun studied law in Bologna between 1265 and 1269, years during which he may have written the *Romance of the Rose* or at least a blueprint of it. Dante himself spent a few years in Bologna, between 1291 and 1293. Rossi also names two Bolognesi who may have personally known both Jean de Meun and Dante: the *notaio* Tommasino delle Querce and the illuminator Oderisi da Gubbio.[51] If Rossi's speculations are correct, we can easily imagine a scenario in which Jean de Meun, who wrote his *Testament* in 1291–1292, sent this poem to his Bolognese acquaintances, who were also Dante's acquaintances, while the latter was in Bologna. This would have given the Italian poet the opportunity to read the literary testament of a great French poet whom he allegedly admired and wanted to emulate.

A more extended comparison between Jean's *Testament* and Dante's *Comedy* would exceed the scope of this study, but one aspect of the cultural relationship between the two poets is worth stressing. Jean and Dante are iconic figures of two sister cultures, and each poet has contributed tremendously to the literary development of the attendant vernacular language. Both authors provide unique literary treatments of the deadly sins and poetic descriptions of the otherworld. Although it is true that compared to Dante's vast moral and poetic undertaking, Jean's approach to ethics might seem schematic, this coincidence is striking and invites further exploration by scholars.

50. Laurent's integral assessment of the two poems can be found in McWebb, *Debating the "Roman de la Rose,"* 422–23.

51. Luciano Rossi, "Dante, la Rose e il Fiore," in *Studi sul Canone Letterario del Trecento: Per Michelangelo Picone,* edited by Johannes Bartuschat and Luciano Rossi (Ravenna: Longo, 2003), 29.

What I retain from the *Testament* as relevant for my present study is Jean's preoccupation with the deadly sins, his obsession with the specular relationship between speech and thought, and the mention of several verbal deviations affecting society. Besides these deviations that I have discussed above, it is worthwhile to mention that the entire work ends with the author's excuse for his prolixity (ll. 2097–108). Jean is expressing fear that his long speech on moral matters might bore his readers, who typically and naturally prize brevity. For the sake of achieving concision in speech even good words must be sacrificed sometimes, and it is commonly said that "biau parler ennuye" ("beautiful speaking is boring"; l. 2105). Thus, Jean prefers to become silent, out of fear that his speaking too much might destroy the effects of what he has already said. The authorial tension between concision and prolixity and Jean's self-portrayal as a penitent sinner will come again under consideration in chapter 4, in my analysis of the transgressive poetic diction of the *Rose*.

FRAMING THE *INFERNO*

All the commentators who have examined Dante's prophetic claims have acknowledged that speech is a concern central to his thought.[52] Bruno Nardi has pointed out that a philosophy of language per se does not exist in Dante, but that the poet elaborated several important linguistic concepts in *Convivio, De vulgari eloquentia* (*DVE*), and *Paradiso.* Analyzing these concepts from a philosophical perspective, Nardi has come to the conclusion that, despite the apparent "discontinuity" in Dante's views, there is a unity of thought in the poet's speculative approach to language as a

52. For groundbreaking studies of Dante's linguistic thought or of the poet's preoccupation with the immorality of speech, see Joan Ferrante, "The Relation of Speech to Sin in the *Inferno,*" *Dante Studies* 87 (1969): 33–46; Steven Botterill, "Dante's Poetics and the Sacred Word," *Philosophy and Literature* 20, no. 1 (1996): 154–62; Giuseppe Mazzotta, *Dante, Poet of the Desert,* and "L'Esilio da Firenze: Il *De Vulgari Eloquenzia* e il cerchio della frode," in *Dante: Da Firenze all'aldilà,* edited by Michelangelo Picone, 223–47 (Florence: Cesati, 2001); Fyler, *Language and the Declining World;* and Barolini, *Dante's Poets* and *The Undivine Comedy.* In the chapter "Ritornerò poeta" from *Dante's Poets,* Barolini argues that the chief concern of Dante's textuality is the question of truth and falsity, a pervasive concern that motivates the poet's assessment of his precursors and of his own literary output. In the *Undivine Comedy,* Barolini discloses the narrative mechanisms by which Dante achieved the supreme artistic paradox: that of "situating the *menzogna* of art within the framework of a prophetic stature that guarantees truth" (13).

medium of communication.[53] This section strives to add a new dimension to Dante's philosophy of language as described by Nardi and to highlight the ethical side of it, in pursuit of further evidence of the poet's unity of thought, this time in the field of abuses of speech. Dante's earlier works feature numerous pronouncements on the ethics of oral communication, pronouncements that constitute valuable hermeneutic tools for the problematic of the verbal sins in the *Inferno.* There are only a few references to sinful uses of language in *DVE* and *De monarchia,* but numerous ones in *Convivio. Purgatorio* and *Paradiso* also provide essential elements in my investigation, as they offer solutions for some of the language abuses punished in Hell and thus round out Dante's treatment of verbal sins.

Chapters 2 and 3 from Book 1 of *DVE* are cast within a pronounced Augustinian framework that allows Dante to define language as a system of signs by which humans represent the concepts forming in their minds.[54] This system of representation arises from the spiritual and social needs to share ideas and feelings: "Now, if we wish to define with precision what our intention is when we speak, it is clearly nothing other than to expound to others the concepts forming in our mind" (1.2.3). Sharing is thus for Dante the basic principle underlying all human utterances. Language, this "distinguished human act," is a meeting of minds and of souls; ideally, it is the vehicle that helps us achieve a perfect, universal communion. Terms such as "intention" and "sharing" belong less to speculative philosophy and more to ethics, a detail that signals Dante's unambiguous placement of the rationale for human speech in a moral context. This ethical setting becomes even more marked when the author discusses the famous biblical episode

53. Bruno Nardi interprets Dante's revisions of his linguistic theories as a remarkable sign of maturity, not as mere inconsistencies (*Dante e la cultura medievale* [Bari: Laterza, 1984]). Stefano Rizzo also argues for an evolution rather than an internal contradiction in the poet's linguistic perspective ("Il *De Vulgari Eloquentia* e l'unità del pensiero linguistico di Dante," *Dante Studies* 87 [1969]: 69–88). For an overview of the major interpretations of Dante's view of language, see Ileana Pagani (*La Teoria linguistica di Dante* [Napoli: Liguore, 1982]), who sums up a wide range of studies from Marigo and Nardi, through Pagliaro and Pézard, to Dragonetti, Contini, and Mengaldo, all of whom have made important contributions to the critical history of *DVE.*

54. Dante's debt to St. Augustine's epistemology of language has carefully been studied by Marcia Colish, who, analyzing all of Dante's works, argues that the Italian poet reformed the artistic language simultaneously with his working out of his poetics of rectitude (*The Mirror of Language: A Study in the Medieval Theory of Knowledge* [Lincoln: Nebraska University Press, 1983], 152–221).

of the Tower of Babel. Until Nimrod's presumptuous attempt at building an edifice designed to reach the sky, this divine abode, people had been able to communicate harmoniously with each other. But since Nimrod's transgressive gesture prompted divine anger, God decreed that from then on humans would start speaking different languages, a penalty with more instructive and far-reaching repercussions than physical death. This linguistic fragmentation would turn out to be a universal barrier to communication and to social concord, a powerful moral lesson for humankind. Albert Russell Ascoli reminds us that for Dante, Babel represents a surrogate of the Fall of humankind and is inextricably linked to the "transgressive pride of Eve, itself a linguistic sin, as Dante specifies, because based upon her conversation with the serpent."[55]

The story of the Babelic confusion is also a good illustration of the principle of *contrapasso* that will become so important to Dante in writing the *Inferno:* speech was the means by which Nimrod united so many people and had them work together in the construction of the transgressive edifice; therefore, the punishment visited on them affected particularly this manifestation of human communication and sociability.[56] The excursus into the Old Testament stories of Nimrod and, later on, Adam elicits from Dante a bitter exclamation symbolic of his polar concern with speech and sin: "Oh, human nature, always inclined toward sin!" (1.7.2). Were it not for the moral framework in which the writer develops his theory of original language, this exclamation would seem odd and inadequate in a scientific treatise on the status of vernacular eloquence, and more appropriate in the moral universe of the *Comedy.* An important aspect to retain from Dante's reaction is that even when he is mainly preoccupied with scholarly matters such as dialects and poetry, he cannot obliterate his concerns with (and about) sin.

55 Albert Russell Ascoli, *Dante and the Making of a Modern Author* (Cambridge: Cambridge University Press, 2008), 143.

56. For Dante, the Tower of Babel represents the third major transgression of the humankind (following the fall and the flood) and gives him the opportunity to develop his theory of Adamic language. This *sacratum ydioma*, "holy tongue," was given to Adam by God himself and was thereafter preserved by the Jews, among whom Jesus would be born. (Dante will subsequently revise this view in *Paradiso* 26.) As for Nimrod, we will find him in Hell among traitors, speaking tongues that nobody is able to understand (*Inf.* 21.77–81). For a thorough study of the ramifications of the biblical symbol of the Tower in the medieval thought on language, see Fyler, *Language and the Declining World,* 38–44.

DVE also reiterates the Augustinian argument for the necessity of speech for humans, a necessity that differentiates us from other species: "Between creatures of different species, on the other hand, not only was speech unnecessary, but it would have been injurious, since there could have been no friendly exchange between them" (1.2.5). Here spoken language is cast between the two polar opposites that mark its potentiality: by virtue of its social nature, speech can promote friendly human interactions (this is its natural function), or it can be injurious to others (and this is unnatural). The view of language as a perverted means of expression that people employ to harm each other will become a dimension fully exploited only in the *Inferno,* but the *Comedy*'s final solution to the sins of speech is already prefigured in *DVE,* which defines speech as a divine gift bestowed on man, who must use it for the glorification of the divine. As a manifestation of reason, speech is a sign of the divinity in us, the most powerful link tying us not only to other people but also to our Creator (1.5.2). All of these aspects representative of *DVE* will be seen at work in the *Comedy,* but in a very different context and in a much more dramatic way.[57]

If the treatise on the vernacular forewarns readers about the impact of sin on speech, *De monarchia* offers them clues about how this relationship can affect individuals on a political level. In discussing the qualities necessary for an exceptional monarch, Dante relies on Aristotle's authority to draw attention to the dangers resulting from the discrepancy between one's words and one's deeds: "And from this one can refute the error of those who believe they can improve the life and morals of others by saying good things but doing evil. They have not noticed that Jacob's hands were more persuasive than his words, even though the former suggested what was false and the latter what was true. Accordingly, Aristotle says in the *Nicomachean Ethics:* 'In matters involving feeling and conduct, words are to be believed less than deeds'" (1.13.4). This view illuminates the placement in Hell of figures such as Jason, Ulysses, Guido da Montefeltro, or Sinon, who illustrate the disjunction between skillful talking and evil deeds and the dire politi-

57. Placing *DVE* in the typically bilingual context of its time represented by the tension between Latin and vernacular as options for the written medium, Ascoli reads this work as an attempt to reconcile "the contingent necessities of historical reality, that is, of a burgeoning vernacular culture in early Trecento Italy, with culturally mandated definitions of poetic *auctoritas* as impersonal, ancient and non-vernacular (i.e., Latin), in order to satisfy Dante's desire for an oxymoronically personal authority" (*Dante and the Making of a Modern Author,* 149).

cal consequences this disjunction brings about. The divorce between artful ways of using speech (*bona loquendo*) and the type of actions to which the misuse of speech gives rise (*mala operando*) counts for the physical location of the above-mentioned characters in the area of fraud.

Seen from a social and political angle, sin receives a definition highlighting the ruinous nature of discord and division: "sinning is nothing else than scorning unity and moving away from it towards multiplicity" (1.15.3). Filtered through Aristotle's *Metaphysics,* this Plutarchian thesis serves Dante to prove that political unity is universally good and natural, whereas plurality, understood as political and social divisiveness, is an unnatural phenomenon tantamount to evil. It is one of the fascinating cases in which Dante takes up classical moral concepts (or characters) and, giving them a new spin (or a new biography), presses them into the service of his own ideas and makes them bear on the reality of his own days. In the Aristotelian quote, sinning, although per se a moral notion, is rather defined in speculative terms, whereas in the moral tracts from Dante's time, the definitions given to sin are very specific and practical. They describe sin not in terms of a universal phenomenon of dispersal, but as particular evil acts related to individuals and their wills. Dante's credit in the appropriation of the classical quote in *De monarchia* is to have implemented it into the concrete ground of the political situation of his country. It is a tendency that we will see best at work in the *Comedy,* where Aristotelian terms such as "incontinence," "violence," and "fraud" will be represented by specific characters, who will illustrate these philosophical terms by their own particular transgressions.

At the other pole of multiplicity and sin stands social harmony, defined as a union of wills, which constitutes "the root of concord, or simply concord itself" (1.15.5). This viewpoint enlightens the treatment of the sowers of discord in the *Inferno,* just as the use of the Aristotelian concept of *ebulia,* "prudence," in *De monarchia* accounts for the link between fraudulent counselors and sowers of discord.[58] Ulysses and Guido da Montefeltro will

58. The poet invokes the Aristotelian term in Book 2, chapter 5.23. By *ebulia,* Aristotle (and then Thomas Aquinas) understood excellence of deliberation manifested in the rectitude of counsel. For the Aristotelian definition, see the *Nicomachean Ethics* 6.9, and for Aquinas, *ST* IIa-IIae QQ. 47–52. As I will highlight in chapter 3, in the section devoted to the fraudulent counselors, a trend in Dante criticism interprets Ulysses as the embodiment of Aquinas's definition of "false prudence."

be assigned to the eighth pouch of Malebolge because they infringed on the norms for prudence and gave fraudulent counsels. In Hell's topography, the ninth pouch is inhabited by the sowers of discord, who, through their intentional wicked words, caused social disruptions and wars. All these links between words, sins, and politics emerge already in *De monarchia,* proving that, just as in his capacity as literary theorist, Dante could not forget the sinfulness of human nature, so in his capacity as a political analyst, he cannot bracket off his moral concerns. This mixed approach to morality is typically Aristotelian, if we consider that the Greek philosopher posits the science of ethics as an integral part of the science of politics, this "master art" that strives to ensure the good of the community at large. For Aristotle, all human sciences have specific ends, but the best of all ends is that of political science, which aims at forming virtuous citizens, capable of selfless acts. Good political governing is so dependent on a good knowledge of ethics that the first prerequisite in the training of a student of politics is the knowledge of the soul and its virtues (*Nicomachean Ethics,* Book 1). For Dante, just as for Aristotle, the good of the city-state overrides the good of the individual, and it is the noble mission of both ethics and politics to ensure the happiness of all citizens. The substantial blending of politics, ethics, and rhetoric will be magisterially achieved in the *Inferno,* where we will find verbally skilled public figures who lost their souls because of their failure to abide by the high standards raised by moral philosophy and politics.

In the series of Dante's prose works, I have left *Convivio* for the end, because through its pervasive concerns with sins, it constitutes an ethical tract in its own right, best prefiguring Dante's moralizing mission in the *Comedy.*[59] In Book 4, where the author portrays himself as carefully studying people's behaviors, he explains that he became so disgusted with the

59. The declared goal of *Convivio* is to enlighten men spiritually and move them to virtue. Of the four *trattati,* "books," of the work, it is especially the last one that deals with ethical matters, but preoccupations with notions such as malice, justice, will, etc., occur in the first three *trattati* as well. Dante firmly believes in the ability of poetry to reform people's mores: at the beginning of the fourth book he asserts that the purpose of the canzone *Le dolci rime* is to bring people back to the straight path. Useful interpretations of the *Convivio* have been provided by Patrick Boyde (*Human Vices and Human Worth in Dante's "Comedy"* [Cambridge: Cambridge University Press, 2000]), who dwells at length on the issue of the twofold happiness of man, and by John Took *(Dante Lyric Poet and Philosopher: An Introduction to the Minor Works* [Oxford: Clarendon Press, 1990]), who analyzes the work as a philosophical point of intersection between Neoplatonism and Aristotelianism.

spectacle of human sinfulness that he eventually decided to adopt a stance and to begin correcting moral errors publicly: "I resolved that I would cry out to those who were walking along this evil path so that they might place themselves back on the right way" (4.1.46–48). A meaningful element in Dante's capacity as an ethicist is the distinction he makes between bad habits and their practitioners. He takes care to mention that he hates not sinners but their sins, and that the blame he addresses to morally weak people has an active value—that of helping them mend their ways. He hates sinners only to the extent that they are tarnished by their unrighteous deeds, but it is a benign form of hate that hopes to cure the diseases of the soul for the benefit of the spiritually ill. The contemporary scene marked by "disorderly mores" and "defects of life" worries Dante, forcing him to appeal to that particular field of knowledge that is best able to help him understand the inner motivations underlying behavioral mechanisms—moral philosophy, which he considers the supreme human science to which all the other ones should be subservient.[60] It is here that individuals wishing to reform their lives should look for solutions to their doubts and problems, for moral philosophy's mission is precisely to teach the rules for good behavior and to drive the vices away.

Along Aristotelian-Thomistic lines, Dante expresses his *morale dottrina* in terms of right/evil appetite, justice/injustice, making the important point that all our decisions and operations (offending or helping someone, fighting or fleeing in battle, remaining chaste or giving in to lechery, for instance) are rooted in the will, this innate function of reason.[61] In this moral scheme,

60. In Book 1, when he discusses the structure of heavens in correlation with human sciences, he assigns moral philosophy to the Crystalline Heaven and quotes Thomas Aquinas's view of the preeminence of ethics with respect to all other sciences (2.14.77–83). Later on, Dante recasts this notion in a metaphorical context, asserting that just as the beauty of the body arises from the orderly disposition of the limbs, so too the beauty of philosophy resides in that branch of it that deals with orderly moral virtues (3.15.77–81).

61. For an overview of Dante's assimilation of Aristotle's and Aquinas's moral theories, see Boyde, *Human Vices and Human Worth*, 77–99. Marc Cogan's *Design in the Wax* also deals with Dante's relationship with Aristotle and Aquinas. Cogan argues that it is indeed Aristotle's ethics that underpins the structure of the three moral realms of the *Comedy*, but not Aristotle as we interpret him today, but the one that the medievals/Dante knew: Aristotle read through the lenses of Aquinas. By virtue of this thesis, Cogan demonstrates that at the root of each of the three realms of the *Comedy* lies the tripartite structure of the appetite—concupiscible, irascible, and intellectual (or of the will)—an Aristotelian tripartition that Dante borrowed from Aquinas.

forms of injustice such as betrayal, ingratitude, falsity, theft, and deceit represent *inumani peccati,* "inhuman sins." Here Dante uses the term *peccato* as a synonym for vice, a rare occurrence in the text of *Convivio,* which privileges the terms *errore morale,* "moral error," or *vizio,* "vice." Given that Dante quotes *Secunda secundae* in *Convivio,* we can assume that he was aware of the Thomistic distinction between vice, as a settled evil disposition of the will, and sin, the actualization of that disposition. *Convivio* is mainly concerned with vices, which it divides into innate and acquired, whereas the *Comedy,* dealing mostly with sinners, will privilege the word *peccato.* (It is worthwhile to mention, however, that in Dante, these two terms—vice and sin—are less technical than in *Summa theologica.*) We have seen that Aquinas's main contribution to the theological debate on speech was to transfer the cause of verbal transgressions from the tongue, a bodily organ, to the will, a spiritual agent. Reflections of this approach are apparent in *Convivio* as well, for, on the one hand, Dante posits the will as the root of good and evil human actions, and, on the other hand, he lists "l'arte di parlare" ("art of speaking") as a rational act. In other words, not only what we do, but also what we say and the way we speak are results of our willful choices. It is illustrative in this sense that in Marc Cogan's interpretation of the structure of Hell, Malebolge (where Dante assigns most of the verbal sins) corresponds to the Aristotelian-Thomistic appetite of the will.[62]

More indications in *Convivio* prepare us to approach the first *cantica* of the *Comedy,* and one of them is of vital importance for understanding Dante's decision to include sins of word among sins of deed in Hell. In a passage emphasizing the attention one should pay to one's actions, and especially to speech acts, Dante defines words as seeds of actions:

> [We must] rather consider how reasonable it is that we should await the proper moment in all our undertakings, and most of all in speaking.... This is why great discretion must be shown in using or in avoiding the use of words—which are, as it were, the seed of our activity—so that they may be well received and fruitful in effect, so as to avoid any defect of sterility on their part. The right moment must therefore be predetermined, both for the one who speaks as well as the one who must listen. (4.2.30–46)[63]

62. Cogan, *Design in the Wax,* 68–73.

63. Dante will splendidly reuse the metaphor of the "germinating" power of words in the context of Count Ugolino's acknowledgment that his words may be the seeds of infamy for his mortal enemy, the archbishop Ruggieri (*Inf.* 33.7–9).

Communication is emphasized as a vital, generative human undertaking, in which words engender actions and are themselves a sort of deeds, for saying is virtually doing, and this intimate equivalence is responsible for the interpersonal or public impact of our initiatives. When, or even before, we speak, we have to carefully consider and assess the effects that our words may produce on their recipient(s) (4.2). This theory contains in a nutshell the doctrine of disciplined speech pioneered by Hugh of St. Victor and taken up by later medieval rhetoricians (including Peraldus and Brunetto Latini). The quote above echoes no fewer than three of the incentives for *custodia linguae* Peraldus posited in his prologue to "De peccato linguae": the tongue as the instrument of reason (incentive two), words as fruits of the mouth (incentive twelve), and the careful consideration of the time when, and the audience to whom, words are addressed (incentive fifteen). In Dante's time, speaking "discreetly" meant thinking beforehand to whom one spoke, what the speaker had to say, when, where, and to what purpose he spoke. Disciplined (or discreet) speech meant screening one's own words through these norms—turned true moral filters—which, if observed, could protect human utterances against all potential sinfulness.[64] Dante further draws attention to the risks a speaker lacking self-control incurs: if the speaker is in a bad mood, for example, "his words can be harmful in many ways" (4.2.47). The lack of self-control is here tantamount to the lack of *custodia linguae,* specifically the kind of (disturbing) situation that the scheme of circumstances is intended to prevent. By the same token, if the hearer is in a bad mood, the words of the speaker, even if they come from a good intention, may be ill received.[65] The passage defining

64. Studying the part played by the rhetorical science in *Convivio,* Marianne Shapiro argues that Dante casts rhetoric and moral philosophy as the very poles of this vernacular work ("On the Role of Rhetoric in the *Convivio,*" *Romance Philology* 40 [1986]: 38–64, at 62).

65. For an extended exemplification of this circumstance, see Brunetto Latini, who in the section "The person to whom you are speaking" develops an impressive list of potential listeners (friends, enemies, princes, knights, parents, priests, nuns, drunk men, wicked women, etc.) and gives advice about the way in which each of these categories should be addressed. Among these classes of listeners, Brunetto singles out the sower of discord and, along scriptural lines, warns his audience not to talk to such a person, because they would only put logs on his fire, and this can have terrible consequences for the city (*The Book of Treasure (Li Livres dou Tresor),* edited by Paul Barrette and Spurgeon Baldwin [New York: Garland, 1993], 209). Brunetto's influence on the civic rhetoric of *Convivio* has thoroughly been studied by Charles T. Davis ("Brunetto Latini and Dante," *Studi Medievali* 3, no. 8 [1967]: 421–50) and Walter Goetz ("Dante und Brunetto Latini," *Deutsches Dante Jahrbuch* 20 [1938]: 78–99). Luigi Mario Ca-

words as seeds of operation ends with a biblical quote positing time as a circumstance to consider when one wants to speak: "And therefore Solomon says in the book of *Ecclesiastes* that 'There is a time to speak and a time to keep silence'" (4.2.48–49), a commonplace quote in the medieval *lingua*-texts (we find it, for instance, in Peraldus, Albertano da Brescia, and Brunetto Latini).

In the *Inferno,* we find several sins that the clerical discourse contemporary with Dante associated with speech: blasphemy, a sin of violence, and at least four more sins (flattery, fraudulent counsel, sowing of discord, and false speech) grouped in Malebolge, the area punishing manifestations of fraud.[66] Distributed apparently randomly among sins of a nonverbal nature such as murder, simony, theft, and the like, the four verbal sins above mentioned form nearly half of the structure of Malebolge and are embedded in the system of fraud in subtle, deliberate connections with the other sins. The presence of verbal transgressions in Hell and the network they establish with the surrounding major sins of deed are essential pieces of information to consider in an analysis of Dante's speech ethics. I treat this topic at length in chapters 3 and 4.

In the structure of Purgatory, modeled on the Gregorian scheme of the seven capital vices, there are no verbal sins, but the preoccupation with speech patterns continues. Models of communication are offered, both on the horizontal level (among individuals), and on the vertical level, in the human relationship with the transcendental. Cato, the guardian of the entry to Purgatory, warns from the outset that flattery is excluded in this realm (*Purg.* 1.92). It seems that the same holds for the practice of swearing; on the second spur of the mountain, Jacopo del Cassero tells Dante that here, the souls trust his sayings, he does not have to swear for them to

pelli ("Ancora del *Tresor* nelle opere di Dante," *Giornale Dantesco* 5 [1898]: 548–56), Giovanni Nencioni ("Dante e la rettorica," in *Dante e Bologna nei tempi di Dante,* 91–112 [Bologna: Commissione per Testi di Lingua, 1967]), and Bruno Nardi (*Dal "Convivio" alla "Commedia"* [Rome: Istituto Storico Italiano per il Medioevo, 1960]) have investigated the role played by rhetoric not only in *Convivio* but also in the other Dantean works, particularly in the *Comedy.*

66. I say "at least," because the sins of divination and betrayal also imply a linguistic element. This element, however, is less marked than in the case of the five sins I have mentioned in the main text; therefore, I do not dwell on diviners and traitors. As far as the cantos depicting Malebolge are concerned, I would like to recall Barolini's remark that in them, Dante questions "the basis of all human representation, to probe relentlessly the fraud inherent in language and indeed in all sign systems" (*The Undivine Comedy,* 75).

believe him (*Purg.* 5.64–65). The repenting sinners meet Virgil and Dante with courteous speech, and Casella goes so far as to welcome the two travelers with Dante's own lyrics, which he recites out of love for the pilgrim. The souls constantly stress the importance and necessity of prayer, the only verbal practice able to break the harshest divine decrees. Moreover, when those in Purgatory pray, they do it mostly for the ones they have left behind, a supreme example of charity (*Purg.* 9.22–24). In his turn, Manfred explains that powerful prayers can break even the curses pronounced by the Church and can shorten the souls' stay on the sacred mountain. Sapìa first evokes the defiant words that, in her early life, she had thrown at heaven in a moment of presumptuousness. Then she adds that if, despite her transgression, she did not end up in hell but was given the chance to repent in Purgatory, it is thanks to the prayers Pier Pettinaio, a holy man, said for her (*Purg.* 13.118–29). The field of the social and political implications of speech is also mined. In the context of his bitter invective against Florence, the poet rails against the shallowness of the Florentine rhetoric of justice, based on a deep disjunction between verbal expression and inner essence. Public discourses about lofty moral ideals seduce with their external, ornamental beauty, but they are highly fraudulent, for they are not rooted in the soul. The tragedy is that this dichotomy between the noble, outer words of the Florentines and the inner language of their empty hearts lies at the very root of the public life of his city (6.130–33).

Far from being exhausted in *Inferno* or *Purgatorio,* the question of transgressive speech is reopened in *Paradiso,* sometimes in dramatic terms. One of these instances occurs in Canto 19, when the Eagle phrases Dante's silent wonder about the principle underlying the salvation of non-Christians: how can a man who has never heard of Christ and *has never sinned in deeds or words* (emphasis mine) be condemned to eternal punishment? (ll. 70–75).[67] The way in which this question is phrased conveys that in Dante's Christian scheme of the final judgment, assessing words is equivalent to assessing deeds even in the case of a non-Christian, with the implication that verbal trans-

67. For a fine analysis of the theological question of the implicit revelation and its bearing on this canto, see Anna Maria Chiavacci Leonardi ("La salvezza degli infedeli: Il Canto XX del *Paradiso,*" in *Regnum celorum violenza pate: Dante e la salvezza dell'umanità,* 193–203 [Montella: Accademia Vivarium Novum, 2002]), who argues that the great question weighing on Dante's mind finds its solution in the Virgilian hero Rifeo, whose presence in heaven proves that the value of baptism is surpassed by the inner, personal relationship with the divine.

gressions can universally cause eternal damnation. Alongside the theory of words as seeds of actions expressed in *Convivio,* this radical view illuminates Dante's decision to imbed sins of word among sins of deed in Hell. Another theme worthy of consideration is the issue of broken vows, treated in cantos 3, 4, and 5 of *Paradiso.* Piccarda Donati, one of the poem's few female characters, justifies her place in a lower sphere of the celestial hierarchy by her unfulfilled monastic vows. The "trilogia dei canti" ("trilogy of cantos") as they are referred to in Dante studies, is intended to criticize the too-great ease and superficiality with which humans make religious commitments, for vows are not idle talk, but a serious matter that should be treated with discernment (*Par.* 5.64–65). Although Piccarda's location is not a punishment proper, the fact that she insists on her lower degree of blessedness raises questions about the consequences of her religious transgression. We can examine her failing under the optic of *indiscretum votum,* "indiscreet vow," a sin of speech defined by medieval moralists as a cancelation of the moral and institutional pact concluded with God. In chapter 19 of his tract on verbal sins, "De peccato indiscretae promissionis" ["On indiscreet promise"], Peraldus considers broken religious vows as the most grievous form of failed commitments and, picking up Proverbs 20 and Ecclesiastes 5, warns that it is better to abstain from making a holy pledge than to break it afterward, because God hates a foolish and disloyal promise. In his subtle and exhaustive analysis of the issue of the broken vows in *Paradiso* 3–5, Mazzotta reminds us that in Aquinas's treatment of this sin,[68] *votum,* "vow" (a word derived from *voluntas,* "will") presupposes three elements: deliberation, resolution of the will, and the promise. This Thomistic definition accounts, in Mazzotta's opinion, for Dante's explicit description of the vow as promise and for the insistent discussion of vows in terms of will in *Paradiso* 3.[69]

Although "indiscreet vow" is defined by medieval moralists as a willful, transgressive cancelation of a previous act of verbal commitment to God, in *Paradiso,* cancelation also works in the opposite direction. Despite her failure to keep her monastic vows, Piccarda is still assigned a place in the Empyrean, which shows that *cancelation* functions in Dante's world not only as a moral error but also as a transcendental act of love: forgiveness—a cancelation, or erasure, of sin—granted by divine justice. The encounter

68. *ST* IIa-IIae Q. 88.1–2.

69. Giuseppe Mazzotta, *Dante's Vision and the Circle of Knowledge* (Princeton, N.J.: Princeton University Press, 1993), 36–46.

with this female character offers Dante the opportunity to express his solution to the problem of the dispensation of vows. A vow cannot be canceled or erased, it can only be permutated, that is, recuperated through a harder commitment (*Par.* 5.46–60). Piccarda's presence in the Celestial heaven proves that, under exceptional circumstances, a potentially mortal sin of word becomes a forgivable transgression.[70]

Paradiso 26 and 27 also offer us important indications about Dante's view of speech. Canto 26 reopens the discussion of the Adamic language from *DVE* and argues that this original tongue was spent by the time the Tower of Babel was built. Through the agency of Adam, "il padre antico" ("ancient father"), Dante conveys his conception of the mutability of the linguistic sign. At the beginning of time, people called God *I,* but later on, they replaced this word with *El,* a shift bespeaking human inconsistency and the instability of language as a semiotic system. Against this background, the tension between speaking, as a law of nature, and the human manipulation of this law is negotiated in the following terms: "Opera naturale è ch' uom favella, / ma così o così, Natura lascia / poi fare a voi secondo che v'abbella" ("It is a natural operation that man speaks, but / whether in this way or that, Nature allows you to / do it as it may please you"; *Par.* 26.130–32).[71] Traditionally interpreted in the context of the linguistic theory of the mutability of the sign, the phrase "ma così o così" may also be read in a moral key: it is natural that man should speak, but the misuse of the divine gift of speech is no longer attributable to nature but constitutes an individual act of choice.

Paradiso 27 further develops this notion. Here, age is placed in relation-

70. It is not the first time Dante suggests that divine decrees can be changed; in the *Inferno,* for instance, Beatrice justifies St. Lucy's request to help the pilgrim by the intercession of a noble lady in Heaven, i.e., the Virgin Mary (2.94–96). In *Paradiso* as well, Dante stresses that sometimes divine counsel willingly lets itself be overcome by love (20.94–96). This notion helps us understand how, although Piccarda and Constance broke their religious vows, they overcame Heaven's severity; it is their intense charitable love that earned them a place in the celestial realm. Noting Dante's fascination with heroic action as a way of overcoming a defective will, Mazzotta explains the poet's kind treatment of Piccarda and Constanza in these terms: "In the absence of self-pity, in their absolute will, in their constant affection for the veil, Piccarda and Constanza are two heroic figures, whose appeasement can be construed as a rebuke to the savagery they have previously suffered" (*Dante's Vision,* 40).

71. Unless otherwise noted, the English translation of the *Comedy* I use is *The Divine Comedy of Dante Alighieri,* translated by Robert Durling (Oxford: Oxford University Press, 1996 *Inferno;* 2003 *Purgatorio;* 2010 *Paradiso).*

ship to language in order to emphasize the corruption brought to the natural purity of speech by old age, viewed as loss of innocence, not as wisdom: "Tale, balbuzïendo ancor, digiuna, / che poi divora, con la lingua sciolta, / qualunque cibo per qualunque luna, / e tal, balbuzïendo, ama e ascolta / la madre sua, che con loquela intera / disïa poi di vederla sepolta" ("This one, while still a babbler, observes fasts, / and later, when his tongue is loosed, devours / whatever food in whatever month, / and this one, while still a babbler, loves / and obeys his mother, and later, with full command / of speech, desires to see her buried"; 27.130–35). Just as food intake increases with age, to the point where it becomes nocuous for the body and turns into gluttony, a sin of flesh, in the same way, the use of language becomes abusive and breaks sacred family ties. Gluttony and murderous speech are placed in a balance here, as equal transgressions committed by way of the mouth. The prejudices of the *mala bocca,* "evil mouth," a biblical phrase Dante uses in *Convivio* as a trope for the misuse of language (4.25), recur thus in *Paradiso,* in this traditional coupling of gluttony with verbal deviations.

That even in *Paradiso,* the *cantica* of the heavenly spheres, we encounter characters speaking of the evils people commit with their wicked tongues/ mouths is less peculiar than it might seem at first glance. The disembodied souls of the holy, besides their harsh criticism of the human manipulation of the divine faculty of speech, often offer themselves verbal models. In the Heaven of Jupiter, for instance, the virtuous souls forming the Eagle utter the same words simultaneously, realizing a perfect communion of wills, in which the words "I" and "mine" dissolve into a collective "us" and "ours" (*Par.* 19.10–12). Their mode of communication suggests that in Heaven, the linguistic signs typically used for the notion of individuality—personal pronouns or possessive pronouns/adjectives—are reinvested with a new function, that of expressing unity in plurality, or cooperation toward the common good, this Aristotelian *telos* of ethics and civic life. (The Eagle's harmony of individualities and speeches stands in sharp contrast with the practices of the sowers of discord from *Inferno,* who—we will see—have used their wills and verbal skills to promote their own selfish, antisocial agendas.) The figures of St. Francis and St. Dominic are offered as paradigms for virtuous speech on earth. They represent genuine, holy preaching, in which words concord with intentions and with deeds. In *Paradiso* 12, they are characterized as two champions of the faith, who were able to convert sinners to a life of virtue with both their words and their actions (ll. 44–45).

Their exemplary lives, Dante conveys, should embarrass and modify the hypocritical behavior of those who preach the words of the doctrine without believing in it, the false preachers harshly condemned by Beatrice in *Paradiso* 29.

But the holy figure who perhaps voices most explicitly Dante's rhetorical ideal is Thomas Aquinas, who in the text praises the merits of St. Francis and outside the text is an authoritative Scholastic voice on the sins of word. Aquinas's way of speaking is characterized as "'l discreto latino" ("discreet Latin"; *Par.* 12.144), a phrase reminiscent of the theory of *discreta locutio* I presented in chapter 1.[72] (Coincidentally or not, Hugh of St. Victor, the pioneer of this theory, is mentioned in the same canto, l. 133). The meaning of the phrase "discreet Latin" becomes even clearer when Aquinas sets out to teach the pilgrim not to judge or speak too quickly, like those who cannot discern between an assertion and a negation:

E questo ti sia sempre piombo a' piedi
per farti mover lento com' uom lasso,
e al *sì* e al *no* che tu non vedi:
ché quelli è tra li stolti bene a basso
che sanza distinzione afferma e nega
ne l'un così come ne l'altro passo;
perch' elli 'ncontra che più volte piega
l'oppinïon corrente in falsa parte,
e poi l'affetto l'intelletto lega.
(*Par.* 13.112–20)

And let this ever be lead upon your feet, to / make you move slowly, like a weary man, to both the *yes* / and the *no* that you do not see: / for surely he is low among the fools who / affirms and denies without distinction in either case, / for it often happens that a hasty opinion turns / in a wrong direction, and then affect binds the / intellect.

Hastiness can cause people to form erroneous opinions and speak in incomplete knowledge of the facts, a serious impediment to just judgment and eloquence.[73] The detailed knowledge of circumstances is of vital im-

72. Durling translates "'l discreto latino" as "judicious words," which slightly departs from Dante's shade of meaning. Not only the word *discreto* but also *latino* is pregnant with meaning, implying that this is the language Aquinas speaks in Paradise. This implication elevates Latin, especially in its theological expression (for Dante read Aquinas in the original) to the rank of a paradisiac tongue, which may further mean that the pilgrim's dialogue with Aquinas takes place in Latin, and that in reproducing his discourse in this canto, the poet translates it into vernacular for his readers. For a review of the languages spoken in the universe of the *Comedy,* see Antonino Pagliaro, "Dialetto e lingue nell'oltretomba," in *Dante nella critica d'oggi: Risultati e prospettive,* edited by Umberto Bosco, 254–70 (Florence: Le Monnier, 1965).

73. The last part of Aquinas's discourse in Canto 13 is fraught with quotes and notions

portance in Aristotelian ethics, the section devoted to justice in particular, which Aquinas echoes here, enjoining the pilgrim not to give in to the temptation of speaking too hastily but to weigh up facts and choose very carefully between "yes" and "no." In the New Testament, Christ had given as parameters for speech only these two, straightforward words, but in the text, Aquinas is implying that even these simple words should be uttered with extreme care when the facts are not sufficiently clear. Those who randomly use affirmative or negative statements are careless speakers, the most foolish of fools. Asserting and denying are the most fundamental acts of speech, and when one performs them without discernment, one speaks indiscreetly, in the medieval acceptation of the term. Opposed to these ill-considerate speakers is Aquinas himself, whose language (*latino*) does make distinctions between positive and negative values and is characterized by Dante as *discreto.*[74]

Further textual instances justify the use of this adjective with respect to Aquinas's discourse. The Dominican theologian feels compelled to clarify his enigmatic words about the members of his order by telling the pilgrim: "Tu dubbi, e hai voler che si ricerna / in sì aperta e 'n sì distesa lingua / lo dicer mio ch' al tuo sentir si sterna" ("You are puzzled, and you wish my words to / make clear, in such open and ample language / as befits your hearing"; *Par.* 11.22–24).[75] Aquinas's wish to explain his diction bespeaks both his fear of being too hermetic and his awareness of the benefits that a message delivered with no ambiguity has. Later on, he again takes precautions to make himself understood perfectly: "Ma perch' io non proceda troppo chiuso" ("But that I may proceed not too obscurely"; l. 73)

---

from *Secunda secundae.* The term "kingly, political wisdom" is treated in Q. 47, Art. 11 as one of the three categories of *prudentia* (the other two being personal prudence and domestic prudence). Even the dangers of the hastiness of judgment to which Dante's Aquinas draws attention are amply treated in IIa-IIae, where the theologian often speaks of the precipitation and levity of mind that can cause unfounded judgments or unjust accusations (Q. 53, Articles 1, 2, and 3, and again in Q. 60, Art. 2).

74. In *Convivio,* Dante actually quotes Aquinas's definition of *discretio* (4.8). The fact that now, in *Paradiso,* he places this concept in the imparadised speech of the great Scholastic theologian is the supreme form of poetic compliment. It is also worth noting that, although semantically *discretio* covers a wide range of intellectual operations, in both *Convivio* and *Paradiso,* this term is used especially in reference to speech. See, for instance, *Convivio* 3.10.48–52.

75. "Io fui de li agni de la santa greggia / che Domenico mena per cammino / u' ben s'impingua se non si vaneggia" ("I was among the lambs of the holy flock that / Dominic leads by a path where one fattens well / if one does not wander"; *Par.* 10.94–96).

and specifies that the two enigmatic lovers he has described in his "diffuse speech" are Francis of Assisi and Lady Poverty (*Par.* 11.74–75). Two cantos later, he passes along his obsession with discreet speech to the pilgrim: "Con questa distinzion prendi 'l mio detto" ("With this distinction take what I said"; *Par.* 13.109).

Dante casts Thomas Aquinas as the antithesis of the verbal sinners from Hell. He is the highly respected theologian who, building on Aristotelian and Christian moral theories, wrote authoritative statements on issues dear to Dante: virtue, justice, sin, speech, and so on. At the same time, he is also the holy man who, in life, imposed himself as a model of virtue, and who, even in the afterlife, teaches values such as *prudentia* and *discretio.* The conscious, almost obsessive care Dante's Aquinas takes of the quality of his discourse draws attention to the poet's own obsession with speech and its social or philosophical functions. People should talk sparingly and with discernment; they should avoid using language for phrasing unjust accusations, incorrect facts, or false syllogisms. Dante himself—in his hypostasis both as a pilgrim and as a poet—takes lessons from Aquinas. Judging or condemning people too hastily and speaking without discernment are transgressions of which Dante, the demiurgic artist, is very well aware. He has just devised a hellish world where personal friends and Catholic popes are tortured for eternity, alongside foes and unbelievers. Speaking too much and too abstrusely, or using hoarse words, are traps into which the author of the *Comedy* himself can fall, while he dramatically struggles to represent a world for which no human words have yet been invented.

The numerous references to the humans' abuse of language scattered in *Purgatorio* and *Paradiso* show that transgressive linguistic behavior is a privileged topic not only in *Inferno,* the *cantica* that most prominently deals with the sins of speech, but of the entire poem. The great ethical project of the *Comedy* also establishes intimate connections with the earlier works, which contain valuable assessments of verbal acts. All of these writings prove that the polarity speech-sin constitutes a constant theme of Dante's moral reflection, and, at the same time, they configure the global vision of the poet's speech ethics.

THREE

Lingua Dolosa, "The Guileful Tongue"

Speaking under the Sign of Fraud

Dolus est fraudulenta deceptio.

{Alain of Lille, *Tractus* 44}

In the Middle Ages, the popular attitude toward guile was highly ambivalent, oscillating between admiration for the cunning intelligence of the trickster, as depicted by the *fabliaux,* and reprobation of the moral act proper. The shade of admiration inherent in the popular perception does not subsist, however, in the ethical tracts on which I base my critical endeavor. Alain of Lille, who in his works systematically confronts the complex issue of fraud, condemns various terms pertaining to the semantic field of deceit and also draws an apocalyptic picture of the world succumbing to the invasion of fraud and evil:

The epigraph reads: "Guile is fraudulent deception." Since there is no English version of the *Tractus,* the translation of the quotes from this text is mine.

While the lightning-flash of crime blasts the earth, the night of fraud darkens the star of fidelity and no stars of virtue redeem the Stygian darkness of that night. The evening of fidelity lies heavy on the world, the nocturnal chaos of fraud is everywhere. Fidelity fades in the face of fraud; fraud, too, deceives fraud by fraud and thus trickery puts pressure on trickery. In the realm of customary behavior, accepted practices are lacking in morality. Laws lack legal force; rights lose their right of tenure. All justice is administered without justice and law flourishes without legality.[1]

In the view of Alain and other medieval moralists, *dolus,* "guile," being a manifestation of fraud, is not an admirable expression of human intelligence but a sin. Thomas Aquinas, for instance, considers *dolus* a species of *falsa prudentia,* "false prudence," and defines it as a dishonest way of dealing with people in everyday situations and problems. Root of all fraudulent activity, guile is the translation into practice of cunning (or craftiness), a translation achieved not only through deeds but also through words, to which the category of guile is fundamentally attached.[2]

Alain of Lille's and Thomas Aquinas's concerns with fraudulent behavior have left indelible marks on Jean de Meun and Dante. In chapter 2, I examined Dame Raison's perception of the world as collapsing under the invasion of fraud and violence. She is only one of the many characters in the *Rose* who contribute original ideas to the discussion of falsehood in behavior or speech. All of these characters make important statements on cheating or seducing, for instance; Ami and La Vieille overtly recommend the use of guileful verbal strategies in love, and Faus Semblant unashamedly makes the apology for lying and double talking. In the *Comedy,* Dante is also highly concerned with the myriad manifestations of guile and deceit. Malebolge, the infernal area receiving fraudulent sinners, is the most complex structure in Hell; it is composed of ten levels corresponding to ten different types of sins of fraud. Four of these sins—flattery, evil counsel, sowing of discord, and falsification of words—are based on the usage of speech.[3] These various manifestations of linguistic fraud can be subsumed

1. Alain of Lille, *Plaint of Nature,* translated and commentary by James J. Sheridan (Toronto: Institute of Medieval Studies, 1980), XI.6.

2. IIa-IIae Q. 55.4–5.

3. I leave hypocrisy and divination aside because in medieval culture they had a more complex outlook than the mere linguistic aspect. Hypocrisy denoted lying mainly through outward appearance and deeds, and it was opposed to religiousness or holiness. What we understand

and analyzed together under the title *lingua dolosa,* a scriptural term that for medieval ethicists denotes rhetorical abilities that showcase human intelligence at its best but are intended to deceive, defeat, or hurt others.

ORNAMENTS OF SPEECH: FLATTERY AND SEDUCTION

A Short History of Flattery

The preoccupation with *adulatio,* “flattery,” starts as early as patristic-era thought with St. Augustine, the first major thinker to analyze this doubtful linguistic practice. However, from his time to that of the late-medieval theologians, there is a substantial lack of concern with this speech act. As in the case of blasphemy, theorizing about flattery owes its recrudescence to texts written in the twelfth and thirteenth centuries.[4] Two of the works that reopen the debate—John of Salisbury’s *Policraticus* (1159, England) and Peter Cantor’s *Verbum abbreviatum* (before 1187, France)—were written in two different cultural contexts but just a few decades apart. Both works enjoyed great success in the late Middle Ages and influenced the thinking of subsequent generations of moral writers.

While mainly concerned with the art of governing, *Policraticus* addresses a wide array of ethical aspects related to the social conduct of courtiers. Worried about the wide dissemination of the habit of flattery at the royal court, Salisbury devotes memorable pages to the practitioners of this type of rhetoric. In the third book of *Policraticus,* chapter 6 is titled “The Multi-

---

today as hypocrisy (saying things that we do not mean) was defined as *bilinguium,* “double talk.” Peraldus treats *hypocrisis* as an offspring of pride and associates it with vainglory, saying that hypocrites pass themselves off as holy because of their love of earthly fame. In *ST* IIa-IIae, Aquinas devotes four articles to hypocrisy (Q. 111.1–4), defining it as that dissimulation whereby “one person simulates another, as when a sinner simulates the person of a just man.” *Inferno* 23, the canto devoted to hypocrites, mirrors the pretense of religiousness essential to the medieval definition. As far as divination is concerned, it is not among the twenty-four types of verbal trespasses established by Peraldus. In Aquinas’s system, it does not have a linguistic side either, being one of the vices opposed to religion and tightly linked to superstition and idolatry (IIa-IIae Q.95).

4. Casagrande and Vecchio point out that monastic culture, by virtue of its emphasis on the divine word, paid scant attention to the sin of *adulatio,* if any. Absent from Cassian’s and Gregory’s typologies of sins, *adulatio* resurfaces forcefully in the moral summae from the twelfth through the fourteenth centuries. This would also explain the fluctuating origin of this sin, considered either a daughter of pride, or of avarice, or of greed (*I peccati della lingua,* 362).

plication of Flatterers Is beyond Number and Pushes Out of Distinguished Houses Those Who Are Honorable."[5] The background against which flatterers are set is social and political, and the habit of praising highly placed people is associated with deceit practiced for the purpose of profit:

> The flatterer is inimical to all virtue, and like a sore upon the eye he fastens himself by his speech to those with whom he bonds. And what is more odious than that fraud and deceit which, under the appearance of love and faith, is exercised against the simple, the credulous, and (what is most detestable) the friendly by perfidious and worthless enemies? Indeed men of this sort all speak towards the end of pleasure, not of truth. They entreat with iniquitous and deceitful words, which subvert those friends who fall into error, repeating "Well done, well done."[6]

In Salisbury's view, it is honorable to seek favor with people, but if in a conversation, one breaks the rules of moderation and exaggerates the worth of the interlocutor for personal profit, one lapses into the heinous mode of sycophantic speech. Flattery, like tyrannicide, is licit when directed against abusive rulers, but it is absolutely forbidden among friends. Warning his audience of the dangerous seductiveness of flatterers, Salisbury not only compares the adulatory speaker with a prostitute who thrives by selling herself, but also gives examples of compliments to be avoided: "my light," "my salvation," "my refuge," "my heart and my life," "invincible commander," "the wisest of those alive," "the most generous and benevolent of all," "mirror of the virtues," and the like.[7] Interestingly, the writer attributes the origin of adulatory speech to the Romans, whom he holds responsible for knowingly and willfully spreading this type of insincere rhetoric throughout Europe. The accusation is occasioned by the Roman habit of reverently addressing a high-ranking political figure with the plural instead of the singular, a form of speech meant to "deceive superiors."[8] Appreciated both for its value as a historical document and for its literary craftsmanship, *Policraticus* played a major role in the political and ethical speculation

5. John of Salisbury, *Policraticus: Of the Frivolities of Courtiers and the Footprints of Philosophers,* edited by Cary J. Nederman (Cambridge: Cambridge University Press, 1990), 19.

6. Ibid., 3.4.

7. Ibid., 3.9.

8. "If it comes to words, the Romans take precedence in such matters over the Greek infidels, since it is the former who were taught the use of flattering allurements to the extent that they readily were transformed into a race of teachers themselves. This nation invented the speech by which we deceive superiors, in so far as we confer distinction on a single person by honouring him in the plural, and by the authority of their name the Romans have transmitted this technique to their neighbours and to posterity" (ibid., 3.10).

of the later Middle Ages. The book seems to have influenced Dante both in his treatment of the sin of flattery in the *Inferno* and in his overall political views.[9] The *Rose* contains a reference to *Policraticus* as well (l. 6690), which testifies to Jean's familiarity with Salisbury's work.

In France, flattery is a major concern for Peter Cantor, who in *Verbum abbreviatum* (The abbreviated word) examines this speech act from a theological perspective. Without mentioning the alleged Roman origin of flattery, he considers the habit of using the plural for the singular as an evil alteration of speech, from both a grammatical and a moral perspective. He deems it a perversion to use plural forms of reverence toward humans when the singular is used in addressing God. By the same token, words of praise should be uttered only in our discourses about God, not in our daily verbal exchanges, when we speak to or about one another. The main line of thought informing Cantor's treatment of *adulatio* is essentially Augustinian; he begins the chapter "Against Flatterers" by defining flattery as "oil" and as false praise that blinds the mind and renders it incapable of perceiving the truth. In this definition, flatterers are vendors of the oil of false praise and disingenuous delight. The tongue of the flatterer—this skillful but mendacious speaker—is described as a *lingua dolosa,* a phrase that owing to Cantor's mediation will consistently be used by medieval philosophers to qualify various instances of fraudulent speech. *Verbum abbreviatum* will be seminal for the subsequent treatment of flattery, and many of its insights into the sinful potential of human language will be developed by West European moralists.

Contemporary with Peter Cantor, Alain of Lille, whose influence on Jean de Meun and Dante I discussed in chapter 1, evolved an original approach to the theme of adulatory speech. In the *Plaint of Nature, adulatio* leaves the realm of theological tracts and enters the sphere of moral poetry. Here, the goddess Natura, the author's spokesperson, bitterly complains about the human propensity to flattery, which she describes in vitriolic terms. A malign sin, springing from envy, flattery is a moral disease affecting especially individuals who live in the proximity of the rich—lay people

9. This is the opinion held by Umberto Cosmo, quoted in Wayne Conner, "*Inferno* XVIII, 66 (*Femmine da Conio*) and 51 (*Pungenti Salse*)," *Italica* 32, no. 2 (1955): 95–103, at 102, and André Pézard, "Du *Policraticus* à la *Divine Comédie,*" *Romania* 70, no. 1–2 (1948): 1–36, 163–91, at 4. The latter contends that Dante was as familiar with Salisbury's work as he was with Boethius's *Consolation of Philosophy.*

or prelates—and who behave like henchmen of princes and like palace dogs. The main method flatterers use to acquire privileges or a better position at the court is cheating. These smooth talkers are genuine artisans of speech, but in a negative sense, for they trumpet insincere praise and forge falsehood.[10] The notion of fraud is emphatically asserted in all the passages describing the sin of flattery in the *Plaint of Nature.* One of these passages is worth quoting, because it analyzes this verbal act from the viewpoint of a philosophy of language that will be echoed by Jean and Dante:

> What, then, is the ointment of flattery but cheating for gifts? What is the act of commendation but a deception of prelates? What is the smile of praise but a mockery of the same prelates? For since speech is wont to be the faithful interpreter of thought, words the faithful pictures of the souls, the countenance an indication of the will, the tongue the spokesman of the mind, flatterers separate, by a wide distance and divergence, the countenance from the will, the words from the souls, the tongue from the mind, the speech from the thought. For externally they smile on many as they whitewash them with praise, while internally they laugh at them in mockery.... Externally they rain down showers of honeyed flattery, internally they are heaving with storms of detraction.[11]

Another major contribution to the medieval debate on flattery is William Peraldus's *SV.* Here, the sin of *adulatio* gains absolute autonomy with respect to the seven capital vices, becoming a sin on its own terms, one of the twenty-four types of immoral speech treated in the section "De peccato linguae." Defined as *perversa laudatio,* "perverse praising" (for praise should be given only to God, not to man), *adulatio* is defined as a diabolical discourse that enables the dishonest man to manipulate his friends and lead them astray. Compared to the chameleon, the flatterer is a seducer enlisted in the service of the devil, for he makes people think of themselves exactly what they want. He is a traitor, who, like Judas, sells his benefactor under the pretense of a kiss and kills him under the guise of friendship. Following St. Augustine's and Peter Cantor's lines of thought, Peraldus compares flattery to toxic honey, to a wind that turns the city of God into the city of the devil, and to a net serving to trap the gullible. Taking up a scriptural quote, Peraldus ultimately defines the flatterer as a *simulator,* "faker," who deceives his friend with his mouth.[12]

10. Alain of Lille, *Plaint of Nature,* XIV.7.

11. Ibid.

12. Peraldo, *Summa virtutum ac vitiorum,* 572.

The highly critical attitude toward flattery expressed by the above-mentioned moralists, and their keen sense that adulatory speech was a plague of the day, shaped Jean's and Dante's views of this disingenuous mode of communication. In chapter 1, I highlighted that the imperative of a specular relationship between truth and speech (a relationship that flattery violates) informs both Jean's definition of words as "cousins of deeds" and Dante's principle of the consonance between reality and words, which he posits as an indispensable condition for truthful speaking.[13] In the next two sections of this chapter, I will analyze the ways in which these philosophical notions operate in the poets' treatment of flattery.

The Art of *Losange,* "False Praise," in the *Rose*

Flattery is a discursive practice consistently debated in Jean's poem, where the characters discuss adulatory speech either to condemn it vigorously, for its deceitfulness, or to recommend it warmly, for the social advantages it can bring along. To the first category of debaters belongs Dame Raison, who openly and insistently criticizes flattery as an expression of immorality. Within her severe condemnation of the love of riches, she describes the greedy man's heart as passionately attached only to material values and therefore imbued with "fainte volontez d'amer" ("fake will to love"). Blinded by the wealth he wants to acquire, a covetous man only pretends to cherish his friends; if he overwhelms them with inflated compliments, it is only for the sake of lucre. Once the hope of obtaining some profit has vanished, his charitable love for others disappears as well. The notion is reiterated several verses later and analyzed from the viewpoint of the flattered, not of the flatterer. Raison notes that those who, by a favorable movement of the wheel of Fortune, suddenly see themselves rich and placed at the top of the social hierarchy, readily attract cohorts of admirers. These quickly acquired "friends" do their best to convince the rich that they will serve them loyally; they proclaim the wealthy men their masters and pledge to shed their own blood to protect them and their families. The newly minted rich naïvely believe all these noisy declarations of love and devotion that, in fact, are void of substance: "Et cil qui tels paroles oient, / S'en glorifient et les croient / Ausi com se fust evangile, / Et tout est flatterie et guile" ("And those

13. For a philosophical approach to Dante's view of language, see Bruno Nardi, "Il linguaggio," in *Dante e la cultura medievale* (Bari: Laterza, 1984), 148–75.

who hear such speeches glorify themselves and believe them as though they were the Gospel. But all is flattery and guile"; ll. 4873–76). One can sense subtle Salisburian echoes in this view that highlights the social dynamics between the economically privileged and the aspirants to a better fortune. The main idea in both Salisbury's and Jean's texts is that where there is wealth, there are circumstantial friends, and along with them, there is adulatory rhetoric. What is remarkable in the *Rose* is that Jean's analytical eye looks not only at those who are practicing flattery but also at those who are victimized by it. Thus, one and the same habit of speech is seen from a twofold angle (of both the duper and the duped), and the psychological mechanism of fraudulent praise is laid bare in all of its workings.

Another reference to flattery sends us back to the mythical world. In evoking the reaction that the diviner Phania had in hearing about her father's enigmatic dream, Raison stresses that Phania preferred to tell him the truth, instead of "flattering" him with a beautiful but false interpretation of the dream (ll. 6513–29). Her father's vision was of ill auspices, and Phania honestly chose to reveal this to him, instead of altering the meaning of the dream for the sake of pleasing him. In this brief mythic episode, flattery is clearly tantamount to mendacious discourse.[14] As a matter of fact, Dame Raison's overall perception of flattery as a form of fraud is so strong that in some places she squarely uses the verb "to flatter" in the sense of "to lie." In an exchange of replies with Amant, for instance, she specifies that she cannot recommend avarice more than foolish liberality because they are both abominable vices, and that she does not wish "to flatter," that is, to lie to her interlocutor about them (l. 5749). The context in which this reply is inserted has nothing to do with praising or making false compliments, since Raison is not extolling any of Amant's qualities. In fact, she does not speak of him at all; she is only sharing her views of prodigality and avarice.

The female character makes an identical use of the verb *flater* in her evocation of the Italian princes Manfred and Conrad, described while playing a chess game. In the middle of her tale, Raison pauses to insert a paren-

14. From a metalinguistic viewpoint, it is worth noting that "to flatter" is surrounded by words belonging to the exegetical vocabulary: *soustille,* "subtle"; *espondre,* "to expound"; *respondre,* "to respond"; *glose,* "to gloss." The contamination of a moral term with the lexicon of biblical hermeneutics may stem from the fact that the same theological texts dealing with the ethics of speech also dealt with the interpretation of Scripture. As a character engaged both in moral and speculative issues, Raison echoes this contamination.

thetical comment meant to assure the audience of the truth of her story: "Car se verité conter os, / Si n'en quier je nullui flater" ("If I dare tell the truth and do not seek to flatter anyone"; ll. 6674–75). Again, the context has nothing to do with making false compliments; it is a technical depiction of the game of chess serving to illustrate the whims of Fortune's wheel. More significantly, in this very passage Jean explicitly quotes *Policraticus,* in which Attalus, the inventor of the chess game, was evoked for the first time. The quote is important as it furnishes literal proof of Jean's familiarity with the first major medieval text that treated flattery in a social context.

Dame Raison's lexicon contains another term related to adulatory speech —*lous* (<Lat. *laus*), "praise," which she uses in the sense of "public praise" when describing the prodigal. These are people who "put wings to money" (i.e., make money circulate at a fast rate) not out of the sheer goodness of their hearts, but because they have an unhealthy obsession with the praise and fame that their liberality can earn them (ll. 5227–29). Raison's negative assessment of the prodigal can be seen as symptomatic of the central role that commendation plays in the civic arena of the time. Being praised in public is not only an agreeable feeling that enhances self-esteem but also an important social accreditation that self-centered individuals, obsessed with attaining worldly fame, strive to acquire. Success and glory are two most valuable civic assets, and the way to appropriate them is to have one's name and deeds praised by others; this is the distorted social mechanism that allows the devious habit of flattery to set in and affect people's lives.

While Raison's position with respect to sycophantic speech is one of condemnation, the recourse to flattery is overtly recommended by Ami, who inveighs against Malebouche and his relatives, *lez lozangiers* (the singers of praise from courtly romances, or simply, people with evil tongues).[15] Ami strongly recommends the use of fraud, stating that one can make gossip and slander stop only if one sides with slanderers, by flattering them and jollying them along. In his exhortation to fraud in speech and deeds, Ami cannot appeal to stern authorities in ethics, as Raison has done with Cicero, Horace, and Cato. He does try, however, to give some authority to his advice by appealing to a strain of popular wisdom that encourages men to use violence as a means of self-protection: "il fait trop bon le chien chuer /

15. As far as Malebouche is concerned, he is no stranger either to the use of flattering speech. Bel Accueil depicts him as one who likes to exaggerate things and spice them up with his flatteries (ll. 14582–84). Here, the latter noun should be read as "lies."

Tant com ait la voie passée ("It is a very good idea to stroke a dog until one has passed by"; ll. 7394–95).

In this form of justification, the notion of *auctoritas* transitions from a solid ethical tradition rooted in Classical antiquity, a tradition represented by Dame Raison, to a dubious type of popular wisdom, which Ami puts at work in support of his devious ideas. This change of authorial references derives from the conflict I have mentioned at the beginning of the chapter, a conflict between a popular justification of fraud (deceit is licit as a means of self-defense or preservation) and a plethora of moral thinkers who attempted to undermine this way of thought by reviving an entire stock of Greek and Roman authorities in ethics. It is a cultural conflict that permeates the entire text of Jean's *Rose* and poses a constant challenge to the reader who wants to find Jean's own stance in this mix of contradictory moral messages.

Flattery is present in the discourse of Faus Semblant as well, when he describes the zeal with which mendicant preachers seek to obtain recommendations that would allow them to gain access into more Christian homes. The means by which the friars persuade the rich to give them these good references is flattery: "Et pour avoir des genz *loanges,*[16] / Des riches hommes *par losanges* / Empestrons que lettres nous doignent / Qui la bonté de nous tesmoignent, / Si que l'en croie par le monde / Que vertuz toute en nous habonde. ("In order to win people's *praise* we tell *flatteries* to rich men and get them to give us letters bearing witness to our goodness, so that throughout the world people will think that every virtue abounds in us"; ll. 11673–78, emphasis added). Faus Semblant's statement is based on a pun on two key words in the French lexicon for flattery, words specialized in opposite meanings: *loange* (sincere praise) and *losange* (insincere praise). Jean skillfully plays on these terms and, by highlighting their antonymy through the rhyme, is able to convey the hypocrisy of the mendicant preachers. Adulatory speaking is germane to the way of life of the fraternal orders, the Dominicans especially, whom Faus Semblant is intended to represent. Through them, flattery participates in a vicious circle: the friars appeal to adulation, a form of verbal fraud, to obtain recommendations that are themselves fraudulent, in that they do

16. Interestingly, the noun *loanges* Faus Semblant uses to work out his pun (*loanges/losanges*) belongs to the same semantic family as *lous,* which we have encountered in Raison's speech. Whereas *losanges* conveys smooth talk in a negative sense, *lous* and *loanges* express sincere praise. This range of terms bespeaks Jean's efforts to assign shades of meaning to closely related words.

not reflect the truth with respect to the mendicants. Such letters depict the friars as depositaries of virtues, when, in fact, they are fraught with vices. This is another elaborate social mechanism whereby deceitful speech enables other forms of fraud to take place. I will return to Faus Semblant in my analysis of *bilinguium,* "double talk."

La Vieille takes a stand on flattery as well. She seems to condemn it not because it is incompatible with her nature (for she does not hesitate to recommend strategies of erotic seduction to young girls), but because male smooth talk has caused her so much suffering. She complains that many of her lovers fooled her with their flattering words: "Trop sont tuit apert menteeur; / Plus m'ont menti li flateeur / Et foi et seremenz jadis, / Qu'il n'a de sainz en paradis!" ("All men are very expert liars. These flatterers have told me more lies, made me more vows and oaths in past times than there are saints in paradise"; ll. 13791–94). For La Vieille, too, flattery is tantamount to lying, as her words explicitly reveal in the equation *flateeur-menteeur,* "flatterer-liar," highlighted again by means of the rhyme.

As if to endorse La Vieille's complaint, later on in the romance, Genius excoriates women for being too sensitive to male blandishments (ll. 16341–47). In his powerful antifeminist diatribe, he states that no other persuasive method is more efficacious with women than flattery. This verbal strategy of seduction has such a powerful effect on ladies because they are naturally weak and naïve, and therefore prone to believe anything, even lies. To convince the audience that his perception of the female gender is correct, Genius resorts to the authority of Titus Livius, whom he quotes to criticize the weaknesses of the female gender, characterized by malice and *meurs pervers,* "perverse ways." Genius sees nothing wrong about the male fraudulent speech; when it comes to flattery, it is not men who are guilty of practicing it, but women for yielding to it.

Starting with Dame Raison and ending with Genius, there is practically no character in the *Romance of the Rose* who does not address the issue of adulation. Raison criticizes this verbal practice and qualifies it as fraudulent, looking at it from both the perspective of the flatterer and that of the flattered. Ami remorselessly recommends smooth talk to Amant, insisting that it is one of the most effective strategies of male seduction. La Vieille curses adulatory speech because it has harmed her, and she forewarns young ladies about the devastating consequences of yielding to an artful male speaker. Finally, to Genius, men's adulatory speech serves to prove how gullible women are. From these varied positions, flattery emerges as an all-encompassing social behavior, adopted by lovers (mostly male), diligently practiced by religious figures, and ardently sought by the rich. Exaggerated or false compliments are mainly used to seduce, to manipulate, and to help guileful talkers obtain what they want.

Flattery represents such a complex phenomenon that, at this point in its historical evolution, French vernacular develops an impressive list of terms in an extraordinary effort to describe the myriad manifestations of this form of fraudulent speech. *Flatterie, blandice, adulacion, lous,* and *loanges* are all terms that medieval French—through its major poet, Jean de Meun—activates to debate a socially nocuous practice. From a terminological perspective, however, it is interesting that, although Jean associates this habit with fraud, he never uses the word "sin" or "vice" to describe it, as he does with Raison's obscene speech. Jean does consider fraud a "vice," but he never explicitly identifies flattering talk as such. He is obsessed with adulation (otherwise he would not have all of his characters speak of it), but in his metalinguistic enterprise he does not go further than harnessing an extended series of synonyms to describe it.

We have seen, however, that in the moral tracts from Jean's time, flattery was considered a grievous verbal transgression. Alain of Lille, Peter Cantor, and William Peraldus define it as a subclass of fraud that is spiritually harmful, vastly diffused, gender-related, and heavy with social implications. All these aspects link Jean's treatment of flattery with the pastoral treatment of *adulatio,* despite Jean's omission of the technical terms "vice" or "sin." The fact that he explicitly acknowledges the sinfulness of only obscenity is an indication either that he considers lewd talk a verbal practice more dangerous than flattery or that he is not really willing to take the doctrine of the moral tracts at face value or seriously. I will return to this issue in chapter 4, when I discuss Jean's "blasphemy."

In the context of Italian moral poetry, about thirty years after the completion of the *Romance of the Rose,* Dante will consider flatterers so immoral that he will reserve for them a place in one of the most gruesome zones in Hell: Malebolge, the area of Fraud. In so doing, he follows the severe line of thought promoted by the theological texts that considered sycophantic speech a mortal sin.

Seducers and Flatterers in *Inferno* 18

In the Inferno, after Dante and Virgil encounter various sinful manifestations of incontinence and violence, they enter Malebolge, the eighth circle of Hell, divided into ten subparts corresponding to ten species of fraud: seduction (and pandering), flattery, simony, divination, barratry, hypocrisy, theft, evil counseling, sowing of discord, and falsification. Most distasteful to God, fraud is located deeper down because, unlike incontinence and violence, it is specific only to man as a being endowed with reason and speech. Thus, whereas in the upper and middle parts of Hell, the damned souls have in common the incapacity to anchor their passions in reason, the fraudulent sinners in Malebolge stand out by a certain type of cleverness they manifested while alive. Their defect lies not in the suppression of intellect, as in the case of the incontinent and the violent, but in the willful perversion thereof. These individuals used their intellectual gifts not in the service of the common good, as they should have, but for the selfish appropriation of the objects of their desires. The chief means by which these sinful souls attained their self-serving purposes was *inganno,* "deceit," a conscious and willful immoral practice intended to harm people.

We have seen that in *Convivio,* among the four types of human operations governed by reason, Dante also listed the *arti di parlare,* "arts of speaking," which he deemed vital for building trustworthy family and social relationships (4.9). In this scheme, the perversion of the intellectual faculties through deceit entails the alteration of the natural functions of human language and thus represents a sin against God. If we examine some categories of sinners in Malebolge, we find them guilty of verbal sins: flattery, evil counsel, sowing of discord, and falsifying of words, so many habits treated by medieval moralists as forms of transgressive speech.

The first cantica of the *Comedy* builds Hell as very noisy place resounding of shrieks, laments, sighs, and wailing, but also as a place where various and strange languages can be heard, spoken out loud by the suffering, angry souls (3.22–27). It is a universe where sinners enjoy exchanging information or opinions—Fra Gomita and Michel Zanche tirelessly talk about Sardinia, for instance (22.89–90)—and where more abuses of language are committed. Thus, the neutrals and the lustful blaspheme (3.103–5; 5.36), and Guido da Montefeltro curses the memory of Pope Boniface (27.70). The avaricious quarrel with the prodigal (7.25–27), and Master Adam engages in a brawl with Sinon over a verbal offense (30.112–29). Symbolic gestures accompany words to enhance their meanings; thus, in the tragic forest of the suicidal, Pier de la Vigna speaks while oozing blood and swears on the tree's roots that he is innocent (13.34–75); in the circle of the thieves, Vanni Fucci makes the fig while uttering impious words against God (25.1–3), and another sinner spits with disgust while speaking (25.138).

But we also encounter souls to whom language is denied or whose ability to speak is altered. Thus, the sullen are unable to form words when they intend to communicate (7.126), whereas Nimrod speaks incomprehensible languages (31.72–77). In the circle of treachery, the giants are mute, and Lucifer uses his three mouths not to speak but to mangle sinners. In the infernal world, the tongue itself, as a symbol of rational speech, becomes a victim (or instrument) of punishment: Curio, Cesar's general and advisor, no longer has a tongue, for it was cut off (28.100–103), and the tongues of two thieves-snakes undergo monstrous mutations (25.133–35). News given in Hell can cause pain, a sign that even here speech is still a psychological force to be reckoned with. Among the violent against Nature, for instance, Guiglielmo Borsiere gives updates on the city of Florence to three Florentines, deeply saddening them with his words (in text, *ci croccia,* "crucifies us"; 16.72); the Pilgrim himself is profoundly affected by the news concerning his future or the fate of some of his friends and acquaintances. Virgil's tongue (here in the sense of words) is described as being able to both "sting" his pupil and cure him (31.1–3).

Constant attention is paid to the ways in which the positive characters use language in their interpersonal communications. When Beatrice addresses Virgil, she praises his *parlare onesto,* "virtuous speech" (2.113); Farinata uses the same adjective in reference to Dante's speech (10.23). The Pilgrim himself is careful not to speak too much when asking questions of Virgil (10.19–21), or he uses his *dolce dir,* "sweet saying," to convince Pier de la Vigna to come out of his silence (13.55). Elsewhere, Dante wonders whether he is not being too vehement when admonishing Pope Nicholas III, then he warns the reader that his words of reprimand will become even harsher (19.88–103). Virgil advises his pupil to choose fitting words when addressing Farinata (10.39) and recommends him to speak courteously with the three Florentines (16.14–15). He chides Dante for listening curiously to the verbal duel between Sinon and Master Adam, and, with a phrase worthy of the *lingua*-texts, tells him that listening to a verbal abuse is a sign of moral weakness (30.130–48).

These clues scattered all throughout the first *cantica* project the underworld as a space where communication plays a fundamental role on all levels: the one between the two visitors, where a lot of explaining needs to be done; the one among the damned souls, who are still very active verbally; the one among the sinners and God (whom they constantly curse); and, finally, the one between the inquiring pilgrim and the confessing souls. From an artistic viewpoint, the last level is the most important, for it serves both as a means of building characters into the text and of advancing the narrative. The poet himself seems to face two major problems, since, on the one hand, he constantly complains about the insufficiency of language, this instrument unable to capture the essence of the otherworldly vision, and, on the other hand, he struggles to convince his readers of the truthfulness of his poetic text, this "ver ch'a faccia di menzogna" ("truth which has the face of falsehood"; 16.124).

Cantos 16–17 introduce a key element in the world of the *Inferno*—the figure of Geryon, "quella sozza imagine di fronda" ("that filthy image of fraud"; 17.7). The monster helps the two wayfarers make the transition from the zone of sins of violence to that of sins of fraud. An absolute embodiment of misleading appearances, he surfaces from the abyss with a human face typical of a just man, but then he creates waves of shock by showing his leonine body ending in a scorpion-like tail. As an emblem of fraud, Geryon is the perfect anticipation of the sins punished in Malebolge, including those of a linguistic nature, for the mouth of a just man would open to form virtuous words. But the monster's treacherous face serves, at best, only to symbolically prefigure man's ability to use reason and speech for fraudulent purposes.[17] Very significantly, Geryon also helps Dante to make another type of transition, from the fictive world of the text to the real one of its critical reception. For it is the first time in the poem that

17. It is worth noting that in *Verbum abbreviatum,* Peter Cantor discusses the significance of the devilish "Geryons" in relationship to the dangers they represent for the unity of the Church. In the chapter "Contra Geryones belluas bicorpores, bicipites in pluribus ecclesiis," the theologian contends that these bi- (or tri-) corporeal creatures mimic the Trinity, one in substance and undivided. Interestingly, in the *Verbum* this chapter immediately precedes the one on flattery ("Contra adulatores"). For detailed analyses of the meanings associated with Geryon in the *Comedy,* see Barolini, *The Undivine Comedy;* Roberto Mercuri, *Semantica di Gerione* (Rome: Bulzoni, 1984); and Paolo Cherchi, "Geryon's Canto," *Lectura Dantis* 2 (1988): 31–44. The latter also provides a list of the most important studies written on Dante's Geryon over the course of time.

Dante relates his vision to the issue of textual truthfulness, as he swears to his readers on the very lines of his *comedy* (a literary term also used for the first time in the text) that the hard-to-believe scene he will recount—the emergence of Geryon—was real, not imagined (*Inf.* 16.124–29). Meaningfully, the specter of the authorial linguistic and literary fraud is dissipated here by an act of speech, on oath positing the poem as an expression of truth.

Forming a large part of Hell, the ten subdivisions of fraud from the "post-Geryon world" are the focus of thirteen cantos of the *Comedy.*[18] The first of these is *Inferno* 18, which depicts both the ditch inhabited by pimps and seducers and the one inhabited by flatterers. The first ditch brings together two types of sinners who share an obsession with erotic relationships, since pimps financially exploit the lust of others and seducers abuse the innocent with calculated words and deeds. On a psychological level, what is common to these two classes of sinners is the deliberation with which they practice their evil methods: panders turn the female body into an object of traffic, selling something that is not theirs, and seducers victimize women by means of premeditated erotic techniques. In the text, the panders are represented by Venedico Caccianemico, a Bolognese credited with the selling of his sister Ghisabella to one of the noblemen of the day (presumably Obizzo d'Este). Venedico confesses to the pilgrim that the place is crowded with natives of Bologna, an assertion obliquely conveying not only Dante's negative view of Bologna but also the high frequency of the practice of pandering. The dialogue between the two is cut short by a horned devil who flays Venedico with both his whip and his words: "Via, ruffian! / Qui non son femmine da conio" ("Away, pimp! here there are no / females to coin" [i.e., for sale]; 65–66).[19] Uttered with sharp irony, this monetary reference is intended to cancel the equivalence between female bodies and money, on which panders base their trade. *Ruffian,* "pimp," is an infamous appellation; here, speech itself becomes an instrument of punishment, and the verbal corrective the devil applies to Venedico restores the proper perspective to the feminine image, by implying that women cannot be equated with profit-bringing merchandise. The base language the devil uses in his apostrophe corresponds to a vile type of commerce, and

18. I borrow the phrase "post-Geryon world" from Barolini (*The Undivine Comedy,* 75).

19. For an explanation of the enigmatic phrase *femmine da conio,* see Conner, "*Inferno* XVIII, 66."

his obscene words serve to highlight the sordidness of a sin based on carnal slavery.

The seducers are exemplified by Jason, a famous mythological character bequeathed to medieval culture as a hero, a paragon of valiance and tenacity. Echoes of this ancient perception resound in the text as Jason is introduced with a reverent high style that Dante reserves only for the major figures of history or mythology (Farinata, for instance, or Capaneus and Ulysses): “Guarda quel grande che vene, / e per dolor non par lagrime spanda: / quanto aspetto reale ancor ritene!” (“Look at that tall one coming, who does not seem to / be shedding any tear for the pain: / how regal is his bearing still!”; 83–85). A winner in the mythological tale of the Argonauts, Jason is presented in the *Comedy* as a defeated man. For, although Virgil admiringly introduces him as a man endowed with courage and wit, he also highlights his darker side, that of a seducer who “con segni e con parole ornate / Isifile ingannò” (“with tokens and elaborate words deceived Hypsipyle”; 91–92). When used in the service of a noble ideal, that of acquiring the Golden Fleece, Jason’s *senno,* “wit,” had a positive connotation; it was the power of the mind capable of overcoming the harshest obstacles. His wisdom, however, becomes guile when through deeds and skillful words he outwits a *giovinetta,* “young girl,” whom he seduces to satisfy his lust. He eventually turns out to be a *lingua dolosa,* a fraudulent speaker, to use Peter Cantor’s synecdoche. Jason’s sin, the deceitful technique he used to ensnare Hypsipyle, is based on the misuse of language, and the adjective *ornate,* “elaborate,” describing his seductive talk, is indicative of this misuse. He practiced his verbal skills to satisfy a carnal desire, and the embellishments he attached to his rhetoric were in fact morally empty and nocuous.[20]

The word *ornate,* used first in *Inferno* 2 to eulogize Virgil’s poetic art, is now recurring in a negative context, drawing attention to Dante’s constant assessment of speech as the main means of social interactions. The same fine words that in poetry serve to convey lofty ideals can be used as a method of persuasion for attaining a vile and selfish goal.[21] What distinguishes

20. In William H. V. Reade’s view, Jason’s sin would consist, rather, in the “*nocumentum proximi* involved in the false promises made to Isifile” (*The Moral System of Dante’s “Inferno,”* 340). (Reade does not mention that in medieval ethics, “false promise” was considered a deadly sin of the tongue; see, for instance, Ardens, Peraldus, and Aquinas).

21. Steven Botterill notes in this respect: “The moral validity of eloquence is not, in Dante’s thinking, a given.... Jason’s *parole ornate* are morally quite different from Virgil’s: instead of saving they betray, instead of embodying the truth, they act as a vehicle of deceit. Their

a beautiful human utterance from another enchanting one, produced in a different context, is the intention that moves the speaker. Virgil used his eloquence to create art, whereas Jason exploited his verbal skills to manipulate and ruin others' lives. The latter is also mentioned in relationship to Medea, his other mistress, whom he abandoned as well, after having made her (false) promises. However heroic Jason's exploits on the Argonautic adventure may have been, they cannot stand Dante's ethical test when they are put in balance with the hero's deceitful ways with women. In the classical tradition, both Jason and Ulysses were individuals endowed with keen intelligence and capable of deeds of great heroism, but with few scruples when it came to attaining their goals. In the conflict between the merit of intellectual abilities and the lack of moral principles, the latter factor prevailed in Dante's perception of the profiles of these mythical characters.[22]

---

ornamental quality is specious, employed to conceal the speaker's malicious and self-seeking intent" ("Dante's Poetics of the Sacred Word," 155–57). The word *ornate,* used to describe both Virgil's and Jason's speeches, has prompted Barolini to contend that classical culture is associated through both Virgil and Jason with linguistic ornament and deceit. Barolini explains Dante's vulgar style in *Inferno* 18 by his intention to dissociate himself from flatterers, to mark a clear distance between fraudulent speakers and himself (*The Undivine Comedy,* 77). Based on the polysemy of the adjective *ornate,* I believe that Dante used it in its esthetic sense to characterize Virgil's elegant style, and in its moral sense to denounce Jason's sweet-sounding (but empty) rhetoric. As is often the case with multivalent words such as this, it is the context that disambiguates the term. *Inferno* 2 disallows the interpretation of Virgil's *parola ornata* as a general symbol of classical linguistic deceit. In line 113, Virgil's speech is described by Beatrice as a *parlare onesto,* a mode of speech on account of which she can come to him in all confidence. She trusts him specifically for the truthfulness of his rhetoric. Along the same lines, in verse 126, Virgil characterizes his own words as "'l mio parlar che tanto ben ti promette" ("my speech promises you so much good"). His words promise to bring comfort and enlightenment to the Pilgrim, a promise that the subsequent narrative of the *Inferno* and the *Purgatory* will fully accomplish.

22. Dante's decision to recast heroic Jason as a manipulative, malicious speaker may have been influenced by Jean de Meun, who has La Vieille lacerate Jason as a perfidious smooth-talker, guilty above all of lying to Medea: "Que refist Jason de Medee / Qui si vilment refu boulee / Que li faus sa foi li menti / Puis qu'el l'ot de mort garenti / … Puis la laissa, li maus trichierres, / Li faus, li desloiaus, li lierrres" ("What did Jason do with Medea? He deceived her shamefully, the false one, when he belied his faith to her after she had saved him from death.… Then he left her, the evil trickster, the false, disloyal thief"; ll. 13233–61). The story is also mentioned in passing in the *Fiore* 161 and 190, where Jason is called *quel disleale,* "that unfaithful man." It is interesting that in the *Fiore* Medea plays to some extent the same role as Hypsipyle in the *Comedy;* she is the one who, despite her *sapïenza,* "wisdom," and *incantamenti,* "spells," was unable to keep the man who had sworn her love and fidelity. Jason is, in this light, one who outwits somebody knowledgeable in matters of guile (Medea or Hypsipyle), a circumstance, however, which neither in the *Fiore*

Although the practitioners of *lusinghe,* "blandishments," share the first circle of Malebolge with pimps and seducers, they are punished in a different ditch.[23] The flatterers are completely immersed in excrement and their heads (or hairdos) can no longer reveal if they are laypeople or clerics. This strange mention can be read in light of Alain of Lille's critique of the prelates' propensity to *adulatio.* In the passage from the *Plaint of Nature* quoted above, clerics are depicted as being equally as prone to smooth talking as laymen. Dante's stress on the undifferentiated physical appearance of these social categories further reinforces the idea that ecclesiastics also practice this depraved way of speech and pay the eternal price.[24]

The pilgrim engages in a dialogue with one of the sinners, Alessio Interminei, who confesses to Dante: "Qua giù m'hanno sommerso le lusinghe / ond' io non ebbi mai la lingua stucca" ("I am submerged down here by the flatteries with which / my tongue was never cloyed"; 125–26).[25] By self-definition a sweet-talker, Alessio turned flattery into a mode of life; he was a con artist, an artisan of speech, as Alain of Lille would have put it. The adjective *stucca,* "cloyed," which Dante uses pejoratively, implies that Alessio's insincere compliments were a constant of his life; they were not rare occurrences, but a consciously cultivated practice, a way of being.[26] Both the labeling of Jason's words as *ornate* and the description of Alessio's *lusinghe* reveal a writer who constantly and perceptively evaluates people's manners

nor in the *Comedy* does excuse Jason, but which may give one more reason for Medea's alignment with Hypsipyle in *Inferno* 18. The fact that Jason is smarter than two clever women only enhances his deceitful ways.

23. In *Inferno* 11, when Virgil explains to his pupil the overall structure of Hell, he refers to this sin as *lusinghe.* The term is interesting in that etymologically it is the Italian cognate of *losanges,* the term used by Jean de Meun to depict the same habit of speech. Thus, the *Rose* and the *Comedy* meet not only in their preoccupation with adulatory speaking but also in the field of the attendant terminology, and, as we have seen with Jason, of the exempla. *Adulatori* or *lusinghieri* are also the vernacular terms *Pungilingua* uses in reference to the practitioners of *adulatio.*

24. For the flattering clerics, the law had established the deposition, a penalty introduced by Gratian in his *Decretals* (1.46.3): "A cleric who is found out in the practice of flattery and scheming is to be degraded" (quoted in Aquinas, *ST* IIa-IIae Q.115.2).

25. These two dense lines remind H. Wayne Storey of the medieval practice of bringing dishonor to a person's reputation by drawing disparaging *graffiti* on public buildings ("*Inferno* XVIII," in *Lectura Dantis Virginiana, I. Dante's "Inferno": Introductory Readings,* edited by Tibor Wlassics, 235–46, Supplement to *Lectura Dantis* 6 [1990], special issue [Charlottesville: University of Virginia, 1990], 244).

26. In Aquinas's interpretation, it is the intention underlying the words that renders flattery a mortal sin (*ST* IIa-IIae Q.115.2).

of speech, as well as his own. In *Inferno* 32, for instance, the poet obliquely places himself in a favorable light, by having Bocca degli Abati say that the pilgrim is a bad flatterer (l. 96). Later on, flattery will be banished from the outset on the mountain of Purgatory, where Cato averts Virgil's smooth talk by telling him that here, in the second realm, blandishments are not necessary (*Purgatorio* 1.92).

But why does Dante punish the habit of flattery in the area of fraud? First of all, let us recall what John of Salisbury, one of the finest analysts of this verbal practice, has said: "Just as the aim of the orator is persuasive speech, and the end of a physician is a medical cure, so the aim of flatterers is sweetly spoken deception."[27] Adulatory speakers enlist the help of rhetorical procedures to convince people to act in a manner that serves their selfish purposes. In their social dealings, they have a well-established goal, but unlike physicians, they do intend not to heal but to harm by deceit. Flattery is defined as perverse rhetoric, a form of eloquence directed at the manipulation of others, and Salisbury does not hesitate to compare it to prostitution: "Having previously bribed the friend with delights, the flatterer creeps up on his fortune in the manner of a prostitute, diminishing his faculties, accumulating the plunder from those things which belong to him, and converting everything to one's own advantage."[28]

Dante's moral values oppose these ways. To recall his statement from *Convivio,* words are to be used with extreme caution, for they contain the seeds of our actions and their consequences. Since speech is intended for, and addressed to, an interlocutor or an audience, it can be used as a powerful tool to control people's minds and actions. Words need to be released with mental discernment, so they may be welcomed by listeners and have positive results in their lives. Anticipating the reactions our utterances will cause is the vital psychological element that ought to shape our discourses before we pronounce them (*Convivio* 4.2).

This is the speech ethics that accounts for the presence among flatterers of Thaïs, the cunning courtesan, whom Dante introduces by recounting the inflated praise she gave her lover, when he inquired about the degree to which he was able to satisfy her: "'Ho io grazie / grandi apo te?': 'Anzi maravigliose!'" ("'Do I / find great favor with you?': 'Marvelous favor indeed!'"; 134–35). Thaïs's overstated reply is deliberately formulated to

27. John of Salisbury, *Policraticus,* 3.10.

28. Ibid., 3.6.

touch her lover's vanity, and thereby, to place herself in a favorable standing with him. What is particular about her reaction is that she goes too far in trying to please him, an excess underlying the ethical definition of adulation; she exaggerates her own pleasure so as to ingratiate herself with her paramour. It is true that a most courteous way of speech should govern, in Dante's opinion, all friendly relationships. Friendships are to be built on civil social attitudes, such as speaking very courteously, serving others, and treating them with kindness and respect. However, Thaïs's reply crosses the boundaries of the most courteous speech; it is a calculated fraud, a lie masquerading as a compliment. Dante defines truth as the quality that "restrains us in our speech from vaunting ourselves as greater than we are and from deprecating ourselves as less than we are" (*Convivio* 4.17.38–39). To be truthful, our words should reflect a personal image proportionate to our true self, and in light of this definition, the same criterion may be extended to our speech about others: the words we use to describe them should be proportionate to the genuine image we have of them.

Thaïs deliberately enlarges the image of her paramour; she praises him as greater than he is, to paraphrase Dante, just as typical flatterers exaggerate the qualities of the individuals of whom they want to take advantage. The outer, verbal projections that sycophantic speakers make of their victims do not correspond to their inner, genuine opinion of them. As a result, the flatterers' words become, to use Peraldus's phrase, toxic honey. The type of *contrapasso* the poet reserves for *lusingatori* echoes the medieval perception of deceitful smooth talkers—they are punished in excrement reflecting the toxic speeches they eliminated through their mouths while alive.[29] In *Convivio,* Dante urges his readers to speak words that are fruit-

29. Both Pézard ("Du *Policraticus* à la *Divine Comédie,*" 6), and Georges Güntert ("Canto XVIII," in *Lectura Dantis Turicensis, I: "Inferno,"* [Florence: Franco Cessati, 2000], 245–59), explain this *contrapasso* by the possible influence of Salisbury, since in *Policraticus* 3.4 *adulatio* is defined as *fetor,* "stench." I would also add that actually Salisbury explicitly defines flattery as "toxin" (3.6). Examining the distinct notions of scatology and obscenity that permeate *Inferno* 18, Barański notes Dante's reluctance to talk about the erotic as opposed to his comfort in talking about the excremental. Both linguistic attitudes are typical of religious texts and represent proofs that Dante "is doing God's work, that he is a *scriba Dei,*" Barański adds (*Scatology and Obscenity in Dante,* 267). For more on the relationship between Malebolge and physiological processes, see Robert M. Durling's splendid article "Deceit and Digestion in the Belly of Hell," in *Allegory and Representation,* Selected Papers from the English Institute, 1979–1980, edited by S. Greenblatt (Baltimore: Johns Hopkins University Press, 1981). An interesting study on the medieval view of excrement has been published by Susan Signe Morrison, *Excrement in*

ful, not sterile, but the only fruit that the flatterers' speeches bear are these toxins in which they are plunged in the underworld.

Medieval moralists often interpreted excrement in an erotic framework. The symbolism of *stercum,* "feces," spanned a wide range of meanings, three of which match the idea of profit and lust associated with Thaïs—bodily pleasure, attachment to material values, and sordidness.[30] In the *Comedy,* Thaïs is from the outset placed in a social context; she is a *puttana,* "whore," who, according to Pézard, was punished by Dante not for this single reply, but because this reply was indicative of a constant practice. Filtered through Cicero's or Salisbury's texts, the Terentian female figure is called to represent in Malebolge the type of female prostitute who turns adulatory speech into a way of life. We also have to recall that in the moral texts of the Middle Ages, flattery was commonly associated with depraved women. In his chapter on adulators, for instance, Peter Cantor reiterates the biblical view according to which flattery is the prostitutes' typical way of speaking: "Mel et lac sub lingua meretricis" ("Milk and honey under the tongue of the whore").[31] Waltherio's *Liber Esopi,* acknowledged as a source for Dante's familiarity with Thaïs, testifies that for the same medieval culture, Thaïs was the prototype of the whore. It is thus easy to understand why this female figure comes to represent the most suitable character for Dante's exemplification of flattery as a long-standing practice in the history of humanity.

In the structure of Hell, Thaïs also offers the key for understanding Dante's placement of adulation between the sins of seduction and simony. Benvenuto da Imola has long ago justified Dante's association of Thaïs and Jason on the grounds of their common obsession with erotic deceit: "Jason exemplifies men who deceive women and Thaïs women who deceive men."[32] The link between seduction and flattery is strong, since both transgressions are based on the use (or rather misuse) of language. To reach his self-seeking goals, the seducer, just like the adulator, often has to mobilize his rhetorical skills. While it is true that both Jason and Thaïs are skillful speakers, for Christian Dante there is a sharp line of demarcation between

the Late Middle Ages: Sacred Filth and Chaucer's Fecopoetics, (New York: Palgrave Macmillan, 2008).

30. Alain of Lille, *Distinctiones dictionum theologicalium, PL* 210, col. 956 B.

31. Peter Cantor, *Verbum abbreviatum,* Patrologia Latina 205, col. 142 A.

32. Quoted in Edoardo Sanguinetti, *Interpretazione di Malebolge* (Florence: Olschki, 1961), 33.

smooth talk and virtuous speech, since sweet-sounding words of love and praise may often be only artful rhetoric placed in the wrong service. This is why in the system of Hell, the sin of seduction, a complex behavioral mechanism that typically enlists the support of language, is placed side by side with adulation. This is also why the first two ditches of Malebolge are depicted within the same canto, and Jason the tempter paves the way for the episodes of flatterers Alessio and Thaïs. The female character also marks the textual transition to simony, a transition easy to understand, if we recall that in the Middle Ages simony was defined as "a prostitution of God's bride, the church."[33]

Inferno 18 is a canto subtly dominated by female figures. Indirectly present in the expression "femmine da conio ("females to coin"; l. 66), which diffusely projects them as nameless objects on the stage of male desires and negotiations, women are then invoked as intellectually endowed persons through Hypsipyle and Medea, both capable, according to legend, of guile and manipulation. The female potentiality for *inganno* evoked in connection with Hypsipyle is then reiterated through the figure of Thaïs, who takes the linguistic side of guile, the *lingua dolosa,* to a high level on a perverse scale of values.

Thaïs is the opposite of Dante's ideal of female speech. At the other ethical pole, the poet casts Beatrice as the perfect model for women's use of language, repairing thus in Limbo, Purgatory, and Paradise, the moral corruption caused by women of Thaïs's stock. When, in *Inferno* 2, Beatrice descends into Limbo to ask Virgil to help the lost and disheartened pilgrim, her way of speaking is described as *soave e piana,* "gentle and soft." Her words, an exemplification of the art Dante calls *cortesissimamente parlare,* "speaking most courteously," are moved not by concerns of self-promotion, nor by simulated love, but by the most genuine form of charity. Beatrice too uses compliments and verbal negotiation when she emotionally pleads to Virgil on behalf of Dante, but she does it in an unequivocally positive

33. Joan M. Ferrante, "The Malebolge (*Inf.* XVIII–XXX) as the Key to the Structure of Dante's *Inferno,*" *Romance Philology* 20 (1967): 456–66, at 462. Peter Cantor furnishes an interesting link between adulation and simony in a passage that I will cite to suggest that the association of flattery with simony in the *Inferno* is not extravagant: "if the retribution for a service and the obtainment of money are simony, *then simony is also the retribution for a sordid submission or deed, like flattery.* Because the retribution was obtained on account of the favors, it is neither a gift of gratitude, which opposes both guilt and money, nor (a gift) of nature" (*Verbum abbeviatum,* 140B; emphasis added; translation mine).

context: in exchange for Virgil's helping her friend lost in the dark wood, she promises to praise the Latin poet before God, as a token of her gratitude. Beatrice restores to speech an exquisite moral quality that seducers and flatterers deny it: generosity in human relationships, altruism manifested through words and deeds, which, in Dante's view, should be beneficial first to others, then to ourselves.[34]

EVIL COUNSEL

"It is unlawful to cooperate in an evil deed, by counseling, helping or in any way, consenting, because to counsel or assist an action is, in a way, to do it."[35] The discussion of the practice of evil counseling is another major intersection between the *Romance of the Rose* and the *Divine Comedy.* In the *Rose,* it is Ami and La Vieille who embody this form of transgressive speech, whereas in the *Comedy,* it is represented by Ulysses and Guido da Montefeltro.

"Preachers of Sin" in the *Rose*

Ami offers Amant detailed instructions on how to cope with the tribulations of love, adopting from the outset the posture of a counselor in heterosexual interactions. Textually, his discourse is a reworking of Books 1 and 2 of Ovid's *Ars amatoria,* a revision possibly facilitated by the French *Art d'Amours,* an anonymous prose translation whose first two books predate the *Romance of the Rose.*[36] The colors in which Ami describes the torments of passion are less dark than Raison's. Unlike her, he does not fear their ability to cloud discernment and does not recommend the total avoidance of erotic involvement. He rather speaks with the confidence of a learned prac-

34. The notion is twice expressed in *Convivio:* first, when Dante speaks of the commandment of his moral and philosophical models, who urge man to put his gifts and benefices at the disposal of others (4.22.1–3), and second, when he quotes Aristotle's definition of man as a civic animal, who is required to be useful not to oneself, but to others (4.27.19–20).

35. Thomas Aquinas, *ST* IIa-IIae. Q. 71.4.

36. Marilynn Desmond proposes a fine reading of Ami's speech, which she considers a vernacular extension of Ovid's *Ars amatoria* filtered through the glosses offered by the French *Art d'amours.* She also analyzes the sequence of the Jealous Husband through the angle of erotic violence and places it in relationship to the visual representation of domestic abuses in the manuscript tradition of the *Rose* (*Ovid's "Art" and the "Wife of Bath": The Ethics of Erotic Violence* [Ithaca, N.Y.: Cornell University Press, 2006], 73–111).

titioner, who has withstood stormy relationships and is now able to teach others how to control them (ll. 7283–84). He is not as bookish and stern as Raison, for instead of invoking the authority of various Stoic philosophers, he buttresses his points of view with numerous popular proverbs. As Marilynn Desmond notes, the Boethian philosophy underlying Raison’s pronouncements is replaced in Ami’s discourse with an Ovidian substratum that sounds more appealing to Amant and his sexual needs (80). At the same time, Ami is less allegorical than the great lady embodying man’s rational faculties, in that he projects himself as a character with a real biography, as a concrete and pragmatic person who speaks with the authority given by his own, solid experience in matters of life. It is an experience that has had its own share of bitterness, however, and this accounts for the sarcastic tone of this new preceptor of love.

In offering to help Amant out of his plight, Ami first suggests an alliance with Malebouche, whose friendship needs to be cultivated because of the great damage that his verbal activities may bring to Amant’s cause: “Mais male bouche trop forfait / Pour s’ordre vill langue despite, / Que il ne puet, des qu’il l’a dite / De sa gueule mal renommée, / Restorer bonne renommée / N’estaindre une parole sangle / S’il l’a meüe par sa jangle” (ll. 7372–78; “But Foul Mouth commits too great a crime with his filthy, vile, spiteful tongue: once he has spoken slander with his mouth he cannot repair it, nor destroy a single word that he has produced with his chatter”). As a fictive construct, Malebouche perpetuates the tradition of the *janglers,* “evil talkers,” from the courtly love poetry and is associated with several abusive speech acts, such as gossip, slander, flattery, false promises, and rumor mongering. Paradoxically, however, he is only an abstract figure who is not given a discursive identity in the poem. The audience is made aware of his malicious habits from the other characters’ reports; Malebouche himself never opens his mouth in the text. He is always referred to as a menacing active presence in the plot, and the lingual habits that are attached to him, although deriving from the tradition of love lyrics, are all social ills identified by the pastoral writers as instances of sinful speech. Thus, Jean’s penchant for paradoxical constructs is already apparent in this personage, who, despite being an integral incarnation of deviant speech, is never given the chance to utter an actual word.[37] The poet’s cultivation of the paradox

37. For an analysis of the role played by this feared character in the plot of the romance, see Leslie C. Brook (“Malebouche dans le *Roman de la Rose* et le *Champion des dames,*” in

as a literary mode will reach a brilliant level in the episode of Faus Semblant, who will eventually murder Malebouche and take over all of his linguistic functions.

If Ami insists on the necessity that Malebouche be reduced to silence, it is not to purge society from a source of linguistic evil, since he himself constitutes such a source. Tellingly, Ami's solutions to the problems posed by the wicked rumormonger are deceitful words and deeds: "Male bouche et touz ses paranz / A cui ja dieus ne soit garanz, / Par barat estuet barater, / Servir, chuer, blandir, flatter, / Par hourz, par adulacions, / Par fausses simulacions, / Et encliner et saluer / Q'il fait trop bon le chien chuer / Tant com ait la voie passée (ll. 7388–95; "One has to trick Foul Mouth and his kin—may God never be their surety!—with fraud: one must serve them, caress, blandish and flatter them with ruse, adulation, and false simulation; one must bow to them and salute them. It is a very good idea to stroke a dog until one has passed by"). The *modus operandi* Ami recommends to the lover relies entirely on encouragements to fraud and violence. On this occasion, the friendly preceptor introduces for the first time the basic tenet of his life philosophy: deceiving deceivers is a praiseworthy thing (ll. 7344–45).[38] By virtue of this moral justification of ruse, Ami advises Amant to offer Malebouche everything, even his own body and soul, but not sincerely. Self-dedication should be only feigned not felt because—and here Ami reiterates his principle—it is legitimate to defraud the fraudulent: "De ceuls bouler n'est pas pechiez / Qui de bouler sont entechiez" ("it is no sin to trick those who are tainted by trickery"; ll. 7355–56). This statement reveals Ami's awareness of the potential transgressiveness of his advice; he obliquely admits that counseling fraud is a sin but tries to excuse himself by invoking a piece of popular "wisdom" according to which deceit practiced on dupers is morally licit. Lines 7344–56 are the most philosophically dense in Ami's agency as a champion of interactive fraud. The excuse (or promotion) of deceit is expressed several times in only twelve short lines introducing three proverbs interrelated by a synonymy of fraud. Besides the two quotes I have given above, there is also: "L'en seult dire, et voirs est, ce cuit,

De la Rose: Texte, Image, Fortune, edited by Catherine Bel and Herman Braet [Dudley, Mass.: Peeters, 2006], 430–34).

38. This statement will have Christine de Pizan outraged in the *Querelle,* insofar as she will interpret it as a direct exhortation to immorality made by the writer himself. For more on this topic, see chapter 4, the pages devoted to Jean de Meun's blasphemies.

/ Encontre vezié recuit” (“Men are accustomed to say, and, believe me, it is true: a cunning man against a crafty one”; ll. 7353–54)

On account of this strongly argued excuse, flattery and *fausses simulations,* “fallacious dissimulations,” are promoted as effective means of reaching one’s purposes. Friendship itself becomes a victim of this Machiavellian scheme in which simulating an affectionate attitude is advocated as the best way to defeat one’s enemies. The problem is that Ami encourages Amant to adopt disingenuous gestures even with other people, like the guardians of Jalousie’s castle or the young lady he loves. With the former, Ami vividly advises Amant to use a wide range of smooth-operating methods, such as producing presents, complaining, lying, swearing, bribing, or dissimulating. Another strategy warmly recommended is corrupting the watchmen (or generally those who stand in one’s way) with presents, for these soften hearts, alter people’s discourses, and change slander into praise.[39] Dealing with watchmen requires verbal skills, Ami maintains, and nothing is more harmful to a lover’s cause than a careless way of speaking. He who wants to win over strong opponents (here the guardians of the castle) should never be a *hastif sermonneur,* “hasty speaker,” but should take time to formulate his request and seize the right moment to speak (for example, when the watchman is in a good mood). In order to get something from people, one also has to touch their most sensitive chord (here *pitié,* “pity”), to impress them with one’s suffering; once people are fooled, one should take advantage of their weakness to one’s personal benefit. It is thus evident that among these persuasive strategies Ami recommends, many are related to the usage of language: complaints, promises, oaths, and prayers. Of these strategies, the one that strikes me as the most fraudulent is the excessive use of promises (“you must promise something by oath,” or: “make a strong promise”), with the intention of never keeping them (ll. 7448–49). It is worth noting parenthetically that recommending the use of false promises seems to be a very fashionable practice in the Middle Ages, since we find it exemplified in the *Comedy* as well, through the figure of Guido da Montefeltro in *Inferno* 27. It should thus come as no surprise that Peraldus treats *indiscreta promisio* as a sin of the tongue, the nineteenth one on his roster of twenty-four verbal transgressions.[40]

39. Dante expresses a similar view when he describes the Bolognese barraters as turning “no” into “yes” (i.e., changing refusal into acceptance) for the sake of money (*Inf.* 21.41–42).

40. See Caput 19, “De peccato indiscretae promisionis.”

In the *Rose,* Ami gives Amant a veritable lesson of rhetoric centered on the standard criteria for proper speaking posited by the ethical tracts, criteria related to the interlocutor as well as to the time and mode of communication. However, the advice concerning these circumstances of speech is now pressed into the service of ruse. Ami's exhortations to fraudulent uses of rhetoric are the exact opposite of the warnings against verbal sins from the pastoral tractates; consequently, the authority of these Christian texts seems irremediably compromised. Considering this opposition from an intertextual perspective, however, it is evident that the problem of sinful speech in Ami's agency emerges mainly from the clash between an eminently Ovidian discourse (transposed into the vernacular) and the normative prescriptions for speaking promoted by the moral tracts from Jean's time. This conflict between a pagan source that, we should not forget, earned its author his political exile, and contemporary regulations of Christian speech will become even more dramatic in the episode of La Vieille.

Like words, deeds too can be falsified, Ami adds, and Amant should not hesitate to turn each situation to his advantage through fraud. When he wants to cry in order to impress ladies but cannot shed a tear, he should use onion juice or other spices for the stimulation of tears. Ami points out that this has always been a very successful practice with women, who, wishing to seduce men, have been fooled themselves by false stories and lying tears produced by men. Mimicking the female gender is another vital part of the masculine arsenal of seduction. A male lover constantly has to adjust his behavior to the behavior of the woman he desires. If she is childish, he has to play childish; if she is wise and mature, he has to behave like a mature person himself. A man should look happy when his mistress is happy, cry when she cries, and praise whatever she praises.[41] He has to flatter her, by eulogizing her looks and manners at all times. When these strategies of seduction do not work, the use of physical force is the only effective solution left at the disposal of a true man: "cueillicz la rose tout a force / et moustrez que vous estes hon, / quant tans iert et lieus et saison, / car riens

41. It is important to note that in the French text, the pronoun used to designate the generic woman for whom Bel Accueil stands is *il,* since the grammatical gender of the noun *Bel Accueil* is masculine. For a thorough study of the implications of this pronominal obfuscation, see Simon Gaunt, "Bel Accueil and the Improper Allegory of the *Roman de la Rose,*" in *New Medieval Literatures,* vol. 2, edited by R. Copeland, D. Lawton, and W. Scase (Oxford: Clarendon Press, 1998), 65–93.

ne leur porroit tant plere / com tel force, qui la set faire" ("pluck the rose by force and show that you are a man; for, as long as someone knows how to exercise it, nothing could please them [women] so much as such force"; ll. 7692–96).

The only place where violence against women is forbidden is the domestic arena, where physical abuses can be detrimental to the relationship between spouses. This exception to the rule of violence comes as a comment on the episode of Le Mari Jaloux ("the Jealous Husband"), used as a negative example of marital behavior (in this episode, the husband's foul language accompanies the emotional and physical abuse of the wife). If, however, a good husband makes a mistake and beats his wife, Ami adds as a corrective to the Jealous Husband's aggressiveness, he should immediately repent and amend his error by making love to her.

Amant's reaction to Ami's pieces of advice confirms the reader's sense that the love preceptor is not someone to be taken seriously: only a hypocrite would do such devilish things, Amant exclaims, apparently outraged (ll. 7798–99). I say apparently, because his reaction should rather be read in light of the ambivalent attitude of medieval Christians toward ruse: that of fascination with the power of the human mind and of repulsion toward a twisted form of intelligence typically associated with the devil. But Amant's scandalized reaction does not diminish Ami's enthusiasm as a counselor of fraud, and the remainder of his discourse offers the reader more surprises. One of these concerns an interesting aspect of the relationship between language and love and occurs when Ami speaks about female venality in the context of male (ineffective) literary creativity. He tells Amant not to bother to send his sweetheart pretty rhymes, motets, or little stories, because nowadays these have become obsolete and useless ways of approaching a lady. In sharp opposition to the Golden Age, when love was sincere and devoid of simony, now it has become a form of commerce wherein women let themselves be conquered only by men with well-filled pockets. The noblest expressions of human language—poetry, tales, songs, in other words all the assets of the literary tradition of *fin'amors*—have become powerless in competition with current mercantile values. As it is the money that talks, not poetry, women now run to embrace men with rich pockets, not with noble hearts and poetic skills.

Jean places the diminishing stature of courtly poetry as a driving force in love within the framework of Ami's depiction of the Golden Age and its end.[42] This is an extraordinary moment in the *Rose,* for it presents the state of the world in terms that will become the hallmarks of Dante's universe in the *Comedy:*

Lors ert amours sanz symonie, / L'uns ne demandoit riens a l'autre, / Quant baraz vint, lance seur fautre, / Et pechiez et male aventure / Qui n'ot de souffisance cure. / Orguieulz, qui desdaingne pareill / Vint avoec, o grant apareill, / Et couvoitise et avarice, / Envie et tuit li autre vice.... / Tantost cil doulereus mauffé / De forsenerie eschauffé, / De duel, de corrouz et d'envie, / Quant virent genz mener tel vie, / S'escourcerent par toutes terres / Semanz descors, contens et guerres, / Mesdiz, rancunes et haÿnnes / Par corrouz et par ataÿnnes. (9530–72)

At that time there was no simony in love; one did not demand something from another. Then Fraud came, with his lance at rest, and Sin and Misfortune, who take no heed of Sufficiency, and, along with them came Pride, equally disdainful in her grand array, Covetousness, Avarice, Envy, and all the other vices.... Immediately these wretched devils, excited by fury, sorrow, anger, and envy when they saw men leading such a life, rushed off through all countries, sowing discord, contention and war, slander, rancor, and hatred through anger and quarreling.

"Fraud" and "sufficiency" are Aristotelian terms consecrated by the moral tracts of the late Middle Ages; they are also fundamental coordinates in Dante's moral system, which posits fraud as one of the axes of Hell and sufficiency as a divide between insufficient love and excessive love, in Purgatory. In Jean's list, fraud is followed by two generic terms with further moral connotations, *pechiez,* "sin," and *male aventure,* "misfortune," which spring from violating sufficiency, the right mean between two extremes. In this passage, Aristotelian theories of morality are intertwined with the patristic list of capital vices (pride, covetousness, avarice, wrath, and sorrow) in an ethical amalgam that will characterize Dante's system of Hell as well. It is very significant that Jean's long and disorderly list of social evils contains several sins of the tongue: sowing of discord, contention, slander,

42. Helmut G. Walther interprets this description, as well as the episodes of Le Mari Jaloux and Faus Semblant, as instances of Jean's veiled criticism of Aquinas's utopian social philosophy. Jean would thus be the first writer to engage in a satirical polemic with Aquinas's teachings that were based on an anthropological optimism that the author of the *Rose* did not share ("Utopische Gesellschaftskritik oder Satirische Ironie: Jean de Meung und die Lehre des Aquinaten über die Entstehung menschlicher Herrschaft," *Soziale Ordnungen im Selbstverstaendnis des Mittelalters* 1 [1979]: 84–105, at 99–104). Richards notes that Walther's study is an important one, being the first to ascertain the concrete textual traces of Aquinas's thought in Jean's poem ("*Les contraires choses:* Irony in Jean de Meun," 390).

and quarrelling, all new indications of the poet's sensitivity to the abuses of speech characterizing his contemporaries.

The surprises offered by Ami's discourse do not end, however, with the picture of the dark days in which Fraud and his companions conquered the world. Forgetting about his own complaint about the decay of morality, the embittered preceptor immediately resumes his office of fraudulent counselor by making more recommendations on the use of ruse and deceit in heterosexual relationships.[43] Cheating is a perfectly moral practice, says this Ovidian love preceptor, giving specific instructions on what a cheater should say or do to appease the suspicions of his lady: he should vigorously deny all the accusations of infidelity; he should swear that he still loves her; he should flatter her and promise that he will always stay true to their love. Not only that, but he should also make some creative efforts and invoke fictitious dreams he had about her, dreams he should romantically tell her before they go to bed.[44]

From an artistic point of view, the textual tension between Ami's complaint about the immorality of contemporary society and his exhortations to a sinful way of life is designed to compromise the personage. His promotion of vices as an effective *modus vivendi* belies his lamentation of the loss of good morals from golden times and undermines the overall ethical value of his teachings. The fraudulent potentiality of human (here male) language is inflated to the maximum, as the ability of speech to convey truth in the relationship between man and woman, and in a broader sense among people, is again deeply impaired. Ami is a "Malebouche," a character whose silencing he has just urged, but he fails to recognize himself as such. Jean's female readership must have had a shock reading his lines in the poem (as indeed had Christine de Pizan), and their trust in male erotic speech must have been seriously shaken.

But was not this the very agenda of Jean de Meun as the author of *Mireor aus amoureus* (Mirror for lovers), as he labels his poem? Jean writes an allegorical text in which all categories of lovers need to see their images

43. This type of conflict occurring within the discourse of a character is shocking as it undermines the very coherence of it. It is a writerly practice that Jean systematically applies to his characters, and we will see it again at work in the discourses of La Vieille, Nature, Genius, and especially Faus Semblant.

44. The suggestive rhyme *songe / mençonges* has been used in criticism to prove Jean's mistrust of the dream as a narrative form. See Renate Blumenfeld-Kosinski, "Remarques sur songe/mensonge," *Romania* 101, no. 3 (1980): 387–90.

reflected. This entails that even those lovers who conquer the objects of their desires through sweet talking, lies, and ruse (because erotic love is, as we have seen, a sin and a form of simony) will recognize themselves in the mirror. Moreover, this text has didactic purposes; it is explicitly written with the goal of instructing people (especially the youth) in matters of love and life. As such, by questioning the truthfulness of erotic speech, the poem undertakes to disillusion young women and make them more alert to the traps set by verbal strategies of seduction. Words are "neighbors with things" and must be "cousins to their deeds," Jean says in his direct intervention in the poem (ll. 15194–96). In other terms, speech should both mirror what is in one's mind and be corroborated by deeds. Ami's activity as a malicious counselor violates this categorical imperative of the harmonious relationship between truth and speech, since his lesson on love abounds with recommendations of linguistic deceit. Amant and, through him, men in general, are urged to use their eloquence in order to lie, charm, or seduce women into their beds, in short, to manipulate. In such dealings, words are no longer expressions of truth but treacherous veils designed to hide it.

In this context, it seems evident to me that this character does not act as a mouthpiece for Jean de Meun, as Christine de Pizan and Jean Gerson will later argue. On the contrary, the dissociation between author and personage is all the more marked since Ami's pieces of advice are so blatantly loaded with fraud that they eventually turn against him and demolish him as a love counselor. The philosophy he teaches, when it was applied to his own life, led to failure, as now Ami is alone, a paradoxical "friend" without friends. If Roger Dragonetti is right when he speaks of Jean's formidable love for language,[45] on account of which the poet explores the word and the sentence in all their potential, it is also true that through Ami, Jean tests all the potentiality for sinfulness of human speech. Taking up virtues of language (oath, praise, or beautiful lyrics), the poet stretches them in the opposite direction to such an extent that they become vices (perjury, flattery, and fallacious verses). The purpose of this moral-linguistic acrobatics is to highlight the ruinous effects of words when they are used by minds intent on fraud and violence. Although in the Ami episode, the pastoral texts on transgressive speech seem to be undermined and ridiculed, the iro-

45. Roger Dragonetti, "Specchi d'amore: Il *Romanzo della Rosa* e *Il Fiore*," *Paragone* 81 (1981): 3–22, at 21.

ny with which Jean portrays this character, a mock love guru, is so evident that the authority of the moral tractates is implicitly restored. The poet ultimately proves to be a fine connoisseur of the contemporary discourse on abusive speech, which he uses in remarkable detail as a means of fashioning his characters and structuring their messages.

La Vieille's Feminine "Ethics" If Ami's sequence focuses on the falsity inherent in the male strategies of seduction, the discourse of La Vieille teaches exactly the same methods from the opposite angle, as she instructs young women on how to ensnare men. In 1959, Lionel Friedman made a remark about La Vieille that is vital in the context of my investigation. Noting that this character's Latin ancestry and her evolution in European romance and courtly literature have been well clarified, Friedman adds that "her connections with moral literature must still be traced."[46] He then indicates as a possible source for La Vieille Peraldus's *SV,* which lists as third among the eight occasions for the sin of lust: "the exhortation of old women or other persons who are counselors of turpitude and a bad example."[47] Friedman's reference to *SV* seems of common sense to John Fleming, who is bolder than Friedman on this matter, as he states: "That Jean de Meun knew this *Summa,* as Chaucer knew it and used it after him, is entirely likely; it was after all, one of the most extraordinarily successful books of the later Middle Ages."[48] More recently, Edwin Craun has analyzed the speech of Geoffrey Chaucer's Wife of Bath (the "heiress" of La Vieille) from the perspective of the medieval tradition of *peccata linguae.*[49] In light of all these critical stances, a reading of La Vielle's speech in relationship to the pastoral discourse on verbal sins becomes an interpretive duty.

46. For a survey of La Vieille's literary genealogy (classical and French traditions), see Luis Beltrán, "The Old Woman's Past," *Romanische Forschungen* 84 (1972): 77–96. For a more complex treatment of the medieval representations of old women, see Gretchen Mieszkowski ("Old Age and Medieval Misogyny: The Old Woman," in *Old Age in the Middle Ages and the Renaissance,* edited by Albert Classen [New York: Walter de Gruyter, 2007]), who also analyzes *De Vetula,* a popular Old French text written about 1250, which might have served Jean in the portrayal of this controversial female figure.

47. Lionel J. Friedman, "Jean de Meung, Antifeminism, and 'Bourgeois Realism,'" *Modern Philology* 57 (1959): 13–23, at 18.

48. Fleming, *The "Roman de la Rose,"* 172.

49. Edwin Craun, *The Hands of the Tongue: Essays on Deviant Speech* (Kalamazoo, Mich.: Medieval Institute, 2007), 33–60.

It is worth noting that in the section devoted to *pravum consilium,* "evil counsel," from "De peccato linguae," Peraldus does not speak of wicked female counselors, but Domenico Cavalca, his Italian translator, pays special attention to them in his chapter on evil counsel. Cavalca is scandalized by the *maladette femmine,* "wicked women," who either cause young men to lose their innocence or yield to "uomini vani e corruttori" ("vain and corrupting men"). He considers these women worse than the devil and warns that after death they will burn in the fires of hell for having fanned other people's fires of lust. He even tells the story of a *maladetta vecchia,* "wretched old woman," who caused a young wife to commit adultery by reassuring her that God could not see sins committed at night. The young lady eventually repented for her sin and saved her soul, but the old woman could not redeem herself and lost hers. Cavalca holds female evil counselors responsible for many sins, wars, brawls, and murders, and asks his readers to avoid these "diavole maladette femmine" ("devilish wicked women") as the worst kind of people and female friends of corruption.[50]

Representing one of the longest and most controversial episodes in the *Rose* (1,806 lines), La Vieille's discourse is an extremely dense celebration of erotic fraud and violence, a glorification of vice achieved through highly obscene speech.[51] Sylvia Huot notes that two medieval copyists of the romance go so far as to shorten this section of the book or to remove it completely.[52] La Vieille touches upon a plethora of hot topics: liberality and loyalty in love (qualities that she spitefully dismisses), manipulation of other people's feelings, exploitation of fleshly pleasures while young, advice on the art of seducing and extorting money from men, women as actresses in the comedy of love, female sexual freedom, the art of cosmetics, and table manners. All these themes are discussed within a circular biographical frame, which allows the character to launch her speech with an evocation of her own promiscuous youth and end it with the unhappy story of her last amorous passion.

La Vieille introduces herself as a woman with great expertise in erotic

50. Cavalca, *Pungilingua,* 190–92.

51. Alastair Minnis offers an extended study of the connections between speech, obscenity, and vetularity in the *Rose* ("From *Coilles* to *Bel Chose*": Discourses of Obscenity in Jean de Meun and Chaucer," in *Medieval Obscenities,* edited by Nicola McDonald [York: Medieval Press/Boydell and Brewer, 2006]).

52. Sylvia Huot, *The "Romance of the Rose" and Its Medieval Readers* (Cambridge: Cambridge University Press, 1993), 35–36, 141.

relationships. She is, in fact, a former prostitute turned an old procuress, who brags about her ability to bring to Bel Accueil as many rich lovers as he wants. She did not need to go to school to take lessons on love, she explains, for at school one studies only theories, whereas life has taught her the practice of love (ll. 12806–9).[53] The rationale for her tutoring Bel Accueil in this domain lies in her desire for revenge against male lovers who made her suffer. While admitting that her body is now in decay and her face all wrinkled, La Vieille remembers that as a young woman she was of an extraordinary beauty that would draw cohorts of paramours into her house. She would fill all of them with hopes by making them promises she knew she could not keep. As a consequence of her false speech, her house was often a site of physical aggressions, where many of her lovers fought with each other, losing their limbs, or even their lives (ll. 12782–93). Her lack of speech ethics is thus posited as the primary cause of violence in a private space that has turned into a site of open confrontations among men. A sin of speech identified by Peraldus as *indiscreta promissio* is underscored as the evil seed of psychological dramas, brawls, bodily mutilations, and death.[54]

As in Ami's case, La Vieille's idea of wisdom is very different from Raison's. For the latter, wisdom implies the ability to discern between good and evil and to opt for the righteous path in life. It means shunning temptations or vices and observing moderation in desires. At the same time, wisdom also

53. We can read La Vieille's self-praise in the context of two sins of the tongue that, as Richards astutely points out, Jean may have borrowed from Aquinas's philosophy of speech: *jactantia* (boasting) and *ironia,* in its medieval sense of self-abasement. Here is how Richards explains Jean's use of these two verbal deviations: "While Jean's part of the *Rose* is rife with dissimulation, the pertinence of Thomas' distinction between boasting and self-abasement is that all of the speakers in Jean's poem are anything but self-ironic, and they certainly all strut onto the stage in the *Rose* as overweening boasters with not the slightest hint of humility about them" ("*Les contraires choses:* Irony in Jean de Meun," 392).

54. La Vieille's narrative of sexual and linguistic transgressions is highly important in the economy of the poem as it grants the character autobiographical substance, a premiere in French literature (Beltrán notes that for the first time the representation of an old woman is enhanced by the addition of a personal background). Owing to La Vieille's biographical "wound"—her past of lust, ruse, and suffering—this section of the poem becomes more credible in the eyes of the audience. The critic deems the traditional interpretation of La Vieille as a spokesperson for Jean's misogyny too simplistic. Through her, Jean is neither offending women nor humiliating men; rather, he tries to bring the two genders together and to abolish the differences between them. By creating this moral confusion between sexes, the poet is "denying the validity of the duality Woman-Man as it was understood in his time" (Beltrán, "The Old Woman's Past," 90–95).

entails the ability to rein in one's tongue and speak with discernment.[55] La Vieille's teachings are diametrically opposed to these moral precepts. She confesses that her wisdom consists in knowing all the rules of the game of love, in which the woman is at times the duped and at others the duper. By virtue of this rich life experience, she has developed a solid corpus of knowledge—her *douctrine*—that she now imparts to Bel Accueil.[56]

One of the first steps the old prostitute takes in her disquisition is to deconstruct two major principles of courtly love: liberality and loyalty. Although being generous and faithful are commandments of the god of love, they are nothing but "false text" and "false letter" (l. 13036), she argues, keenly aware of the discrepancy between an unattainable ideal of love and its debasement in a society based on mercantile values. The problem with this argument is that the falseness of which La Vieille accuses courtly love represents the very essence of her being.[57] Just as for Ami it was morally licit to trick the trickster, so for La Vieille it is natural that a woman set her heart on several lovers, a notion that runs like a leitmotif throughout her speech. In this scheme, a woman should never offer her heart but sell it, and sell it well, to the man who offers the highest price for it. Deviant forms of speech—perjury, lies, and false promises—are strongly recommended as constitutive elements of the erotic game. These speech acts form the linguistic weaponry that any woman should master if she wants to seduce a man. Women should not be reluctant to swear falsely, for even God cannot take seriously a love oath uttered by a woman, but he readily forgives her: "S'ele est perjure, ne li chaille: / Dieus se rit de tel serement / Et le pardonne liement" ("If she perjures herself, it doesn't matter; God laughs at such an oath and pardons it gladly"; ll. 13128–30). To justify her endorsement of

55. Melinda Marsh Heywood interprets La Vieille as an ironic reworking of Boethius's Lady Philosophy, Jean's source for Dame Raison ("Lady Philosophy and La Vieille: Old Women, Aging Bodies, and Female Authority in Late Medieval French Literature" [PhD diss., University of Pennsylvania, 1997]). In Heywood's view, the distortions of the *Consolation* in La Vieille's speech serve Jean as *loci* for articulating a strong misogynistic discourse. For a complex study of the myriad ways in which the medieval imagination shaped the concept of woman, see Joan Ferrante, who also briefly analyzes La Vieille in contrast to Dame Raison (*Woman as Image in the Medieval Literature* (New York: Columbia University Press, 1975), 116–17).

56. Jean attaches an ironic slant to several terms pertaining to La Vieille's religious vocabulary: besides *douctrine,* used several times, we also encounter *endouctriner,* "to indoctrinate"; *sermonner,* "to sermonize"; and *preeschier,* "to preach," all used satirically.

57. The lover-narrator introduces her in the text as a *fausse vieille,* "a hypocritical old woman" (l. 12992).

such verbal acts, La Vieille invokes the pagan gods, with Jupiter at the forefront, who made of amorous false swearing a current practice.[58] In ancient times, it is because men saw their gods betraying their words that mortals felt justified in lying and making false promises, the character argues.

Across this veiled critique of mythic morality, perjury is obliquely condemned at the very moment that it is recommended. Once again, Jean weaves a contradiction into the intimate nature of a character so as to undermine his/her claims to moral truth and wisdom. La Vieille vividly advocates perjury, but, by invoking the values of the pagan world in which the gods themselves were compulsive liars, she implicitly subverts the very morality of the practice of swearing. From an artistic point of view, this constant discursive self-sabotage is a brilliant performance, and Jean develops this technique to the point that it becomes the hallmark of his art concerned with moral themes. Both Ami and La Vieille (and later on, Faus Semblant) strongly recommend the use of deceit in deeds and words, but the foundation of their recommendations is compromised by their highly doubtful moral outlook, or by the very contexts in which these recommendations are made. In La Vieille's case, perjury is legitimized by the mores of the ancient world, but to a Christian, this world populated by numerous gods is a priori mendacious. Thus, this form of legitimization simply does not stand, and the trust in human language is again sapped.

La Vieille reinforces her distrust of verbal communication by stressing that one must be a fool to believe the words of a lover just because (s)he swore they were true. Since lovers have changing hearts, they easily recant their vows: "Juene genz ne sont point estables; / Non sont li vieill souventes foiz, / Ainz mentent seremenz et foiz" ("Young men are in no way stable—nor, often times, are the old—and therefore they belie the oaths and faith that they have given"; ll. 13146–49). Consequently, a woman who loves only one man deserves all the suffering and torments of passion because fidelity is worthless. However experienced or versed in erotic tricks she may be, she cannot keep her lover for too long, for men have unstable hearts and are masters in the art of deceptive talk, adds the old woman as she enlists again the support of ancient myths. Aeneas repeatedly swore fidelity to Dido, but ended up betraying his words and abandoning her; because

58. For a more extended analysis of the way in which La Vieille recycles classical mythology, see Renate Blumenfeld-Kosinski, *Reading Myth: Classical Mythology and Its Interpretations in Medieval French Literature* (Stanford, Calif.: Stanford University Press, 1997), 58–62.

she trusted his fallacious speech, when he left, she suffered so much that she committed suicide. Phyllis also waited in vain for Demophon to keep his promise; he never came back to her, so she hanged herself. Paris had declared fidelity to Oenone in writing but was quick to forget his vows when he fell in love with the beautiful Helen. Jason belongs to the same gallery of perjurers in love, for he abandoned Medea after swearing that he would never leave her. For having trusted his passionate but mendacious words, when he left her, her suffering became so unbearable that she lost her mind and went on a killing rampage.[59] This long list of tragic mythical exempla meant to illustrate the currency of perjury among men becomes a new means of authorizing the female manipulation of the same verbal practice. The implication is that since men have remorselessly been employing verbal deceit from the beginning of time, why should not "modern" women do the same? Since all men cheat, lie, and frequent several women, why should not women act in the same way?

Because La Vieille's discourse indirectly projects the quintessential woman as ridden with vices, *Rose* criticism has typically viewed it as an occasion for Jean to structure his misogynistic views. The very length of this character's speech would establish her as an embodiment of the garrulous female, a topos in medieval literature.[60] We have to consider, however, that the length of La Vieille's disquisition is rather due to the Ovidian subtext (*Ars Amatoria* 3, the long speech of the male author to young ladies), from which Jean borrows extensively. Then we also have to remember that the old madam's discourse is strongly feminist and offers Jean the occasion to insert in his text disparaging statements about men. La Vieille justifies women's disingenuous ways as defensive reactions to male aggression and deceptive methods, and she depicts men as prototypical jerks. She piles up insult upon insult in describing them, whether she speaks of her own lovers or of the unfaithful men of classical antiquity. The old procuress not only curses men, but sadistically imagines physical tortures to which she would submit them if she could (ll. 12913–27).[61]

59. Both the love story between Phyllis and Demophon and that between Paris and Oenone are evoked succinctly, whereas those between Aeneas and Dido, and Jason and Medea, respectively, are told with a wealth of details. The last two couples are mentioned in Dante's *Comedy* as well.

60. R. Howard Bloch discusses the medieval conception of "women as riot," and exemplifies it with a few references to Jean de Meun's poem (*Medieval Misogyny and the Invention of Western Romantic Love* [Chicago: Chicago University Press, 1991], 17–22).

61. Sarah Kay pertinently labels La Vieille's speech as "the vocabulary of misogyny turned

In the *lectio* component of her speech, however, La Vieille teaches women how to render themselves agreeable to their male companions, namely how to dress up, how to eat, how to walk, and especially how to speak. Within the context of the usage of speech, she draws attention to the importance of being a smooth and sweet talker. Women ought not only to know songs and games but also to avoid all quarrel and contention. If they want to cry in front of a man in order to impress and manipulate him, they can do so, but in no circumstances should they betray their thoughts through words or deeds (ll. 13387–88). This piece of advice is reasserted in the context of the lesson on table manners, when women are strongly advised not to drink beyond measure, because they can lose not only verbal but any kind of control: “Et bien se gart qu'el ne s'enyvre / Car en homme ne en fame yvre / Ne puet avoir chose secree / Car puis que fame est enyvree, / Il n'a point en li de deffense, / Ainz jangle tout quanqu'el pense” (ll. 13453–58; “Now a lady must be careful not to get drunk, for a drunk, man or woman, cannot keep anything secret; and when a woman gets drunk, she has no defenses at all in her, but blurts out whatever she thinks and abandons herself to anyone when she gives herself over to such bad conduct”).[62]

However wicked the intention of a woman is, the appearance of decency must always be preserved; this is La Vieille's message. The constant interplay of essence and appearance that she recommends as a behavioral strategy in love confers tones of comedy to this section of the poem. Her advice is couched in moral language but placed in an immoral context. The old prostitute urges women, for instance, to go to church, but not for religious purposes. The church (just as festivals, weddings, parties, and other social occasions for fun) is only a good place for ladies to show themselves

---

against its authors” (“Women's Body of Knowledge: Epistemology and Misogyny in the *Romance of the Rose,*” in *Framing Medieval Bodies,* edited by Sarah Kay and Miri Rubin [Manchester: Manchester University Press, 1996], 218). I also agree with Nadine Bordessoule, who, analyzing La Vieille as an “impertinent woman,” argues that through her, Jean not only contributes to the late-medieval collapse of courtly love lyrics but also initiates a new, progressive discourse on the female condition (“*Fine Words on Closed Ears:* Impertinent Women, Discordant Voices, Discourteous Words,” in *Reassessing the Heroine in Medieval French Literature,* edited by Kathy M. Krause [Gainesville: University of Florida Press, 2001], 123–32).

62. The link between excessive food or drink and verbosity was common in the Middle Ages. Both Robert de Sorbonne (*De confessione*) and Laurent d'Orléans (*Somme le Roi*) treat verbal deviations along with gluttony as sins of the mouth (*peccata gulae*). For more on the link between *affluentia ciborum-inundatio verborum,* see Casagrande and Vecchio's chapter “La lingua tra *gula* e *loquacitas*” (*I peccati della lingua,* 141–68).

to men and enlarge the pool of amorous aspirants. In another instance, she warns that a woman should not readily yield to any man who makes her promises (*prometierres,* l. 13651), but should first verify whether he speaks with good intentions, springing from a pure heart, or, on the contrary, he has dishonorable plans about her.[63] But next, La Vieille teaches women how to take advantage of that man, how to dupe him with their words and get at his money. Language is thus wide open to all possibilities and can be used in any fraudulent ways, as long as these ways serve a woman's purposes. Even if a young lady has a thousand suitors, she has to promise her virginity and faithfulness to each and every one of them (ll. 13213–26). La Vieille encourages female speakers to swear falsely on God and the saints (she does so herself, several times in her discourse) and goes so far as to give women the actual words to say in fooling their lovers:

Cele qui puis a lui s'acorde / Et qui tant set de guiles faintes, / Dieu doit jurer et sainz et saintes / K'ainc ne se vost mais otroier / A nul, tant la seüst proier, / Et die: "Sire, c'est la soume, / Foi que doi saint Pere de Romme / Par fine amour a vous me don, / Car ce n'est pas pour vostre don. / N'est hons nez pour cui ce feïsse, / Pour nul don, tant grant le veïsse. / Maint vaillant homme ai refusé / Car mout ont maint a moi musé. / Si croi que m'avez enchantee: / Male chançon m'avez chantee!" / Lors le doit estroit acoler / Et baisier por mieux affoler. / Mes s'el veult mon conseil avoir, / N'entende a rien, fors a l'avoir. (13682–700)

In giving in to him, she, who knows so many wily ruses, should swear by God and by the saints that she has never wished to give herself to anyone, no matter how well he may have pleaded; then she should say, "My lord, this is my all; by the faith which I owe to Saint Peter of Rome, I give myself to you out of pure love, not because of your gifts. The man isn't born for whom I would do this for any gift, no matter how greatly he desired it. I have refused many a worthy man, for many have gazed adoringly at me. I think you must have cast a spell over me; you have sung me a wicked song." Then she should embrace him closely and kiss him so that he will be even better deluded.

Within this new lesson of rhetoric, no limits are imposed on female speech; rather, all of the moral rules are broken, since it is a woman's natural duty to lie, make false promises, and even shore everything up with biblical names as tokens of "truth." Everything is allowed in language, as lying, per-

63. The noun *promettieres* (very likely a coinage of Jean's) is hilarious, as it conveys that erotic promises were such a widespread habit that its practitioners acquired their own technical denomination, very much as liars who derive their name from the practice of lying, or flatterers who acquire theirs from practicing flattery.

jury, and blasphemy are fostered and raised to the level of a verbal art to be taught or imparted from generation to generation. The old woman's advice on female verbal behavior challenges the entire pastoral tradition on moral speech; she recommends what the authors of texts on *peccata linguae* forbid.[64] Through her agency, feminine language becomes sacrilegious language.

On a terminological level, La Vieille manipulates a rich word bank of fraud. A plethora of terms such as to cheat, to lie, to fake, to pretend, to perjure oneself, to hide, to dissimulate, flatterer, traitor, false, and disloyal create a linguistic web of deceit within which the character moves with nonchalance and which paves the way for the textual emergence of Faus Semblant. This lexicon of fraud is constantly paralleled by one of violence and obscenity, as the old madam evokes her wild lustful appetite and performances, or teaches sexual techniques in precise detail. The culminating point of La Vieille's discussion about violence occurs at the end of her discourse in the romance, when she recounts the story of her last amorous passion. The depiction of the relationship with her last lover (presumably her pander) takes a sadomasochistic turn when she describes him as despising her, beating her cruelly and then making love to her. She is now cursing him but also admitting that she enjoyed this mixture of violence and make-up sex so much that she became addicted to it.[65]

From the beginning of her disquisition, when she evoked her youthful beauty, erotic successes and victims, to this last personal anecdote, La Vieille uses language as a medium for remembering her amorous exploits, thereby transferring her sexual transgressions from life into the fabric of her discourse. What in her youth was a sin of flesh now becomes a sin in language.[66] The generic polarity of La Vieille's discourse, articulated as both an

64. Chaucer transferred many of La Vieille's linguistic transgressions to the Wife of Bath. For a subtle article on the deviant speech of Chaucer's female character and its relationship to Jean's La Vieille, see Edwin D. Craun, "*Allas, Allas! That evere Love was Synne:* Excuses for Sin and the Wife of Bath's Stars," in *The Hands of the Tongue,* 33–60.

65. The term La Vieille uses in reference to her last lover is *ribaud,* which Armand Strubel glosses as proxenete (765). A compelling analysis of La Vieille as a literary embodiment of female subjectivity in its relationship to desire is offered by Marilynn Desmond, who reads the old woman's speech in contrast to its main Latin source: the discourse on love from Ovid's *Ars Amatoria* 3. Desmond argues that by recasting Ovid's ironical message about eroticism as teachings, Jean inscribes the creation of La Vieille as an important phase in the vernacular reception of Ovid's book (*Ovid's "Art" and the "Wife of Bath,"* 125).

66. For a study of Jean's use of allegory in connection with his conception of sexuality, see Maureen Quilligan. Starting from the premise that all narrative allegory "focuses on the pro-

autobiographical confession and a mock sermon (Jean ironically qualifies her speech as *preeschier,* "preaching," l. 12743, and *sermonner,* "giving a sermon," l. 14552), allows the character to achieve logical coherence, since the confession serves her as a springboard for her teachings. That is to say, it is by authority of the confessed mistakes and heterosexual experience that she can tutor others in love. Thus, if she urges women to be their own secretaries, careful not to set up two amorous *rendez-vous* at the same time, it is because she failed in aptly scheduling her own encounters. If she instructs women on how to be their own accountants, it is because she herself was not able to keep the books of the material gains she had extracted from her lovers, and now she is completely broke.

The same generic bipolarity, however, serves Jean to dismantle La Vieille morally as he fashions her textually, for while the confessional component of her speech substantiates her teachings, it also works at cross-purposes with them. Specifically because La Vieille's confession projects her as a prostitute, a sinner in flesh, the same confession disqualifies her as a valuable preceptor/"preacher."[67] Her relationship to speech is so complex that La Vieille seems to resist any definition or classification. The medieval ethicists of speech, however, had a solution for such an ambiguous case of language use; they called it *peccati predicatio,* "the preaching of sin," and defined it as an abuse of language consisting in the public promotion of transgressive behaviors.[68] In their capacities of "benevolent" counselors, both Ami and La Vieille are preachers of sin, in that they use obscene language and strongly recommend the use of violence or fraud in human relationships. Through these characters' statements on the guile intrinsic to erotic games, Jean deconstructs the traditional code of courtly love, based on a series of gestural and linguistic attitudes that for him were mere fallacies. Love, this noble feel-

cess of language as its final subject," Quilligan argues that Jean uses obscene words in order to explode the conventions of courtly love that would have prevented him from speaking freely of the "limbs" ("Words and Sex: The Language of Allegory in the *De planctu naturae,* the *Roman de la Rose,* and Book III of the *Faerie Queene,*" *Allegorica* 2 [1977]: 195–216, at 195). Quilligan focuses only on Raison's and Genius's linguistic abuses, without taking into consideration La Vieille's speech.

67. Desmond also notes that La Vieille's evocation of her past undercuts the effectiveness of her instruction in love, as she ultimately advises Bel Accueil to "remain aloof from desire as a way of retaining control" (*Ovid's "Art" and the "Wife of Bath,"* 111).

68. See for instance *De lingua,* f° 208ᵛ, which describes the preacher of sin as an ape and minister of Satan, representing an evil perversion of the offices of pastor and teacher. For more on this sin see Casagrande and Vecchio (*I peccati della lingua,* 159–62).

ing, has lost its genuine essence and is now reduced to a struggle for power between men and women, a struggle in which each party competes to outwit the opposite sex through cunning and craftsmanship. As an evil counselor, the female character goes a step further than Ami, as she presses even religious language into the service of deceit and appropriates moral notions only to compromise and ridicule them. Both La Vieille and Ami (joined later by Faus Semblant and Genius) make of *peccati predicatio* an agenda and a way of textual life.[69] This moral ambiguity that allows the characters to distort the sacred function of preaching into exhortations to vices becomes a shrewd artistic device meant to ensure the cohesion of this dense polyphonic poem. Without this necessary discursive concatenation, the poem's scaffolding might have failed, undermined as it was by its hybridity and the shock of the opposing theses it conveyed.

But if we think that Jean is done with the issue of old women as soon as La Vielle leaves the stage, we are wrong. He comes back to them in a very surprising place, toward the end of the poem, to make a final point about them. Before approaching the rose in order to conquer her sexually, Amant pauses and becomes reflective, launching into a disquisition about the usefulness of erotic experimentation, a natural process that typically hinges on two principles: experimenting with young girls (what Jean calls “the new path”), or, even more profitable for young men, experimenting with old women (“the old road”). Amant/Jean starts by quoting Juvenal and Ovid's theory that sleeping with an old woman is a sure and fast way of making a fortune. He then warns that the man must be very careful not to do or say anything that looks like a ruse. For, unlike young women, who are gullible and believe all male lies as if they were sayings from the Gospel, old women, having been flattered and abused verbally and emotionally in their youth, have developed a very fine ear in detecting men's phony speeches. The epithets Jean uses to depict the erotically experienced old ladies are again highly corrosive: *corriace,* “hard-headed”; *chenues,* “hoary”; *malicieuses,* “evil”; *madrees,* “cunning”; “versees dans l'art de tromper” (“versed in the art of deception”): a very impressive list, obviously drawn with a lot of dislike and cynicism. This new parenthesis in the text offers a fresh word bank of fraud, as it minutely studies the ploys and tactics used in male-female

69. The conflict between La Vieille's (or Ami's) transgressive language and the norms for disciplined speech posited by the ethical tracts may also be accounted for from an intertextual perspective, since these two sections of the poem are a parodic distortion of Ovid's *Ars Amatoria.*

interactions. To Jean's credit, he lampoons not only the mores of aging women but also the theatrics deployed by false male lovers:

Li flajoleeur … / Qui par paroles les detiennent / Et as oreilles leur taborent, / Quant de leur grace avoir laborent, / Et souspirent et s'umilient, / Joignent les mains et merci crient / Et s'enclinent et s'agenoillent / Et pleurent si que tous se moillent, / Et devant euls se croicefient / Pour ce que plus en euls se fient, / Et leur promettent par faintises / Cuer et cors, avoir et servises, / Et leur fiancent et leur jurent / Les sainz qui sont, seront et furent, / Et les vont ainsi decevant / Par parole ou il n'a que vant. (21479–94)

These deceivers are those who detain the ladies with lies and drum into their ears their pleas for grace, who sigh and abase themselves, clasping their hands and crying out for favor, who bow down and kneel and flood everything with their tears, who cross themselves before their ladies so that they will have greater trust in them, who promise in sham their heart, bodies, possessions, and services, who pledge themselves and swear by all the saints that ever were, are, or shall be, and go around, thus deceiving with words that are only wind.

Jean further compares the male deceiver to a bird catcher, who hides like a thief in the bushes and spreads his snare for the bird, luring her there with sweet sounds. The foolish bird hears this enchanting music, but because she does not know how to answer the *sophisme,* "sophism," that has deceived her through a "figure of speech" (ll. 21502–04), she throws herself into the net. In contrast to such stupid birds, standing for inexperienced young girls, old women do not fall into this sort of traps; rather, they detect them immediately from the speeches they hear and the faces of their male predators. Jean emphatically reiterates the notion that experienced ladies are so afraid of being tricked again that they listen to male speeches very suspiciously and do their best to detect the lies that may hide therein. Such women, who have been fooled many times before and, therefore, think that all men want to deceive them, weigh each word said to them very carefully.

Once again, what is at stake in this parenthetical disquisition about the advantages of experimentation with females of all ages is not so much male erotic success, but the ability of language to secure a safe, pristine space, in which true love may spring and flourish. It is a new textual instance in which speech and fraud are placed in a perfect rapport of equivalence in the context of heterosexual relationships. Thus, even toward the end of the poem Jean stays true to his depiction of a corrupt world where genuine love is an obsolete reality that has been replaced by sex and money, just as language, this tool created to be a mirror of truth, has become a vile shelter for lies of all forms. What this passage also conveys obliquely is a hermeneutical suggestion or solution to the hotly debated problem of Jean's performance as a moralist, as a "teacher" of morals (I borrow this term from Jean's critics in the *Querelle de la Rose*). In lifting up the beautiful veil of rhetoric and revealing beneath it the ugly face of falsehood, Jean is sensitizing his readers to the snares of eloquence and of language, in general. As it will become again apparent in the (different) context of Faus Semblant, persuasive rhetoric is a dangerous tool of manipulation and spiritual destruction. Jean Gerson and Christine de Pizan will be wrong in accusing Jean de Meun of teaching vices. By revealing the fraudulent mechanisms that sustain love declarations or pseudo-Christian teachings, Jean is compelling his readers to mature in front of eloquence and to react to it similarly to the suspicious old women who cautiously weigh everything said to them. This is also how he wants his public to read his poem, with maturity and discernment, careful to distinguish between true virtues and the vices that, through the twisted workings of the satire, may masquerade as virtues.

Evil Counselors in the *Inferno*

Although in the episodes of Ami and La Vieille, Jean condemns the deviant use of rhetoric only obliquely, at the time when he was building these characters into his poem, the practice of counseling the use of fraud and violence was considered a mortal sin. Echoes of the moralists' severe condemnation reverberate in the *Comedy,* where this speech act is punished in Hell and represented by the tragic figures of Ulysses, Diomedes, and Guido da Montefeltro. A close reading of *Inferno* 26–27, the narrative of which unfolds in the eighth pouch of Malebolge, gives rise to two main hermeneutical difficulties. The first one stems from the apparent absence of the name of the sin punished in this location. In *Inferno* 11, where Virgil provides the taxonomic list for the transgressions of lower Hell, he does not specify the names of the sins assigned to pouches eight and nine but refers to these trespasses as *simile lordura,* "similar filth" (l. 60).[70] This strongly

70. The ambiguity of the phrase arises not so much from the noun *lordura,* "filth," for medieval ethics typically defined sinfulness as moral filth, as from the enigmatic *simile,* "similar." This adjective suggests that the sins from *bolgias* eight and nine are similar in their sordidness to those punished in the previous *bolgias,* since the phrase *simile lordura* occupies the last posi-

pejorative but vague phrase is partially disambiguated in the narrative of the ninth pouch, which focuses on the "seminator di scandalo e di scisma" ("sowers of schism and discord"; *Inf.* 28.35), a textual denomination generally accepted by scholars. For the eighth *bolgia,* however, the label *consiglio frodolente,* "fraudulent counsel," given in the text in reference to Guido da Montefeltro's sin, has not been as widely accepted, mainly because it does not seem to fit Ulysses, who is in the same pouch. As *Inferno* 26 does not name the sin for which the Greek warrior is punished (an omission that only compounds the mystery of the phrase *simile lordura*), Dante's interpreters have felt justified in disambiguating Ulysses's trespass in various ways: fraudulent counsel; *astutia,* "astuteness"; *falsa prudentia,* "false wisdom"; *superbia,* "pride"; *vana curiositas,* "vain curiosity"; betrayal; or evil use of *ingegno,* "intellect."[71]

The second hermeneutical node related to *Inferno* 26–27 derives from the nature of the *contrapasso* (the tongue-shaped flames enveloping the sinners) and has also engendered heated debates. Here, however, the *contrapasso* has best served the interpreters defending the thesis of Ulysses being punished for wrongful use of speech, since there is a figural correspondence between the tongue, an organ used to utter words, and the souls represented as tongues of fire.[72] Evil counsel, a scriptural term, was a common notion

tion in a long enumeration, in which the adjective *simile* functions as a deictic pointing back to the previous terms in the enumeration.

71. For an overview of the major interpretive engagements with Dante's Ulysses, see Anthony K. Cassell, "*Ulisseana*: A Bibliography of Dante's Ulysses to 1981," *Italian Culture* 3 (1981): 23–45, and more recently, Massimo Seriacopi, *All'estremo della "Prudentia": L'Ulisse di Dante* (Rome: Zauli, 1994). The latter offers ample recollections of the main discussions around Ulysses from the early commentators to the most recent. For an analysis of the interpretive flaws in the problem of Ulysses, see Barolini, who highlights the paradoxes inherent in the arguments of either the "pro-" or the "contra-Ulysseans." Those who glorify Ulysses forget the relevant fact that he is punished in Hell, whereas the "moralists" deny to Ulysses his thematic significance for the whole poem (*The Undivine Comedy,* 49–51).

72. Among the early commentators, Pietro Alighieri notes that the source for the *contrapasso* is the famous passage from the Epistle of St. James (3:5–8), where the tongue is described as a dangerous fire, harboring a great destructive potential (*Super Dantis ipsius genitoris Comoediam Commentarium,* edited by V. Nannucci [Florence: Garinei, 1844], 232). Richard Bates and Thomas Rendall have further substantiated Pietro's reference to the biblical source and concluded that the epistle is undoubtedly the source that served Dante in his figuration of the *contrapassso* for fraudulent counselors ("Dante's Ulysses and the Epistle of St. James," *Dante Studies* 107 [1989]: 33–44, at 35). Giuseppe Mazzotta makes a splendid connection between this *contrapasso* and Alain of Lille's description of rhetoric as *ignis in ore* from *Anticlaudianus*

in the Christian literature before Peraldus and Cavalca, but it is only with these authors that this speech act becomes a moral category within well-structured systems of verbal sins. The two theologians examine this ethical class by means of psychology, philosophical definitions (mostly metaphorical in Peraldus, more concrete in Cavalca), and exempla (a few in Peraldus, very numerous in Cavalca). Dante also treats fraudulent counsel as an ethical category by placing it in Malebolge and by enacting it through Ulysses and Guido da Montefeltro. My interpretation of *Inferno* 26–27 through the lenses of the medieval debate on the sins of the tongue will invalidate the critical position according to which Ulysses and Guido are not punished for *consiglio frodolente,* because there was no such moral category in the Middle Ages.[73] An examination of Peraldus's and Cavalca's theories of speech reveals that *pravum consilium* was an ethical class tightly connected with fraud.

Maria Corti and Bruno Porcelli have made important assertions about Dante's possible connections with the medieval theorists on the sins of the tongue. Corti has placed Ulysses's trespass in relationship to the topos of the *lingua ignea* from the pastoral tradition, and Bruno Porcelli has linked the sin of the eighth *bolgia* to the notion of *pravum consilium* as defined by William Peraldus. Recalling previous works by Siegfried Wenzel, Franco Mancini, and Carlo Delcorno, who have highlighted textual links between Peraldus's *SV* and the *Comedy,* Porcelli argues for Peraldus's influence on Dante's decision to incorporate the category of *consiglio frodolente* into the moral structure of Hell.[74] Although Porcelli does not analyze the treatment

(*Dante, Poet of the Desert,* 92). For Piero Boitani, too, this form of retribution figures a "tragedy of language" ("Beyond the Sunset: Dante's Ulysses in Another World," *Lectura Dantis* 9 [1991]: 34–53, at 38). In the same vein, James G. Truscott speaks of the flames as punishing the "misuse of the gift of counsel in speech" ("Ulysses and Guido: *Inferno* XXVI–XXVII," *Dante Studies* 91 [1974]: 47–59, at 54). More recently, Edwin Craun has pointed out that, along with the sword, fire is a central biblical representation of the tongue, "recast endlessly in medieval texts." In Craun's view, the metaphorical description of the tongue as fire is meant to illustrate the destructive power of speech (*The Hands of the Tongue,* ix).

73. It is mainly John Ahern who has denied the existence of *consiglio frodolente* as an established moral concept: "Nor do most readers realize that there is no Christian tradition of a sin of Fraudulent Counsel" ("Dante's Slyness: The Unnamed Sin of the Eighth Bolgia," *Romanic Review* 73, no. 3 (1982): 275–91, at 275). For a synopsis of the controversy around *fraudulent counsel,* see Michael Papio's note in the *Dante Encyclopedia,* edited by Richard Lansing (New York: Garland, 2000), 422–23.

74. Porcelli, "*Peccatum linguae*" 425–26.

of this sin in the Peraldian text, a closer look at "De peccato linguae" reveals subtle affinities with *Inferno* 26.

Peraldus assigns *pravum consilium* a central position (the twelfth vice) in his scheme and posits five reasons that should move people to the detestation of this speech act: 1. it is rooted in fraud and injures friends; 2. it is practiced by people capable of all evils; 3. it is self-destructive; 4. it is highly harmful to the Church; and 5. it upsets God and attracts divine punishment. Peraldus attempts to define *pravum consilium* through a description of the moral profile of the perpetrator, the *pravus consiliarius.* Compared to a traitor, the evil counselor uses deceitful words to betray the confidence of the people who seek him for spiritual guidance, and he harms his friend through fraudulent speech: "Pravus consiliarius proditor est. Decipit enim eum qui in eo confidit; scilicet eum qui ab eo consilium petit; quod non est parvum peccatum. Unde Prov. 26, Sicut noxius est qui mittit laceas et sagittas in mortem: ita vir qui *fraudulenter* nocet amico suo" ("The evil counselor is a traitor. For *he deceives* the one who trusts him and turns to him for counsel; and this is no small sin. Hence, the Proverb: 'like a mad man who casteth firebrands, arrows and death'—so is the man who does harm to his friend *through fraud.*").[75]

Endowed with *astutia,* evil counselors are expert in vices, and their verbal activity stems from great malice. Since they commit more evils than they can amend in a lifetime, there is no sin that hinders man's salvation more than evil counsel. *Pravum consilium* has tragic consequences not only for one's soul but also for the integrity of two major institutions—the militant Church and the body politic:

> Pravi consiliarii quasi omnia malum faciunt: sic tamen ut nihil mali fecisse videantur. Ipsi dant palmas in faciem Christi et in membris eius dicentes : "Prophetiza nobis, Christe, quis est qui te percussit ?" . . . quasi Dominus ignorare possit astutias eorum. . . . [P]eccatum istud multum nocivum est Ecclesiae Dei. Unus enim malus consiliarius destruit quandoque totam unam patriam. . . . [I]lli qui astuti sunt ad dandum consilia nociva aliis, in consulendo sibiipsis iusto Dei consilio fatui inveniuntur.[76]

The wicked counselors do evil like any other things, but *they do it in such a way as to look like they did nothing wrong.* They strike Jesus's face and limbs, saying: "Prophesy to us, Christ, who it is that beat you?" . . . as if God could not know *their ruse*. . . .

75. Peraldo, *Summa virtutum ac vitiorum,* 579; emphasis added.

76. Ibid., 579–80; emphasis added.

This sin is very harmful to God's Church. For an evil counselor destroys an entire country at one stroke.... They who are *astute* in advising others, in giving counsel to themselves are shown to be fools in God's just judgment. (emphasis added)

Cavalca deepens Peraldus's insights into this sin. In *Pungilingua,* the chapter devoted to evil counsel—"Del peccato de' mali consilieri e confortatori al male"—is significantly longer than Peraldus's section on *pravum consilium,* bespeaking the importance the matter of evil counsel had for the Italian moralist.[77] *Male consigliare,* Cavalca argues, has two subspecies corresponding to its two possible roots. It can be caused by ignorance when the counselor, on account of his poor judgment and advising skills, gives a piece of advice that further developments will prove wrong. This type of evil counsel is epitomized by a blind man who guides another blind man on the road and both fall into a ditch. And if physical blindness is so debilitating for the general health of the body, spiritual blindness is even more nocuous, for it causes prelates and clerics to give poor advice to Christians and to place the Church in danger.[78] Although it is caused by ignorance, not by an evil intention, this type of *male consigliare* is still a sin, because evil counselors are motivated by material profit, losing sight of an important moral precept: that one should not commit oneself to a mission if one is not well prepared or qualified for it. In this instance, Cavalca speaks of the negligence of those who, in need of advice, do not search for the best counselor but are satisfied with random advisors. Seeking good guidance in life is paramount, for a counselor is like a physician of the soul. If it is natural for a sick man to look for the best physician for his bodily condition, it is all the more urgent for a Christian to find the most appropriate counselor for afflictions pertaining to the soul.

The second species of evil counsel is even more harmful, because it is prompted by *malizia* and executed in perfect awareness and with delibera-

77. For an overview of Cavalca's ethical theories, see Francesco Falco, *Domenico Cavalca moralista* (Lucca: Tipografia del Serchio, 1982). More recently, Carla Casagrande has analyzed the relationship Cavalca established between disorders of the soul and moral transgressions ("Motions of the Heart and Sins: The *Specchio dei peccati* by Domenico Cavalca, OP," in *In the Garden of Evil: The Vices and Culture in the Middle Ages,* edited by Richard Newhauser [Toronto: Pontifical Institute of Medieval Studies, 2005]), and Carlo Delcorno has investigated Cavalca's narrative techniques in the vernacular ("Modelli agiografici e modelli narrativi: Tra Cavalca e Boccaccio," in *La Novella italiana: Atti del Convegno di Caprarola, 19–24 settembre 1988* [Rome: Salerno, 1989]).

78. Cavalca, *Pungilingua,* 181.

tion: "Ma vie più sommamente e più pericoloso e diabolico è il peccato di quelli, i quali saputamente ed a malizia danno mali consigli, ed a male inducono e confortano. E questo peccato è grave più e più, secondo la qualità della perversa intenzione di chi consiglia, o secondo il male che ne seguita, o può seguitare" ("But most of all and most dangerous and devilish is the sin of those who, knowingly and maliciously, give evil counsels, and drive and encourage people to do evil. And the gravity of this sin depends on the quality of the perverse intention of he who gives advice, and on the evil that ensues or may ensue").[79] Focusing on this second type of evil counsel, Cavalca isolates two important criteria in his definition of *male consigliare:* 1. malice as the root of evil advising and 2. its consequences. Either the perverse intention that underlies advising or the dire consequences that may derive from a piece of advice enable a moralist to identify a counsel as malicious. The speech of the evil counselor is fraudulent (a *parlare fraudolentemente*) and has diabolic roots, because just like the devil, the perverse counselor makes evil pass off as good: "sotto spezie di bene e di cosa lecita, a male induce e consiglia" ("under the guise of good and of a licit thing, he incites to, and counsels, evil").[80] The terms Cavalca uses to describe this deceit that takes place in language are strikingly similar to Dante's description of Geryon as a "sozza imagine di froda" ("filthy image of fraud"; *Inf.* 17.7): the monster has the face of a just man, but the lower part of his body is that of a dragon. Taking up Dante's imagery and transferring it to speech, we could label the verbal activity of the fraudulent counselors as Geryonic; their words bear the appearance of righteousness, whereas the essence of their speech is sheer evil.

The verbal suggestion of an advisor motivated by evil intentions is an unjust counsel—*iniquo consiglio*[81]—that eventually turns against the perpetrator himself. Most often, the deceiver falls into the trap set by his fraudulent suggestions, since Divine Justice not only alters the wicked advice but also ridicules the counselor's *astutia* by changing the course of events and reestablishing equity.[82] For instance, it is known that the Pharisees and leaders of the Jews advised the slaying of Christ in order to stop people from be-

79. Ibid., 182. Since there is no English version of *Pungilingua,* the translation of the passages I quote is mine.

80. Ibid.

81. Ibid., 183.

82. "Comprende Iddio i savi colle loro astuzie, e dissipa, e perverte i loro consigli, sicchè non gli possano reducere ad effetto.... Sono alquanti enfiati d'umana stoltizia e sapienza che vedendo che Iddio co' suoi giudici impedisce i suoi mali desideri, s'assottigliano con astuti consigli

lieving in him, but the exact opposite of their plan occurred, as people began worshipping Christ, and the new faith spread from Judea into the Roman world.[83]

For Cavalca, the biblical archetype of the evil counselor is the serpent, which advised Adam and Eve to taste the forbidden fruit, thereby deceiving them and causing them to sin. The fall of humankind from its Edenic state is thus the result of an astute counselor who, with skillful words, prompted two human souls to break a divine interdiction (*trapassar il segno* is the phrase Dante uses to describe the same event in the *Paradiso*). In a Christian world, the counselors who, like snakes, use their words to induce other people into evil, in fact betray those who trust them. The virtual betrayal that hides underneath friendly counseling makes it imperative for everyone to take extreme care in choosing counselors: "molto si debbe l'uomo guardare d'avere mali consiglieri e procurare d'avergli buoni."[84] The same imperative prevails for Dante when he analyzes the social consequences of the counselors' words and draws attention to the risks that political leaders incur when they choose inadequate advisors: "I am speaking to you, Charles and Frederick, and to you other princes and tyrants! Beware who sits by your side and offers advice, and count how many times a day your counselors call your attention to this end of human life" (*Convivio* 4.6.113–16).

---

e pensano di contrastare al consiglio ed alla disposizione di Dio. Ma per mirabile modo Dio sapientissimo gli conchiude sì, e comprende che al tutto per quella astuzia e per quella via, e per quello ingegno e consiglio, col quale credevano contrastare a Dio, sì fanno venire fornito il consiglio divino, sicchè appunto serve alla disposizione di Dio ciò che per l'umana astuzia gli contraddice" ("God knows the sages with their ruses, and dissipates, and alters their counsels, so that they cannot carry them out.... There are some inflated with human stupidity and wisdom who, seeing that God with his judgments prevents their evil desires, become subtle with astute counsels and think they can counter God's judgments and disposition. But in an awesome way, God the most wise thus controls them, and understands that entirely through that astuteness, and through that mental subtlety and counsel, with which they thought they could oppose God, the divine judgment is thus carried out, in such a way that God's disposition is served exactly by what opposes it"; ibid., 183–84).

83. Cavalca reproduces several biblical stories (from both the Old and the New Testaments) as exempla of wicked counsel, stories meant to illustrate the catastrophic repercussions of perverse suggestions. At the end of these stories, he concludes: "Or così potremmo contare molte istorie, per le quali si conchiude, e mostra che molti mali e guerre, e grandi ingiustizie sono fatte per gli consigli ed impronti" ("Now this way we could tell many stories, through which one concludes, and proves that many evils and wars, and great iniquities are done through counsels and suggestions"; ibid., 188).

84. Ibid., 189.

In Cavalca's view, the only perfect counselor is Christ. He is the only one who does not betray and who, in his great wisdom and charity, cannot err in his advice. As to the degree of gravity of evil counseling, no other sin seems to be more dangerous for one's soul and for social harmony and peace. In Peraldus this notion was mentioned only in passing, whereas in Cavalca it is amply developed and reiterated throughout the chapter:

E dico, che singolarmente questo peccato si grava per gli mali di colpa e di pena che ne seguita; che tutto dì per continua esperienza veggiamo, che uno male consigliere più guasta e dannifica in uno punto che non racconcia e non edifica tutto il tempo della vita sua in ciò che, consigliando ed ordinando una guerra, n'escono danni e guasti ed omicidi, e danni tanti e mali tanti e di colpa e di pena.... Sicché chi ben guata, nessun peccato è, che tanto impedisca la salute dell'uomo, quanto questo, per lo molto danno e male che ne procede, del quale tutto è tenuto a restituzione chi consigliò ed ordinò; senza la quale nessuno assolvere lo può, se egli è in istato che restituire possa. Ma pognamo che non possa, rade volte avviene che questi consiglieri di guerra bene si pentino e bene finiscano.[85]

And I say that the gravity of this sin may be gleaned from the evils of guilt and punishment that ensue; which we see every day by ongoing experience, for an evil counselor does more damage and harm at one moment than he can mend and build in all of his life, inasmuch as, by recommending and ordering a war, there follow so many harms and damages and murders, and so many harms and so many evils of guilt and punishment.... So that, if we consider things well, there is no other sin that hinders man's salvation more than this one, because of the harms that follow, for which he who gave advice and orders is called to atonement, if he is able to make amends, without which atonement no one can absolve him. But let us suppose that he cannot make amends; then it rarely happens that these war counselors repent well and end up well.

The moralists then minutely describes the economic and social disasters that can result from evil counsel: when a perverse piece of advice leads to war, many men lose their properties and become thieves or fall ill; women, by losing their families, become whores. All this collective sinfulness attracts divine anger and results in terrible punishments. Since every human being needs guidance in life, the individuals who assume the spiritual function of *consiglieri* take on a great responsibility. If they are bad counselors through poor judgment, they fail like a blind man leading the blind. If they are bad counselors through malice, they distort a Christic function and lose their souls.

85. Ibid., 186.

Cavalca's treatment of *male consigliare* as a form of fraudulent speech rooted in malice helps us better understand the narratives of the eighth pouch of Malebolge. In Dante's system of Hell, the disposition toward evil that is *malizia* is punished in Malebolge; fraudulent counsel is located in the eighth pouch of Malebolge as a sin of malice. Here, Dante encounters the mythic hero Ulysses and the Italian condottiere Guido da Montefeltro, both represented as tongue-shaped flames.

Ulysses What is particular about Ulysses's soul is that it is entwined in death with Diomedes, his companion from the Trojan War. Whereas every other soul inhabiting this pouch is enveloped by an individual flame, the souls of these two mythical heroes share the same, forked, flame. The only difference is that the horn of the flame representing Ulysses is bigger than the one hiding Diomedes. The reasons for the two Greeks' presence in this pouch are three, explains Virgil: the ambush of the horse, the "art" that caused Deïdamia's pain at the loss of Achilles, and the story of the Palladium (*Inf.* 26.55–60).

Evidence gathered by most modern critics supports the view that all three crimes involve, more or less manifestly, deceitful rhetorical habits related to Ulysses.[86] Sinon, thanks to whose lies the Trojans accept the horse into their city, is instructed by Ulysses on how to speak and what to say. The Trojan horse itself is a major fraud, and the way it is introduced into Troy is based on verbal fraud and manipulation. Cavalca's identification of a malicious counsel based on the consequences deriving from that counsel applies very well to this mythical episode. The destruction of the city following the success of Ulysses's stratagem confirms that Sinon's persuasive advice to the Trojans to accept the horse, a verbal performance orchestrated by Ulysses, was a malicious one. In the second crime as well, we deal with a fraudulent form of persuasion, with verbal suggestions that bear the appearance of truth but hide the repulsive face of a lie. Ulysses lures Achilles into joining him in the war with skillful words depicting the bright side of it: personal military fame. Ulysses does not mention what war really entails, the hideous, fatal side of it, but we know that Achilles will die on the battlefield,

86. According to James C. Truscott, the trap of the Trojan horse is based on an "implicit suggestion of false promise" ("Ulysses and Guido," 62). Truscott qualifies Sinon's speech to the Trojans as "eloquence commanded by Ulysses," and Giorgio Brugnoli calls Sinon "l'agente di Ulisse" ("Ulysses' agent"; "Dante Filologo: l'esempio di Ulisse," *Studi Danteschi* 3 [1998], 25).

triggering the great pain of Deïdamia, his wife. It seems that every time Ulysses opens his mouth, people around him die or suffer. As to the third crime evoked—the one related to the Palladium—David Thompson points out that, on the one hand, Dante's text does not mention the word "theft," and on the other hand, the giant Antenor, not Ulysses, is the real author of the theft.[87] Thompson does not exclude the possibility that Antenor stole the Palladium at Ulysses's and Diomedes's promptings. Thus, it is likely that even in this mythic episode Dante saw an indication of malicious counsel.[88]

In short, all three sins indicated by Virgil in relation to Ulysses and Diomedes involve verbal suggestions with a tragic consequence; in this case, the destruction of Trojan civilization. But we remember from Cavalca that God alters human counsels and turns tragedies into seeds of new prosperity. There is a divine counsel (here, in the sense of judgment and decision) that changes and corrects wicked human counsels (understood as verbal suggestions), and we see this correction at work in Dante's interpretation of the myth. Ulysses's and Diomedes's words targeted and ultimately caused the defeat of the Trojan nation, but Divine Providence intervened and turned the demise of the Trojans into the birth of a new people, the Romans. For in Dante's reading of the mythical events, the ambush of the horse made it possible for the noble seed of the Roman nation to spring (ll. 59–60).

In the story of Ulysses, Dante reserves for this character a completely different end than the one we know from Homer. Instead of ending peacefully in his country, surrounded by his faithful family, Ulysses abandons everything again and sets out on new adventures. Despite his old age, he is animated by one main desire: experience of the world, not only in a geographical sense but also in a moral one. He wishes to become expert in human vices and worth. A major element in Dante's reworking of the myth is the way in which Ulysses enlists the support of his crew for his adventurous projects—he talks to them.[89] The reproduction of this speech is made in

87. David Thompson, "A Note on Fraudulent Counsel," *Dante Studies* 92 (1974): 151.

88. As regards the real author of the theft, Thompson relies on an Italian source contemporary with Dante: Guido delle Colonne, who in *Historia destructionis Troiae* maintains that, although Ulysses was eventually accused of stealing the Palladium, it is Antenor who actually did it.

89. In Alan Deyermond's view, many aspects of *Inferno* 26 (including the forbidden voyage, the captain's address to the sailors, and the death of the crew) echo Alexander the Great's adventures in search for the Antipodes, adventures described by the *Libro de Alexandre* (ll.

Hell by Ulysses himself, who recounts to Virgil with what words he convinced his men to follow him:[90]

"O frati," dissi, "che per cento milia
perigli siete giunti a l'occidente,
a questa tanto picciola vigilia
d'i nostri sensi ch'è del rimanente
non vogliate negar l'esperïenza,
di retro al sol, del mondo sanza gente.
Considerate la vosta semenza:
fatti non foste a viver come bruti,
ma per seguire virtute e canoscenza."
(*Inf.* 26.112–20)

"O brothers," I said, "who through a hundred / thousand perils have reached the west, to this so / brief vigil / of our senses that remains, do not deny the / experience, following the sun, of the world without / people. Consider your sowing: you were not made to live / like brutes, but to follow virtue and knowledge."

Ulysses's handling of the ethical vocabulary projects a shadow over the moral quality of his speech; there is a tension between the notions *vice* and *virtue* that he withholds from his crew. He reserves for himself the expertise in vices, whereas to his men he speaks only about virtue and knowledge. The wish to be an expert in human sinfulness is itself intriguing, for how can one be an *esperto* other than by experiencing the vices, by exploring the entire spectrum of evil inclinations? The tradition of Ulysses *hortator scelerum* on which Dante relies excludes the option of the Greek's gaining expertise in vices only by watching them in others.[91] Ulysses's desire to

---

2288–99). In these lines of the famous Spanish poem, Alexander's misfortunes are compared with Ulysses's. Deyermond argues that Dante knew this poem from his teacher, Brunetto Latini, who had spent some time at the court of Alfonso el Sabio, where the *Libro de Alexandre* was well known ("El Alejandro medieval, el Ulises de Dante y la busqueda de las Antipodas," in *Maravillas, peregrinaciones y utopias: Literatura de viajes en el mundo romanico* [València: Universitat de València, 2002], 28–29).

90. Ulysses's speech to his aging crew represents one of the factors of controversy around Ulysses. Massimo Seriacopi points out that the early commentators did not consider this discourse a trap; only the modern interpreters have done so. Seriacopi himself considers that Ulysses's *orazion* is free from any sign of deceit, despite the hero's blatant persuasive qualities. The prevalent opinion among modern critics is, however, that the *orazion* is a fraud. (Seriacopi, *All'estremo della "Prudentia": L'Ulisse di Dante* [Rome: Zauli, 1994]).

91. As to the sources for Dante's story of Ulysses, critics have indicated two main texts: Virgil's *Aeneid,* where the rare references to Ulysses are mainly negative, and Statius's *Achilleid* (Mark Musa, "Virgil's Ulysses and Ulysses' Diomedes," *Dante Studies* 97 (1978): 187–93). Brugnoli finds in *Achilleid* I the most significant of Ulysses's fraudulent discourses, most of which are addressed to people of good faith who trust him—the good king Licomedes and the young Achilles ("Dante Filologo," 27–38). Suzanne C. Hagedorn also points out that it is in this part of *Achilleid* (1.472) that Ulysses is described as "sleepless in counsel" (*Abandoned*

become a specialist in *li vizi umani* is one of the most interesting things he says about himself. Other than Dante, who at the end of his poetic journey through the three realms will be the *Comedy*'s true expert in vices and virtues, there is only one other being who can lay claim to expertise in sins in the Inferno. This is Minos, the monster who judges the newly arrived souls in Hell and who, with the flicking of a tail, sends the souls to specific infernal areas (*Inf.* 5.7–12). Ulysses's plan to become an expert in human sinfulness, far from being a noble ideal, tarnishes him and dooms him to Hell.[92]

Isidore of Seville's thought on sin can best explain the ambiguity of Ulysses's moral profile. The medieval theologian notes that it is typical only of the hypocrite to masquerade his vices as virtues through slyness. Whereas all other sins can be committed by simple-minded people, deceit and hypocrisy can be practiced only by those endowed with a superior type of intelligence that allows them to disguise their evil habits into virtues.[93] At the same time, we should not forget that both "De peccato linguae" and *Pungilingua* posit the expertise in vices as a main characteristic of the depraved advisor. Cavalca's treatment of malicious counsel validates the *orazion* as a form of linguistic fraud. The moralist defines the notion of *consiglio* as "una esaminata ragione d'alcuna cosa fare, o non fare" ("a well-considered reason for doing or not doing something"; 190). When giving a piece of advice, one has to take into account four considerations: one, what is expedient and useful; two, what is easy; three, what is certain; and four, what is safe. By the same token, in order for one to give good counsel, one has to choose and recommend the useful and necessary thing instead of the nonuseful, the easy instead of the difficult, the certain instead of the uncertain, and, finally, the safe instead of the dangerous (190).

In the address to his crew, Ulysses does not observe any of these req-

---

Women: Rewriting the Classics in Dante, Boccaccio and Chaucer [Ann Arbor: Michigan University Press, 2004], 57).

92. In this light, I cannot agree with Mario Trovato, who reads *Inf.* 26. 90–105 as "il momento giulivo della conversione di Ulisse alla sapienza; distacco non solo dal mondo del peccato, ma degli affetti più puri" ("the climactic moment of Ulysses's conversion to wisdom; detachment not only from the world of sin but also from that of the most pure feelings"; "Il Contrapasso nell'ottava bolgia," *Dante Studies* 94 [1976]: 47–59, at 49). There is not enough evidence in the text to support a moral conversion of Ulysses; there is, indeed, a detachment from family life and love of country, but the idea of expertise in vices undermines Trovato's claim that Ulysses also detached himself from the world of sin.

93. Isidore of Seville, *Sententiarum libri,* Patrologia Latina 83, cols 537–738.

uisites for good counsel. The new adventures in which the Greek asks his fellow men to accompany him are neither useful nor necessary to them, but to himself alone. This new enterprise is not easy since it requires the exploration of land hitherto uncharted. It is a project that involves dangers, for the sailors do not know what awaits them beyond Hercules's pillars. These pillars are markers beyond which no living man has ever ventured; they are signs of a divine interdiction. Like the evil-counseling serpent in the biblical story told by Cavalca, Ulysses has his companions transgress this interdiction—a new *trapassar del segno* of which he is the unique cause. The end result of his exhortations is the death of the entire crew. Ulysses's speech to his men has a Geryonic dimension insofar as his high-flown rhetoric manipulates and promises something it cannot offer. This is why, in Hell, the character is punished in the "post-Geryon world," to take up Barolini's phrase. Unmoored from the context of the Malebolge, Ulysses's speech could convince readers of its sincerity, but the fact that this speech is framed by the infernal area of fraud undermines its claims to sincerity and nobility.

Giuseppe Mazzotta points out that the weakness of rhetoric is that it promises things whose fulfillment depends on extradiscursive conjunctures.[94] In this context, the end Dante reserves for Ulysses and his crew highlights the *orazion*'s emptiness and speciousness. The words of the "little speech" fall into the same category as Jason's; they seduce because they promise but eventually give nothing in return. Like Jason's, Ulysses's words are merely *parole ornate* that deceive through their false beauty. Ulysses's speech is Geryonic, inasmuch as his dual rhetoric seduces but ultimately leads to disaster. As a symbol of human failure, the shipwreck marking the death of the sailors invalidates the nobility to which the *orazion* lays claim. Thus, although I do acknowledge Ulysses's intelligence, my sense is that we have to focus not on the intellectual but on the moral type Dante proposes through him. The classical nobility conveyed by the *orazion* is what Ulysses could have represented, had he really converted his vices into virtues. But the Greek's statements in the "little speech" are different from his actual deeds. This is why he is not among the *spiriti magni* in Limbo but is punished in Hell in the spiritual area of fraud.[95]

94. Giuseppe Mazzotta has devoted memorable pages to the connection between Ulysses's rhetoric and fraud (*Dante, Poet of the Desert,* 69–106).

95. As to Dante's relationship to Ulysses, excellent studies have been written over the years

Guido A companion of Ulysses in Dante's underworld, in the sense that they share the same location and the same punishment, is Guido da Montefeltro, an important political leader in Dante's time. Famous for his political cunning, Guido was a public figure whose movements and gestures could have hardly escaped popular attention. One of his publicly known gestures was his conversion to Franciscanism, a conversion that occurred in his later years and earned him Dante's esteem in *Convivio.*[96] A vague echo of this esteem still resonates in *Inferno* 27, where Guido's speech is couched in courteous terms. Here, the soul reverently asks the travelers to give him news about Romagna, his native land. It is worth mentioning that Guido does not inquire about the fate of his relatives, but about the state of his country. He wants to know whether Romagna is at war or not. Like his reverent speech, this noble concern for the good of the earthly community to which he belonged projects Guido as an almost positive figure. Prompted by Virgil, Dante gives Guido disturbing news about the sociopolitical situation of the Italian cities, torn apart by war, *mal governo,* and *tirannia.*

Against the dark background of this ethical-political denunciation, Guido introduces himself as a renowned politician, whose works had been not those of a lion but of a fox.[97] A professional of moral and political duplicity, Guido was well aware of the spiritual consequences of his methods; therefore, he says, when he grew old, he had a moment of *metanoia* and took shelter in religious life.[98] His new status as a penitent was, however, in-

by Jurij Lotman, John Freccero, Giuseppe Mazzotta, Teodolinda Barolini, and others. Repeating their theories about the (non) identity between Ulysses and Dante would be, as Barolini justly points out, echoing what is by now "critical dogma." I will only quote the latter, who, analyzing the Ulysses theme in rapport with Dante's writerly undertaking, reaches the conclusion that "Ulysses reflects Dante's conscious concern for himself.... [He is] the lightning rod Dante places in his poem to attract and defuse his own consciousness of the presumption involved in anointing oneself God's scribe" (*The Undivine Comedy,* 52).

96. *Convivio* 4.28.40–43. Critics point out that at the time when *Convivio* was written, news about Guido's last fraudulent action had not yet spread.

97. As far as the phrase *di volpe* is concerned, a good deal of light is shed on its medieval meaning by Alain of Lille's dictionary, where the word *vulpes,* "fox," designates *homines fraudulenti,* "fraudulent men" (*Distinctiones dictionum theologicalium,* col. 1011B).

98. For Lino Pertile, who does not trust Guido's rhetoric, this conversion is not a deeply felt act but a cold, calculated move meant to win the ultimate prize in life—salvation ("*Inferno* XXVII: Il Peccato di Guido da Montefeltro," *Atti dell'Istituto Veneto di Scienze, Lettere ed Arti* 141 (1982–1983): 153). In Pertile's view, Guido and Ulysses are punished for their astuteness, and Guido's reproduction of the black cherubim's phrase (*consiglio frodolente*) is just an attempt to minimize his sinfulness and shift the pilgrim's attention from him to the pope (153–54, 163).

terrupted by a last temptation offered by Pope Boniface VIII, who, unable to conquer the city of Palestrina, appealed to him for advice. In exchange, *il gran prete,* "the great priest"—for whom now, in Hell, Guido reserves the harshest words—offered the counselor the promise of absolution.

The terms of negotiations between the two men reveal their awareness of what was ultimately at stake: eternal salvation, the supreme Christian good. Boniface's great promise translates his acknowledgment of the fact that what he was asking of his counselor was not something right but an encouragement to evil, a *confortare al male,* as Cavalca would have put it. The earthly "shepherd," who is supposed to be the supreme spiritual guide, the most honest of counselors, comes in all awareness to ask for the endorsement of an evil plan. Boniface is a Jack-of-all-trades type of politician who comes to another reputedly malicious politician to ask for a suggestion that he does not expect to be righteous. For both men, religiosity and sacred concepts are just masks that fall off when greed or deeply ingrained patterns of corruption are activated.

The words that Guido, the former political advisor, uses to describe the pope's mental state—*guerir, febbre,* and *ebbre*—are remarkably similar to Cavalca's lexicon of counseling as healing. Guido himself, at hearing Boniface's request, is conscious of what is expected of him; the term *peccato* he uses in his dialogue with the pope indicates this awareness. He knows that, by giving the pope the advice he needs to conquer the city (and only devious ways will work here), he commits a moral transgression. Manipulating words and their effects was presumably one of Guido's best *opere di volpe.* Here, his sin consists in teaching Boniface how to make false promises (*indiscreta promissio*!). The sin of *male consigliare* is in a synonymic relationship with the inducement into evil (*confortare al male*) in Cavalca's ethical system, and this synonymy illuminates Guido's placement in the same zone with Ulysses. Through their verbal suggestions, both Ulysses and Guido induced other people into transgressive actions. As a spiritual advisor, Guido realized that the pope was a morally ill man; the series of words with medical resonance and the half-medical, half-moral term *consiglio* placed in the middle of this series contribute to the idea of fraud as illness. And yet, instead of healing the pope with a truly Christian message, Guido aggravated his fever and state of frenzy with the exhortation to further sins.

After death, however, one has to give account for one's malicious advice. Cavalca repeatedly warns that unrighteous counselors never end up well; the divine penalty for evil counseling is, unavoidably, the loss of the soul ("il misero consigliere pure ne pierde l'anima").[99] This severe moral pronouncement is splendidly exemplified in the dramatic account of Guido's death, when St. Francis comes down to take his soul to heaven but is "defeated" by a black Cherub, who establishes that the friar's place is with the infernal orders. As a religious man, Guido was supposed to know that the divine punishment for the kind of *peccato* of which he spoke to Boniface was very serious. The same holds for Boniface, who, as a leader in spiritual matters, knew what type of risks and consequences sins incurred. Otherwise, the entire discussion about absolution from sins as a recompense for Guido's help would have been futile. And yet, the papal power eventually turned out to be a kind of fraud as well, for the pope was unable to deliver the absolution he had promised to his political counselor.

Both Dante's handling of this episode and *Pungilingua*'s treatment of *male consigliare* convey the notion that no human promise, judgment, or decision can compete with higher, divine laws. Cavalca asserts that very often evil counselors themselves fall into the traps they set: "Sicchè eglino per giusto giudicio di Dio caggiono in quella fossa ed in quello lacciulo ch' eglino apparecchiavano per altrui. Sicchè bene si verifica il detto de' Proverbi, che chi ordina lo iniquo consiglio, sì gli torna in capo" ("So those men, through God's fair judgment, fall into the same ditch and trap they were preparing for the other. Therefore, this confirms the saying of the Proverbs: the unfair advice turns against the head of he who gave it").[100] The way in which the corrupt Franciscan friar ends can be seen as an exemplification of Cavalca's warning, since Guido, the promoter of false promises, falls prey to Boniface's own (impossible to keep) promise of absolution. The forgiveness of sin granted by the corrupt father of the Church availed Guido nothing at the moment of his death, for the devil still prevailed over St. Francis in the conflict for the counselor's soul.[101] Both Dante's text and Cavalca's treatment of malicious counsel tell us that, however great the power of forgiveness held by ecclesiastics is, there is a greater power above the Church, which, if the Church is corrupted by wicked leaders, annuls the ecclesiastic

99. Cavalca, *Pungilingua*, 183.

100. Ibid.

101. Analyzing the brief explanatory speech that the devil gave during this battle (a speech cited by Guido himself), Gabriele Muresu reaches the interesting conclusion that this battle actually never happened; it is only Guido's invention ("La Rancura di Guido da Montefeltro (*Inferno* XXVII)," *Studi Danteschi* 70 [2005]: 47–86, at 84–85). I cannot agree with Muresu's conclusion, since Guido's presence in Malebolge actually proves that the devil had the "last word" in the battle for the sinner's soul.

absolution and ridicules the so-called wise. No power in the world, however great and cunning that power may be, can change God's laws; therefore, the prelates' capacity for absolution is stymied when it contravenes fundamental moral rules such as justice and charity. This is the lesson that *Inferno* 27 sets forth and this is also the conclusion that Domenico Cavalca, Dante's contemporary, reaches in his chapter devoted to evil counselors:

> Or ecco dunque, come Iddio perverte i consigli umani; e, come dice il Salmista: Il suo consiglio sta fermo in eterno. Sicchè, come dice la Scrittura: Non è consiglio, nè prudenza, nè sapienza contra a Dio.... Che poichè immutare non si può il divino consiglio e la divina sentenza, in ogni cosa dobbiamo inchinare le spalle, e sottometterci alla sua santissima volontà. Or questo sia detto contro agli stolti savi del mondo che credono con loro astuzie fuggire, o impedire i giudici, o i consigli divini.[102]

> So this is how God alters human counsels; and, as the Psalmist says: His counsel stays firm in eternity. Therefore, as the Scripture says: There is no advice, no prudence, no wisdom against God.... For since the divine counsel and the divine sentence cannot be changed, in everything we do we have to bend our backs and submit to his most sacred will. And this is to be said against the foolish wise of the world who believe that they can shun or circumvent divine judgments or counsels with their ploys.

A reading of *Inferno* 26–27 from the perspective of the pastoral discourse on *peccata linguae* proves that the sin punished in the eighth pouch of Malebolge is *consiglio frodolente.* Ahern's argument that "neither *consiliari male,* nor *pravum consilium* are synonymous with *consiglio frodolente*" is not tenable, since in the *trattatistica morale* of the time *pravum consilium* was tightly connected with, and defined in terms of, fraud.[103] Of all the features of *pravum consilium,* for Dante the most salient one was fraudulence. This aspect was also the most relevant to his ethical system (to Malebolge, in particular). The two main moral readings I have proposed—Peraldus and Cavalca—demonstrate that the other transgressions that critics have posited as alternatives—*astutia,* injustice, betrayal—are not different from *consiglio frodolente,* but typical traits of it. Far from being a "preposterous misnomer," as Anna Hatcher has argued, *consiglio frodolente* is an appropriate label for the sin punished in the eighth pouch of Malebolge.[104] Writ-

102. Cavalca, *Pungilingua,* 185.

103. Ahern, "Dante's Slyness," 276.

104. Anna Hatcher, "Dante's Ulysses and Guido da Montefeltro," *Dante Studies* 88 (1970): 109–17, at 110. One of the reasons why Hatcher argues against this denomination is the distinction she makes between "the use of fraud in counseling" (as embodied by Ulysses) and "counseling the use of fraud" (as personified by Guido da Montefeltro). This distinction is, however,

ten after "De peccato linguae" and before *Pungilingua,* cantos 26 and 27 of the *Inferno* mark an exceptional moment in the history of an important moral concept linking speech, ethics, politics, and salvation. With the psychological sharpness germane to a moralist, Dante lifts up a modern ethical category and applies it like a psychoanalytical grid not only to his contemporaries but also to the cultural material of classical antiquity. Thanks to the poetic enterprise of the *Comedy,* the notion of *pravum consilium* leaves the stern and abstract sphere of the medieval ethics in Latin and enters the realm of vernacular poetry, coming to life through the memorable characters of Ulysses and Guido da Montefeltro.

A text written in Renaissance France by a fine analyst of secular history, Michel de Montaigne, may also shed light on the pairing of Guido with Ulysses in *bolgia* eight. In Book 1, chapter 5 of his *Essays,* where Montaigne analyzes the classical Roman philosophy of war in contrast to the Greek one, he notes that whereas for the Romans a war had to be won through military virtue and prowess, for the Greeks, it was more glorious to win a war through guile and fraud. He remarks that the *anciens Florentins,* "medieval Florentines," were the proud heirs of the Roman war ethics, and he exemplifies this viewpoint with a historical anecdote highlighting Florentine ethical qualities in combat.[105] Montaigne's text is a splendid lens through which we can look at *Inferno* 26–27 and understand why a medieval Florentine poet, whose life was deeply marked by wars, punishes a Greek warrior famous for his cunning in the same *bolgia* with an Italian *condottiere* who sinned by adhering not to the Roman war philosophy, a natural cultural heritage, but to the Greek one. In the *Inferno,* Ulysses represents the remote origin of fraudulent verbal practices, whereas Guido, the presence of these practices in contemporary Italy. If Peraldus and Cavalca sketch out the moral profile of the malicious counselor, in *Inferno* 26–27 Dante gives his readers concrete examples of fraudulent counselors in action, examples that continue to fascinate generations of readers.

---

inoperative, since the medieval notion of evil counsel is extremely elastic and encompasses both meanings. A reading of the dozen of exemplary stories told by Cavalca to illustrate this sin reveals a much greater variety of fraudulent facets than these two detected by Hatcher.

105. Michel de Montaigne, *Les Essays,* edited by Pierre Villey (Paris: Presses Universitaires de France, 1992), 26. Since the Florentines believed that attacking an enemy by surprise was unfair, they would take care to warn their enemies of an attack at least one month in advance by having their war bell "Martinella" sound continuously (ibid., 26).

BILINGUIUM, "DOUBLE TALK," IN FAUS SEMBLANT'S DISCOURSE

The problem of Faus Semblant in criticism of the *Rose* is similar to "il problema di Ulisse" in Dante studies. Over the course of time, the two characters have sparked a considerable amount of controversy among critics and caused passionate polemical writings. If the question related to Ulysses concerns the exact sin for which Dante punished him in Hell, the controversy around Faus Semblant debates the rationale for his very textual genesis. *Rose* interpreters have sought to understand and explain why Jean created this evil character, who has little to do with the plot of the romance. Some of the critics (C. S. Lewis and William W. Ryding, in particular) argue that Faus Semblant is an unnecessary personage, generating a great deal of extraneous and irrelevant poetic material; some others offer strong arguments for the necessity of his presence in the text.[106]

Like Ami and La Vieille, Faus Semblant is a hybrid literary construct, displaying not only abstract moral features but also a biography grounded in the social realities of the time. As a poetic artifact he presents such a complex intertwining of allegorical and concrete traits that if I operate a disjunction between allegory and history, it is only for analytical purposes. Even within the framework of *allegoresis,* Faus Semblant is not a typical representative, in the sense that he cannot be interpreted as the personification of a single vice in the old-fashioned mode of Prudentius's *Psychomachia.* He embodies so many vices and crimes that he becomes the absolute allegory of human evil, in all of its hideous manifestations. On the level of the plot, at the promptings of the god of love, who repeatedly calls him

106. In her groundbreaking study of the semiotic structures of deceit in the *Rose,* Susan Stakel sees Faus Semblant as the main site where Jean articulates his literary treatment of moral duplicity (*False Roses: Structures of Duality and Deceit* [Saratoga, Calif.: Anma Libri, 1991]). Richard K. Emmerson and Ronald B. Herzman ("The Apocalyptic Age of Hypocrisy: Faus Semblant and Amant in the *Roman de la Rose,*" *Speculum* 62, no. 3 [1987]: 612–34) interpret the controversial character as a key element for understanding the poem's apocalyptic framework, while Sarah Kay (*The Romance of the Rose* [London: Grant & Cutler, 1995]) reads this section of the poem as the locus where two essential literary techniques (allegory and irony) converge. Finally, Kevin Brownlee argues that Faus Semblant's discourse is vital to the poem because it provides "one of the most important meditations on the status of language" ("The Problem of Faus Semblant: Language, History, and Truth in the *Roman de la Rose,*" in *The New Medievalism,* edited by Kevin Brownlee and Marina Scordilis-Brownlee [Baltimore: Johns Hopkins University Press, 1991], 253).

"devil," Faus Semblant himself reveals that he works for Antichrist, does not fear God, and will be active on the social stage "tant comme li mondes dure" ("as long as the world lasts"; l. 12345).

If on an allegorical level he is the personification of sheer evil (or the devil himself), historically, he is rooted in Jean's own time. The writer casts Faus Semblant as the representative of the mendicant friars (Dominicans, especially), who played a central and controversial role in the religious arena of the thirteenth–fourteenth centuries. By virtue of his historically grounded biography, Faus Semblant acquires a distinctive social identity: he is a preacher and a confessor. However, these two ecclesiastic functions are deeply altered, insofar as he admits to leading a deeply immoral way of life: "Mais en quelque lieu que je viengne, / Ne comment que je m'i contiengne, / Nient plus fors barat n'i chaz. / Ausi com dant Tyberz li chaz / N'entent qu'a soriz et a raz, / N'entent je a riens fors a baraz" ("But whatever place I come to, no matter how I conduct myself, I pursue nothing but fraud. No more than Tibert, the cat, has his mind on anything but mice and rats, do I think of anything except fraud"; ll. 11069–74).

Why Jean builds into his poem such an immoral character and why the author's view of the mendicant friars is so radically negative are questions that can best be answered by a fresh look at a source dear to Jean: William of St. Amour.[107] Passionately engaged in criticism against the fraternal orders that had acquired teaching positions the University of Paris, William wrote several antimendicant texts that rapidly earned him both popularity and enemies. The most notorious of these texts, *De periculis novissimorum temporum* (On the dangers of the last times), written in 1256, would fuel the conflict between the secular clergy and the fraternal orders for many years to come.[108] The author was outraged by the great religious and social privileges of the Franciscan and Dominican orders and by the extremist

107. Following upon a suggestion made by Ernest Langlois, Penn Szittya notes that Faus Semblant's discourse is heavily charged with William of St. Amour's antifraternal ideas (*The Antifraternal Tradition in Medieval Literature* [Princeton, N.J.: Princeton University Press, 1986], 186). It is worth adding that as a result of the influence of William's texts on Jean, the Faus Semblant episode itself would be considered subversive by some of its readers. Sylvia Huot notes that some scribal editors of the *Rose* warned that this episode was not suitable for wide dissemination and consequently removed the passages they considered ideologically too dangerous (*The "Romance of the Rose,"* 17).

108. For the text of *De periculis* I use *De Periculis novissimorum temporum,* edited by G. Geltner (Paris: Peeters, 2008), whereas for the other works I rely on *Opera omnia* (Constance, 1632).

Christian movement initiated by Joachim of Fiore. Although these religious have great rhetorical skills, William admits, their rhetoric is nothing but poison, for it does not spring from the heart but from a devilish thirst for powers and privileges. These false preachers corrupt people's morals and drive them away from true faith, for they are corrupt and heretics themselves.[109] Because the intelligence and the oratorical talent of the friars are real, people of good faith cannot recognize them as false preachers but succumb to their diabolical power of seduction. *De periculis* further draws attention to the heretical climate of the day and calls for Christians to unmask the friars as false apostles prefiguring the coming of the Antichrist. Feeling compelled to teach his audience how to recognize them, William draws a long list of *signa,* "signs," based on which the friars can be identified as forerunners of the Antichrist.[110]

The *Signa* in the "Rose"

Jean praises William's work, expressing sympathy for its oppressed and exiled author (ll. 11510–18). The name Faus Semblant itself was suggested to Jean by a character in Rutebeuf's *Complainte de William de St. Amour* (William of St. Amour's complaint). Jean actually assimilated many of William's *signa* for identifying a hypocritical preacher and used them as representational devices for patterning the textual behavior of Faus Semblant. Pinpointing these signs is not without a challenge, for Faus Semblant's speech is not mono-vocal. In many places he speaks as a fraudulent ecclesiastic, whereas in many others he goes in the opposite direction and assumes the voice of the moralist, criticizing and exposing the false religious. The longest passage exhibiting a complete and overt identification between Faus Semblant's words and William's voice is the discussion of licit mendicancy (ll. 11291–512). Here Jean names William twice and examines six cases of morally justified beggary, using all the arguments and examples furnished by *De periculis.* It is an interesting case of medieval intertextuality,

109. "And yet their counsels will become exceedingly dangerous, since ultimately they will be men of degenerate manners and of corrupted faith.... Eventually, as they will lead the Christian leaders and people in the said ways away from the prelates' counsels and later from obedience to them, so they will easily send them into error, both against good customs and against faith" (*De periculis,* 65).

110. For an in-depth analysis of the historical context, the agenda, and the afterlife of *De periculis,* see Geltner's introduction to his edition of the text (1–29).

in which the (translated) text of *De periculis* substitutes for (or becomes one with) that of the *Rose* in a brilliant manner.[111] Jean's stroke of genius in this passage is to place Faus Semblant in a direct relationship with William of St. Amour in the realm of fiction, where the antifraternal writer and the mendicant friar have a sort of close encounter. Faus Semblant tells how, through ploys, his mother, Hypocrisy, had William exiled on account of his antihypocritical writings. In these writings, the false friar complains, "Master William of St. Amour" wanted him, Faus Semblant, to renounce mendicancy and his life as a drunkard, and to go to work (ll. 11510–22). This is one of the strongest textual connections between the *Rose* and *De periculis,* a connection that turns William into a character who interacts with Faus Semblant in the fictive world of the poem. Needless to say, Faus Semblant opposes Master William's wishes and refuses to work, choosing instead the garment and practices of a corrupt mendicant friar (ll. 11523–28). Jean's reference to a direct relationship between Faus Semblant and William of St. Amour projects the latter as a moral authority, who in his texts sets high behavioral standards, and the former as a knowledgeable individual, who is aware of these texts and ethical imperatives but who refuses to comply with them. Thus, Jean subtly pays homage to William, by obliquely acknowledging his influence over the textual evolution of the hypocritical friar in the *Rose* and by revealing to his readers that the literary product called "Faus Semblant" was designed with the ideological contribution of the antimendicant writer.

Besides the love of fine foods and the thirst for other temporal goods, attachments that, in William's opinion, characterize the false friar (signs twelve, sixteen, twenty-one, twenty-seven, and twenty-nine in *De periculis*), and to which Faus Semblant confesses freely, another salient aspect of his self-revelations is that he does not act alone in the social arena. He constantly speaks of his likes, either by using the third person plural pronoun "they," when he presents them as a dangerous crowd that he takes pain not to upset with disparaging words, or by using the inclusive pronoun "us," when he asserts his affiliation with this evil social force. Faus Semblant's cohorts, although depicted as a vague presence—*mes amis,* "my friends"; *mes compagnons,* "my companions"; *mes frères,* "my brothers" (and the last

111. See also John V. Fleming: "it is possible that Jean actually thought of himself as carrying on, in a formal sense, the task begun by Guillaume [de St. Amour] a generation before him" (*The "Roman de la Rose,"* 164).

term is not accidental)—are always there, in the outside world, lurking in the background, never manifesting themselves, but constantly invoked as an unsettling and menacing power. This apocalyptic image closely echoes William's portrayal of the friars as a multitude of *pseudopredicatores,* "false preachers," and *antichristi,* "antichrists," embodying the millennial prophecies of the New Testament.[112]

One of the main actions of this large and evil mob is *penetratio domos,* "intrusion into homes" (sign one), a violent action exerted by friars able to enter everywhere, even places from which they are normally excluded. In the *Rose,* after confessing to the god of love that he can be found either in the cloister or in the world, Faus Semblant admits, however, to his preference for open and intensely populated areas, where he can make more victims: "Es bours et es chastiaus, as citez / Ai mes sales et mes pales / Ou l'en puet corre a plain eslais, / Et di que je suis hors dou monde; / Mais je m'i plunge et m'i affunde / Et m'i aese et baigne et noe / Mieus que nus poissons de sa noe" ("I make my halls and palaces in towns, castles, and cities, where one can run with a free rein. I say that I am out of the world, but I plunge into it and immerse myself in it; I take my ease and bathe and swim better than any fish with his fin"; ll. 11710–16). It is worth noting the cynicism with which Jean highlights the contradiction between Faus Semblant's adherence to a worldly life style and his purported isolation from the world.

Apart from the friars' unsettling presence in the *saeculum,* there are two other aspects connected with the mendicant orders that render them dangerous: their persuasive eloquence and the ease with which they get in touch with people from all social estates (signs two, fourteen, fifteen, and twenty-six in *De periculis*). In William's view, both seduction and social skills rely on the care with which the typical friar is "composing" his public figure, and we see these aspects at work in the *Rose* as well. For, in order to ensure a better circulation from one level of society to another, Faus Semblant is constantly and carefully building his external image, an image based on deceptive physical outlooks and formidable linguistic skills:

112. William has a particular scheme about Salvation History, a scheme that posits three major phases of persecution against the Church. The first one, which took place in the time of the first martyrs of the Church, was a *persecutio violenta;* the second one, which took place in the time of Augustine and Hilary, was a *persecutio fraudulenta;* whereas the third one, close to William's time, was a persecution performed by hypocrites and predicated upon the conjunction of violence and fraud. William casts the friars as the agents of the third persecution, insofar as they are both simulators of pastoral care (fraudulent ecclesiastics) and perpetrators of violence.

Trop sai bien mes habiz changier, / Prendre l'un et l'autre estrangier: / Or sui chevaliers, or sui moines, / Or sui prelaz, or sui chanoines, / Or sui clers, autre heure sui prestres, / Or sui deciples, or sui mestres, / Or chastelains or forestiers; / Briement, je sui de touz mestiers. / Or sui princes, or resui pages, / Et sai par cuer trestouz langages. / Autre heure sui vieulz et chenuz, / Or resui juenes devenuz. / Or sui Roberz, or sui Robins, / Or cordeliers or jacobins. (11191–204)

I know very well how to change my garment, to take one and then another foreign to it. Now I am a knight, now a monk; at one time I am a prelate, at another a canon; at one hour a clerk, at another a priest; now disciple, now master, now lord of the manor, now forester. Briefly, I am in all occupations. Again I may be prince or page, and I know all languages by heart. At one hour I am old and white, and then I have become young again. Now I am Robert, now Robin, now Cordelier, now Jacobin.

In light of this detailed portrayal foregrounding his chameleon-like nature, Faus Semblant reveals himself as a dynamic actor on the social stage. The masks that he changes with great ability provide him direct access to all the individuals with whom he wants to interact. By collapsing differences in both the religious and lay hierarchies, by blurring distinctions between professions, and by asserting his outstanding linguistic talent, the character is in fact affirming his universality as an agent of evil, as the all-invasive incarnation of sin.[113] The three elements on which his identity is based—family lineage, wearing apparel, and verbal activity—all point in this direction. As son of the world-governing Fraud and of Hypocrisy, Faus Semblant is genetically predisposed to a fraudulent existence; his wearing apparel, a type of language itself, is highly deceptive; and finally, his verbal activity consists of nothing but lies and threats.

In William's scheme, another sign of the friars' composing their fraudulent public image is the care they take to be perceived as virtuous persons and holy pastors. A tool in this fabrication of a false social and moral outlook is the request for letters of commendation (sign five), a request routinely accompanied by the false preachers' intolerance to any kind of criticism (signs three and seventeen). These notions surface in Faus Semblant's discourse within the framework of his confessed hatred of honest work and poor people (ll. 11673–79). The hypocrite asserts not only his unwillingness to accept criticism from others but also his determination to kill any-

113. See also Stakel: "Faus Semblant identifies himself and his cronies with avarice, hypocrisy, cruelty, pride, gluttony—all of the seven deadly sins, in fact, except lust" (*False Roses,* 48). Actually, Faus Semblant is not innocent with respect to lust either, since he has a relationship with Constraint Abstinence, who is introduced in the text as his concubine (and who is pregnant!).

one who would dare oppose his agenda and methods. The propensity to murder of Faus Semblant and of the *antichristi* whom he represents is first verbalized, when he warns about the fate awaiting those who do not follow him, then actually enacted on two separate occasions: the slayer of the Norman soldiers and the heinous extermination of Malebouche.

Nowhere is Faus Semblant's penchant for fraud and violence more evident than in the scene that depicts him killing Malebouche during his pious act of confession. Since the rumormonger represents a danger for Amant's conquest of the rose, Faus Semblant and his concubine, Astinance Constrainte, decide to eliminate him. Before returning to Faus Semblant's house, where Malebouche is lodged, the two hypocrites premeditate their act and debate how best to kill him. They wonder if they should make themselves known to him or assume false identities. Eventually, they choose the latter option and disguise themselves as pious pilgrims. With meticulous care, Astinance Constrainte puts on a robe of cameline and passes herself off as a Beguine, whereas:

> Faus samblant qui bien se ratorne / Ot aussi com pour essoier / Vestuz les dras frere Soier: / La chiere ot mout simple et piteuse / Ne regardeüre orgueilleuse / N'ot il pas, mais douce et paisible. / A son col portoit une bible. / A pié s'en va sanz escuier, / Et pour ses membres apuier / Ot ausi com par impotence / en sa main destre une potence / Et fist en sa manche glacier / .i. bien tranchant rasoir d'acier, / Qu'il fist forgier en une forge / Que l'en apele coupe gorge. (12086–100)[114]

> False Seeming, who was also equipping himself well, had dressed, as though to try it out, in the clothing of brother Seier. He had a very simple, compassionate face without any appearance of pride, a sweet, peaceful look. At his neck he carried a Bible. Afterward, he went off without a squire, and, to support his limbs, as though he had no power, he used a crutch of treason. Up his sleeve he slipped a very sharp steel razor, that he had made in a forge and that was called Cut-Throat.

The detailed description of the religious attire of the two criminals and the compassionate looks they display while pretending to be holy people serve to highlight the disjunction between appearance and moral essence, the divorce between the outer self and the inner self. Their external image and the pious speech they skillfully deliver to gullible Malebouche before killing him turn out to be deceptive codes meant to warn the reader about the dangers represented by what William labeled "falsi fratres sub habitu

114. "Frere Soier" is a nickname based on a pun (*soie,* "silk") and standing for the Dominican friars, reputed for their love of silk garments.

sanctitatis" ("false friars beneath the habit of sanctity"), whom he identified with the mendicant orders. The slaying of Malebouche in the midst of his act of confession enacts William's message about the religious persecution by hypocrites.

The several "signs" we have seen attached to the figure of Faus Semblant suggest that Jean projected this character in the wake of William's highly negative perception of the fraternal preachers. My comparison between the two texts does not exhaust all the places in which Jean inserted William's *signa* into the portrayal of Faus Semblant; more indices can be detected in the friars' appetite for sophistical reasoning or carnal delights, for instance. Out of the forty-one signs posited in *De periculis* there is hardly one that cannot be identified in Faus Semblant's speech in the *Rose.* It takes great literary craftsmanship and industriousness to give life and textual body to a roster of notions from another author's work. Jean not only does so, not only does he devise a character who walks and acts following this long lists of identifying signs, but at the same time, he paradoxically creates one of the most original personages of the entire French tradition. The means by which the poet achieves this literary performance is an almost obsessive concern with the character's devious speech.

The Traps of Rhetoric

For William, a friar's gift of eloquence is one of the most important signs that enable true Christians to identify that friar as false, and Faus Semblant repeatedly illustrates this point of view.[115] The character declares that his ecclesiastical skills are exceptional, and that his long experience in preaching attests to his magisterial expertise in the use of religious language (ll. 12354–57). Beyond this mere declarative level, there are indeed several passages in which the personage aptly quotes, and glosses on, scriptures. In reality, however, Faus Semblant uses his ecclesiastical privileges and knowl-

115. "The second sign is that apostles do not deceive the hearts of simple men; [gloss: the false] extol their ways by ornate words, with which they deceive the hearts of simple men" (*De periculis,* 113). Or later on: "The fourteenth sign is that true apostles, unlike false ones, do not strive for eloquence or an ornate arrangement of words" (121). This notion recurs in a subsequent text: "Common people think that those Preachers are holy who have an erudite tongue in preaching and an elegant eloquence.... But the words of the Holy Preachers do not spring from talent or skills but from sacred inspiration" (*Pericula imminentia Ecclesiae generali,* in *Opera omnia,* 393; translation mine).

edge for the purpose of defrauding people, as he himself admits: "Mais de religion sanz faille, / J'en lais le grain ct preng la paille. / Pour genz enbascher y abit: Je n'en quier sanz plus que l'habit" ("But without fail, I leave the kernel of religion and take the husk. I dwell in religion only to trick people; I seek only its habit, no more"; ll. 11219–22). The sermons he allegedly delivers to his audience are in sharp contrast with his moral depravation, and his discourse in the poem unrelentingly highlights the contradiction between what he says and what he truly thinks or does.

Faus Semblant establishes a genetic affiliation with fraudulent language from the very beginning of his textual activity. Not only is he introduced in the poem through a sin of speech signaled by the god of love: "c. mile foiz t'es parjurez" ("you have perjured yourself a hundred thousand times"; l. 10947), but he is also the son of an evil allegorical couple. The lineage of the character, with Fraud as the father and Hypocrisy as the mother, preordains his textual life and circumscribes his evolution in the narrative within essentially immoral parameters. The dialogue with the god of love reveals the discrepancy between Faus Semblant's sermons and his inner structure:

> «Car si com tes habiz nous conte, / Tu sambles estre .i. sainz hermites! » / (Faus samblant): « C'est voirs, mes je sui ypocrites. » / (Li dieus d'amours): / «Tu vas preschant astinance! » / (Faus samblant): «Voire voir, mais j'emple ma pance / De tres bons morsiaus et de vins / Tels comme il affiert a devins. » / (Li dieus d'amours): «Tu vas preschant povreté. » / (Faus samblant): «Voire, riches a poesté. / Mais combien que povres me faigne / Nul povre je ne contredaigne. » (11234–44)
>
> As you tell us of your habits, you seem to be a holy hermit / —It is true, but I am a hypocrite. / —You go around preaching abstinence / —True, indeed, but I fill my paunch with very good morsels and with wines such as are suitable for theologians. / —You go around preaching poverty. / —True, abundantly richly. But however much I pretend to be poor, I pay no attention to any poor person.

The god's brief remarks seem to have the mere function of prompting long denials from Faus Semblant, who is compelled to introduce and characterize himself. This humorous dialogue is designed to emphasize the contradiction between appearance and moral essence, between truth and lie, and to dismantle conventional systems of signs—the clothes and the words—commonly regarded as faithful indicators of social identity and moral profile. The hypocritical character not only gives many details about his preaching skills but also boasts about his ability to speak all languages: "sai par cuer trestouz languages" ("I know all languages by heart"; l. 11200), a clear parody of the Apostles' glossolalia. His manipulation of speech in fraudulent ecclesiastic activities is best seen at work when he brags about systematically breaking the secrecy of the confessional. For, in Faus Semblant's view, pastoral care must be directed primarily at the rich, since they are much more sinful than the poor and therefore in more need of his guidance. But he admits to using the privileges that he gains as a confessor for fraudulent purposes, since he blackmails the sinners over their moral errors and is willing to give pardon only to those who pay for his silence.

Along these lines, it is worth noting that in the *lingua*-tracts, ferreting people's secrets is a sin (*secreta revelare*), and in Peraldus's system, this sin is all the more serious when committed by religious figures. Faus Semblant makes of *secreta revelare* his political and social agenda, as this practice is one of his main means of making a living. It is evident all throughout the text that the sins mainly associated with this character are of verbal nature. Through him, they invade the lives of the rich and the poor, the young and the old, the native and the foreigner. Faus Semblant's statement "I know all languages by heart" is an ironic allusion to Pentecost, but on a symbolical level it can also mean: "I speak the inner language of every soul; I therefore know how to relate to people and manipulate them." Faus Semblant's statement seems a verbatim translation of Peraldus's definition of double talkers: "Bilingues sunt pseudo apostoli variis linguis loquentes" ("Double talkers are false apostles speaking various languages"; 582).

Further textual clues reveal Jean's goal of exposing the corruption of religious rhetoric. One of the constants of Faus Semblant's speech is the care he takes to make explicit the gap between his words and his deeds. Besides the programmatic avowal "Mout est en moi muez li vers: / Trop sont li fait au diz divers" ("The tune is very much changed in me; my deeds are very different from my words"; ll. 11223–26), he admits to preferring prayer to work. But then he immediately adds that his prayers are in sharp contrast with what he does behind people's backs. When he speaks about chivalry as an eminently honest social class, he curses all the honest people for the harmony between their sayings and their actions. He also bluntly warns the god of love about his own deceitful way of talking: "Ne ja certes pour mon habit / Ne savrez o quel gent j'abit; / Non ferez vous voir as parole, / Ja tant n'ierent simples ne moles ("Certainly by my habit you would never know with what people I dwell, any more that you would from my words, no matter how simple and gentle they were"; ll. 11076–79).

Faus Semblant constantly establishes for himself the textual posture of a double dealer, who says one thing and does the opposite. As such, he is also a skillful double talker, in the Peraldian sense of the word—a person whose outer speech does not correspond to his mental scheme. Although the words of the hypocrite seemingly convey simplicity (in the medieval sense of honesty), they are in fact "double," because what the hypocrite says is different from what he thinks. Like snakes, the sinners by *bilinguium* have two tongues, Peraldus asserts.[116] One is the outer tongue that proclaims the good intention, and the other one, the inner tongue that speaks the evil thought. The words of double talkers seem simple, to wit honest, but are in sharp contrast to their *verba interiora mentis,* "the inner words of the mind," which translate the intent of wrongdoing. The sin of double talk has extremely dangerous consequences for the public life, Peraldus adds, and it is all the more grievous when committed by those who teach the Christian doctrine.

All throughout his discourse, Faus Semblant casts himself as the embodiment of religious hypocrisy and double talk. His immorality is predicated upon the split between his words and his deeds, between his outer speech and his cast of mind. It is this logical discrepancy that accounts for the highly contradictory statements he makes in the poem. The critics who have tackled the "problem" of Faus Semblant have noted the paradoxes inherent in his discourse, paradoxes generated by the oscillating stances he takes with respect to his own theses.[117] He curses noble people for not being as hypocritical as he is, but later on, he compares the hypocrite with a pig returning to his vomit and explains how a hypocrite can be recognized. He abhors working but opposes mendicancy. He speaks in favor of William of St. Amour in the quarrel against the mendicant friars but then complains that he feels personally threatened by his book. He vituperates against the Eternal Gospel that he considers full of errors, then he expresses regret that it was not more popular. He deplores the state of the Church and praises the University as a defender of Christianity, but then he brags about being one of the Antichrist's boys.

116. Peraldus, *SV,* 582.

117. Several critics have argued that Faus Semblant's discursive bipolarity damages him as a fictive construct, in that it undermines his credibility. See, for instance, C. S. Lewis (*The Allegory of Love* [New York: Oxford University Press, 1936]), William W. Ryding ("Faus Semblant: Hero or Hypocrite?" *Romanic Review* 60 (1960): 163–67), and Lee Patterson ("*For the Wyves Love of Bathe*: Feminine Rhetoric and Poetic Resolution in the *Roman de la Rose* and the *Canterburry Tales,*" *Speculum* 58, no. 3 (1983): 656–95).

These unrelenting shifts should not surprise us in a hypocrite; they are to be accounted for in light of the malicious habit of *bilinguium* germane to this type of person. Domenico Cavalca tags as *bilingui*, "double talkers," those who "first say one thing, then another, and thus twist the words as it pleases them, they say and unsay things; they lack steadfastness in their speech, and therefore generate many scandals."[118] In the wake of this definition that applies in spectacular ways to Jean's hypocritical personage, I respectfully disagree with Lee Patterson, who considers Faus Semblant a representational failure. The conflicting positions on which Faus Semblant's speech is patterned have prompted Patterson to assert that "these crude juxtapositions make it impossible for Jean to portray either the ethos or language of hypocrisy. As a speaker, Faus Semblant dissolves before the pressure of the inherited rhetorics that jostle side by side in his discourse, dissipating any coherence of the character before it can coalesce."[119] I believe that Peraldus's and Cavalca's pronouncements on the practice of double talk undermine Lee Patterson's stance. In my opinion, the shifts in perspective that characterize Faus Semblant's discourse are a mimetic tool for representing his duplicitous nature.[120] Here, the "jostling of rhetorics" works not to demolish the character but to figure him forth. Particularly because the change of perspective is a recurrent motif, the spotlight falls on the personage's patterns of speech, and his ideological oscillations reveal a premeditated literary technique that Jean uses to convey *bilinguium* and hypocrisy. Emmerson and Herzman have noted that "Faus Semblant is unique not because of his hypocritical nature, but because his hypocrisy is so blatant."[121] My opinion is that this blatancy is a deliberate representational strategy adopted by the writer. Jean knew the mendicant friars in the realm of reality, but the close reading of this section of the poem proves that in creating Faus Semblant he also drew on the energies of two important cultural traditions: that of antifraternal literature, as best expressed by William of St. Amour, and that of the moral writings of his time.

118. Cavalca, *Pungilingua,* 199.

119. Lee Patterson, "For the Wyves Love of Bathe," 672.

120. Referring to the same contradictory statements made by Faus Semblant, Geltner makes an adequate analogy with the "Cretan liar's dilemma, a moving field of deceit" (Geltner, "Faux Semblants: Antifraternalism Reconsidered in Jean de Meun and Chaucer, " *Studies in Philology* 4, no. 101 [2004]: 364 and 376). In a similar vein, Sarah Kay argues that this personage presents the readers with "the conundrum of the hypocrite who unmasks himself, and so solicits belief, and yet remains a hypocrite, and so places himself beyond it" (*The Romance of the Rose* 29).

121. Emmerson and Herzman, "The Apocalyptic Age of Hypocrisy," 627.

All throughout the Faus Semblant section in the *Rose,* the authorial stress on his speaking habits is too evident and cultivated to be a deficiency of craftsmanship, as Patterson argues. The constant bipolarity of Faus Semblant's speech is not a factor of mimetic dissolution but the hermeneutical key to the character. His discourse is indeed paradoxical, but *paradoxia* is, as Charles Presberg has pointed out, an artful discourse that is both trope of thought and rhetorical strategy. Rooted in Plato's definition of the dialogue as the art of simultaneously arguing the opposite sides of a question, the paradoxical discourse uses "the categories of language and logic to question and mock the very categories that undergird language and logic as discursive systems."[122] Thus, in analyzing Faus Semblant, we not only have to consider what the character says and does, but across his fluctuating moods and statements, we also have to see what *the writer* does with this character and with the text. Faus Semblant's textual figure is constructed along paradoxical lines as a *coincidentia oppositorum.* His long and contradictory disquisition is designed as a dialectical space in which each argument can be seen from both sides. The writer casts this disquisition in the medieval mold of a dialogue between the two sides of man—the inner and the outer—each with its attendant speech, the mental and the aural, here constantly in disagreement. This carefully cultivated linguistic duality is a textual rendering of double talk and hypocrisy, which need to be deciphered as such by the reader. Only by having Faus Semblant constantly bounce from one ideological position to its opposite, from one assertive statement to its denial, can Jean reveal the true nature of the personage and expose the potentially fraudulent resources of (religious) language.

Faus Semblant's speech is the embodiment of Presberg's definition of "paradoxy." Through this character, Jean constantly mocks language and logic as human institutions, unmasking both their seductions and their weaknesses. The target audience of the *Romance of the Rose* will now be more on guard against external signs of sincerity and religiousness and more inclined to look for the true intentions underlying words or deeds. Far from being a literary fiasco, as some have suggested, the portrayal of Faus Semblant is so accomplished and has played such an important role in the history of West European literature that George Puttenham took

122. Charles Presberg, *Adventures in Paradox* (University Park: Pennsylvania State University Press, 2001), 2.

up this name as a technical term referring to a figure of speech. In *The Art of English Poesie* (1589), Puttenham uses "False Semblant" as a specialized phrase to designate allegory, which he defines as speaking "otherwise than we think, in earnest as well as in sport; under covert and dark terms, and in learned and apparent speeches; in short sentences, and by long ambages and circumstances of words; and finally as well when we lie as when we tell the truth."[123]

SOWING OF DISCORD AND FALSIFYING OF WORDS IN THE *INFERNO*

The "Seminator di Scandalo e di Scisma" ("Sowers of Scandal and Schism")

Aware of the importance of maintaining social and political harmony, the intellectuals of the Middle Ages draw constant attention to the tragic consequences arising from the disruption of this harmony. Alain of Lille defines "concord" as that virtue on account of which fellow countrymen live together in respect of all the legal institutions. He also defines the notion of "discord," but in a more spiritual way, as that form of dissension separating people previously bound by ties of charitable love.[124] In the historical context of late medieval Italy, Albertano da Brescia also warns about the dire consequences of the verbal practice of sedition: "Be warned not to say anything seditious, anything which would bring the city to ruin. Where there is sedition, there is a divided city. The Lord says. Every kingdom divided against itself is ruined and a household divided against itself collapses."[125] Brunetto Latini, another leading Italian intellectual of the time and Dante's own teacher, voices his concerns about an ill-governed city in the following terms: "So that I know none / Whom I would wish to see / Have my city / Entirely in his control, / Or that it be divided; / But all in common / Should pull together on a rope / Of peace and of welfare,

123. George Puttenham, *The Art of English Poesy: A Critical Edition,* edited by Frank Whigham and Wayne A. Rebhorn (Ithaca, N.Y.: Cornell University Press, 2007), 271.

124. Alain of Lille, "Tractus de virtutibus, de vitiis et de donis Spiritus Sancti," *Mediaeval Studies* 12 (1950): 20–56, at 32, 41.

125. Albertano da Brescia, *De doctrina loquendi et tacendi,* 23 March 2005, http://freespace.virgin.net/angus.graham/Loquendi.htm.

/ Because a land torn apart cannot survive."[126] In Brunetto's view, a man is naturally predestined to own and transform the geographical environment in which he is born. Within this economic framework of land ownership, man thrives not only with respect to nature but also inside a complex network of social relationships. One defines oneself with respect to the world, first by relating to one's family, then by expanding this interrelational net to the *commune*. Nature, man, and society constitute key terms in a philosophical worldview that prompts Brunetto to air a political statement. Loathing both tyranny, dangerous for the abuses it can engender, and division, which can lead to political extinction, he calls for his fellow citizens to pull all on a single, allegorical rope—that of prosperity and harmony.

Albertano's and Brunetto's concerns with discord testify to the profound effects the political divisiveness of Italy had on its intellectuals. It should then come as no surprise that Dante is preoccupied with the notions of social harmony and discord as well. Following Aristotle and Aquinas, he defines "concord" in philosophical terms, as "the uniform motion of more wills than one" (*De monarchia* 1.15). For Dante, the politically engaged poet who deems that universal peace is the highest good of humankind, unity, first within the family then within the city-state, is the indispensable condition for the attainment of happiness. Social harmony is as vital to man as the synergic functioning of body and soul, and it should characterize any form of human organization, from family, through city and kingdom, to the entire human race. In a passage from the same political tract, a passage promoting the ideal of a unique empire guarantor of the security of the world, Dante tackles the problem of political division from a religious angle and invokes the same scriptural quote as Albertano and Brunetto: "Every kingdom divided against itself shall be made desolate"; *De monarchia* 1.5).

Dante's concerns about political divisiveness acquire deeper prophetic tones in the *Comedy:* first, in the pilgrim's colloquia with Ciacco and Cacciaguida, and then more dramatically in the *bolgia* of the sowers of discord. When addressing Dante, Ciacco, a Florentine punished for gluttony, excoriates his native city for its reputed viciousness: "La tua città, ch'è piena / d'invidia sì che già trabocca il sacco" ("Your city, which is so full of envy / that the sack already overflows"; *Inf.* 6.49–50). Ciacco's words imply a disjunction between himself and his birthplace, since he calls Florence not

126. Brunetto Latini, *Il Tesoretto (The Little Treasure),* edited and translated by Julia Bolton Holloway (New York: Garland, 1981), ll. 170–79.

"my city," but Dante's ("la tua città"), as though he wanted to disown it out of repulsion.[127] When the pilgrim inquires about the fate awaiting the inhabitants of so divided a city (and about the cause of this tragic division), Ciacco answers that the plight of Florence is due to the moral depravity of its denizens, who are tormented by three great evils: envy, pride, and covetousness. This state of affairs is at the root of the hatred and bloodshed that will lacerate Florence for many years to come, prophesizes Ciacco. Overwhelmed by the news, Dante further asks about the destiny met in the afterlife by Florentines of good faith, such as Farinata, Tegghaio, Mosca, Jacopo Rusticucci, and others, who had dedicated their lives to the promotion of the common good. To his great dismay and sorrow, he learns that all of them are punished deeper down in Hell, for the darkness of their hearts (*Inf.* 6.85–86). (Ciacco's words actually anticipate Dante's meeting with Mosca, one of the evoked Florentines, in the *bolgia* of the sowers of discord.)

Another meaningful episode takes place in cantos 15–17 of *Paradiso,* which narrate the pilgrim's encounter with Cacciaguida, a forefather of Dante's, also native to Florence. Cacciaguida's description of the civil setting in which he was born stresses Florentine peace and concord almost tautologically: "A così riposato, a così bello / viver di cittadini, a così fida / cittadinanza, a così dolce ostello, / Maria mi diè, chiamata in alte grida" ("To so peaceful, to so comely a life of citizens, to / so loyal a citizenry, to so sweet a dwelling, / Mary gave me, invoked with loud cries"; *Par.* 15.130–33). Cacciaguida's Florence stands in sharp opposition with Ciacco's; it is an Edenic place where social relationships are imbued with beauty, trust, and kindness. It is virtually an embodiment of Alain's view of fraternal love as the cornerstone of civic concord. In contrast to these golden, peaceful times, Cacciaguida describes Dante's city as torn apart by bloody family and political rivalries (*Par.* 16).[128] Ciacco's and Cacciaguida's discourses

127. Even the name with which the sinner introduces himself represents not so much a personally assumed identity as a linguistic habit of his acquaintances: "voi cittadini mi chiamaste Ciacco" ("you citizens called me Ciacco"; *Inf.* 6.52).

128. When he mentions the "broken stone" to which Florence offered a victim, he refers to the statue of the Roman god of war, Mars, the former protector of the city, whom the Christian Florentines had replaced with John the Baptist. The popular superstition held that many of the social and economic plights of Florence were due to Mars's wrath for having been betrayed. The sacrificial victim to which Cacciaguida is alluding is the Count of Buondelmonte, a young nobleman, whose vicious murder in 1215 would lead to the conflicts between Guelphs

on Florence offer an important topical picture of the sociopolitical background of the city, and at the same time they provide a useful glimpse into Dante's rationale for the inclusion of the sowing of discord in the moral structure of Hell.

Bruno Porcelli has already noted that the order "fraudulent counsel-sowing of discord," corresponding to pouches eight and nine of Malebolge, matches Peraldus's scheme, where *pravum consilium* is immediately followed by *seminantium discordiae,* "dissemination of discord" (426). Although Porcelli does not deal with the latter sin, I adhere to his opinion that the correspondence between Dante's arrangement and Peraldus's is too great to be a coincidence. A closer look at Peraldus's tract shows further remarkable congruencies with Dante's *contrapasso* for the sowers of discord. "De peccato linguae" describes sowing of discord as rooted in *malizia* and considers this verbal sin most hateful to God because it causes enmity *inter fratres,* "among brothers," and is opposed to the Christic model. Christ loved the body of the Church more than his own, which he offered as a sacrifice for her welfare; therefore, those who break the unity of the Church do more harm than they would do if they tore apart their own bodies. Just as the greatest injury one can inflict to the human body, this organic whole, is laceration or rupture, so the greatest harm one can do to the body of the Church is division. Peraldus does not neglect the civic side either, considering that one word of a seditious man suffices to cause a great social conflict that can lead to the disintegration of the entire body politic. Disseminating discord is a diabolical enterprise, for, unlike Christ, who came onto earth to make peace and unify, the devil came to divide and disperse.[129]

Peraldus's words seem to be graphically illustrated in the round of the

---

and Ghibellines, the cause of Florence's tragic history and of Dante's own exile. The assassination of Buondelmonte was allegedly a decision sanctioned by Mosca dei Lamberti with the words "a thing done has a head," words reported by the Florentine chronicler Giovanni Villani (1277–1348). We will see that in *Inferno 28,* Dante quotes Mosca's phrase literally.

129. "Ex uno verbo quod dicit ille qui discordiam seminat, quandoque nascitur discordia tanta, ex qua distruitur patria una. Unde magnae malitiae est seminar semen tale, cum ex uno gradu illius, talis messis surgat. Ad Cristum et ad servos eius pertinet unire e pacificare. Hac de causa filius Dei venit in mundum, ut pacem reformaret in mundo. Ad diabolo vero pertinet dispergere" ("Sometimes, such a great discord arises from one word uttered by a sower a discord that an entire country is destroyed. Hence, sowing such a seed is indicative of great malice, because from a single movement of this seed grows such a crop. It behooves to Jesus and his servants to unite and pacify. This is why the son of God came into this world, to reform peace in the world. In truth, it behooves to the devil to cause dispersal"; Peraldus, *SV,* 581).

"seminator di scandalo e di scisma." On the bottom of the infernal valley, pained shadows walk in a circular path, watched by a devil who splits their bodies with a sword. A passage from Book 3 of the *Convivio* explaining the perfection of wisdom through an analogy with the human body is highly meaningful for the choice of this *contrapasso:* "just as the beauty of the body derives from the degree to which its members are properly ordered, so the beauty of wisdom, which, as has been said, is the body of Philosophy, derives from the order of the moral virtues" (15.77–81). Since the perfection of wisdom, which consists in the impeccable order of moral virtues, is similar to the beauty of the human body, which results from its wholeness, we can infer that the lack of a specific virtue in an individual is similar to a body deprived of one of its limbs or of its internal cohesion. The missing link in the moral profiles of the "seminator di scandalo e di scisma" is the virtue of concord, in the acception that Alain assigned this term. As a result, Mohamed is cleft from the throat to the belly and his intestines hung out, Curio no longer has a tongue, Pier da Medicina's nose and one ear are sectioned, Mosca dei Lamberti's hands are severed, and Bertrand de Born is decapitated and holds his head in front of his torso.[130] After the terrible pain of the mutilation, the wounds heal, but since the souls follow a circular path, every time they pass in front of the devil, this one reopens their wounds and the atrocious pain resumes.[131] Peraldus's comparison between

130. In his masterful analysis of the aesthetics of Hell as an "antiaesthetics of being," Warren Ginsberg speaks of the infernal metamorphosis as a "process of unbecoming" and stresses the souls' materiality as the condition that enables the "unforming of the damned." In Ginsberg's view, the damned are matter in which form has failed, and their punishments are metamorphoses of loss. Although Ginsberg applies his view particularly to the transformation of the thieves, his analysis can be very well exemplified by the punishments of the sowers of discord, given that: "The very degree the damned have become material . . . indicates the degree each sinner has turned to nonbeing" (*Dante's Aesthetics of Being* [Ann Arbor: University of Michigan Press, 1999], 116–26).

131. In *De monarchia,* Dante describes the relationship between parts and whole in terms of systemic unity: "Again, the purpose of the part is related to the purpose of the whole as the part is related to the whole. . . . What is good for the part of an organization is not greater than what is good for the whole organization, but rather the contrary is true" (1.6.1). Although this notion is discussed in connection with humanity ("mankind in its entirety is a kind of whole"), it can be extrapolated to the *contrapasso* reserved for the sowers of discord. In the natural order, bodies cannot function properly without a good working of their parts, but in the case of the scandalmongers these parts are either detached or defective. It is also interesting that in the same political treatise, Dante defines sin itself in terms of (lack of) unity and dispersal: "sinning is nothing else than scorning unity and moving away from it towards multiplicity" (1.15).

the body of the Church and the human body enlightens Dante's choice of this form of *contrapasso.* Mohamed's intestines figure the religious intestinal strife he caused while alive, and Alì's face, cleft from chin to forehead, stands for the disfigurement he brought to the harmony of the faith.[132]

The Peraldian references to the civic dimension of discord can be seen at work in the portrayals of Curio, Mosca, Pier da Medicina, and Bertran de Born, all intended to embody the division of political nature. Curio is the famous Roman general who advised Caesar to cross the river Rubicon, an action that led to civil war:

"Questi è desso, e non favella.
Questi, scacciato, il dubitar sommerse
in Cesare, affermando che 'l fornito
sempre con danno l'attender sofferse."
Oh quanto mi pareva sbigottito
con la lingua tagliata ne la strozza,
Curïo, ch'a dir fu così ardito!
(*Inf.* 28.96–103)

"This is he, and he cannot speak. / He, an exile, drowned Caesar's doubts, affirming / that one prepared always suffers from delay." / Oh how dismayed Curio seemed, with the tongue / cut out of his throat, he who was so bold to speak!

The verbs Dante uses to describe Curio's sway on Caesar's political decision—*affermare* and *dire* (the latter accompanied by *ardito,* which enhances the stylistic effect)—point to the oral dimension of Curio's moral error, a dimension that the *contrapasso* reserved for this (now tongueless) character only confirms.[133] It is his speech to Caesar that prompted the civil war that

132. It is well known that for medieval Western Europe, Mohamed was a Christian preacher who, deluded in his ambitious expectations, caused the first great schism in the body of the Church. Alì, his cousin and son-in-law, was held responsible for the creation of a new schism within Islam. The type of sin Mohamed and Alì represent is of a verbal nature, and this can be inferred from what Justinian says about the method underlying his conversion to Christianism: "'l benedetto Agapito, che fue / sommo pastore, a la fede sincera / mi dirizzò *con le parole sue*" ("the blessed Agapetus, the highest / shepherd, directed me to the pure faith with his words"; *Paradiso* 6.16–18; emphasis added). Just as words serve to convert a person to true faith, in the same way, they can be abused and pressed into the service of heresy and schism. Whereas in *Paradiso* Justinian embodies the first case, in Hell Mohamed and Alì represent the latter.

133. In Dante's time, the belief that divine providence punishes evildoers in the limbs in which they have sinned was common. In her study on the practice of blasphemy in the Middle Ages, Corinne Leveleux invokes numerous stories describing verbal sinners whose dead bodies were discovered either without tongues or with huge tongues covered by worms. Among the late-medieval sources that Leveleux cites is Vincent of Beauvais, who in *Speculum morale* warns that those who commit verbal sins will end up in Hell, where they will be tortured in their very

would destroy the Roman unity. Through Curio, Dante also establishes a textual link between evil counsel (as embodied by Guido and Ulysses in *bolgia* eight) and sowing of discord, thus echoing Peraldus's association of the two sins.[134] Curio's transgression lay in an act of political counseling, but, although this act was not grounded in fraud, it is more grievous than Ulysses's and Guido's because it led to civil war.

In *Inferno* 28, the portrayal of Mosca dei Lamberti also brings into focus an act of speech. The words with which the Italian politician endorsed the murder of Buondelmonte are inserted in the text as a free discourse, introduced by the verb of assertion *dire,* "to say." More specifically, when Mosca beseeches the pilgrim not to forget him, he speaks of himself in the third person, and at same time he quotes himself: "Ricordera'ti anche del Mosca, / che disse, lasso! 'Capo ha cosa fatta,' / che fu mal seme per la gente tosca" ("You will remember Mosca, too, who said, / alas, 'A thing done is done,' the seed of evil for the / Tuscans"; 106–09). Cast in the shape of a micro-discourse within a discourse, the infamous words "capo ha cosa fatta" are now branded by Mosca himself as an evil seed that germinated into the disruption of the political balance in Tuscany. Intertextually, the metaphorical self-comment harks back to Dante's image of words as seeds of human actions from *Convivio* 4.2. For the phrase Mosca uttered while alive was a political sanction that would bear fruits of hatred and war between two Christian families, citizens of the same country.

---

tongues (*La Parole interdite. Le blasphème dans la France médiévale (XIIIe–XIVe siècles): Du péché au crime* [Paris: De Boccard, 2001], 146). It is worth adding that this is a scriptural notion already harnessed by Peradus, who, quoting St. John, warns Christians that the hellish *cruciatus linguae,* "suffering in the tongue," should be a strong reason why they should watch what they say (reason number ten on his agenda for *custodia linguae*).

134. The notion of *malizia* as the origin of specific sins of the tongue, such as evil counsel and sowing of discord, harks back to Peraldus, and it is worth noting that both Dante and Cavalca follow this moral pattern. (Cavalca asserts that both *male consigliare* and *seminare discordie* are rooted in malice and argues that the many exemplary stories he has given to illustrate evil counseling also apply to the sin of dissemination of discord.) In recent Dante studies, several interpreters have highlighted the affinity between the two sins. Truscott notes that both the counselors of fraud and the sowers of discord are evil counselors, since they all use the gift of language to cause "schism" ("Ulysses and Guido," 70). Along the same lines, Ferrante maintains that the impact of evil counsel in this circle of Malebolge is even stronger than in the eighth pouch, as it is shown to produce divisions in both church and state (*The Political Vision of the "Divine Comedy"* [Princeton, N.J.: Princeton University Press, 1984], 186). Mazzotta also points to the association between city and language in the circles of the lower Hell (*Dante, Poet of the Desert,* 72–73).

Both the oral aspect of the dissemination of discord and the connection with malicious counseling reemerge in the discourse of Bertrand de Born, the famous martial poet of the Provençal lyric:

E perché tu di me novella porti,
sappi ch'i' son Bertram dal Bornio, quelli
che diedi al re giovane i ma' conforti.
Io feci il padre e 'l figlio in sé ribelli:
Achitofèl non fé più d'Absalone,
e di Davìd coi malvagi punzelli.
(*Inf.* 28.133–38)[135]

And that you may take back news of me, know / that I am Bertran de Born, he who gave the young / king the bad encouragements. / I made father and son revolt against each other: / Achitophel did no worse to Absalom and David with his evil proddings.

Bertran's significance for the political view of the *Divine Comedy* has thoroughly been examined by Teodolinda Barolini, who, collating the Provençal poet with Dante's Sordello, has highlighted the reasons for Dante's negative assessment of Bertran in the *Comedy.*[136] Analyzing the Provençal *vidas,* "biographies," of the warmonger troubadour, Barolini concludes that the key to understanding Dante's Bertran are the *vidas'* exaggerated accounts of Bertrand as a counselor for Henry the Young. More significantly, Barolini says, these texts argue that the Provençal poet caused political disruption and conflicts by means of his poetry. In addition to the biographical testimonies, I believe that *Inferno* 28 offers us more indications of Bertran's misuse of language. Not coincidentally, the vocabulary Dante places in the character's speech is reminiscent of the medieval lexicon for the sins of the tongue. The phrase *i ma' conforti,* "evil incitements," which hints at Bertran's alleged office of political counselor, conveys the sin of evil counseling. In fact, *male confortare,* "incitement to evil," are the very words that Domenico Cavalca uses to translate Peraldus's notion of *pravum consilium.*

135. Craun notes that the reference to Achitophel was a topos in the pastoral debate on the sowing of discord. It was present, for instance, in the works of Peraldus, Etienne de Bourbon, and pseudo-Vincent of Beauvais (*Lies, Slander and Obscenity,* 51). Danuta Shanzer posits as a possible source for Bertran's punishment Alain of Lille's *Anticlaudianus,* where the allegorical figure of Discord is beheaded ("The Punishment of Bertran de Born," *Yearbook of Italian Studies* 8 [1989]: 95–97).

136. In Barolini's view, Dante intends Sordello as a symbol of political and linguistic unity (two ideals that Sordello attained through his poetry), whereas Bertrand was Sordello's polar opposite, since he used his poetry to foster divisiveness ("Bertran de Born and Sordello: The Poetry of Politics in Dante's *Comedy,*" PMLA 94, no. 3 (1979): 395–405, at 402).

Another important indication of Dante's relationship to the moralists of transgressive speech is the label "seminator di scandalo e scisma" that he applies to the sinners punished in the ninth pouch. Both *scandalo* and *scisma* represent moral categories well defined in the Middle Ages. Alain of Lille defines *scandalum* as: (1) the act of inducing another into evil through words or deeds, and (2) saddening or offending someone.[137] Thomas Aquinas echoes Alain's definition in virtually identical terms: "While going along a spiritual way, a man may be disposed to a spiritual downfall by another's word or deed, in so far, to wit, as one man by his injunction or example, moves another to sin; and this is scandal properly called."[138] The textual clues offered by *Inferno* 28 point significantly to the wrongful verbal practices underlying the activities of those who sow discord either on a religious or on a political level. Implicit in Mohamed's and Alì's portrayals (for how is faith spread or distorted other than through the medium of speech?), the linguistic side of dissemination of discord is explicitly expressed in the poetic representations of Curio, Mosca, and Bertran de Born. The latter is to be interpreted in opposition not only to Sordello, but also to Dante. In *De vulgari eloquentia,* when Dante establishes equivalences between the exponents of the Provençal lyric and the poets of vernacular Italian (Arnaut Daniel and Cino da Pistoia, in love poetry; Guirault de Borneil and Dante himself, in moral poetry), he concludes that there is no Italian equivalent for Bertran de Born in the field of war poetry. If Dante the literary historian leaves vacant the place reserved for Italy's poetry of war, Dante the poet marks an even greater distance with respect to this lyric genre. By placing dissemination of discord in one of the lowest and most repulsive circles of Hell, and by having the warmonger Provençal troubadour represent this sin, Dante makes clear that he has transcended the temptation of using poetry for spreading the wicked seeds of social and political discord. Had he yielded to this temptation, the harshness and bitterness of his exile would have justified it, and his great artistic talent would have served him well. But the good company of his *coscïenza pura,* "pure conscience," the one that he evokes in the same *Inferno* 28, has helped him resist this temptation. In a consciously anti-Bertranian attitude, Dante turns the genius of his poetry toward the Christian ideals of harmony and peace. In the fictional realm

137. Alain of Lille, *Distinctiones dictionum theologicalium,* Patrologia Latina 210, cols. 685–1012, at 936.

138. *ST* IIa-IIae Q. 43.1.

of the *Comedy,* the pity the pilgrim feels toward Geri del Bello, his own kinsman punished in the same *bolgia* as Bertran, is the pity of a man rising above earthly laws of blood and revenge and striving to the higher values of Christian charity.

The Verbal *Falsador*

“On the side opposite Truth, enmity-causing Falsehood stood in strained pose. Her face, darkened with the soot of ugliness, bespoke no gifts given her by nature; rather old age, subjecting her face to the hollows of wrinkles, had gathered it all over into folds.... This one, secretly lying in wait for the picture of truth, disgraced by deformity whatever truth graced by conformity.”[139]

We have seen that in the *Inferno,* forms of transgressive speech such as flattery, fraudulent counsel, and sowing of discord are punished in lower Hell. With the sole exception of blasphemy, a sin of violence, all the other verbal transgressions are assigned to the area of Fraud. The most striking absence in this list of sins seems to be *mendacium,* “lie,” one of the most basic and debated sins of the tongue. In the biblical tradition, lying was considered the progeny of the devil, and in consonance with this scriptural view, Dante has Malacoda, one of the devils from the circle of barraters, lie to the pilgrim and his guide that there is a bridge that can lead them to the next circle, that of the hypocrites. As we will find out in *Inferno* 21, in fact all the bridges of the sixth pouch are broken.[140] But despite this fictional enactment of the sin of *mendacium,* Dante does not use the denomination “liars” for any category of sinners he depicts in the text. What he uses instead is a series of terms interconnected through the notion of falsity: *la*

139. Alain of Lille, *Plaint of Nature,* 218.

140. Alain of Lille’s definition of “liar” illustrates the medieval perception of this type of speaker: “The liar is called false, hence in the Gospel Jesus says about the devil that he is a liar himself and the father of it, that is, of the lie. He is called guileful, hence the Psalm, the liars are in swaying, that is, guileful in their denials” (*Liber,* col. 856). In *Inferno* 23, Dante inserts the biblical definition of the devil as the father of lies in the context of hypocrisy: “Io udi’ già dire a Bologna / del diavol vizi assai, tra’ quali udi’ / ch’elli è bugiardo e padre di menzogna” (“In Bologna I once heard many / vices of the devil told, among which I heard that he / was a liar and the father of lies”; ll. 142–43). The point here is that one does not need to have a theological training, like the Bolognese students, to know that the devil is the prototypical liar; this was common knowledge.

falsa, "the false woman" (in reference to Potiphar's wife); "'l falso Sinon Greco di Troia" ("false Greek, Sinon of Troy"); *dire falso,* "to speak falsely"; "non fosti sì ver testimonio" ("you were not such a true witness"); *spergiuro,* "perjurer"; all used in *Inferno* 30, the last of the thirteen cantos devoted to Malebolge. Trying to fill in the gap created by Dante's omission of the name of the sin (a situation similar to that from *Inferno* 26–27), early commentators volunteered the phrase "falsari di parole" ("falsifiers of words") for the category of sinners represented by Sinon and the wife of Potiphar.

The omission of the sin's name is again rather atypical for Dante, who is usually very thorough in distributing and naming moral errors. A fresh look at the way in which the major medieval authors on *peccata linguae* defined the relationship of speech to falsehood will help me untie this new hermeneutical knot. In the ethical texts, the sin of *mendacium* was typically associated with *perjurium,* "perjury" (and sometimes with *falsum testimonium,* "false testimony") on account of their common element of falsehood.[141] In Peraldus, Aquinas, and Cavalca, although *mendacium* and *perjurium* are treated distinctly, they are allied and investigated by means of a common lexicon of intentional falsehood. Peraldus starts from St. Augustine's definition of lying as "falsa significatio vocis cum intentio fallendi" ("using a word to make someone believe something untrue, with the intention to deceive";[142] and, recalling the biblical image of the devil as the archetypal liar, evolves an original approach to the problematic of lying. Among the reasons that should prompt the detestation of this vice abominable to God, Peraldus first lists the natural repulsion to false things. To be more specific, he draws an elaborate parallel between lying and counterfeiting money:

> Quantum praevalet bonus denarius denario falso, tantum praevalet homo verax, homini falsi et mendaci. Unus bonus denarius valet centum falsos, unus homo verax centum mendaces. Unde multum melioraret se aliquis, si remoto peccato mendacii vera de caetero loqueretur: quia cui non displiceat si aliquem de denariis suis invenit falsum? Quis est qui non potius velit habere denarios bonos quam falsos?[143]

141. According to Casagrande and Vecchio, long before the medieval constitution of the systems of verbal sins, *mendacium, perjurium,* and *falsum testimonium* formed an inseparable sin-triad. However, medieval texts showed little interest in *falsum testimonium,* privileging instead the other two transgressions (*I peccati della lingua,* 251).

142. Peraldus, *SV,* 558.

143. Ibid. The same analogy occurs in another Peraldian text, *De eruditione principum* (On

> Just as the good dinar has more value than the forged one, so the man who tells the truth is worthier than the false and lying man. A good dinar is worth one hundred forged ones, and a man who tells the truth [is worth] one hundred liars. Therefore, every man would better himself if, casting away the sin of lying, would always say true things. For who does not hate to discover that one of his dinars is false? Who would not have true coins rather than false?

For Peraldus, a liar is a traitor who breaks the bonds of trust and deceives those who confide in him. He is worse than a thief, for the thief harms only the body, by stealing temporal goods necessary for the physical welfare, whereas the liar harms the soul, by inducing it into error. The wrong appetite of a thief is more understandable than the appetite of a liar, because the thief longs for good material things (which do not belong to him), whereas the liar desires spiritually evil things. Lying is thus worse than stealing, because the motivation for theft comes from self-concern, whereas the motivation for lying springs from the will to do wrong to others. Finally, lying is a devilish sin rooted in malice and able to do a great deal of harm both to the militant Church, who speaks the message of truth, and to society as a whole.[144]

Another socially disruptive speech for Peraldus is *falsum testimonium,* a subclass of lying that offends not only God (whose name is invoked as a token for the oath), but also the judges and those against whom the testimony is spoken and who are, in fact, innocent. Although treated separately from lie and false testimony, *perjurium* is also defined in terms of falsifying the truth, and its practitioners are labeled *falsarii,* "falsifiers":

> Si quis sigillo alicuius domini sibi commisso ad confirmandam aliquam veritatem, uteretur ad aliud confirmandum, ipse falsarius iudicaretur et excommunicatus

---

the erudition of the prince), where the moralist instructs the prince to control his speech as he would control money forging in the state (quoted in Casagrande and Vecchio, *I peccati della lingua,* 284).

144. Like Peraldus, Aquinas takes up the Augustinian definition of lying as a false signification by words but also introduces the Aristotelian tripartition of lying into officious, jocose, and mischievous. The intention to deceive belongs only to the latter class, which represents the perfection of lying (*ST* IIa-IIae Q. 110.1–2). Perjury is also described in terms of falsehood: "That perversity in swearing which is called perjury takes its species chiefly from falsehood. Lack of truth, lack of justice, lack of judgment; by the very fact that a man swears indiscreetly, he incurs the danger of lapsing into falsehood" (Q. 98.1). The noun "falsifier" does not appear, however, in Aquinas's handling of these types of verbal fraud, as it did in Peraldus, nor is the parallel between money and words drawn.

est.... Sic quam Deus permiserit hominibus ut assumant nomen suum ad confirmationem veritatis, si utant nomen eius ad confirmandum falsum ipsi falsarii suunt."[145]

If he who has the seal of his master, [a seal] entrusted to him for the confirmation of a truth, uses it in order to confirm something else, he will be judged as a falsifier and will be excommunicated.... Thus, since God allowed men to use His name to confirm a truth, if they use His name to confirm something false, they become falsifiers themselves.

Peraldus's terminology recurs in Cavalca's *Pungilingua,* which uses the analogy with falsifiers of seals and coins to lobby for harder legal punishments for perjurers. If the falsifiers of the papal seal are justly excommunicated and the falsifiers of coins or letters are rightfully condemned to burn at the stake for their crimes, it is all the more necessary to institute tougher penalties for perjurers, for they falsify God's name by swearing on it to promote a lie. As a consequence of their verbal alterations of truth, perjurers lose their souls and are doomed to Hell for having worked against both human and divine justice. In *Pungilingua,* the notion of verbal falsity inherent in perjury reemerges in the chapter on the "peccato del bugiare" ("the sin of lying"), which immediately follows the section on perjury.[146] Lying alters the human being in that part of the body that was divinely appointed for the expression of truth: the tongue, Cavalca says. Thus, liars have false tongues and are worse than the handlers of forged coins, for those who accidentally get a false coin are reluctant to use it out of fear of legal sanctions, whereas liars use false words with no shame or fear whatsoever (69–70).[147]

Peraldus's and Cavalca's treatments of perjury and lying can enlighten our understanding of Dante's treatment of the sinners from the last ring of Malebolge. Here, alchemists are assembled with impersonators, falsifiers of objects, money forgers, and those who speak falsely (*dire falso,* in the text), grouped by Dante under the generic noun *i falsador,* "falsifiers," introduced in *Inf.* 29.57.[148] The link between the sin of falsifying and Dante's central

145. Peraldus, *SV,* 558.

146. In this, Cavalca faithfully follows Peraldus's arrangement, where *perjurium* occupies the fourth position and *mendacium* (with its appendix *falsum testimonium*) the fifth.

147. Cavalca, *Pungilingua,* 69–70.

148. Robert Durling offers as possible sources for Dante's series of *falsador* the Old French *Tristan* or Gottfried von Strassburg's *Tristan* ("Dante among the Falsifiers," in *Lectura Dantis: "Inferno,"* edited by A. Mandelbaum, A. Oldcorn, and Ch. Ross [Berkeley: California University Press, 1998], 393). Roberto Sarolli tells us that Luigi Pietrobono was the first to identify the

notion of *malizia* is established through a metaphor associating this pouch with the island of Egina: "Non credo ch'a veder maggior tristizia / fosse in Egina il popol tutto infermo, / quando fu l'aere sì pien di malizia" ("I do not believe it was a greater sadness to see / in Aegina the whole people sick, when the air / was so full of malice"; *Inf.* 29.58–60). Here, *malizia* denotes the biologically infested and contagious quality of the air, but even in this sense, the term may be read as a grim reminder that we are still in Malebolge, the deep infernal zone where sins of malice are condemned. *Malizia* as a pathological quality of the air is also reminiscent of Dante's (and the general medieval) conception of sin as disease.

It should thus come as no surprise that people who spoke falsely from malice, as Peraldus and Cavalca describe liars and perjurers, can be found side by side with other types of forgers in the last division of fraud. Numerous textual indications reveal Dante's reasons for the alignment of impersonation with fraudulent speech. Mirra, who in the myth took a fictitious identity to sleep with her father, is depicted as "falsificando sé in altrui forma" ("counterfeiting herself in another's shape"; *Inf.* 30.41). With a variation of the same phrase, Gianni Schicchi's sin is described as "falsificare in sé Buoso Donati" ("counterfeiting in himself Buoso Donati"; l. 44). We have just seen that in the *lingua*-texts, the sin of lying is tantamount to forging one's identity, to falsifying one's tongue, more exactly. The same definition of lying as assuming a false identity underlies Dante's introduction of Potiphar's wife, described as "la falsa ch'accusò Gioseppo" ("the false woman who accused Joseph"; l. 97), and of Sinon, labeled as "'l falso Sinon Greco di Troia" ("false Greek, Sinon of Troy"; l. 98).

According to Genesis 39:6–23, the wife of Potiphar, the Egyptian wealthy man for whom Joseph was working, unsuccessfully tried to seduce him. Outraged by the young man's rejection and using as evidence the garment Joseph accidentally lost trying to avoid her, she told her servants that Joseph had attempted to rape her. Using the same proof, that is, Joseph's garment, to support her story, she lied again, this time to her husband, about what had happened. Thus, by inventing the story of the attempted rape, the woman constructed an *altered* reality (in the etymological sense of *to alter,* that of creating *another* fact), and by imagining herself within

---

four types of sinners punished in this circle ("Moglie di Putifarre," in *Enciclopedia Dantesca,* 6 vols. [Rome: Istituto della Enciclopedia Italiana, 1970–1984]).

this fabricated reality, she falsified herself just like Mirra—she imagined a "raped self" that did not correspond to the factual truth. The medium that Potiphar's wife used to accomplish this substitution of realities was the words she uttered to substantiate her accusation against Joseph, a lie that would change Joseph's destiny and thereby the fate of the Jewish people. It is this biblical narrative that determines Dante to declare the Egyptian woman *falsa,* an adjective referring to her entire identity, not only to this isolated act of speech that incriminated Joseph.

The use of the adjective 'false' recalls the story of Vanni Fucci, punished in the circle of the thieves. Vanni evokes how he escaped a death sentence when someone else was unjustly accused of robbing the church in Pistoia: "falsamente già fu apposto altrui" ("it was falsely blamed on others"; *Inf.* 24.139). This line, too, establishes a link between someone's identity (*altrui*) and an act of speech (the false accusation) that caused great harm to an innocent person. Both Vanni Fucci's confession and the episode of Potiphar's wife confirm the malicious power (and consequences) of words when they blur the natural lines between true and false. In Vanni Fucci's story, some inaccurate words sent an innocent man to death, just as in the biblical story an unjust accusation had sent Joseph, another innocent man, to prison.

Along the same lines, the figure of the Greek drawn from the myth of the Trojan horse (and we remember from *Inferno* 26 Dante's fascination with this story) is introduced through the adjective *falso,* followed by an ironical phrase enhancing the expressive effect of the adjective: "greco di Troia." Obviously, Sinon was a Greek … from Greece, but by mocking him Dante alludes to the fictitious identity Sinon built for himself in order to enter the city and convince the Trojans to accept the gift of the horse (a great fraud itself): he passed himself off as a defector of the Greek cause who wanted to side with the Trojans. The medium he used in this enterprise was his artful, Ulyssean rhetoric. Sinon is in fact a *falsa lingua,* to take up Peraldus's synecdoche, a person who uses his eloquence in fraudulent ways to enforce another, major fraud—the Trojan horse, a horse that is not what it seems to be. Once again, words, gifts, and identities shift in a complex Geryonic interplay to deceive and harm others. For, Sinon's artful lies eventually caused the fall of Troy and the destruction of the Trojan civilization.

In the text, this mythological figure engages in strife with one of Dante's contemporaries, a reminder of the immunity of sin to history. At hearing himself named a false Greek from Troy by master Adam (a famous English money forger), Sinon reacts violently, "forse d'esser nomato sì oscuro" ("perhaps resented being named so darkly"; l. 101) and strikes Adam in his aching belly. Sinon's violent reaction to the verbal insult is clear evidence of the powerful effect of words on the human psyche, since name calling always triggers psychological (and here also physical) consequences. When Adam strikes Sinon back, the latter uses his words as a tool for revenge and upsets Adam by reminding him that the arm with which he struck was not so fast when he went to the stake to be burnt for money forging (ll. 109–10). In a strongly realistic vein, the two sinners swear at each other with an impressive eloquence of evil and curse the two organs responsible for their wicked words: Sinon curses Adam's tongue and Adam Sinon's mouth.[149] The verbal duel between the two is worth quoting for the wealth of linguistic references it offers:

> E l'idropico: "Tu di' ver di questo,
> ma tu non fosti sì ver testimonio
> là 've del ver fosti a Troia richiesto."
> "S'io dissi falso, e tu falsasti il
> conio,"
> disse Sinon; "e son qui per un fallo,
> e tu per più ch'alcun altro
> demonio!"
> "Ricorditi, spergiuro, del cavallo,"
> rispuose quel ch'avëa infiata l'epa;
> "e sieti reo che tutto il mondo
> sallo!"
> "E te sia rea la sete onde ti crepa,"
> disse 'l Greco, "la lingua, e l'acqua
> marcia
> che 'l ventre innanzi a li occhi sì
> t'assiepa!"
> Allora il monetier: "Così si squarcia
> la bocca tua per tuo mal come suole
> ché, s'i' ho sete e omor mi rinfarcia,
> tu hai l'arsura e 'l capo che ti duole,
> e per leccar lo specchio di Narcisso
> non vorresti a 'nvitar molte parole."
> (*Inf.* 30.112–29)

And the hydroptic: "You say true there, but you / were not such a true witness where you were asked / for the truth at Troy." / "If I spoke falsely, you falsified the coinage," said / Sinon, "and I am here for one fault, but you for more / than any other demon!" / "Remember, perjurer, the Horse," replied he of the / swollen liver; "and let it be bitter to you that the / whole world knows of it!" / "And to you bitter be the thirst that cracks," said / the Greek, "your tongue, and the stagnant water that / makes of your belly a hedge before your eyes!" / Then the coiner: "Your mouth gapes because of / your disease, as usual; for, if I am thirsty and liquid swells me, / you have burning fever and a head that aches, / and to lick the mirror of Narcissus you would not / need to be invited with many words!"

149. The two anatomic references are reminiscent of the first phase of the medieval discourse on *peccata linguae,* a phase in which the tongue and the mouth were held directly responsible for malicious utterances.

The first verses in this passage persistently revolve around the dynamic truth/falsehood and offer us the complete terminology for Sinon's verbal sins: the word *ver* occurs obsessively in three separate positions (as noun, adjective, and adverb) and is played against the synonyms for falsehood: "non … sì ver testimonio," *dire falso, falsare,* and *spergiuro.*[150] This list of terms spans the sin-triad of false speech associated by Peraldus and Cavalca in their tracts: false testimony, lying, perjury. All three varieties of verbal fraud apply to Dante's character, not just the sin of lying. This may be one of the reasons why Dante avoided using the label "liars" for this type of sinners; the complexity of the process whereby speech appropriates semiotic falsehood extends beyond simple lying. Lies can be uttered in a public place, in front of official authorities, and thus they acquire false testimonial connotations, or they can be shored up by an oath and become perjury.[151] Sinon's skillful speech crossed the line between truth and falsehood and enabled the Greek warriors to trespass the boundary separating them from the Trojans—the walls of the city. For this, he is intended by Dante as a prototypical transgressive speaker who now, punished in Hell, is set as a moral counterexample.

An important element in the *tenzone* between Master Adam and Sinon is the verse that synthetically establishes the equivalence between falsifying words and counterfeiting money: "S'io dissi falso, e tu falsasti il conio" ("If I spoke falsely, you falsified the coinage"), a line recalling the association of counterfeiters with liars from the world of fiction. Both this verse and the composition of this ring of sinners point to the common medieval comparison of words to money, a comparison drawn on the basis of their function as signs. Money and words were considered to be semiotic systems referring to specific segments of reality: the linguistic sign stood for the mental concept, while the monetary sign for merchandise. The comparison

150. Regarding the word *spergiuro,* Truscott believes that it was suggested to Dante by Virgil's text (*Aeneid* II, 195–96), where Sinon is described as guilty of perjury or false oath ("Ulysses and Guido," 64). Brugnoli points to the relationship between Ulysses and Sinon in the *Aeneid* and stresses that Sinon was instructed by Ulysses on what to tell and how to speak ("Dante filologo," 36–37).

151. It is also worth noting that Dante's perception of Sinon was common in the literary culture of the Middle Ages. In Alain of Lille's *Plaint of Nature,* for instance, we see Sinon "arming himself with subterfuges for a sinuous speech" (217). What for Alain was sinuous speech for Dante becomes transgressive speech, since the deceitful Greek is punished in Hell, in the deepest ring of Fraud.

became possible because the same texts dealing with the sacred function of words as conveyors of truth were also concerned with the sins of usury and avarice, which had a direct relationship with money. In fact, the analogy words-coins was a conflation of Aristotle's economic theory, as expounded in *Politics,* and Augustine's doctrine of words as vocal signs, as expressed in several of his works (*Confessions, On Christian Doctrine,* and *On The Trinity*). According to Joël Biard, in the Middle Ages both the name of the coin and the image engraved on it were essential components of the monetary sign, since they represented a warrant for its value:

> The name constitutes the monetary sign as such, by institution. The noun designates this founding linkage. The image is an essential element, as well. It points to the authority that holds monetary power. But the image is not a mere sign of identification, nor a mere duplication of the noun. The image guarantees the value, and thus becomes sign, *of the signifying character* of the coin. Since there is a convention in the rapport of equivalence thus established between coin and merchandise, a *warrant* is necessary. The image testifies to this warranty.[152]

In *Inferno* 30, the semiotic value of the coin is alluded to by master Adam, who explains his sin in metaphorical terms: "io falsai / la lega suggellata del Batista" ("I falsified the alloy sealed with the Baptist"; ll. 73–74). Adam's oblique reference to the *fiorini* is in fact Dante's subtle way of highlighting the seriousness of the sin of counterfeiting. Here, the Florentine coin is designated not by its name but by the symbolic image it bears, that of John the Baptist. Master Adam's sin appears even viler since the image on the coin did not represent a political leader of the day, but a biblical hero and a martyr for the Christian faith. Master Adam used the sacred image of the Baptist as a token for his fraudulent action, just as the perjurer takes, according to every standard definition of perjury, God's name as a guarantor for false words. Dante is likely to have taken up the comparison between monetary sign and linguistic sign from Peraldus's treatise on the sins of the tongue.[153] For nowhere in the *Comedy* has this synonymy been established

152. Joël Biard, "Signe monétaire et signe linguistique: La critique de la chrématistique dans l'école buridanienne," in *Les philosophies morales et politiques au Moyen Âge: Proceedings of the 9th International Congress of Medieval Philosophy,* edited by B. Carlos Bazán et al. (New York: Legas, 1995), 1424; emphasis Biard, translation mine). Biard does not mention Peraldus in his exemplification of medieval intellectuals who took up this comparison, but the French Dominican could further substantiate Biard's claim.

153. Another important piece of evidence for Peraldus's stamp on this canto is adduced by

as clearly and explicitly as in *Inferno* 30, the canto of the falsifiers of words and metals.[154] Peraldus used the comparison words-coins to describe two sins of speech: *mendacium* (with one of its subclasses, *falsum testimonium*) and *perjurium.* For him, lying, false testimony, and perjury represent acts of falsifying words, acts similar to the operation of forging coins. Sinon and Potiphar's wife, whom Dante selects to represent the false speakers, are guilty of these particular sins of speech, and they are grouped with the false coiners. Sinon's phrase "S'io dissi falso, e tu falsasti il conio" establishes an explicit rapport of equivalence between speaking falsely and forging coins. Thus, *Inferno* 30 is another place where the world of the myth is brought back to life with a new meaning and pressed in the service of a Christian cause. Just as in Ulysses's case, through the figure of Sinon, the intrinsic value of eloquence is dramatically called into question. Being a skillful speaker avails nothing when speech is built on a web of lies and deceit that causes only disasters. As Dante himself warns in *De monarchia,* "in matters of feeling and conduct, words are to be believed less than deeds" (1.13.4).

For the last circle of Malebolge, Peraldus and Cavalca furnish the necessary key to understanding not only Dante's alignment of money with words but also the connection between falsifying and treason, the following sin in the structure of Hell. According to the two speech moralists, betrayal is based on a verbal sin called "secreta amici revelare" ("disclosing a friend's secrets"). But we recall that the sin of perjury is itself defined as an act of treason: Peraldus labels the perjurer a traitor, and Cavalca posits Judas as the prototypical perjurer. In *Inferno* 28, Dante also describes the act of political betrayal in terms of lying: "a Ceperan, là dove fu bugiardo ciascun Pugliese" ("at Ceperano, where every Apulian was a liar"; ll. 16–17). The citizens of Puglia are called liars because they were disloyal subjects and betrayed their king, as the historical documents testify.

Opposed to legendary figures such as Ulysses, Jason, and Sinon, who not only are fraudulent speakers but also come from a pagan world popu-

---

Shoaf, who argues that Peraldus's image of "false water" lies at the root of Dante's portrayal of the avaricious Master Adam ("Dante and Peraldus," 311–13).

154. An interesting example of the influence of money on language occurs in *Inferno* 21.37–42, the canto of the barraters, described as people who for the sake of money change "no" to "yes." For a thorough investigation of Dante's financial imagery, see chapter "Commerce and Language," in Joan Ferrante's *The Political Vision of the Divine Comedy,* where the author argues that for Dante language was a basic form of exchange, like commerce, and thus subject to similar kinds of abuses.

lated by "dei falsi e bugiardi" ("false and lying gods"), is the Christian language of faith, the unique depository of truth. In *Convivio,* Dante repeatedly describes faith as immune from mendacity, and in *Paradiso,* the truth of Piccarda Donati's words is reinforced by the phrase "alma beata non poria mentire" ("a blessed soul could never lie"; 4.95). As a *scriba Dei,* Dante himself is aware of the dangers he incurs in his assiduous attempts to describe a vision that can easily be judged as mendacious, and consequently, he takes numerous precautions to assure the reader that the story recounted in the *Comedy* is authentic.[155] One of these instances occurs in *Paradiso* 17, when Cacciaguida invests the pilgrim with the mission of recounting his otherworldly journey. Cacciaguida asks Dante to tell the whole and unaltered story of his ultra-terrestrial experience: "Ma nondimen, rimossa ogne menzogna, / tutta tua vïsion fa manifesta" ("But nonetheless, putting aside every falsehood, / make manifest all your vision" (ll. 127–28).[156] Unlike liars and perjurers, who pervert the gift of speech, Dante places his verbal art in the service of a transcendental cause and, in response to Cacciaguida's injunction, posits his poem as a vehicle of Truth, similar to the sacramental rhetoric of the Bible.

155. For an extended and superb analysis of these textual precautions, see Barolini, *The Undivine Comedy,* which centers specifically on the narrative strategies Dante uses to secure the credibility of his story.

156. We can read these lines as an intratextual response to the poet's address to the reader from *Inferno* 13: "s'ì vederai / cose che torrien fede al mio sermone" ("you will see things that would / make you disbelieve my speech"; ll. 21–22).

FOUR

Blasphemy and the Poetics of Violence

JEAN DE MEUN'S APOLOGIES AND THE *QUERELLE DE LA ROSE*

"Et plus puni devroient estre / devant l'empereour celestre / Clerc qui s'abandonent as vices, / Que les genz lais, simples et nices, / Qui n'ont pas les vertuz escriptes, / Que cil tienent vils et despites" (*Roman de la Rose* 18667–73).[1]

In the previous chapters I have detailed the ways in which, under the cover of the personages he impersonates, Jean challenges the ideological and linguistic conventions of his time. Through the agency of Faus Semblant, he conveys antireligious and heretical ideas; through Dame Raison and La Vieille, he encourages the use of unrestricted (and sometimes blasphemous) language. Several of his characters express viewpoints that undermine the sacred institution of marriage, and the plot itself ends with a scandalous sexual act: Amant's rape of a rose bush standing for the virgin young woman he has hitherto pursued. But in the midst of this explosive material, Jean decides to drop off all disguise and to make a few writerly

1. "Clerks who abandon themselves to vices should be more punished before the celestial emperor than should lay people, simple and ignorant, who do not have described for them in writing the virtues [read habits, behaviors] that the clerks consider low and despicable."

comments on his artistic enterprise. In lines 15139–306, for the first and only time in the poem, he steps out of his fictive world and boldly assumes his own, authorial voice. Jean justifies this move by a wish to apologize for his lampoons against the female gender, for his criticism of men of religion, and also for his foolish language. He admits that in the course of his poem, he has often violated the rules for decorous speech and voiced unorthodox notions; then, he explicitly directs his apology to the readership and, very significantly, to the Catholic Church.

Jean's concern about his deviant language gives rise to several critical questions: Was the freedom of speech a right that the vernacular poet could use without incurring certain (ethical or legal) risks? Could the authority of the literary text be so powerful that, if misused, it would pose a threat to the authority of the Church? Can we find in the Catholic readership of the *Rose* a personality with a strong background in ethical writings able to cast light on Jean's self-confessed literary abuses? We can answer these questions by situating the apologetic segment of the poem in relationship to Jean Gerson's polemical texts in the *Querelle de la Rose* and to some of the moral tracts he wrote outside of the *Querelle*. Between 1400 and 1409, Gerson produced several texts on verbal sins, which, to my knowledge, literary critics have not yet considered in their discussions of the *Querelle*. These texts deal either with specific transgressions: *Contre le péché de blaspheme* (Against the sin of blasphemy], *Contre les tentations de blaspheme* (Against the temptations of blasphemy), *Contre les fausses assertions des flatteurs* (Against the false assertions of flatterers), or with the more generic theme of the government of the tongue: *Pour qu'on refrène sa langue* (For the guard of one's tongue) and *De custodia linguae et corde bene ruminanda* (On the government of the tongue and the well meditating heart].[2] Gerson's constant preoccupation with the abuses of language establishes him as a continuator of the tradition of *peccata linguae* from the High Middle Ages. The fact that many of the ideas he develops in these tracts also emerge in his contributions to the *Querelle* suggests that his virulent attack against the *Rose* is deeply rooted in his activity as an ethicist of speech.

2. For the modern edition of these texts, see Jean Gerson, *Œuvres complètes,* edited by Palémon Glorieux, vol. 7 (Paris: Desclée and Cie, 1966): *L'Œuvre française (292–339): Contre le péché de blaspheme* (293, 3–5 [text number followed by page numbers]), *Contre les tentations de blaspheme* (336, 412–16), *Contre les fausses assertions des flatteurs* (325, 360–63), and *Pour qu'on refrène sa langue* (331, 400–404). For *De custodia linguae,* see vol. 9 (1971): *L'Œuvre doctrinale (423–91),* 427 (under "Quaestiones" 4, 64–72).

Fleming makes the important point that Gerson is the first modern critic of the poem, the first person who needs to be convinced that Jean de Meun was a true catholic and a theologian; until Gerson's time the poet had been widely acknowledged as a moralist in morally conservative circles. Jean's public image would dramatically change in the following centuries, and Fleming accounts for this change in the following terms: "There was a widespread reaction against 'obscenity' in many European circles in the late Middle Ages and the Renaissance, which probably helps account for the naughty reputation of the *Roman* by the 16th century."[3] The more recent study by Casagrande and Vecchio in the field of moral theology compels me to add that this public current against obscenity was the result of the major changes that the medieval texts on *peccata linguae* had caused over time in the Westerners' attitude toward language.

The "Confession"

The *Romance of the Rose* had an extraordinary fortune in medieval European culture. About three hundred French manuscripts of it are known (an unusually high number for a medieval piece of writing), and many other manuscripts have survived in translation in several European languages.[4] An important detail accompanies the fate of the French versions of Jean's sequel: some of them have come down to us as moralized rewritings of it. Just as the Middle Ages recuperated a famous (but controversial) classical poet like Ovid, in the form of texts called *Ovide moralisé* (Moralized Ovid), in the same way, some of the first copyists of Jean's *Rose* felt compelled to alter the original version, by removing controversial passages and/or by adding to it more stressed moral tones. These ideological adjustments seem to be at odds with Jean's professed program in the *Rose*—that of providing a sound education to the French youth in matters of life and love. In order to solve the paradox posed by a self-professed moral piece of writing that needed to be further ethicized by its copyists, we have to take a closer look at what Jean himself has to say about his work. The poet assesses his diction in the following terms:

3. Fleming, *The "Roman de la Rose,"* 47–49, 135.

4. For a list of the surviving manuscripts of the *Rose,* see Badel, *Le "Roman de la Rose",* or Huot, *The "Romance of the Rose."*

Mais ainz que plus m'en oiez dire, / Ailleurs vueill un petit entendre / Pour moi des males genz deffendre, / Non pas pour vous faire muser, / Mais pour moi contre euls escuser. / Si vous pri, seigneur amoreus, / Par les geus d'amours savoreus, / Que se vous i trouvez paroles / Semblanz trop baudes ou trop foles, / Par quoi saillent li mesdisant / Qui de nous aillent mesdisant / Des choses a dire ou dites, / Que cortoisement les desdites. / Et quant vous les avrez des diz / Repris, retardez ou desdiz, / Se mi dit son de tel manière / Qu'il soit droiz que pardon en quiere / Pri vous que vous me le pardoingniez / Et de par moi leur respoingniez / Que ce requeroit la matire / Qui vers teus paroles me tire / Par les propietez de sai: / Et pour ce teus paroles ai.... / Et s'il y a nule parole / Qui sainte eglise tiengne a fole, / Presz sui k'a son voloir l'amende / Se je puis souffire a l'amende. (15158–306)

But before you hear me say anything more, I want to move aside a little to defend myself against wicked people, not so much to delay you as to excuse myself to them. Therefore I beg you, amorous lords, by the delicious games of love, if you find here any speeches that are too bawdy or silly and that might make slanderous critics who go around speaking ill of us rise up over things that I have said or will say, that you will courteously oppose them. Then when you have reproved, prevented, or opposed these speeches, if what I say is of such nature that I may justly ask pardon for them, I beg you to pardon me and to reply to them through me that my subject matter demanded these things; it draws me toward such things by its own properties, and therefore I have such speeches.... And if I make any utterance that Holy Church may consider foolish, I am ready at her wish to amend it if I am capable of making the amend.[5]

Although this is a small excerpt encapsulating only the core of Jean's self-defense, on the whole the apology spans no fewer than one hundred sixty-six verses (ll. 15140–306), a telling measure of the author's feeling of guilt. Structurally inserted at the midpoint of the poem, the segment represents a spectacular move on the part of a medieval poet. If we consider Paul Zumthor's assertion that the most difficult task of a medievalist is to find poetic subjectivities, in other words, medieval authors who had the wit to say "I," we will grasp the full significance of Jean's decision to introduce himself to his readers. The poet's unique assumption of his own voice, in defiance of all the other characters whom he has impersonated hitherto, raises in the reader the awareness of an exceptional moment of both textual and extratextual nature. It is the moment when the "producer" of the show

5. The word "change" Dahlberg uses is somewhat unfaithful to the spirit of the original, since in the text, *amende,* "amend" (noun), or *amender,* "to amend," has a stronger moral connotation.

and, at the same time, the actor able to play magisterially so many different parts unexpectedly removes all masks, discloses his true identity, and speaks in his own, authorial voice. Strategically, it is an ingenious move, for once the writer steps out of the world of fiction and compels his readers to focus on the significance of this event, the attention of the audience shifts from the text to the writer.

Jean's *excusacion* is important from a twofold perspective: that of the artificer who slips out of the bounds of literary fiction and objectively evaluates his text as a linguistic artifact, and that of the remorseful Christian, who raises issues of morality related to the process of literary creation and then apologizes to the Church. Jean's discourse in the first person reveals an unexpected facet of his personality—that of a self-declared penitent sinner who problematizes the flaws of his literary craftsmanship. And what vices does Jean identify in his art? His direct address to the readership posits as a motivation the need for self-defense, a need prompted by his virtual detractors. At a first instance, by admitting to having dropped some bawdy and silly words, the writer seems to apologize for some seemingly harmless slips of the tongue. Without being sure that these words are really blameworthy, he nevertheless realizes that they might upset his admirers, so he leaves the assessment of his linguistic boldness to them. If they deem that Jean's language offers reasons for apologies, they should not only forgive him in their hearts, but also defend him publicly, against his potential calumniators. Placing his defense into his admirers' mouths institutes an ingenious dialogic technique that allows the author to address not only his supporters but also, obliquely, his enemies. He asks his faithful readers to courteously reply to his potential critics that if he has used low language throughout the poem, he has not done it by levity of mind, but because the topic of the poem has required so.

Jean invokes the excuse of the stylistic decorum to legitimize his use of coarse language; if his speech is sometimes uncouth, it is because what he is talking about is so base. To justify his bold verbal choices, he invokes the principle of literature as a mimetic art, and, in an ingenious move, blends the requisite of narrative veracity with the moral imperative of telling the truth. The classical authority that serves him best here is the Roman historian Sallust, whom Jean does not hesitate to paraphrase freely and who gives him the opportunity to dramatize his own status as a reporter of contemporary events and mores:

Car chose est droituriere et juste, / Selonc l'auctorité Saluste / Qui nous dist par samblance voire: / "Tout ne soit il samblable gloire / De celui qui la chose fait / Et del escrivain qui le fait / Veult metre proprement en livre, / Pour mieus la verité descrivre, / Si n'est ce pas chose legiere, / Ainz est mout fort de grant maniere / Metre bien les faiz en escrit, / Car quiconques la chose escrit, / Se dou voir ne vous veult embler, / Le dit doit le fait ressembler; / Car les voiz as choses voisines / Doivent estre a leur faiz cousines. "/ Si me couvient ainsi parler / Se par le droit m'en vueill aler. (15181–98)

This procedure is just and right according to the authority of Sallust, who tells us in a true judgment: "Although there may not be the sane glory for him who performs a certain deed and for him who wants to set down the deed accurately in a book, the better to describe the truth, still it is not an easy thing to set down deeds in writing; it requires great strength of technique, for if anyone writes something without wishing to rob you of its truth, then what he says must resemble the deed. Words that are neighbors with things must be cousins to their deeds." Therefore I have to speak thus if I want to proceed in the right way.

Poetry is placed one on one with history in Jean's rewriting of Sallust, since that which for the Roman author was the task of the historian now becomes the duty of the poet. He who writes poetry, just like the chronicler who writes objectively about history, has to preserve the truth in his verse. Just as the historian faithfully and truthfully depicts the events that he is witnessing, so the poet has to represent the facts of his world with no alterations. There is a genetic affiliation between language and reality, words and deeds belong to the same ontological family, and whoever makes of truthful writing a moral obligation must place reality and text in a specular relationship. Sallust's description of the daunting task of the historian serves Jean as a springboard from which to launch his apologetic display and to justify his language. It is the ethical requisite of telling the truth that renders writing a difficult enterprise, the author warns his readers.

The Sallustian paraphrase ushers us into the core of Jean's self-defense, and what at first seemed an excuse for some unhappy lexical choices now reveals something much deeper. Narrowing the field of his targeted audience, Jean ends up addressing only two segments of it, the ones he knows he has criticized most: women and the religious figures of the day. In the discourses of La Vieille and Le Jaloux, Jean has drawn a horrendous picture of feminine mores, whereas through Faus Semblant he has mounted a virulent attack against the mendicant orders. It is this set of discourses that he alludes to, mindful that not only his language, but also the content of his sayings, may discontent some. The writer argues that he has not only voiced the historical truth in his book, but he has also taken care to instruct and correct depraved women and hypocritical friars. His text is not only a chronicle of mores that immortalizes people and events, but also a didactic work, intended for the correction of bad morals. The issue of textual truthfulness becomes even more specific when Jean counters the potential charge of lying about women by invoking the long-standing misogynistic tradition on which he has heavily relied. There can be no place for lies, he maintains, in a long series of writers who have said the same things about women in different epochs and in different places of the world. Again, writing equates telling the truth, and Jean contends that he is lying to the extent that so many erudite figures from the past have lied about women, which cannot be. The Horatian tenet of *docere delectandi* that Jean is quick to invoke gives him afresh the opportunity to reflect on his text as an artifact. In his criticism of women, he has faithfully reproduced what the authorities said, and then he has contributed some remarks of his own to this impressive written tradition. Being an integral part of the artistic *delectatio* he owes to the readership, his personal contribution to the misogynistic discourse is just part of the poetic game (ll. 15199–246).

Beyond the diplomatic move of devolving the responsibility for his virulent criticism of womankind to his predecessors, there is another element in Jean's relationship to misogynistic literature that compels attention. For Jean, writing poetry entails not only immortalizing the truth but also creating something new, and creation involves playing, having fun. The description of poetry as *geu,* "game," is an important factor in Jean's direct address, not only because it has the value of a profession of artistic faith, but also because it is meant to attract the sympathy and the understanding of the reader. Jean calls himself a poet, who, like all other poets, has to play according to some rules. One of these rules requires that the author bring something new in the material he is treating in order to please the public. Although the few personal remarks about women—"moz mordans et chenins" ("biting and hateful words"; l. 15203)—might displease the ladies who recognize themselves in the picture, the same remarks, however, might please a larger body of society that is morally upright, Jean adds to his defense.

The same mechanism of argumentation takes place in the justification of the criticism against hypocritical friars, only that here the emphasis is placed no longer on tradition, but on the poet's own spirit of observation.

His attacks are not aimed at truly religious people, he carefully mentions, but at those who, under the appearance of sanctity, are corrupt and arrogant people. As a Christian, Jean is better than they, therefore entitled to criticize them, because he at least overtly admits to being a sinner (l. 15262), whereas the hypocritical, depraved friars present themselves as holy men. This is how the poet justifies the *saiete,* "arrows," he shoots from the bow of his art, the *fers,* "iron," of his sword. The powerful imagery of attack is telling about Jean's awareness of the linguistic aggressiveness to which he resorts in his vituperation of the mendicant orders. It is an awareness that culminates with his apology to the Church, the only official institution toward which the writer feels he can be held accountable, and for the sake of which he is ready to mend his verbal abuses. Language as strike, arrow, and sword is justified, as in the case of the criticism of depraved women, by ethical purposes. It is a means by which the writer-moralist assumes the difficult task of eradicating social evil. The poetic language is corrupt because it deals with corruption; it is violent because it deals with violence.

The fact that the only direct intervention of Jean in the poem ends with an address to the *Sainte Eglise,* "Holy Church," bespeaks the poet's ultimate concern: his words might have upset many, and he is well aware thereof, but what really seems to matter to him is the sanction of the Church. All the linguistic trespasses confessed hitherto are now related to the reception the ecclesiastical authority may give to his book. A hermeneutic question that arises here is the semantic value of *paroles foles,* "silly words," an ambiguous phrase that lends itself to multiple interpretations. Does Jean mean that the Church might consider his attack against the friars excessive? That she might consider it untruthful? But he has just specified that he did not say anything in his critique that was not legitimized by other books, proven by experience or by reason. Once again, the issue of the text as a speaker of truth surfaces in a vital point of the writerly discourse. Taking into account the generality of the phrase and the other instances in which Jean uses the adjective *fol/fole,* it is more likely that the expression describes the poet's overall usage of language. Writing during a time when so many new words were entering the vocabulary of the vernacular and when the ecclesiastical authorities were taking drastic measures to police lay speech, Jean sets his anxiety in relationship to the ethical dimension of his writing. Here, the concerns of the poet are coupled with that of the Christian, an element of novelty in literature, and the drama that arises is that the sharp tongue of the satirist, which Jean has inherited from his cherished classical authors, clashes with the medieval Christian ideals of disciplined speech. It is the awareness of this clash that motivates the author to intervene directly in the text and to invoke the authority of the Church.

The *Testament* brings more indications about the way in which Jean wanted his allegorical love poem to be read and assessed. At the beginning of the testamentary text, he contrasts this new poem to the output of his youth, in which many readers took delight. The youthful writings were born out of vanity, whereas the *Testament* is a work of self-redemption that aims at amending the previous works, which have been of little spiritual profit to him (ll. 5–8). In this first move, the poet seems to obliquely confess that writing the *Rose* was a mistake, attributable to the erring of a young heart worthy of forgiveness. In a second move, however, this self-incriminating posture changes visibly, as the author raises a very important hermeneutic question. Although this question is cast in general, impersonal terms, it can also be read in an autobiographic key. Since the seven liberal arts, law, and theology are based on *maintes paroles,* "many words," Jean reminds us, some glossing is necessary for the profit of the public. Those readers and commentators who see the worst in the texts of the *acteurs* are committing a villainous act, since they should see therein only what is "le plus sain" ("soundest/healthiest"). (The word *acteurs* is to be taken here in its typically medieval double meaning, of both "authors" and "authorities.") If the dead writers could, they would defend themselves in the face of their detractors. Unless the authors say obvious errors, no one should criticize them; they have studied so much for our salvation that one must gloss their sayings very favorably (ll. 77–80). Jean himself is aware of his status as an *actor* (both an author and an authority), but one who is still very much alive and who, very astutely, assumes in these lines the posture of a reader, not of a writer, most likely in order to enhance the sense of objectivity he wants to attach to his oblique self-defense. If the authors did a good thing in instructing us, then we, as readers, Jean warns, would be very ungrateful and rude if we spoke ill of them or of their learning.

The nature of this hermeneutical section of the *Testament* becomes more personal, and at the same time more passionate, when Jean is addressing such a potentially inept, hateful reader in a very direct and aggressive way: "Tu qui contr'eulz ne fines de ton venin vuidier, / Ne sces espoir leur textes jusqu'au vif desvuidier, / Et pour ce te devroies d'eulz blasmer refroidier, / Car je cuit que leur fautes sont en ton fol cuidier" ("You who do not manage to empty yourself of the venom against them [the authors] / You have no hope in spinning the essence off their texts, / Therefore you should cool off in blaming them / For I think their mistakes lie in your own foolish judgment"; ll. 85–88). If among the countless goods that the authors have said or done there is, accidentally, one bad thing, this does not diminish the value of their works, and no single author owes any apology, for authors have opened to us the way to all the sciences (ll. 89–96).

The tone of these lines is too passionate not to be read in an autobiographic key, and there are several aspects that compel attention here in that they hark back to the "young, vain" Jean: as in the *Rose,* the question of written language is problematized, since this medium of communication is cast again as a tool intrinsically prone to misunderstanding, whether it is used in the seven liberal arts, in law, or in theology. When he defends the *auctores,* he diplomatically identifies himself with their readership, but this only serves him to defend himself better, under the shield of objectivity. Here again, Jean is a double dealer, both a writer (an authority) and a reader of authorities. More importantly for us, he implicitly casts himself as a self-reader; a conscientious writer who goes over his older texts and looks at them with a mature, and at the same time honest, scrutinizing eye. The problem of potential misinterpretation of the written word can easily be solved or avoided, Jean suggests, with the proviso that the reader has a grain of good will, for charity, respect, and gratitude are owed to educators who have set things in writing. And we have seen that this is how Jean views himself: as a French Sallust, a historian of mores who cannot lie and who feels obliged to instruct his readers; therefore, he owes no apology to anyone (a clear hint at the *excusacion* from the romance). Like in the *Rose,* if misinterpretation occurs, it is not because the text is evil (despite some minor, possible flaws), but because the (mis)interpreter, or detractor, holds in himself the vices or mistakes he sees in the text.

I find it imperative to reassert that what Jean is debating here is the status of Christian didactic writing that uses the vehicle of artistic imagination in the service of truth, the kind of writing he himself has produced. His art, read *Rose,* may seem now, in retrospect, a product of youthful vanity, but there should be no doubt that the program at the heart of the poem, its entire design, is Christian and educative, since it is intended for our *sauvement,* "salvation." This is the key word of the hermeneutical part of the

Testament, and it is on account of this design that Jean invites, moreover demands, that his early poetry be favorably interpreted.[6]

The "Trial"

But did Jean's excuses and self-explaining convince his virtual judges of his good intentions? The answer to this question comes not from his contemporaries but from his posterity, given that Jean's self-exculpation will be answered by the Church with one of its finest voices, that of Jean Gerson. The high ecclesiastic dignitary will respond to Jean de Meun's "confession of sins" in terms that establish one of the most fascinating facts of the cultural history of France. From the viewpoint of its time of composition, Jean's *Rose* belongs to the golden age of *peccata linguae,* and the poem will be judged specifically under the optic of the sins of the tongue by a moral theologian who lived more than one century after Jean de Meun.[7]

Gerson was a prominent ecclesiastic personality of his time; as a chancellor of the University of Paris, he initiated many reforms with political implications and, as an author of theological writings, he gained notoriety and respect all throughout Europe. He was also a gifted preacher, very much concerned to draw Christians from the clutches of sin.[8] Besides nu-

6. Hill also argues that the *Testament* should not be interpreted as a corrective to the *Rose.* Rather, the *Testament* represents an evolution with respect to the love poem, as many moralizing themes from the *Rose* were reopened and fully exploited in the testamentary text (*The Medieval Debate,* 51).

7. For an overall account of the role Jean Gerson played in the *Querelle,* see Renate Blumenfeld-Kosinski's detailed study "Jean Gerson and the Debate on the *Romance of the Rose,*" in *A Companion to Jean Gerson,* edited by Brian P. McGuire (Boston: Brill, 2006). Another interesting approach is David Hult's analysis of Jean Gerson and Christine de Pizan as "censors" of the *Rose* who illustrate the close link between "the problems of shameless speech and shameful reaction" ("Words and Deeds: Jean de Meun's *Romance of the Rose* and the Hermeneutics of Censorship," *New Literary History* 28, no. 2 [1991]: 345–66, at 361).

8. For a detailed account of Gerson's life and public activity, see McGuire, *A Companion to Jean Gerson.* Daniel Hobbins has recently written a book on Gerson, in which he also analyzes the theologian's view of rhetoric as applied to preaching and ethics (*Authorship and Publicity before Print: Jean Gerson and the Transformation of Late Medieval Learning* [Philadelphia: University of Pennsylvania Press, 2009], 111–19). Hobbins focuses on two Gersonian works: *On the Two Kinds of Logic* and *On the Modes of Signifying,* without taking into consideration the texts of a more pastoral nature that I have mentioned above. These texts can further substantiate Hobbins's claim that Gerson granted "a mighty role to rhetoric, which masters the interpretation of scripture and sharpens the moral arts," serving "a deep moral purpose: to stir the passions through preaching and writing" (*Authorship and Publicity before Print,* 116).

merous sermons dealing with vices, Gerson also wrote two ethical tracts, called *Le profit de savoir quel est péché mortel et véniel* (The profit of knowing which is mortal sin and which is venial) and *Examen de conscience selon les péchés capitaux* (Examination of conscience according to the capital sins), both dated 1400–1401. In these two texts, among the traditional capital vices, he treats several sins of word: blasphemy, flattery, detraction, garrulity, lie, and perjury.[9] He defines such practices *abus de la parole,* "abuses of speech," and does not hesitate to consider them potentially mortal sins dooming the soul to hell.[10] Two of these sins—flattery and blasphemy—he finds so grievous that he devotes separate texts to them. In *Contre les folles assertions des flatteurs* (1409), he studies the catastrophic impact that flattery has on political leaders. Worried about the ambiguity of words, which often are "equivoquez et se prennet aultrement en ung lieu que en ung aultre" ("equivocal and can be mistaken one for another"),[11] Gerson warns his readers that, typically, those who flatter political rulers also give them evil advice that can lead either to immorality at the highest administrative level or to social conflicts and even war.

Against blasphemy Gerson wrote two tractates: *Contre le péché de blaspheme* and *Contre les tentations de blaspheme,* both dated again 1400–1401. In the first of these tractates, he describes profanatory speech as the most serious and dangerous sin, worse than eating meat on Good Friday or during fasting, worse even than murder. Bitterly deploring the fact that the practice of blasphemy is so widespread in France, Gerson considers responsible for this sin not only those who actually utter impious words but also those who listen to them without punishing the blasphemer(s). Blasphemy is the language of the devil and the damned, and it always attracts divine wrath; this is how Gerson accounts for the outbreaks of the plague, wars, famine, and other tribulations that affect Christianity. By the same token, blasphemy is an evil practice requiring severe punishments by both religious and civil authorities. After briefly noting that the French and other European legislations include the death penalty for the most serious forms of blasphemy, the theologian proposes six steps to curb this wicked verbal practice in France. These measures are organized mainly around three solu-

9. Both texts can be consulted in Gerson, *Œuvres complètes,* vol. 7: *Le Profit* (328, 370–89) and *Examen* (330, 393–400).

10. Gerson, *Le Profit,* 381.

11. Gerson, *Œuvres complètes,* 7:361; translation mine.

tions: religious education of society, diligent execution of the laws by the forces of order, and parental control of speech in families. In *Contre les tentations de blaspheme,* this sin is approached from a more psychoanalytical angle. Here, Gerson studies the causes responsible for blasphemous speech (suggestion of the devil, physical exhaustion due to fasting or overwork, intoxication of the body, bad habit, etc.), and, invoking examples from the lives of the saints, he proposes efficient remedies the sinners can use to bridle their tongues (making mental fun of the tempting devil; taking care of one's health through medication and proper diet; reserving time for reflection on divine matters, etc.).

In 1403, to sum up his ideas about the misuses of speech, Gerson writes *Pour qu'on refrène sa langue,* a treatise in which he warns again of the dangers of undisciplined speech and proposes "remedies," that is, ways in which people can control their unruly tongues. This text represents the core of Gerson's thought on sinful speaking, his moral philosophy in matters of verbal conduct. Whereas in the tracts on blasphemy he has focused on the vertical axis of speech (human words against things divine), here the author is concerned exclusively with the horizontal dimension of language; namely, how the usage of words can forge or break human relationships. Following St. Augustine, Gerson argues that in the context of interpersonal communication, human language has four good purposes (to instruct, avoid fraud, correct morals, and express compassion) and two main negative uses (loquacity and detraction). Prompted by excessive curiosity and self-indulgence, loquacity (or speaking to quench one's verbal appetite) is vain speech, which can easily degenerate into gossip and bad-mouthing. Loquacity is also a perverse sin, whereby the perpetrators take delight in ruining other people's reputation:

> Mais signes sont au contraire quant on parle par loquacité, car on ne puet fin mectre en ses parolles, aincoys comme l'eaue du molin quant le verital est ouuert qui ne regarde ou elle coule ne qu'elle doiue abatre ou non, et sans mesure; auec ce se on a indignacion souuent contre ceulx desquelx on parle et une crueuse leesce et un ris maling et une maniere mordant et comme dessirant et sans edificacion des oyans, a la guise des chiens qui se rechignent ou qui rongent une charongne.[12]

But it is obvious when one speaks out of loquacity, since one cannot put an end to one's words, just like a mill when the shutter is open and the water flows out

12. Gerson, *Œuvres complètes,* 7:401.

without measure, not caring where it flows nor whom it may knock down. Along with this, often comes a feeling of hostility against those about whom one speaks, a cruel joy, an evil laughter, and a biting way, that only tears apart the listeners without instructing them, just as dogs balk at, and gnaw, a corpse. (translation mine)

Taking away another man's good name by calumny is more abominable than taking away his life, for one's reputation is a spiritual good superior to one's body, a material good; therefore, loquacity can be a mortal sin, the author concludes. Gerson's speech analyses from the ethical tracts are fundamental data to be considered in any interpretation of his standpoint in the incendiary debate around the *Romance of the Rose.* His view of blasphemy (definitions, measures suggested, outraged tone of the moralist) accounts for the accusation of blasphemous speech directed against Jean de Meun in the *Querelle.* Along the same lines, the definition of loquacity from *Pour qu'on refrène sa langue* helps explain the repeated excoriation of Jean as a garrulous writer. Speaking excessively and enjoying it, the cruel joy, the malicious laughter, and the biting irony that only misinform the listeners are all features of the loquacious speaker that characterize, in Gerson's view, the poetic style of Jean de Meun. Chronologically, with one exception (the text against flatterers, dated 1409), all the other Gersonian writings on abusive speech precede the main text against Jean de Meun, written in 1402.[13]

The *Vision* is a judicial allegory unfolding at the Court of Holy Christianity, where Chasteté (Chastity) and Eloquance Theologienne (Theological Eloquence) accuse Jean de Meun (here designated as the Fol Amant—Foolish Lover) of crimes against morality. The supreme judge is Justice Canonique (Canonical Justice) and the universal court of Christianity is composed of allegorical characters representing Mercy, Truth, Faith, Sound Judgment, Reason, Knowledge, Humility, Conscience, and the four cardinal virtues. Both the framework and the selection of the characters leave no doubt as to the angle from which the defendant is being tried; we are inside a highly theological setting in which moral virtues shore up the canonical law. It is evident from the outset that we are not dealing with literary criticism on the part of Gerson, but with severe moral judgment. Justice Canonique holds the place of God on earth and is the judge appointed to pronounce the final verdict, whereas Eloquance Theologienne is the pros-

13. Gerson, *Le traictié d'une vision faite contre le Rommant de la Rose,* hereafter referred to as the *Vision.*

ecutor, by virtue of his excellent rhetoric.[14] Chasteté plays the role of the plaintiff who, deeply hurt by the offenses of Fol Amant, asks the high court to find a remedy and put an end to his misdeeds. The word *remedy* in Chastity's vocabulary provides us with the first clue to the moral portrayal of Jean de Meun in this debate. In the ethical encyclopedias of the time, *remedium,* "remedy,"' functioned as a technical term designating the solution offered to the problem of vices. (In Peraldus's *SV,* each of the capital vices, including those of the tongue, was offered several healing remedies; Gerson himself had used this term with the same meaning in his ethical treatises.) Thus, Jean de Meun, under the name of Fol Amant, the very character he contrived in his poem, is from the outset introduced to the audience as a malefactor on whom punitive actions ought to be imposed by legal ruling. Chasteté levels the specific charges against Fol Amant in a proper judicial form, as a petition drafted in articles corresponding to the most controversial characters in the *Rose.*

Article one addresses the problem of La Vieille, the devilish old prostitute who uses lewd language to advise young girls to seduce men and sleep with them outside marriage. Articles two, three, and four criticize Le Mari Jaloux, who speaks against marriage, indiscriminately bad-mouths women, and reprimands the men embracing the religious life for laying aside their basic nature. These four articles provide us with the first reason why Gerson, through the agency of Chasteté, is so upset with Jean de Meun. La Vieille and Le Jaloux undermine two vital institutions of Christian society: marriage (which grants morality to intimate relationships between man and woman) and the organized structures of religious life— the church and the cloister. Gerson takes issues not only with the content of La Vieille's and Le Jaloux's discourses but also with the way in which the two abominable characters speak; they use obscene words that pollute the hearers' souls and spread the evil seed of lechery.

With the issue of improper language, Chasteté moves on to another key figure in the *Romance of the Rose:* Dame Raison, God's worthy daughter representing intellectual abilities, the noblest side of man. As an allegorical character in the poetry of Alain of Lille or Guillaume de Lorris, Raison had given speeches characterized by wisdom and exemplary language, Ger-

14. Although *Eloquance (Theologienne)* is a feminine noun, Gerson casts this allegorical character as a man.

son reminds us. In Jean's sequel, however, this lofty literary model is turned into a quirky lady, who, in lubricious terms, airs unconventional views of human anatomy and sexuality. Thus, speaking through the mouth of this controversial female character, Fol Amant is guilty of nothing less than blasphemy. His encouraging people to speak bluntly about everything, including the male genitalia (which are openly and shamelessly named by Dame Raison), is a crime. Far worse, Fol Amant mixes up base words with holy and spiritual notions, to the confusion and corruption of the faithful. Gerson admits to having a hard time calling Jean's poem a "book"; to him it looks like an obvious fraud, something that is not what it seems to be. He compares it to a harpy, a woman with a virginal, very beautiful face, but with a fish-like body that displays "a stomach and other parts which are very ugly."[15]

Sensitive to this fraudulent, Geryonic dimension that he attributes to the *Rose,* Gerson does not let himself be ensnared by the charms of the literary fiction. The characters in the poem are just masks behind which the real danger has one face—that of their creator. Jean de Meun's literary strategy, that of speaking through characters, although very ingenious, can fool nobody, contends Gerson; it is a technical device unable to excuse the inflaming ideas and words expressed in the *Romance of the Rose.* Despite his undeniable literary artistry, Jean de Meun is a blasphemer, and the type of poetry he writes declares war on all virtues:

> Il, en sa personne, nomme les parties deshonnestes du corps et les pechiés ors et villains par paroles saintes et sacrees, ainssy comme toute tele euvre fut chose divine et sacree et a adourer, mesmement hors mariaige et par fraude et violence; et n'est pas content des injures dessusdictes s'il les a publiees de bouche, mais les a fait escripre et paindre a son pouoir, curieusement et richement, pour atraire plus toute persone a les veoir, ouÿr et recepvoir. Encores y a pis: car afin que plus subtivement il deceust, il a mesley miel avec venin, succre avec poison, serpens venimeux cachiés soubz herbe vert de devocion: et ce fait il en assemblant matieres diverses, qui bien souvent ne font gueres a son propos si non a cause dessusdicte, et pour ce qu'il fut mieulx creu et de plus grande auctoritey de tant que il sambleroit avoir plus veu de choses et plus estudié.[16]

15. Gerson, *Vision,* ll. 483–84. For the French text of the *Vision* and its English translation, I use Christine McWebb, ed., *Debating the "Roman de la Rose": A Critical Anthology* (New York: Routledge, 2007).

16. Gerson, *Vision,* ll. 91–103.

In his own name, he names all the shameful body parts and villainous sins using holy and sacred words, as if these works were divine and sacred and to be worshipped through fraud and violence and even outside of marriage. He is not satisfied with simply enunciating the above-mentioned insults, but has [*sic;* has had] them written down and embellished as much as possible in a luring and lavish manner in order to attract everyone to see, hear, and accept them. The matter becomes still worse, since in order to deceive more skillfully, he mixes honey with venom, sugar with poison; there are venomous serpents hidden beneath the green grass of piety. He does this by assembling various topics which often have nothing to do with his argument, aside from the above-mentioned objective, and thus one believes him more easily and attributes greater authority to him, so that it seems as though he has seen and studied more than he in fact has.

All the modern critics of the *Rose* agree that Jean's sequel is a compilation of disparate materials that sometimes seem to have no relevance to the plot. But Gerson considers this artistic flaw from the viewpoint of the moralist, not from that of the literary critic. The poet's loquacity aims at conferring more weight to his message and thus at enhancing his dangerous influence on the readership. Jean de Meun is a perverse writer because in order to deceive successfully, he mixes up moral defects with positive values, so that the readers do not realize that they are being corrupted and perverted themselves. Human souls are the Lord's most precious houses, and there is nothing more perilous than dissolute words or images that enflame them, Gerson argues.[17]

Relevant in the *Vision* is the recurrence of the notion of evil-inducing speech from *Contre les tentations de blaspheme,* where Gerson draws attention to the dangers represented by those who speak of indecent or immoral things in front of young people. Like obscene paintings, indiscreet words can move the youth to do the shameful things about which they hear; therefore, one must take very diligent care that nothing be said or done before children that can expose them to base temptations. Gerson gives several examples of adults with negative behavior: those who speak boldly against faith, in jest or otherwise; those who speak about marriage secrets, or make other people speak about them, or even perform them in the pres-

17. By images, Gerson means the obscene miniatures accompanying contemporary manuscripts of the poem. The notion of dangerous (visual) art expressed in the *Querelle* is not an isolated occurrence in Gerson's service as a defender of Christian values; he repeatedly asked the public authorities to remove from public places images that were "suggestive of evil" (James L. Connolly, *Jean Gerson: Reformer and Mystic* [Louvain: Uystpruyst, 1928], 87).

ence of their children or the others; and finally, those who display vile images or dissolute paintings.[18]

In the *Vision,* Gerson describes Jean de Meun's poetry in the same terms: it is a dissolute art that, depicting or alluding to shameful acts, encourages people, especially the young and immature ones, to mimic them. It is an art that treats holy, religious ideas with derision and thereby undermines the foundation of the Christian faith. The perils represented by the poet's verbal abuses are all the more dangerous since they are fixed in writing and thus become able to cause an even more widespread evil in space and time. Jean de Meun is a heretic and a blasphemer, for there is nothing more dangerous than disseminating a perverse doctrine in the souls of Christians, as the author of the *Rose* does, and this author, by using vile words in describing holy things, commits as much irreverence toward the divinity as if he threw Jesus' body under the feet of the swine or on a heap of dung. Gerson goes so far as to compare Jean with Mohamed, the Muslim prophet, a heretic who deliberately and maliciously blended Christian teachings with his own evil errors. Thus, on account of the great crimes of blasphemy and heresy, not only the *Romance of the Rose,* but also the other works of Jean's foolish youth, should be burnt, destroyed.

To buttress this request, Eloquance Theologienne, Gerson's spokesperson in the allegory, draws an interesting parallel with the fate of the Roman poet Ovid and his well-known *Ars amatoria.* For having used dissolute words and conveyed immoral notions, Ovid was tried by a court of law and banished from the empire. Although his work, too, had the excuse of the dream as a literary framework and had used the method of speaking through characters, and although Ovid wrote a second book, *Remedia amoris,* to amend his earlier mistakes, the Roman authorities still decided to exile him, because his writings were too serious a threat for Roman morals. Jean de Meun's book, Gerson argues, is far worse than Ovid's *Ars amatoria,* and it is unacceptable that such a despicable work should be tolerated, read, and praised. If the Romans, who were pagans, deemed right to condemn a Roman pagan writer for his depraved book, it is all the more necessary to destroy Jean de Meun's work when he is a Christian author who does spiritual harm to his Christian readers.

The notion of writing as an aggressive act occurs several times in the *Vision,* as Gerson describes the many ways in which Jean de Meun is vio-

18. Gerson, *Vision,* 415–16.

lent. The author of the *Rose* first violates the noble laws of human language, by using smutty talk all throughout his poem. Then he violates the sacred rules of rhetoric, which concern the speaker, the interlocutor, and the time of one's speech. These rhetorical rules, Gerson notes, were transgressed in the construction of several allegorical characters, who deviate from their true nature and make unpardonable mistakes. For instance, Raison's highly philosophical speech should have been addressed to a wise cleric, not to a foolish lover; Nature was not supposed to speak about things alien to her, such as the Christian mysteries; and Venus should not have sworn on the flesh of God. The *Rose* professes to be an educational book, when in fact it subverts the very grounds of the Christian doctrine by disseminating heretical ideas.

All throughout the *Vision,* the idea of education is uppermost in Gerson's mind, and there is hardly a page that does not emphasize the importance of providing the young generation with sound moral lessons. Literary art should be not only an informative but also a formative art, but Jean's poem does not form good Christian citizens; it deforms them. It is by introducing to young readers immoral characters such as Fol Amant, Ami, La Vieille, and Faus Semblant that rapines, robberies, civil conspiracies, and many other great crimes occur. These abominable things can happen by imitating bad examples from literary texts; therefore, such writings as those of Jean de Meun are a grievous danger to the great kingdom of France. Evil speaking and writing corrupt moral virtues insofar as they suppress the praiseworthy feeling of shame that prevents people from imitating the sins they see, hear, or read about. (Again, this idea seems to be an echo of the tracts on blasphemy.)

The author of the *Rose* is also guilty of snatching materials from other writers and forcing them to suit his own interests. Thus, he commits a double act of violence: first, against his own text, which he turns into a compilation of alien sources, and second, against the source-texts he uses, which he misinterprets and alters to the point that they become unrecognizable. He is an inept continuator of Guillaume de Lorris's work, since Guillaume did not borrow from other writers but composed an original piece of poetry where there was no room for filth. Furthermore, although Jean de Meun draws his inspiration from Alain of Lille's great and virtuous book *Plaint of Nature,* he uses this text in an erroneous way and turns Alain's Nature and Genius into evil characters who exhort people to commit sins. By these procedures he drags his readers into profligacy and condemns them to perdition (*pousser,* "to push," and "tirer a dissolution"—"to draw/drag into dissolution"—are the two verbs with a connotation of violence that Gerson uses).

The preaching of sins, or *peccati predicatio,* as it was technically called in the medieval tracts on verbal sins, was an extremely grievous abuse of speech because it worked at cross-purposes with the goals of Christian teachings, based on the cultivation of moral virtues. Gerson points out that in the *Plaint of Nature,* neither Nature nor Genius preaches sins, as they do in the *Romance of the Rose,* and that this is a very perverse way of using literary characters and the written moral tradition. Jean should have used these personages in a positive way, to send out an unequivocal instructive message. The model he should have followed is the Bible, which spells out unambiguously what is a vice and what is a virtue.

Jean's collapsing of the two antithetical moral categories of good and evil is a recurrent reason for discontentment in both Gerson's and Christine de Pizan's texts against the *Romance of the Rose.* Both critics stress that it is extremely dangerous for society when an author professing to write a didactic work, as Jean de Meun does, misleads his readers about what is good and what is bad, about what is morally correct or incorrect. Jean is sending mixed and confusing signals to his readers about how they should behave in family or in society. He extols the practices of flattery and deceit to the point that he seems to recommend them, and he raises the sin of lechery to the rank of virtue.[19] The situation is all the more upsetting when the poet was a man of great erudition and of great literary talent who put his learning and art into the service of evil. By blurring the lines between right and wrong, by presenting vices as exemplary virtues, the poet failed as a teacher of morals, and his book represents even one hundred years after his death a public disgrace and a threat to society. Thus, far from being a true educator, Jean de Meun was in fact an incorrigible sinner, Gerson bitterly concludes.

These harsh lines highlight that the picture emerging from the collation of Jean's self-exculpation with the judgmental documents of the *Querelle*

19. For a study of the medieval topos of vices masquerading as virtues, see Richard Newhauser, "On Ambiguity in Moral Theology: When the Vices Masquerade as Virtues," in *Sin: Essays in the Moral Tradition in the Western Middle Ages,* edited by Richard Newhauser (Ashgate: Variorum, 2007).

is the portrait of a particular type of sinner—not one in flesh (as Christine de Pizan speculates), but one in speech, more precisely in the written word; a sinner by the medium of poetry. Gerson was aware of Jean's post-*Rose* "conversion" (possibly as outlined in the *Testament*), but he never specifically addressed the apologetic segment of the *Rose;* on the contrary, he totally disregarded it.[20] He was interested not so much to find mitigating circumstances for the morally decayed art of Jean de Meun but to demolish it. Even if he had read Jean's self-exculpatory lines, he was not willing to believe a writer who, through his poetic characters, had advocated the use of fraudulent verbal practices and thus gambled the veracity of his own didactic enterprise. The posthumous judgment of Jean de Meun by Gerson (and his ally, Christine de Pizan) is implacable; although they concede that the poem has some good parts, they lobby for the total destruction of it because it throws its readers into the arms of the devil. People are naturally too weak to need encouragement and exhortation to vices; they need a kind of literature that teaches them good, not perverse, morals. Readers must be offered texts that unambiguously depict pure, just, and virtuous attitudes, both in private and in public life, not texts that seduce Christians into sin. Along these lines, Gerson ultimately holds Jean guilty of being a "teacher" of vices, who forcibly drags and pushes people into the filth of carnality, and who blows into the fire of sin through his lecherous words and by using the authority and example of his own person. In a highly outraged tone Gerson accuses poor Jean of having "killed, murdered, or poisoned thousands and thousands of people through various sins" and of continuing to do so day after day with his foolish book.[21]

However exaggerated Gerson's accusations are, one of the points he makes is true: books may continue to exist long after their authors' deaths, and literature has a unique ability of fixing things in writing and sending them down to next generations. What is encapsulated in a book, especially

20. Gerson quotes Jean's testamentary statement literally: "In my youth, I have written many a text out of vanity," and expresses his awareness that the poet allegedly repented during his lifetime and thereafter wrote books of true faith and holy doctrine (ll. 120–21, 178–79). Gerson might have known of the *Testament* from Christine de Pizan's explicit reference to it, in her letter to Pierre Col from October 2, 1402. In this letter, she interprets the testamentary statement as referring to the *Rose,* not to the ballades, *rondels,* and *virelais* that Pierre Col had attributed to Jean but that, as Christine is quick to remark, had not been preserved (McWebb, *Debating the "Roman de la Rose,"* 149).

21. *Vision,* ll. 190–97.

in a skillfully written one, escapes the laws of time and is saved for posterity. But the danger is that, immortalized in such eloquent and successful literary texts, sin is brought back to life every time a sin-inducing book is opened and read, and literary tradition may thus become a channel for the transmission of evil. Expressed in dramatic terms that describe poetry as a potentially destructive art, Gerson's campaign against the dangers of literary texts is not an isolated fact. Dante's *Inferno* had depicted a similar peril in one of its most celebrated cantos. The moral risk emphasized by Gerson and Christine de Pizan in the *Querelle de la Rose* is one that Francesca and Paolo actually took, as they read a well-written book and, under its influence, committed adultery and lost their souls. A cursory look at Francesca's description of her moral error may help us better understand what Fleming calls Gerson's "peculiarly obdurate and obtuse stand" against Jean's poem:[22]

> Noi leggiavamo un giorno per diletto
> di Lancialotto come amor lo strinse;
> soli eravamo e sanza alcun sospetto.
> Per più fïate li occhi ci sospinse
> quella lettura, e scolorocci il viso;
> ma solo un punto fu quel che ci vinse.
> Quando leggemmo il disïato riso
> esser basciato da cotanto amante,
> questi, che mai da me non fia diviso,
> la bocca mi basciò tutto tremante.
> Galeotto fu 'l libro e chi lo scrisse:
> quel giorno più non vi leggemmo avante. (*Inf.* 5.127–38)

We were reading one day, for pleasure, of / Lancelot, how Love beset him; we were alone and / without any suspicion. / Many times that reading drove our eyes / together and turned our faces pale; but one point / alone was the one that overpowered us. / When we read that the yearned-for smile was / kissed by so great a lover, he, who will never be / separated from me, / kissed my mouth all trembling. Galeotto was the / book and he who wrote it: that day we read there no / further.

This fragment depicts Francesca and Paolo as they were reading the Old French romance *Lancelot du Lac.* From the outset the literary text is presented as a sort of third "character" in the scene. The solitude Francesca mentions (*soli eravamo*) is in fact a false one; it is solitude only with respect to other fleshly beings, for the characters in the story they are reading will prove to be the most powerful and dangerous presence. The two readers are in fact not alone but with the knight Lancelot and his queen Guinevere, in

22. Fleming, *The "Roman de la Rose,"* 67.

a blend of life and literature that will have fatal consequences.[23] Francesca and Paolo display toward the text an attitude that somehow anticipates the sinful outcome of their encounter; they read for entertainment (*per diletto*) and become so captivated by the love scene between Lancelot and Guinevere (an adulterous love, as we know), that they look several times at each other and turn pale. Again, the emphasis Dante places on the effects of the book is clear; it is *quella lettura* that prompts Francesca and her brother-in-law to look into each other's eyes and that empties their cheeks of blood. What they see in the text affects them in a personal way and to the highest degree; the fallacious process of identification between the readers and the characters of the romance has thus begun.

It will reach its climax when Francesca and Paolo visualize the adulterous kiss between Guinevere and Lancelot. It is this precise moment of their reading that makes them yield to the temptation woven around them by the literary love story: "ma solo un punto fu quel che ci vinse."[24] It is likely that Francesca and Paolo had been attracted to each other before they started reading—their isolation from other people in order to read together is indicative in this respect. The literary description of Lancelot's falling in love ("come amor lo strinse") made them feel personally concerned and brought them even closer together; but it is only the visualization of the literary kiss that "overcame" them (*ci vinse*). Here, the power of literature becomes so seductive that it acts almost like an aphrodisiac on the two readers. They are unable to go on with their reading, and they materialize what in the book had been an immoral but fictitious kiss into a kiss of their own, as immoral as the literary one, but this time real. The verb *vincere* Dante uses to describe the book's effect has a strong ethical connotation—the text is the conquering enemy who defeats moral principles or considerations. As Renato Poggioli expressively put it, this moment of defeat marks "the descent from literature to life, from fiction to reality, from romanticism to realism; or more simply, from sentimental fancy to moral truth."[25] The moral

23. As the documents of the time tell us, the adulterous relationship between the two will be discovered by Gianciotto Malatesta, Francesca's husband and Paolo's brother, who will kill both of them.

24. For the complex way in which Dante thematizes the notion of point throughout the *Comedy,* raising it from erotic and temporal to divine and eternal, see Franco Masciandaro, "Notes on the Image of the Point in the *Divine Comedy,*" *Italica* 54, no. 2 (1977): 215–26.

25. Renato Poggioli, "Tragedy or Romance? A Reading of the Paolo and Francesca Episode in Dante's *Inferno,*" *PMLA* 72, no. 3 (1957): 313–58, at 338.

of the episode seems to be offered by Francesca herself, the deluded victim of courtly literature: "Galeotto fu il libro e chi lo scrisse." The role of go-between assigned to Gallehaut in the adulterous love story from the French romance was played, in Francesca and Paolo's lives, by the book they were reading and its author.[26] Francesca's outcry of sorrow and regret blames both literary tradition and writer as agents of sin.[27] Through her story of literary taste, lust, and death, Dante condemns the fictional literature's tendency to depict immoral attitudes that offer wrong models to superficial readers.[28]

Literary texts represent or emulate life—a mimetic relationship in which art is the one that "copies," that is, depicts human nature. But in its turn, literary tradition is itself capable of affecting lives—another mimetic relationship in which people from the realm of reality may imitate what they see depicted in literary outputs. Writing—*fabula* or even *storia*—is not without risk, for the writer is the empowered agent who mediates the transfer of significations from lives to other lives, from past to present, or to future. An artist can influence people's lives in ways that can evade both geographical divisions and temporal barriers. *Lancelot del Lac* was written many years before Dante's time, and in French, but in Dante's episode of the carnal sinners, it ends up corrupting two contemporaries of Dante's, in an Italian city.

26. I find incorrect Mark Musa and Anna Hatcher's assumption that Francesca was not a victim of literary influence, but knowingly exploited the power of literature to seduce Paolo: "instead of being aroused by the text, she was exploiting it for the purpose of satisfying her pent-up passion" ("The Kiss: *Inferno* V and the Old French Prose *Lancelot*," *Comparative Literature* 20, no. 2 [1968]: 97–109, at 108). There is no indication in the text to sustain such an interpretation.

27. This condemnation comes as the culmination of the entire visit of Virgil and the pilgrim to the circle of the lustful, among which are punished legendary lovers, such as Semiramis, Dido, Cleopatra, Achilles, Tristan, all figures immortalized by the literary tradition. Poggioli argues that literature plays an important part in Dante's selection of examples of lustfulness because the poet intended to warn that "history and poetry, or literature in general, by preserving and transmitting through the written word the love stories of old, may lead us into sin" ("Tragedy or Romance?" 336).

28. In Susan Noakes's view, Dante did not necessarily condemn the French romance per se but rather the faulty way in which Francesca and Paolo read the love story (the Lancelot text the two failed to read to the end provides a clear condemnation of adultery). Thus, their fault is primarily intellectual, insofar as they are blind to the text's meaning. Their second mistake is that, instead of realizing that the text they were reading is just a literary fiction, they wanted to emulate it ("The Double Misreading of Paolo and Francesca," *Philological Quarterly* 62 [1983]: 221–39, at 226).

The ability of books to circulate in space and time and the persisting danger that even good books may be misread and misinterpreted increase the responsibility of writers as moral agents. Dante's swooning at the hearing of Francesca's tragic love story conveys, in Francesco d'Ovidio's view, Dante's fear that he too "could become a Gallehaut to somebody else."[29]

Within this perspective, Gerson's criticism of Jean de Meun, of his obscene language, and more importantly, of the confused moral message of the *Rose* become fully understandable. The kind of danger for morality Dante saw in the literary texts depicting sinful love is identical to the threat Gerson perceived in Jean's *Rose.* In fact, by condemning this poem, Gerson was condemning all (potentially) immoral literature. If in Dante's terms (with reference to Brunetto Latini), through writing man makes himself eternal, through the same art, human trespasses are preserved and transmitted through the ages. In the texts Gerson wrote against speech transgressions, he did not deal with the potential presence of these transgressions in literary texts, or with the repercussions that the verbal misconduct of a poet could have on his audience; the tracts on sins as a medieval genre with specific rules would not have allowed him to do so. The debate around the *Rose,* however, gave Gerson the unique opportunity to first look at abuses of speech from an original angle, that of poetry in the vernacular, then to verify his own theories about speech from the ethical tracts. And, as we have seen, in Jean's *Rose* he found plenty of supporting examples.

THE SIN OF BLASPHEMY IN THE *INFERNO*

"Quelle que fût la diversité de leurs opinions sur sa consistance et son contenu, les juristes médiévaux définirent toujours le blasphème comme un 'crimen,' sans jamais cesser de voir en lui un 'peccatum.'"[30]

The problem that Gerson identifies in Jean de Meun's ethical message (the fact that the poet does not clearly separate vices from virtues) does not

29. Quoted in Poggioli, "Tragedy or Romance?" 358. Noakes brings an inspired nuance to D'Ovidio's interpretation of the pilgrim's swooning and argues for Dante's awareness that both *Vita Nuova* and the *Comedy,* despite the noble intentions of their author, can be misread, even in the sense that the readers may see in the text the opposite of the meaning intended by the author ("The Double Misreading," 229).

30. "Whatever the diversity of their opinions on its consistency and its content, the medieval jurists always defined blasphemy as a crime, without ever ceasing to see in it a sin" (translation mine) (Leveleux, *La Parole interdite,* 220).

exist in the *Divine Comedy,* whose very structure depends on the separation of sins from virtuous deeds. But Dante struggled as well with problems related to his poetic art and inserted numerous instances of self-reflective postures in his great work. Mazzotta has analyzed in depth these instances and accounted for them through Dante's awareness of the "treachery" of his figurative language. The prophetic stature Dante assumes in the *Comedy* makes him vulnerable to the possibility of blasphemy and heresy, since the language of faith that he speaks is highly metaphorical and therefore may give rise to the same interpretive errors that Dante condemns in his treatment of heresy. Since Mazzotta debates these issues of authorial transgressions and credibility over three chapters of *Dante, Poet of the Desert,* I will not reopen them here. I agree with his conclusion that "whether we believe that the poem is a stone that edifies our faith, or is an artifice that barely conceals the grave—is a question that Dante poses, but it remains necessarily an open one."[31]

The aspect on which I intend to focus in this section of my study is another connection between the *Comedy* and the medieval debate on transgressive speech, a connection that can account for the way in which the Italian poet embedded the sin of blasphemy in the structure of his underworld. In the system of Hell, largely modeled on the three Aristotelian dispositions toward evil—incontinence, violence, and fraud—blasphemy is treated as a sin of violence against God and aligned with sodomy and usury.[32] At first glance, this grouping may seem peculiar in that it associates a verbal trespass with a sin of flesh and with a socioeconomic practice relatively legal (money-lending at interest). A look at the cultural context reveals, however, that the association of blasphemy with sodomy was not unusual in the writings of the moral analysts. Some of them also promoted the analogy between blasphemy and usury. Rather, what is unusual in the *Inferno* is that the sin of heresy, which in medieval interpretations was typically conflated with blasphemy, is treated as different from the latter and punished as a "lighter" transgression, on the borderline between the sins of incontinence and those of violence.

31. Mazzotta, *Dante, Poet of the Desert,* 318.

32. The circle of violence itself is divided into three subcircles, punishing violence against others, against oneself, and against God (*Inf.* 21. 28–32). This tripartition originates in Isidore of Sevilla, whom Aquinas quotes in his *Summa theologica:* "Isidore (*De Summo bono*), in giving the division of sins, says that man is said to sin against himself, against God, and against his neighbor" (Ia-IIae Q. 72.4).

To a modern reader, the term *blasphemy* conveys a rather vague notion of speaking ill of things divine, a profanation of the sacred. Etymologically, blasphemy comes from the Greek *blasphemein,* a compound between the verb *blaptein,* "to injure." and the noun *pheme,* "reputation." In Greek mythology, the degree of seriousness of blasphemy and the punishment it attracted depended on the sensitivity of the god whose reputation was offended by the words or attitudes of the mortals. [33]

In Hebrew society, blasphemous speech incurred death. Since here blasphemy meant the pronunciation of God's name in a disrespectful way, God's personal name (*Yahwe*) was removed from ordinary speech and replaced with Lord (*Adonai*). [34] In the New Testament, the term "blasphemy" is recorded as having been used by the members of the Sanhedrin, who tried Jesus as a blasphemer. The authors of the Gospels, however, widened the scope of this noun to encompass offenses against the Holy Spirit and actions against Christ and his followers. At the same time, this expansion of blasphemy's meaning had the technical disadvantage of diluting the essential traits of this religious transgression. Thus, due to the lack of a clear definition in the Old Testament, accompanied by a too great semantic dilution in the New Testament, the term "blasphemy" will gradually acquire a degree of obfuscation that will continue into early Christianity.[35] The ap-

33. The goddess Athena, for instance, took offense at Arachne's boasting of being a better weaver and punished the young woman by turning her into a spider. Dionysos was deeply angered by the Minyades (princesses of Orkhomenos in Boetia, Central Greece), who spurned Dionysos's worship, calling him a false god (for their blasphemy, the god changed them into bats). For the same type of offense he punished Orpheus, a bard of Pieria in Thrake (Northern Greece), by having the Bakkhantes tear his limbs off. The examples of blasphemous actions, gestures, or words are numerous in Greek mythology, and the punishments they incur are severe. Within the same Hellenic ethos, even more frightening than the testimony of mythology is that of history, which brings along its own cases to exemplify the serious, at times deadly, impact this type of transgression had on its perpetrators. Philosophy itself was often considered blasphemous, and its practitioners were prosecuted for their beliefs; the classical example of this was Socrates. Deeming that Socrates's teachings subverted the religious values of the Athenian youth, the state authorities prosecuted the philosopher for blasphemy and sentenced him to death.

34. In Leviticus 24:16, the godly voice orders Moses to isolate from society a man who had cursed God and to have him stoned to death. Despite the seriousness of the punishment it advocates, the Old Testament gives no example of words or speeches to be considered blasphemous. The omission seems to be deliberate on the part of the authors of the sacred books, who did not want to sully their own texts with impious words (Leonard W. Levy, *Treason against God: A History of the Offense of Blasphemy* [New York: Schocken Books, 1981], 30).

35. This is how Levy describes the semantic confusion inherent in the term: "Under Chris-

proach to this sin becomes more analytic only in the fifth and sixth centuries, owing to the systems of capital sins by Cassian and Gregory, who both introduce blasphemy into their classifications, albeit in different ways (in Cassian's eightfold scheme of capital sins, blasphemy is a daughter of pride, whereas in Gregory's septuagenary it is an offspring of wrath). But despite these inclusions, the bulk of the moral texts from the early Middle Ages pay scant attention to sacrilegious speech. The reasons for this lack of interest seem to lie, first, in the vagueness of the concept, and second, in the fact that the texts on sins were typically produced in monastic settings that, by definition, could not abide blasphemous practices.[36]

On a legal and practical level, however, the habit of speaking ill of divine matters was sanctioned with a severity reminiscent of the Old Testament. In the sixth century AD, Justinian's *Corpus iuris civilis* introduced a section on blasphemy that accounted for the famine, earthquake, and pestilence of his day as signs of divine anger triggered by the society's failure to punish blasphemers. This belief determined Justinian to decree death for the sin of blasphemy. In the ninth century, Charlemagne reinforced the provision on blasphemy from Justinian's code, thus initiating a legal tradition faithfully followed by his close successors. In 1140, Gratian's *Decretus* still made dozens of references to blasphemy, and some others to perjury and lying. By the thirteenth century, the legal punishments against this crime of speech became much more lax; no condemnation to death was pronounced against the blasphemer, and only financial penalties were imposed. In Dante's time, verbal sacrileges against God or the Virgin Mary were distinguished from lighter profanities—those against the saints—and penalized with a larger amount of money.

It is historically attested, however, that between the thirteenth and the

tianity, *blasphemy* became so bloated with meanings that it burst all bounds, becoming almost meaningless. By the year 400, *blasphemy* was hardly more than a vile epithet, and in a confused way similar to the concept of heresy. The word *heresy* originally meant factionalism, which was a form of blasphemy to early Christians because it exposed the true faith to contention, even scorn. Eventually, *heresy* became the more encompassing term. Not until the time of Thomas Aquinas in the thirteenth century did the church coherently define blasphemy, although even then it continued as a peculiar species of heresy.... For early Christians both offenses blurred in meaning and blended with faction, sedition, schism, apostasy, and sacrilege" (*Treason against God,* 31–32). Levy fails to note that Peraldus is the first to have clearly distinguished, a few decades before Aquinas, between blasphemy and heresy.

36. Leveleux, *La Parole interdite,* 100.

sixteenth centuries, verbal impieties directed at divine entities and religious matters were such a widely disseminated practice in France and Italy that canonists felt compelled to promulgate laws against blasphemy. These legal efforts at stemming the tide of impious speech paralleled the moralists' attempts at educating Christians in matters of sinful versus virtuous language. Actually, in Corinne Leveleux's opinion, the lawmakers' preoccupation with blasphemy was grounded in the proliferation in the thirteenth and fourteenth centuries of pastoral tracts on the sins of the tongue.[37] It is the major moral summae written during Dante's lifetime—all of which included analyses of verbal trespasses—that revived the interest in the nature and consequences of blasphemy. Omitted by Alain of Lille in his twelfth-century treatise on vices, blasphemy becomes a common denominator of the thirteenth-century tracts of moral theology. It will also become a constant category in the manuals of confession of the time.

William Peraldus begins his tractate on *peccata linguae* with blasphemy, which he considers the most serious verbal crime, which should be punishable by death. Citing St. Augustine, he distinguishes three types of sacrilegious attitudes: 1. attributing to God something that is not his; 2. negating any of God's attributes; 3. usurping something that belongs to God. After this schematic citation of the Augustinian tripartition, Peraldus adds his own development: "Nos autem hic blasphemiam intelligimus verbum in contumeliam Dei prolatum, ut cum aliquis iratus, vindicare se volens de Deo, aliqua membra de ipso nominat, quae nominanda non sunt" ("We, on the other hand, understand blasphemy as a word uttered to insult God, as, for instance, when someone, being angry and willing to take revenge against God, names parts of Him that are not to be named").[38] Another essential element in the Peraldian treatment is the division of blasphemy into two categories—of the mouth and of the heart: "Duplex est blasphemia. Quaedam est oris, et quaedam est cordis" ("Blasphemy is of two kinds. Up to one point it is of the mouth, and up to one point it is of the heart"). The latter type occurs when one allows ungodly thoughts to take root in one's heart, which is the site where feelings of love (not of hate) for God should be located. The common denominator of these two types of blasphemy is the feeling or state of anger that causes the blasphemer to seek revenge against God. Grounded in wrath and scorn toward things divine, blasphe-

37. Ibid., 103.

38. Peraldo, *Summa virtutum ac vitiorum*, 538.

my is a diabolical kind of speech, recognizable by the horror it arouses in listeners. Guilty thereof are not only blasphemers but also those who listen and condone blasphemies in society.[39]

Thus, two implications are present in the Peraldian analysis: the threat that blasphemers represent to the moral health of society, and, on a transcendental level, the denial of salvation to those who commit blasphemous acts. The moralist foreshadows that those who after death will go to hell will keep blaspheming because of the great pain to which they will be subjected: "Illi qui in inferno erunt, blasphemabunt Deum propter magnitudinem dolores" ("Those who will be in hell will say blasphemies against God because of the intensity of their pain").[40] Other elements that are worth mentioning in Peraldus's text can illuminate Dante's treatment of blasphemy in the seventh circle: the perversity specific to blasphemers and the superior gravity of this sin with respect to heresy. In Peraldus's view, blasphemers are extremely perverse because instead of assuming the blame for their evil deeds and praising God for their good ones, they invert the terms and attribute what is good to themselves, holding God responsible for their wicked works.[41] The perversity of blasphemy is all the more obvious when compared to heresy, for heretics sincerely believe in their ideas, deeming them correct, while blasphemers know that what they say is wrong and still say it: "Haereticus enim ea loquitur de Deo, quae credit esse vera: blasphemus vero contra conscientiam suam de Deo dicit quae scit non esse dicenda" ("For the heretic says about God things he believes to be true, whereas the blasphemer, although he knows he is not telling the truth, says things he knows should not be said"). By the same token, "maius etiam peccatum videtur esse blasphemia, quam haeresis" ("it is evident that the sin of blasphemy is even more serious than heresy").[42] Blasphemy ultimately reduces man to an infra-animal condition and deserves the heaviest of punishments. Many elements of the Peraldian view of blasphemy resound in Dante's text:

Puossi far forza ne la deïtade
col cor negando e bestemmiando quella,
e spregiando natura e sua bontade;

e però lo minor giron suggella
del segno suo e Soddoma e Caorsa
e chi, spregiando Dio col cor, favella.
(*Inf.* 11. 46–51)

39. Ibid., 542.

40. Ibid.

41. Ibid., 540.

42. Ibid., 542.

One can use force against the Deity by denying it / and cursing it in one's heart or by scorning Nature / and its goodness; / and therefore the smallest subcircle stamps with its seal Sodom and Cahors and whoever speaks with scorn of God in his heart.

The elements of scorn and violence, the twofold nature of the offense—of the heart and of the mouth—just as the different placement of heretics, punished higher up in Hell than blasphemers, suggest that Dante took his cue for the sin of *bestemmia* from Peraldus rather than from Aquinas, as is traditionally held.[43] It is true that *Secunda secundae* establishes comparative relationships between blasphemy and other sins, such as perjury and murder, for instance, but the overall approach to blasphemy is slightly different from Peraldus's. In the Thomistic definition, the sin of blasphemy lies in disparaging the surpassing goodness of the divinity, and as such it is opposed to the confession of faith.[44] Just as faith is predicated not only on an attachment of the heart but also on verbal declarations and works of charity, so unbelief can actualize itself in words or deeds.[45] Along with heresy and apostasy, blasphemy is therefore a symptom of unbelief, which can manifest itself in two ways, as an inner disparagement (blasphemy of the heart) or as an oral declaration (blasphemy of the mouth), the latter representing the perfect form of blasphemy.[46] To my knowledge, the relationship between Peraldus's *Summa vitiorum* and Aquinas's *Secunda secundae* has not been studied yet, and to analyze it here would exceed the scope of my presentation. But many original items from Peraldus's definitions of vices recur in Aquinas, and it is hard to believe that when he wrote his *Secunda secundae,* Aquinas did not glance at the most prestigious ethical tract written in the first decades of the thirteenth century by another (very famous) Dominican writer.

43. See for instance Federigo Tollemache in the *Enciclopedia dantesca,* 1:611.

44. Q. 13.1.

45. Q. 12.1.

46. Just as Peraldus before him, Aquinas foretells the countless curses of the damned in the underworld: "Now those who are in hell retain their wicked will which is turned away from God's justice, since they love the things for which they are punished, would wish to use them if they could, and hate the punishments inflicted on them for these same sins. They regret indeed the sins which they have committed, not because they hate them, but because they are punished for them. Accordingly, this detestation of Divine justice is, in them, the interior blasphemy of the heart: and it is credible that after the resurrection they will blaspheme God with the tongue, even as the Saints will praise Him with their voices" (*ST* IIa-IIae Q. 13.4).

Interestingly, Aquinas too detects a kernel of perversity in blasphemers, but he follows a different interpretive path than Peraldus. Blaspheming is committing an act of fraudulence, a falsehood in one's intellect, whereby one denies something befitting God or asserts something unbefitting him. Blasphemy, the opposite of the confession of faith, is an inverted praise, for it represents a distorted version of what in the holy is "vocalis laus Dei" ("the verbal praise of God"). The fraud of the blasphemer is greater than that of the perjurer since the latter only invokes God's name in confirmation of a falsehood, whereas the former utters something false about God himself. Thus, blasphemers are even worse than murderers, because they do harm to God directly.

The fraud factor from Aquinas's analysis of blasphemy does not persist in Dante's conception of this sin, just as the poet's treatment of heresy evidently departs from Aquinas's line of thought. In the Thomistic system, heresy and blasphemy are species of unbelief, and although they do differ by the note of disparagement present in blasphemy and absent from heresy, the two species fundamentally overlap. In fact, one of the reproaches that modern analysts level against Aquinas is precisely that, in the separation of heresy from blasphemy, the theologian stopped halfway through: "Thus, having begun with the element of disparagement as the basis of a distinction between blasphemy and heresy, Thomas Aquinas ignored it thereafter and left heresy and blasphemy as interchangeable as ever."[47]

As a matter of fact, by punishing blasphemers lower down in Hell than heretics, Dante seems to go counter to an entire trend of late medieval thought. The theologians of the time, on the rare occasions when they took care to differentiate the two sins, considered heresy much more preoccupying than blasphemy. The reason lay in the contemporary religious tensions of the High Middle Ages, a time marked by intense heretical movements challenging the unity of the church. As Levy points out, "Blasphemy was not a threat to the church. Heresy was.... God could not be harmed, although he might avenge himself on those who tolerated blasphemers. The heretic, however, could harm the church by dividing it and winning away its adherents."[48] The superior gravity of heresy with respect to blasphemy is not reflected in Dante's structure of Hell, which reverses this polarity by lo-

47. Levy, *Treason against God,* 52.

48. Ibid., 56.

cating the blasphemers lower down than the heretics. There is a certain relationship between blasphemers (punished in the seventh circle) and heretics (assigned to the sixth circle), but this relationship is mediated by two other rings: of the violent toward others and of the violent toward oneself. For Dante, heresy is a sin of incontinence causing people to seek religious ideas beyond the traditional faith, whereas blasphemy stems, as in Peraldus's definition, from a violent inner state.[49]

Inferno 14–16

Blasphemous speech emerges early on in the *Inferno* as a constant verbal attitude of the damned. Against a very noisy background of laments and cries that will accompany the pilgrim and Virgil all along their journey, the curses of the dead are noted by the poet as early as the third canto, in an effort to highlight the deep despair of the inhabitants of Ante-Hell. The image is powerful and reenacts Peraldus and Aquinas's prediction of the fate awaiting blasphemers after death: "Bestemmiavano Dio e lor parenti, / l'umana spezie e 'l loco e 'l tempo e 'l seme / di lor semenza e di lor nascimenti" ("They cursed God and their parents, the human / race and the place and the time and the seed of their / sowing and of their birth"; *Inf.* 3.103–05). The infamous speech of these souls leaves nothing untarnished in the universe. Their hate, verbalized in the afterlife as it has been in life, touches not only the Cre-

49. In recent Dante criticism, the problem of the loose proximity between the circle of the heretics and that of the violent has been raised in interesting terms. Highlighting the differences between heresiarchs and schismatics in the system of Hell, Cogan identifies the heresiarchs from the sixth circle as Epicureans and Photinians (in the Middle Ages, Pope Anastasius V was mistakenly assimilated to the latter). What both classes of heretics had in common was the denial of the possibility of salvation (*Design in the Wax,* 64). Both heresy and blasphemy are, in Cogan's interpretation, sins of the irascible appetite, and what unites them on an imagistic level is the element of fire present in the tombs of the heretics and in the rain that torments the blasphemers. In the case of the heretics, the fire would indicate the specific type of passion that underlies the sin of heresy: despair, one of the five passions at the root of the irascible appetite. Despair is responsible for the overcoming of reason that leads to heresy. The link between heresy and blasphemy, which Cogan shows has somewhat been preserved by Dante, comes from the tradition of the medieval texts, those of Thomas Aquinas mainly, that aligned the two sins. But Dante's debt to this traditional approach vis-à-vis blasphemy stops here, since the poet decides not only to dissociate but also to geographically distance the two otherwise similar sins. Moreover, unlike Aquinas, he considers the sin of blasphemy more serious than heresy, thereby reinforcing Peraldus's view.

ator, but also the created, humankind, and themselves as representatives of it, even the origins of their own lives. Speech here nullifies the attachment to a creating God, family ties, human dignity, self-respect, and the seed of life . . . this symbol of all potentialities. The *bestemmia* of the damned translates the most intense state of hate into the most perverse form of speech. Cursing is the systematic reaction of the souls in Hell to their new condition, and blasphemy, before being a sin punished in the system, is enacted as a verbal practice. For Dante, noting the verbal abuses of the sinners in the underworld is an artistic task as important as describing the various *contrapassi* or the discourses of the characters with whom the poet engages in conversation.

The blasphemy directed at God is recorded one more time in dramatic terms in the circle of the carnal sinners to describe the intensity of their suffering. Here, the torments give rise again to cries and words of hate: "Quando giungon davanti a la ruina, / quivi le strida, il compianto, il lamento; / bestemmian quivi la virtù divina" ("When they come before the landslide, there the / shrieks, the wailing, the lamenting; there they curse / God's power"; *Inf.* 5.34–36).[50] One of the most fascinating encounters in the *Comedy* is depicted in this canto—that with Francesca and Paolo. In fine words redolent of the rhetoric of courtly love lyrics, Francesca graciously and generously answers Dante's invitation to tell her story. Her speaking manner translates the delicacy of her inner structure, the graciousness and the benignity she sees in the pilgrim are in fact her own qualities, and the desire to please her two visitors bespeaks her noble nature. However, her fine qualities are in sharp contrast with her situation in the afterlife, just as her refined discourse is in strange opposition to the blasphemies Dante has just ascribed to the carnal sinners. Is thus Francesca a blasphemer too, she, so gracious and benign? To answer this question we have to consider that Francesca is not only a careful speaker, she is also a very responsive human being. Her adultery is a reaction to the book she was reading, the telling of her story is a response to the visitors' desire to learn it, and her blasphemies—the blasphemies of the block of souls to which she belongs—are responses to their new condition. Francesca's mention of the impossibility of praying for the pilgrim's peace only heightens the drama of the episode. Her

50. Pierre Mandonnet, who reads Dante in a theological key, interprets these sinners' impious utterances as blasphemies against the Holy Ghost, the most grievous type of blasphemy in the New Testament (*Dante le théologien,* 302–3).

adultery drew God's implacable enmity, and as a consequence, prayer—this expression of remorse, willingness to reform, and opportunity to ask for favors—is denied to her. Thus, on account of their feud with God, *i peccator carnal,* to whom Francesca is assimilated, cannot pray, they can only curse, and this is a hellish mechanism from which the female character cannot escape.

After having been made aware of blasphemy as a constant verbal habit in Hell, we arrive to the circle of the violent against God, a circle whose description spans four cantos. Blasphemy is assigned to the first subdivision of a ring that punishes three different classes of sinners: on a plane of burning sand, one group of souls lies supine, another one moves restlessly in a circle, and a third one is seated. All three groups are desperately trying to protect themselves from a merciless rain of fire. Although fewer than those moving in a circle, the damned lying supine have looser tongues, the poet carefully mentions (*Inf.* 14.25–27).[51] Thus, before we come to know the nature of their sin, we are prepared for it by an allusion to these sinners' propensity to verbalize their feelings. Dante's attention is drawn by the impressive stature of a man who seems immune from fire, holding a contorted but at the same time scornful attitude. The intriguing character intervenes directly with clues about his identity:

"Qual io fui vivo, tal son morto.[52]
Se Giove stanchi 'l suo fabbro da cui
crucciato prese la folgore aguta
onde l'ultimo dì percosso fui—
o s'elli stanchi li altri a muta a muta
in Mongibello a la focina negra,
chiamando 'Buon Vulcano, aiuta, aiuta!',
sì com' el fece a la pugna di Flegra,—
e me saetti con tutta sua forza,
non ne potrebbe aver vendetta allegra."
(51–60)

"As I / was alive, so I am dead. / Though Jove tire out his smith, from whom he / wrathful took the sharp thunderbolt that struck me / on the last day— / and

51. "Quella che giva 'ntorno era più molta, / e quella men che giacëa al tormento, / ma più al duolo avea la lingua sciolta" ("The flock that was walking was largest by far, and / fewest were those lying to be tortured, but their / tongues were looser to cry out"; *Inf.* 14. 25–27). Could this be an indication that in Dante's time the practice of sodomy was even more widespread than that of blasphemy? The quote is also an index of the intensity of the blasphemers' torment. While the other groups try to protect themselves from the fiery rain either by moving around or by exposing their backs, the blasphemers are pinned to the ground, their faces and chests exposed.

52. The phrase "Qual io fui vivo, tal son morto" is ironical, as Giuseppe di Scipio notes (*Inf.* 14. 180).

though he weary the others, turn after turn, at / the black forge in Mongibello, calling, 'Good Vulcan, / help, help!' / as he did at the battle of Phlegra—and strike me / with all his force, / he could not have happy / vengeance thereby."

The character's self-portrayal conveys arrogance and ambition, since his entire confession is obsessively turning around one idea: how the mightiest of gods could not defeat him no matter what. As he speaks, the soul tries his best to slight the god's power, depicting him as impotent and forced to beg the aid of another, subaltern god. The repetition of the verb in "Buon volcano, aiuta, aiuta!" stresses Jove's powerlessness, and the adjective *buon* functions here as an element of *captatio benevolentiae.* The entire evocation is meant to conjure up the image of a begging Jove, the opposite of the all-mighty chief of the pagan pantheon. Ridiculing a deity is, undoubtedly, a blasphemous gesture, irrespective of the cultural setting in which the act takes place, and Virgil's harsh rebuke, which castigates the arrogance of the character and uncovers his identity, further clarifies the nature of his sin:

"O Capaneo, in ciò che non s'ammorza
la tua superbia, se' tu più punito;
nullo martirio, fuor che la tua rabbia,
sarebbe al tuo furor dolor compito."
Poi si rivolse a me con miglior labbia,
dicendo: "Quei fu l'un d'i sette regi
ch'assiser Tebe; ed ebbe, e par ch'elli abbia,
Dio in disdegno, e poco par che 'l pregi;
ma, com' io dissi lui, li suoi dispetti
sono al suo petto assai debiti fregi."
(63–72).[53]

"O Capaneus, since your pride / is not extinguished, you are punished more; no / punishment, other than your rage, would be / suffering of a measure with your fury." / Then he turned back to me with a better look, / saying: "This was one of the seven kings who / besieged Thebes; and he had, and seems still to have / God in disdain, and respects him little; but, as I / said, his spite is the ornament his breast deserves."

Virgil's words leave no doubt as to the sin of which the king-warrior is guilty. On account of his *superbia,* Capaneus had, and still has, a scornful attitude toward the divinity. Virgil's repetition of the verb *avere* in two

53. In classical mythology, Capaneus was an outstanding warrior against Thebes. He was notorious not only for his gigantic stature and physical strength but also for his arrogance (which was eventually sanctioned by Jupiter with death by lightning). Dante presumably knew the story from Statius's *Thebaid* (for more on this, see Edward Moore, *Studies in Dante: Scripture and Classical Authors in Dante* [New York: Greenwood Press, 1968], 243–55).

different tenses—past and present—corresponds to Capaneus's own *Qual io fui vivo, tal son morto,* while the text subtly changes the name *Giove* to *Dio.* An accumulation of artistic means serves to figure linguistically Capaneus's transgression: the moral elements of *superbia* and *disdegno,* which echo the adjective *dispettoso* from line 47, are themselves reinforced by the clause *poco par che'l pregi.* By means of this remarkable wealth of lexical clues, the poet seeks to build the figure of a blasphemer who would otherwise be difficult to interpret as such. Capaneus's blasphemy is a matter of attitude rather than of language, for he utters no malediction against the deity he scorns. Had it not been for Dante's care to emphasize almost tautologically the disdainful attitude of the character—this *sine qua non* index of the medieval definitions of blasphemy—we might have failed to recognize Dante's Capaneus as a blasphemer. His transgression may have been clearly perceived as blasphemy in the framework of Greek mythology but not necessarily in the context of medieval ethics; we have seen that the medieval moralists had a different outlook on blasphemy than the classical Greeks, for whom this transgression consisted essentially in injuring a god's *reputation.*

The Greek baggage with which Capaneus comes to Dante poses a problem to the poet, since this type of transgression does not perfectly fit the contemporary view of blasphemy as Dante wants to represent it in his Christian design. To make Capaneus's misdemeanor suitable to the poetic illustration of *bestemmia,* Dante slightly alters the fabric of Capaneus's sin, by adding a few, revealing touches to it. Along with the frequent allusions to scorn we have read in the text, there is one more element that helps us identify this character as a blasphemer, an important clue furnished again by Virgil's rebuke, which mentions twice the wrath underlying Capaneus's transgressive behavior. Both *rabbia* and *furor* are strong words in Italian, and here they are meant to help us better understand the nature and the gravity of the sin. Let us recall that in Peraldus's definition, a wrathful inner disposition is the key factor leading to sacrilegious speech. Blasphemers are essentially people who are angry at God and who use words to take revenge against a power they otherwise cannot overcome. Irreverent, violent speech is the only, illusory means by which they can inflict pain on the untouchable entity against whom their hate is directed. Capaneus's anger at the deity he despises so intensely and his verbal attempt to diminish the image of this deity are two important leads pointing to the nature of his sin: *blasphemia.*

We have seen that Dante's decision to use this mythological figure to represent the sin of blasphemy—a sin "reinvented" in Dante's own time—is problematic. Why did the poet choose a character coming from the world of the mythical pagans to embody a sin consecrated by the Christian world? The answer lies in the same motivation that made Dante choose Ulysses and Diomede to represent the fraudulent counselors, or Sinon the Greek the falsifiers of words. It is their symbolic value for the medieval cultural community that made these characters so suitable for Dante's purposes. Just as Ulysses and Sinon were for medieval culture symbols of human guile and the seductiveness of rhetoric, so Capaneus was emblematic of the power of a mortal king at war with, and eventually punished by, a supernatural power.[54] And just as pagan, mythological Ulysses dies in Dante's reworking of the myth "as it pleased" the Christian God—*com' altrui piacque*—so Capaneus, the one who defied Jove, is punished among the blasphemers against Dante's God. Neither in the case of Ulysses, nor in that of Capaneus, has Dante for a single moment confounded Zeus/Jupiter with God; the two entities come to overlap because what matters to Dante is the essential idea of respect for the sacred. The notion of divinity is so powerful in the poet's mind that the words used to represent this notion—*Giove* or *Dio*—become interchangeable. As Giuseppe Mazzotta has shown, Capaneus (just like Ulysses) provided Dante one more site in which he could Christianize secular history or what the poet interpreted as such.[55]

As if Dante felt that his choice of Capaneus as a blasphemer was a risky writerly decision (for how will Christian poetry convincingly condemn a sin of the tongue so widely disseminated in the late Middle Ages, by invoking a remote, mythological figure?), in the Malebolge Dante has the sin of blasphemy enacted by a thief, in a manner more powerful than any possible injurious words. In the seventh ring of Malebolge, the pilgrim and his guide watch in horror how a sinner bitten at the neck by a serpent turns in-

54. Capaneus is also mentioned in Alain of Lille's *Plaint of Nature* (216–17), where we see Genius paint legendary people to illustrate what is specific about humankind. Besides Helen, Turnus, Hercules, Plato, and Cicero, for instance, Alain also mentions Capaneus's gigantic stature, Ulysses's foxlike cleverness, and Sinon's sinuous speech. This selection is representative for the panoply of mythical or historical figures of which medieval readers were so fond. It is worth noting, however, that Dante views Capaneus, Ulysses, and Sinon as more complex human beings than Alain did, since Dante basically reinvents new identities for these characters and brings them back to life in original ways.

55. Mazzota, *Dante, Poet of the Desert,* 22–25.

stantly into ashes and then retakes his former shape. Like all infernal punishments, this process is cyclical and meant to take place in eternity. Each time the sinner undergoes his inescapable transformation, he experiences tremendous physical pain and psychological trauma.[56] As far as his identity is concerned, we find out from his self-introduction that "Io piovvi di Toscana, / poco tempo è, in questa gola fiera. / Vita bestial mi piacque e non umana, / sì come a mul ch'i' fui; son Vanni Fucci / bestia, e Pistoia mi fu degna tana" ("I rained down from Tuscany, not long ago, / into this fierce throat. / Bestial life pleased me, not human, mule that I / was; I am Vanni Fucci the beast, and Pistoia was a / worthy lair for me"; *Inf.* 24.122–26).[57]

Although Vanni is cast primarily as a thief, he displays a more complex poetic figure. What characterizes him is not, as we would expect, a certain guile that the sinners of Malebolge display, but a pure and openly confessed animality. His violent nature is textually rendered by an accumulation of words such as *vita bestial, non umana, mul, bestia, tana.* Critics have justly noted that as a fictive character he would have better fitted among the violent of the seventh circle. His impulsive nature and the propensity toward a merely instinctual mode of life are doubled by an overweening pride. Recognized by the pilgrim, Vanni Fucci first confesses his shame and embarrassment at being seen in his hellish position; then, he predicts the defeat of the White Guelphs by the Black Guelphs, a prediction that concerns Dante in the keenest way.[58] The purpose of Vanni's prophecy is to hurt his visitor and,

56. As in Canto 14, where the punishment of the violent against God made the pilgrim note the horrible art of justice (l. 6), here too, the severity of the punishment evokes the power of God's just vengeance. "Oh potenza di Dio, quant' è severa, / che cotai colpi per vendetta croscia!" ("Oh the / power of God, how severe it is, what torrents of / punishment it pours forth"; ll. 119–20).

57. In 1293, he allegedly robbed the treasury of San Jacopo in the Church of San Zeno, Pistoia, and got away with the theft when another person was wrongly convicted of it. On account of this biographical information, George Economou notes the opposition between human justice and divine justice that Dante wants to emphasize in the Vanni Fucci episode. Whereas earthly justice is characterized by shortcomings caused by human abuses in words and deeds, in the realm of heavenly justice, false impressions of guilt and innocence are dissipated by testimony given *sub species aeternitatis* ("*Inferno* XXIV," in *Lectura Dantis Virginiana, I. Dante's "Inferno": Introductory Readings,* edited by Tibor Wlassics, Supplement to *Lectura Dantis* 6 [1990], special issue [Charlottesville: University of Virginia, 1990], 314).

58. In May 1301, the Blacks were banished from Pistoia, as a result of a vote endorsed by Dante himself. Just a few months later, in November 1301, with the help of Charles of Valois, the Blacks reentered Florence and in April 1302 expelled the Whites and brought Florence under their administrative and legal rule. According to the legend, the city of Pistoia had been

thus, to take revenge for having been seen in a humiliating situation: "E detto l'ho perché doler ti debbia!" ("And I have told you this that it may grieve you!"; *Inf.* 24.151). The reply is placed in a privileged position, as it concludes not only the prophecy but also the entire canto, and it is meant to echo Vanni's confession of shame from lines 133–35: "Più mi duol che tu m'hai colto / ne la miseria dove tu mi vedi, / che quando fui de l'altra vita tolto" ("It pains me more to be caught in the / wretchedness where you see me than when I was / taken from the other life"). Shame is worse than physical death for Vanni, and no offender or offense directed at him can get away unpunished. As a matter of fact, his ability to feel shame, a feeling that has moral overtones, could be interpreted positively, as a kind of remorse for what he did, which earned him this condition. His hurt pride, however, is a measure not of his feeling of dignity but of his overweening ego. As though punishing Dante were not enough, at the end of his prophecy, angry Vanni does not withdraw humbly from the visitors' sight but makes an unexpected, obscene gesture: "il ladro / le mani alzò con amendue le fiche, / gridando: 'Togli, Dio, ch'a te le squadro!'" ("the thief raised his hands / with both the figs, crying: 'Take them, God, I'm / aiming at you!'"; *Inf.* 25.1–3). Like any other semiotic system, gestural language can be "translated" as well, and by placing words in the character's mouth the poet ensures that his audience "reads" Vanni's message correctly. It is a message with sexual connotations directed at God, a wrathful gesture of defiance that, resembling Capaneus's arrogant and contumelious attitude that Dante evokes here, is an essential key for understanding Vanni's moral profile: "Per tutt' i cerchi de lo 'nferno scuri / non vidi spirto in Dio tanto superbo, / non quel che cadde a Tebe giù da' muri" ("Through all the dark circles of Hell I saw no spirit / so proud against God, not him who fell from the wall / at Thebes"; *Inf.* 25.13–15).

The comparison with the blasphemer from the circle of the violent against God maximizes the meaning of Vanni Fucci's gesture. The contempt for God, the anger that calls for revenge, the sacred name pronounced here irreverently, the provocation hurled at the divinity, and the sexual meaning of the gesture are all manifestations described by medieval theologians as forms of blasphemy. Let us recall Peraldus's definition, which best synthesizes them and which contains not only the elements of *contumelia,*

founded by the remnants of Catiline's army, an origin that also accounts for Dante's negative assessment of Pistoia in *Inferno* 25.

verbum, ira, vindicare de Deo, specific to blasphemers, but also the potential sexual aspect of blasphemous words. In his definition, the theologian is referring to Christ's genitalia, frequently ridiculed by obscene speakers, but, as the analysts of medieval blasphemy tell us, sexual references were also often made to the blasphemer's own private parts. Documents from the end of thirteenth-century Italy testify to the frequency of the gesture of making the fig, as well as to its blasphemous nature on account of which the perpetrators were actionable.[59] Interpreting Vanni Fucci's obscene gesture in the context of medieval Italian society, Ignazio Baldelli notes: "Gestures alluding to the most intimate parts are extremely injurious and even of blasphemous content. Thus, in this society, the gesture of making the fig was the supreme offense; and, if addressed to God, the most atrocious blasphemy."[60]

The simple fact that Vanni pronounces God's name *in Hell* is a profanatory act of speech, if we take into account the medieval sense that God's name was to be uttered rarely, in appropriate circumstances, and only with extreme caution and reverence. This attitude came from the beliefs that, on the one hand, the creator of the world and language could not be subsumed to his own creation, and on the other hand, the divine name was the most important legacy bestowed on man, as it was an effective way to prove the falsity of other gods. Abusing God's name(s) was, therefore, a highly transgressive act.[61] Thus, Vanni Fucci's naming God in the middle of his

59. As similar examples of what was interpreted as impious and offensive gestures, Alain Cabantous notes spitting in heaven's direction or gnashing one's teeth (*Blasphemy: Impious Speech in the West from the Seventeenth to the Nineteenth Century* [New York: Columbia University Press, 2002], 12).

60. In the original: "I gesti alludenti alle parti più intime sono supremamente ingiuriosi e sono di contenuto fin blasfemo. In questa società dunque il gesto di fare le fiche era l'ingiuria suprema; e, se rivolta a Dio, la bestemmia più atroce" (Ignazio Baldelli, "Le 'fiche' di Vanni Fucci," *Giornale storico della letteratura italiana* 114 [1997]: 1–38, at 10; translation mine).

61. Cabantous points out that the rationale for the medieval condemnation of blasphemy mainly derived from the importance attached to the Word. In the Christian scheme of things, "speech opens humanity to the possibility of transcendence and is bestowed with a highly specific intention: that it be placed in the service of glorifying the divine, as emphasized in the second commandment to which the line from the Lord's prayer 'hallowed be Thy name' answers.... And just as the authentic and necessary spoken prayer will be 'heard' in the sense of hearkened to or answered because listened to by God, so the impious word will call forth the often dreadful and immediate punishment of the one who has travestied the essential function of language" (*Blasphemy,* 6).

obscene gesture appears all the more impious and can be read in contrast to Dante's constant care not to name Christ in the *Inferno.*

Another essential element of the medieval view of blasphemy present in this episode is the participation of the will in the sinful utterance. In Aquinas's theory, intention is the key factor that identifies blasphemy as a mortal sin. Impulsive blasphemers, who utter impious words inadvertently, on the spur of the moment, are less blamable than those who knowingly, with a full exercise of their will, pronounce injurious words against the divinity. Dante portrays Vanni Fucci as a speaker who aims at a certain effect; his prophesying the defeat of the Whites in order to upset the pilgrim proves that his words are not due to chance but deliberate. His use of language is as perverse as his will, both when his evil omen hurts the feelings of a human being and when his impious words offend the divinity. Even his lubricious gesture is unambiguously interpreted as transgressive in the order of Hell, since the snakes resume their attack on Vanni, and once again, the poet "translates" for the reader the significance of this attack: "Da indi in qua mi fuor le serpi amiche, / perch' una li s'avvolse allora il collo, / come dicesse 'Non vo' che più diche'" ("From then on snakes have been my friends, / because one of them wrapped itself around his neck, / as if to say, 'I won't let him say more'"; *Inf.* 25.4–6). It is also worthwhile to mention that the snake's attack occurs not after Vanni prophesizes the defeat of the White Guelph faction, but after he makes his blasphemous gesture. The phrase "Non vo' che più diche" may thus refer not only to the prophecy but also to the sacrilegious gesture against God. As to the artistic manner in which the poet-*artifex* builds this personage, we have to note the brilliant way in which language—the same language that Vanni abuses in so many ways—is made to turn against him. For, ironically, the horrendous portrayal of the character, lavishly described as animal, nonhuman, beast, mule, is not made by Virgil or the pilgrim, but by the character himself.

If Dante first cast Capaneus, the mythological warrior-king, as an emblematic blasphemer meant to represent the universal value of this sin of speech, now he casts Vanni Fucci as a historically anchored blasphemer, who illustrates this sin in contemporary society and in the Italian vernacular. D. L. Derby Chapin notes that as a leader of the Blacks, Vanni Fucci represents the symbol of an apotheosis of power, self-will, and pride, who challenged the power of God by literally stealing sacred images: "Like Satan, by claiming for his own what belongs to God, he loses his resemblance to God. In rejecting Christ as a model, he becomes an imitator of the Devil and takes on a resemblance to him and to the beast whose name he bears."[62]

In *Purgatory* 13, the portrayal of the Sienese Sapia Salvani is also grounded in reality, not in myth. She, too, is an Italian contemporary of Dante's, but unlike Vanni Fucci, a blasphemous thief in life and a blasphemous speaker after death, she provides in the text the remedy for the sin. On the purgatorial mountain, Sapia makes amends for her human failings. Her main human defect was foolishness, she says, in that she would rejoice more at the others' misfortune than at her own good luck. More perversely, she felt joy even when her own countrymen were defeated at the battle of Colle, in which her own nephew died. Out of joy, she felt so empowered that she challenged God with the words "Omai più non ti temo!" ("Now I fear you no more!"; l. 122). At the end of her life, however, she repented of her treasons and benefited from the charitable prayers of a man. The *sante orazioni,* "holy prayers," that Ser Pier Pettinaio said on her behalf reversed the terms of her blasphemy and reestablished the sacred function of language—reverent communication with the transcendental. While Francesca da Rimini is in Hell, at war with God and incapable of uttering a prayer, Sapia is on the purgatorial mountain, because repentance earned her peace with the divinity, just as the verbal intercessions of the hermit quickened her salvation. Through Sapia, Dante restores to the dialogue with God its true nature, for blasphemy, an inverted form of speech, is now replaced with reverent language. Sapia is only one of the numerous characters in *Purgatory* who allude to the power of prayer in the process of salvation and to the ability of this type of speech to accelerate the souls' ascension to the terrestrial paradise.

In Hell, however, the sin of blasphemy, as a sin of word, is assimilated by Dante with sodomy and usury, an association that may seem odd to a modern reader. For what do blasphemers have in common with homosexuals and usurers? The main clue of the alignment of these three sins is offered by the text itself. In *Inferno* 11, which contains the so-called map of Hell, Virgil defines "art" as divine; since art imitates nature, and nature is God's daughter, art too has a divine origin. In light of this definition, the seventh circle of Hell suggests that blasphemers offend God directly, whereas sodomites and usurers indirectly: the former by offending nature, and the lat-

62. D. L. Derby Chapin, "Io and the Negative Apotheosis of Vanni Fucci," *Dante Studies* 89 (1971): 19–31, at 28.

ter by offending art (here understood as craft, profession, or industry). The view of nature and art(s) as originating in the Creator is a solid Scholastic acquisition, with roots in Abelard and Alain of Lille (to name just two of the contributors to this view), but what made this theory so popular in the Middle Ages was an impressive number of moral texts that developed ideas about *deviations* with respect to nature and art.

If blasphemy is an insult to God through the medium of language (spoken or unspoken), sodomy is an offense as base as the first, only the medium is different: the flesh substitutes for words. According to recent research in the history of law, the association of blasphemy and sodomy was not uncommon in the Middle Ages, and it had roots in the famous *Novella* 77 of Justinian's code, written with the purpose that "Ut non luxurietur contra naturam neque iuretur per capillos aut aliquid huiusmodi neque blasphemetur in Deum" ("One shall not lust against nature, nor swear on the hair of his head or anything like that, nor shall commit blasphemy against God").[63] In the wake of this document, early-modern juridical texts treat blasphemy and homosexuality on a par and attach them the same legal penalties.[64] In the moral texts of the time, as well, we find connections that justify Dante's placement of the blasphemers beside the sodomites. In the widely circulated twelfth-century treatise *Verbum abbreviatum,* Peter Cantor metaphorically describes sodomites as "muti a laude dei" ("mute to God's praise").[65] Later on, Peraldus will take up this analogy and will add that at the last judgment God will take away the sodomites' voices so they cannot defend themselves. Another important association of language with sex (especially inverted sex) is made by Alain of Lille, who in the *Plaint of Nature* describes intimate relationships in terms of grammar and stigmatises sodomy as follows:

The active sex shudders in disgrace as it sees itself degenerate into the passive sex. A man turned woman blackens the fair name of her sex. The witchcraft of Venus

63. Quoted in Leveleux, *La Parole interdite,* 168; translation mine. The integral text of *Novella 77* can be consulted in Justinian, *Corpus Iuris Civilis,* edited by Rudolf Schoell and Wilhelm Kroll (Berlin: Weidmann, 1954), or at http://upmf-grenoble.fr/Haiti/Cours/Ak/Corpus/Nov77.htm.

64. Leveleux mentions Ludovicus Montaltus with *Tractatus de repprobatione sententiae Pilati* (Treatise on the reprobation of Pilate's sentence) and Tiberis Decianus with *Tractatus criminalis* (Treatise on criminal matters). See *La parole interdite,* 169–70.

65. Cantor, *Verbum abbreviatum,* PL 205. 335B.

turns him into a hermaphrodite. He is subject and predicate: one and the same term is given a double application. Man here extends too far the laws of grammar. Becoming a barbarian in grammar, he disclaims the manhood given him by nature.... For the human race, fallen from its high state, adopts a highly irregular (grammatical) change when it inverts the rules of Venus by introducing barbarisms in its arrangement of genders. Thus man, his sex changed by a ruleless Venus, in defiance of due order, by his arrangement changes what is straightforward attribute of his. Abandoning in his deviation the true script of Venus, he is proved to be a sophistic pseudographer. Shunning even a resemblance traceable to the art of Dione's daughter, he falls into the defect of inverted order.[66]

Akin to blasphemy, which perverts language by turning it away from prayer and confession, sodomy is, in Alain's view, a dysfunctional grammar, in which the genders are inverted, and the relationship between subject and predicate reversed.[67] Blasphemy and sodomy also meet on the common ground of the referential function of language; for, just as blasphemies cannot be retold or reproduced, neither in speaking nor in writing, in the same way sodomitic acts cannot be described. In the Middle Ages, both blasphemy and homosexuality are categories of *nefandum,* that is, things impossible to say or describe. Reproduced, blasphemous words would tarnish the ears and souls of hearers, and describing details of homosexual relationships would pollute Christian mores and subvert the very foundations of society. Examining the medieval concept of *nefandum,* Jacques Chiffouleau notes that it was as much a literary *topos* as a moral and juridical category. He also points out that among the classes of *nefandum,* sodomy was considered to have the most serious social implications in that it threatened the soundness of family life.[68]

Another perversion subversive of the divine and social orders was money-lending at interest. In Thomas Aquinas's ethics, usury was a sin simi-

66. Alain of Lille, *Plaint of Nature,* 67–68, 133–34.

67. André Pézard offers an interesting analysis of the sin of Brunetto Latini, arguing that this is blasphemy, not sodomy; more exactly, by preferring French to Italian vernacular in the writing of his *Book of Treasure,* Latini became guilty of linguistic apostasy. In Pézard's view, the three courteous Florentines from *Inferno* 16 are also guilty of blasphemy (*Dante sous la pluie de feu (Enfer, XV)* [Paris: Vrin, 1950], 236). Richard Kay offers a different interpretation here and posits as sin the opposition to the Holy Roman Empire ("The Sin(s) of Brunetto Latini," *Dante Studies* 112 [1994]: 19–31).

68. Jacques Chiffouleau, "Dire l'indicible: remarques sur la catégorie du *nefandum* du XIIIe au XVIe siècle," *Annales. Economie, Sociétés, Civilisations* (1990): 289–324, at 295–96.

lar to sodomy, insofar as it also acted against nature. Natural laws required that money should increase from natural goods, not from their own perverse propagation. Usurers were instruments of the devil because they did not sell money but time. They did not work themselves to earn their daily bread but made time work for them.[69] We know that in medieval thought time was considered a divine function, and thus its dilation for the purpose of lucre was an extremely grievous sin against the divinity. In his well-known essay on the opposition between the time of the Church and the time of the merchant, Jacques le Goff cites a meaningful view of usury expressed by William of Auxerre (1160–1229):

The usurer always acts against the law of universal nature, for he sells time, which belongs to all creatures. Augustine says that each creature needs to offer herself; the sun needs to offer himself in order to illuminate; by the same token, earth needs to offer all she can produce, and the same holds for water. But nothing offers itself in a way more conform to nature than time; wittingly or unwittingly things have time. Therefore, since the usurer sells what necessarily belongs to all creatures, he hurts all creatures.... This is one of the reasons why the Church pursues usurers.[70]

69. *Verbum abbreviatum,* which stigmatises the sin of usury in vitriolic terms, is indicative of this perception: "Et sicut diabolus talentum peccati non vult sibi reddi (quia quanto diutius detinetur, tanto amplius multiplicatur), sic nec fenerator talentum pecuniae creditum proximo, qui etiam dando ad usuram pejor est exactore diabolo, quia diabolus auctor omnis malitiae talentum suum, non alienum, mutuum dat; fenerator vero dando mutuum talentum pecuniae, non suum, sed Dei, et quo proximus gratis esset juvandus, et ob hoc sibi collatum nequiter dat ad usuram, qui etiam tempus vendit, ut propter dilationem temporis majorem, plus lucri recipiat" ("And just as the devil does not want to get a reward for his sinful help (for the more the reward is delayed, the more it increases), so the publican does not want to get the interest for the loan immediately. But he who gives money in order to make profit is worse than the exacting devil, because the devil, being the author of all evils, makes a loan with his own property, not with someone else's, whereas the publican, by lending the property of money, does not give his own property but that of God. And since a neighbor should be helped in a disinterested way, and the money-lender is rich through the grace of God, it results that the publican commits an injustice when he lends money, for he sells time in order to make more profit from the dilation of it" (PL 305.157B; translation mine).

70. "L'usurier agit contre la loi de la nature universelle, car il vend le temps, qui est commun à toutes les créatures. Augustin dit que chaque créature est obligée de faire don de soi; le soleil est obligé de faire don de soi pour éclairer; de même la terre est obligée de faire don de tout ce qu'elle peut produire et de même l'eau. Mais rien ne fait don de soi d'une façon plus conforme à la nature que le temps; bon gré, mal gré les choses ont du temps. Puisque donc l'usurier vend ce qui appartient nécessairement à toutes les créatures, il lèse toutes les créatures.... Et c'est une des raisons pour lesquelles l'Église poursuit les usuriers" (*Summa Aurea,* III, 21, fol.

"'L tempo fugge che t'assonna" ("the time is fleeting that holds you asleep") sounds one of the most celebrated phrases in the *Paradiso* (32.129), a human time that, as Gianfranco Contini has pointed out, for Dante runs back toward the source of eternity.[71] Along these lines, it is likely that what Dante condemns through the sin of usury is not so much the abuse of money, as some have suggested, as the abuse of time.[72] And if, in the wake of Justinian's *Ut non luxurietur,* it was natural in Dante's time to associate blasphemy with sodomy, it was also natural to equate usury with blasphemy and heresy. In 1311, the Council of Vienne decreed usury as grievous a sin as heresy and blasphemy. What Dante ultimately did in the circle of the violent against God was to offer an extraordinary synthesis of disparate trends of moral thought; he tightly mainstreamed three discrete types of perversions and grouped them on account of their common nature of violations of divine attributes—speech, life, and time. Blaspheming the name of the Highest Good is abusing the sacral function of language; having intercourse with people of the same sex violates the natural laws of the body and threatens life itself by blocking the possibility of procreation; moneylending at interest is an unnatural interaction with time, a debasement of the notion of value from the divine through the human to the diabolical. In the text, the verb Virgil uses to describe usury is *spregiare,* "to despise," the same element that appears in the definitions of blasphemy (Dante's Capaneus hates God "e poco par che'l pregi"). All three sins are acts of violence that, directly or indirectly, do harm to the Supreme Being, and that affect the everyday life of the entire community.[73]

Like all the other sins punished in the *Inferno,* the triad blasphemy-sodomy-usury is seen from a twofold perspective—transcendental and mundane. In addition to offending God, these transgressions also had dev-

225v, quoted in Jacques Le Goff, *Pour un Autre moyen Age: Temps, travail et culture en occident. 18 essays* [Paris: Gallimard, 1977], 46–47).

71. Gianfranco Contini, *Un' Idea di Dante: Saggi Danteschi* (Turin: Einaudi, 2001), 205.

72. Among the interpreters who stress the notion of usury as abusive usage of currency are Ferrante (*The Political Vision of the "Divine Comedy"*) and Lisa Freinkel ("*Inferno* and the Poetics of *Usura,*" *MLN* 107 [1992]: 1–17).

73. Ferrante remarks that all the sinners representing the violent against God are set against social backgrounds: Capaneus is a king, the sodomites are statesmen or teachers, and the usurers belong to leading Italian families involved in the economic life of the community. Thus, the three sins these souls embody are as many constant threats to the social order and concord. (Capaneus, for instance, is the figure of the "human anarchist"; *The Political Vision,* 159–60.)

astating consequences on the immediate level of public life, for according to medieval interpretations, the sin(s) of the individual had deep repercussions on the fate of the multitude.[74] For medieval society, blasphemy was more than just a form of phonic pollution; what was truly at stake was the core of the Christian religion with which medieval communities identified themselves. It was an infraction that could not go unpunished, because it offended the ecclesiastical structures, the profound beliefs of worshippers, and the moral values of Christian society. Thus, indirectly, profanatory speech also had repercussions on the representatives of political power, who were considered symbols of divine authority.[75] Blasphemies were acts of lèse-majesté that were affecting leading political figures as much as they were affecting the ineffable majesty of God. Moreover, under the influence of Justinian's *Novella,*[77] there was the sense that natural calamities were a direct result of blasphemies gone unpunished; therefore, it was the immediate duty of the juridical systems in place to keep such criminal acts under control, for the failure to limit the blasphemous phenomenon would have meant political and institutional inability to keep society under control.

74. See, for instance, Peter Cantor (chapter 4, "Peccatum unius saepe redundant in universitatem," of the *Verbum abbreviatum*), PL 305.217C.

75. Illustrating this perception is John of Salisbury's *Policraticus,* especially chapter 25, in which he describes the prince as an image of the deity.

Conclusion

In the preceding chapters, I sought to bring to the fore those features of the *Romance of the Rose* and the *Divine Comedy* that show the degree to which literary culture in the vernacular was sensitive to the animated medieval debate on *peccata linguae.* In their own specific ways, both poems laid claim to offering moral lessons about the usage of language. The reading of these poems through the lenses of the medieval ethicists of speech has highlighted the great extent to which Jean and Dante absorbed aspects—ideas, images, quotes, and specialized terms—of the rich tradition of the *lingua*-texts. The most salient feature common to the two poets is their adherence to the Scholastic principle of the will as the root of evil speech acts. In the *Rose,* the textual site that exemplifies this principle is Dame Nature's discourse, which is rich in moral notions cast in Scholastic phraseology. Nature's most important postulate is that human deeds or words do not happen by necessity; individuals choose themselves what to do or what to say: "Ainz font bien ou mal franchement, / Par leur voloir tant seulement ("Instead people do good or evil freely, through their will alone"; ll. 17265–66). By virtue of this pronouncement and of her overall analysis of man's vices, I consider Nature as the most important mouthpiece of Jean as a moralist. Not only does she express philosophical opinions that are incongruent with her allegorical essence (and that would have better suited Dame Raison), but she conveys a view of human morals so cynical that it can only belong to Jean de Meun as a satirist of contemporary society. Will is the agent of verbal sins for Dante, as well. In *Convivio,* he argues that *l'arte di parlare,* "the art of speaking," being a rational act, is rooted in the will; by the same token, the abuses committed through the medium of speech stem from the will. To reinforce this notion, in the *Comedy,* with the sole exception of blasphemy, a sin of violence, all the other verbal abuses are punished as sins of fraud in Malebolge, an area that, as Cogan has proven, corresponds to the appetite of the will.

One of the most important achievements of Jean and Dante as moralists of speech is the vernacular lexicon they develop or implement. The ethical category of *peccata linguae* or *verbi* was an important part of the medieval discourse on human morality, but this discourse was developed in Latin. Peter Cantor, Alain of Lille, William Peraldus, Vincent of Beauvais, and Thomas Aquinas wrote their texts on sins in academic Latin, whereas Jean composed the *Rose* in the langue *d'oïl,* and Dante wrote *Convivio* and the *Comedy* in the Florentine dialect. For both poets, the use of the vernacular was the result of a deliberate choice and was intertwined with didactic purposes. In the *Rose,* Amant insists that Dame Raison instruct him in French, not in Latin (ll. 5835–37), a demand to be read in correlation with Jean's marked concern to be understood when he expounded moral or speculative principles. In the passage debating the relationships among predestination, divine foreknowledge, and free will, he stresses that these relationships are not easy to explain to lay people (l. 17110). Jean's task becomes at this point to explain and "translate" into the vernacular a Scholastic discourse routinely written in Latin (and we have historical and textual evidence that he was an outstanding translator). Jean was actually doing in poetry what Laurent of Orléans was doing in a specialized moral tract, with this significant difference that Jean's extraordinary linguistic creativity and verve enabled him to do a better job than Laurent. I have noted that where Laurent proposes two vernacular terms for the translation of a verbal sin into French (flattery, for instance), Jean uses five terms. It is no small achievement to enrich the moral lexicon of a Romance vernacular in poetry more than an ecclesiastic writer does in a moral tract proper.

Likewise, Dante had access to the corpus of philosophical and moral knowledge of his time through the mediation of Latin. He too explained, exemplified, and "translated" notions about sins into the vernacular. Analyzing Dante's relationship to William Peraldus, Mancini has noted that Dante is a *traduttore-traditore* of Peraldus. We have seen how many controversies the term *consiglio frodolente* has aroused in Dante studies; such a moral category did exist in the medieval tracts, but what in Peraldus was the sin of *pravum consilium,* for instance, for Dante becomes *fraudulent counsel.* Cavalca, the Italian translator of Peraldus's "De peccato linguae," published his *Pungilingua* after Dante's death, but his vocabulary of lingual transgressions is very similar to Dante's terminology for the verbal sins punished in Hell. The two thus meet in a common effort of transferring the discourse on *peccata linguae/verbi* from the context of academic Latin to that of the living language of lay people. Yet Dante preceded Cavalca's work in a conscious and constant agenda of "italianizing Scholasticism."[1]

In the poetic treatment of verbal sins, Jean and Dante are brought together by their significant contribution to the cultural movement of "vernacularization" of the pastoral discourse on transgressive speech. Chapter 1, where I presented Laurent's and Cavalca's works, demonstrated that the *Rose* and the *Comedy* are contemporary with, and sometimes even pre-date, pastoral undertakings, which shows how open, receptive, and responsive Jean and Dante are to the currents of thought of their times. The main difference between Dante's assimilation of ethical theories about speech and Jean's is the way in which these theories are imbedded in the poetic texts. In medieval studies, it has become a stereotype to say that the medieval man was a creator of systems, but Dante confirms the validity of this assertion once again; in the *Inferno,* he creates his own rigorous system of sins, with internal, hierarchical relationships, and within it, he forges a micro-system of verbal transgressions arranged in precise, deliberate order. Jean, on the other hand, despite thematizing the vices of the tongue, adopts a nonorganized framework, in which the moral terms—vices or virtues of language—do not always occupy the same positions in the structure; rather, they are constantly revised and rearranged (what is vice for one character is virtue for others). La Vieille's and Ami's notions of morality stand, for instance, in sharp contrast with Reason's. I have noted that this was one of the main charges leveled by Christine de Pizan and Jean Gerson in the *Querelle:* that Jean de Meun failed to give clear moral instruction to his readership. Christine even

1. Giovanni Gentile, *I Problemi della Scolastica* (Bari: Laterza, 1923), 38.

compared Jean de Meun with Dante and gave the latter as the perfect model of a true moral writer.[2] It is a comparison out of which Jean comes ruffled, since it is made with the explicit purpose of diminishing his stature as a moralist with respect to Dante's exemplary one.

With all due respect, I do not endorse Christine de Pizan's conclusion. Despite being designed as a romance featuring malicious characters who employ obscene language and encourage the use of fraud and violence in daily actions, the *Rose* remains a strongly didactic book, written with the declared purpose of educating readers. The great paradox of Jean's ethics is that he aims at ridding his audience of vices while apparently encouraging it to practice them. Behind these encouragements, however, we cannot fail to notice the strong ironic vein of Jean's sayings, his constant mocking of the weaknesses of human nature. If by being so corrosive, he shakes his readers up, it is because he wants to awaken them. If he challenges their intelligence, it is because he wants to make them think twice before they speak or act. The explosive content of some of the episodes should never be taken without a grain of salt, since the credibility of each controversial speaker is undermined by himself/herself. The moral risk for readers exists at moments, when the sinful speakers persuasively preach the doctrines of aggression, lust, and deceit. But by constantly contradicting themselves while they speak, these characters put themselves in highly ridiculous positions and oblige the readers to distance themselves from such postures. When Jean builds these personages into his text, he also plants in them the seed of self-destruction in the sphere of credibility, for what they say (the *peccati predicatio,* "preaching of sin") goes against who they are (human failures). The contrast between essence and appearance is a common denominator in the profiles of La Vieille, Ami, Faus Semblant (in his capacity as a mendicant friar), Genius (in his hypostasis as a priest), and creates irresistible comic effects that, while ensuring the great success of the book, render readers more witted. If we want to understand Jean's design better, we have to place him in the tradition of the Menippean satire, this comic genre whose main representatives are Petronius's *Satyricon,* Martianus Capella's *The Marriage of Philology and Mercury,* and Fulgentius's *Mythologies.* The traditional Menippean satire delights in multiple viewpoints of the same topic or theme; it creates unreliable narrators, authors of questionable authority, and texts

2. McWebb, *Debating the "Roman de la Rose,"* 176.

with ever-shifting perspectives; it ultimately undermines the consistency that a reader expects of a work and makes the interpretation of that work problematic. Jean raises all these artistic features to heights never attained before and offers French culture the first Menippean satire in the vernacular.

The problem of the inept reader who might misinterpret the poem and take from it wrong lessons, a problem identified by Christine de Pizan and Jean Gerson, is offered a solution in the *Testament,* where the author asks that the *aucteurs* be glossed benevolently and respectfully, for they put their learning and creativity in the service of their readers' education. This poetic text that Jean wrote in his old age deserves much more attention than I could offer it in chapter 2 and can be studied from at least three perspectives: as a versified tract on the seven deadly sins, an extraordinary literary undertaking, unique in medieval French literature; in its relationship to the *Rose* in search for more internal evidence for the authorship of Jean de Meun; and as a possible source of inspiration for the *Divine Comedy* in the field of what Barbara Newman calls with a beautiful phrase "imaginative theology."[3]

In *Paradiso,* Dante explicitly warns that uninstructed readers should not embark on the journey with him (2.1–18), but in the *Rose,* Jean never addresses such entities. Not because from the height of his extraordinary erudition he can envision only a reader who is as witty as he, but because his poem, written in what he calls the "sweet language of France" (a low one, sometimes, it is true) is designed to be understood even by the less educated. By using low language, Jean aims at gaining access to that segment of readership who uses the same level of speech in daily communications; the degree of instruction of his audience matters less, for he is writing the *Rose* with the declared purpose of instructing the laity. Even when, out of passion for the Scholastic doctrine of will and sin, he forgets about the plot and goes on explaining this doctrine in the smallest detail, it is not to bar uneducated readers from access to his book. On the contrary, after he warns that clarifying these theological concepts is not an easy matter, he does his best to explain them for everyone to understand. With his great linguistic skills and philosophical penchant, he translates the *latino discreto* of the pastoral and philosophical masterpieces of his time into the clearest French vernacular. It is an intellectual endeavor that prefigures Dante's

3. Newman, *God and the Goddesses,* 305.

agenda in *Convivio*—that of giving light to those who are in spiritual darkness and intellectual obscurity. The problem of Jean's approach to ethics is inextricably linked to that of hermeneutics; the discourses in the poem cannot be taken in isolation and should never be read as autonomous texts, independent from the romance as a whole, as Christine de Pizan confesses to have done.[4] A thorough investigation of Christine's and Jean Gerson's reading techniques exceeds the scope of my study but remains a desideratum, for there are many things left to say about the deficiencies of their methods of interpretation.

Although Jean de Meun does not forge an original moral system as Dante will, in chapter 2 I showed that we can glean Jean's view of speech ethics from disparate passages throughout the *Rose* and the *Testament.* If Dame Nature speaks about the will as the agent of verbal abuses, Dame Raison raises the important issues of obscene speech and the divine origin of language, and Genius vituperates against feminine verbosity; these three discourses are the textual *loci* in which Jean asserts his own opinions or tastes. The question of Jean's antifeminism is one of the main hot controversies around the *Rose.* In an attempt to exculpate the poet from the charge of misogyny leveled at him as early as the Renaissance, Lionel J. Friedmann took great care to show that Jean's attacks against women are only literary clichés and cannot be explained by his so-called "bourgeois realism."[5] Friedman's investigation fails, however, to consider all the voices who speak against women in the *Rose;* he discusses only the case of Jealous Husband and briefly mentions Genius. I have evidenced that we retrieve misogynistic ideas not only in these two discourses, but in several others: in La Vieille's, in Nature's, in Jean's apologetic speech toward his readership, and even in the final part of the poem when Amant speaks about the erotic benefits a man can gain from experimenting with both young and old women (ll. 21455–540). What is clearly transparent throughout these discourses is Jean's profound distaste for women's wicked manipulation of speech.

The major moral and psychological issue that both Jean and Dante confront in their works is that of fraud, this despicable perversion of the intellect "displeasing to God," as Dante put it (*Inf.* 11.26). It is in the sphere of fraud that the main corpus of verbal transgressions takes place, and it is thus this sphere that occupies most of the poets' attention. For Jean, words

4. McWebb, *Debating the "Roman de la Rose,"* 119–20.

5. Friedman, "Jean de Meung, Antifeminism, and 'Bourgeois Realism,'" 20–23.

are neighbors to things and must be cousins to their deeds; for Dante, as well, words must reflect inner speech and be corroborated by deeds. The categorical moral imperative *Mental language=Spoken language=Deeds* informs both Jean and Dante's philosophy of language, and it is on the articulation of this philosophical principle that the two poet-moralists build into their allegorical poems the manifold manifestations of the *lingua dolosa,* this supreme fraud-producing verbal agency. All the instances of fraudulent language I examined in chapter 3—flattery, evil counsel, double talk, sowing of discord, and falsifying of words—represent as many violations of this categorical imperative.

But then again differences occur at the level of the artistic treatment of these sins. As I have pointed out, Jean is a satirist in the tradition of the Roman poets, for whom *ridendo castigat mores* was the most effective ethical strategy; this is why he does not assume the *overt* status of a moral judge, as Dante does, and rarely uses the words "vice" or "sin." Jean laughs at sins and mocks sinners; Dante sends them to Hell. The former is a humorist, reveling in glittering lampoons fueled by human stupidity and vices, whereas the latter is a solemn moralizer, speaking of mortal sins and salvation in a grave tone. Similar to a mirror in a funhouse, the *Rose* lays bare the truth about the workings of speech even as it seems to distort it through discourses given by quirky characters; in the precise geography of the *Comedy,* uses of speech send souls to Hell or Heaven. Jean writes a "lovely romance" for lovers, in which the erotic art is considered from every single angle; Dante imagines a literary universe so strict, within a theological poem so difficult, that those embarked on a *picciolettta barca* cannot follow him.

While studying the verbal sins debated in the two poems, I have sought to constantly emphasize Jean's and Dante's relationships to their sources in the domain of ethics. Whereas the *Quellenforschungen* in Dante studies are rich and do justice to the influences exerted by some of the most important moralists of the time—Alain of Lille, William Peraldus, and Thomas Aquinas—the study of Jean's sources is an obviously underexplored territory. Ernest Langlois's groundbreaking work, *Origines et sources,* was published more than a century ago and at points corrected by John V. Fleming in 1969; it begs to be followed by studies that examine not only the *Rose* but also the *Testament* in light of the most recent findings about medieval ethics, such as the ones published by Carla Casagrande, Silvana Vecchio, Siegfried Wenzel, and Richard Newhauser, who in the last three decades or so have brought to light amazing facts about the medieval tractates on sin. By looking for Peraldian and Thomistic echoes in the *Rose,* my work has taken but a small step in the vast field of Jean de Meun's debts to the authors of these moral tractates.

As to Dante's relationships to contemporary ethicists of speech, my study has highlighted that his sources are mainly two: one located in the pastoral production on sin—Peraldus, more exactly, whose *Summa vitiorum* Dante knew (directly or indirectly); and the other one lodged in the more speculative theology of the time, as represented by Aquinas's *Summa theologica.* There are Peraldian traces in Dante's handling of all the five verbal abuses punished in Hell. I have also underlined that among the moral writers of the time, Aquinas was the only one who systematically assigned degrees of gravity to sins and compared verbal trespasses to sins of flesh or of intellect; he also argued that it was a heretic error to consider all pains of hell equal. The hierarchy of sins and punishments that constitutes a fundamental principle of the Thomistic system also represents the hallmark of Dante's infernal universe. As a moralist, however, Dante was also deeply original. He took painstaking care to build an idiosyncratic architectonics of sins, and as a poet, he went further than Aquinas could: he imagined a scale of hellish punishments with a remarkable wealth of details and an evident concern for variety and symbolism. Rather than detecting the ultimate, absolute wellspring for Dante's treatment of transgressive speech, it seemed more challenging to me to discover why he chose five specific sins—blasphemy, flattery, fraudulent counsel, sowing of discord, and falsifying of words—to punish in the Inferno. Among the factors that may have determined his selection of these particular sins (out of the twenty-four discussed by Peraldus, for instance), three seem salient to me: (1) the historically attested and large diffusion of these five sins in Dante's own day; (2) their social and political implications; (3) Dante's own potential relationship to them.

In chapter 4, I analyzed the connection between violence, another psychological site for sin in the *lingua*-texts, and poetics. The pastoral and theological discourse on *peccata linguae* represents for the French and Italian poets an object of reflection that eventually leads to self-reflection, as it ultimately compels the poets to examine themselves, that is, their own use of (written) speech. This inevitably leads to a distancing process with respect to the tracts on verbal sins, especially in the case of Jean de Meun. Such distance is unavoidable (and even predictable), since according to these tracts one was not even allowed to make a joke (Radulfus, Peraldus, Cavalca, to name just a few, put joking on the "black list" of the sins of the tongue). Fleming has highlighted one of the typical features of Jean's art: his parody of sacred texts and his overall ironic manipulation of religious discourse.[6] I am going to add that complying with the dictates of the *lingua*-texts faithfully would have required Jean to renounce himself, to deny his humoristic and satiric bent, sacrifices he was not willing to make. He chose to go against these dictates, to embrace some of the vices condemned in the moral texts (obscenity, blasphemy, garrulity, irony), and, as we have seen, in doing so he risked putting himself in conflict with the Church (hence, his "confession of verbal sins" from the apologetic segment of the poem). Hill is correct when she notes that Jean disperses acerbic comments on aspects of contemporary society among the speeches made by his characters, instead of voicing them in his own name, because he seeks to raise himself above criticism.[7] I have underlined that Gerson's attacks in the *Querelle* stand as testimony to Jean's ambivalent relationship to the contemporary ethics of (written) speech: he assimilates it at the level of some of the characters, but enters in conflict with it at a personal, artistic level. Gerson's tracts on verbal abuses, most of which precede, or are contemporary with, the *Vision*—his main document against the *Rose*—prove that he examined (and judged) the poem through his lens as a speech ethicist; a tardive but fascinating response to a literary text that was written during the golden age of *peccata linguae* and in which the author himself apologized for inappropriate language.

Dante's awareness of the standards imposed by contemporary speech ethics translates itself not only in the distribution of several sins of the tongue in the structure of the Inferno, but also in the constant care he takes to stress the difference between him and the perpetrators of these sins: unlike Alessio, he is not good at flattering; unlike Ulysses and Sinon, he does not use language for fraudulent or violent purposes; and unlike Bertrand del Born, he does not use his poetic talent to sow political division. Dante the pilgrim safely passes by the blasphemers and fraudulent speakers in Hell; he cleanses the seven capital sins marked on his forehead by ascending the mountain of Purgatory; and, finally, he takes lessons of wisdom and rhetoric from his dearest masters in the heavenly spheres. If Dante the poet

6. Fleming, *Reason and the Lover,* 60.

7. Hill, *The Medieval Debate,* 61.

committed verbal transgressions in the fabric of the *Comedy,* forgiveness for them comes from the sacred poem itself, an exceptional work of art into the making of which "ha posto mano e Cielo e terra" ("both Heaven and earth have set their hand"; *Par.* 25.2).

Lionel Friedman labeled Jean de Meun's *Rose* a "comedy," a literary work with a happy ending.[8] I feel compelled to add that, since the poetic material of this comedy is human nature, with all its weaknesses in thoughts, words, and deeds, it is a *Human Comedy.* Dante takes up the same material and, after punishing it in Hell for mortal sins, filtering it through the purgatorial fires of repentance and prayer, elevates it and redeems it to create a *Divine Comedy.* If Jean solves (or hopes to solve) the problem of his sinful authorial speech by staging a confession of sins and then an apology to the Church, Dante restores the pristine qualities of human language and of his own poetic discourse by turning them into instruments of glorification of the divine. The problematic of sinful speech opened in *Inferno* in dramatic ways finds closure in the third *cantica* of the *Comedy.* Paradiso proposes itself as the realm in which words can no longer "sin," they can no longer be transgressive, since the rules of language are reinvented and speech is no longer a matter of individual will; it is the pure, collective thought reflected in the mirror of the godly mind. *Verbum Dei.* The Word made not flesh, but POETRY.

8. Friedman, "Jean de Meung," 15.

Bibliography

PRIMARY SOURCES

Aelred de Rievaulx (Ethelred of Rievaulx). *L'Amitié spirituelle.* Translated and introduced by Sister Gaëtane de Briey. Vie Monastique 30. Abbaye de Bellefontaine, France, 1994.

Alain of Lille. *The Anticlaudianus of Alain of Lille. Prologue, Argument and Nine Books.* Translated by William H. Cornong. Philadelphia: University of Pennsylvania Press, 1935.

———. *Distinctiones dictionum theologicalium.* Patrologia Latina 210, cols. 685–1012.

———. *Plaint of Nature.* Translation and commentary by James J. Sheridan. Toronto: Institute of Medieval Studies, 1980.

———. *Summa de arte predicatoria.* Patrologia Latina 210, cols. 120–90.

———. "Tractus de virtutibus, de vitiis et de donis Spiritus Sancti." *Mediaeval Studies* 12 (1950): 20–56.

Albertano da Brescia. *De doctrina loquendi et tacendi.* Web. 23 March 2005. http://freespace.virgin.net/angus.graham/Loquendi.htm.

Augustine of Hippo. *Against Faustus.* Translated by Richard Stothert. Web. 10 September 2011. http://www.logoslibrary.org/augustine/faustus/index.html.

———. *Concerning the City of God against the Pagans.* Translated by Henry Bettenson. New York: Penguin Books, 2003.

———. *Concerning the Teacher (De magistro).* Translated by George C. Leckie. New York: Appleton Century Company, 1938.

———. *Confessions.* Oxford: Clarendon Press, 1992.

———. *On Christian Doctrine.* Translated with an introduction by D. W. Robertson Jr. New York: Liberal Arts Press, 1958.

———. *On the Trinit, Books 6–15.* Edited by Garreth B. Matthews. Translated by Stephen McKennsa. Cambridge: Cambridge University Press, 2002.

Boethius. *Consolation of Philosophy.* Translated by Joel C. Relihan. Indianapolis, Ind.: Hackett, 2001.

Brunetto Latini. *The Book of Treasure (Li Livres dou Tresor).* Edited by Paul Barrette and Spurgeon Baldwin. New York: Garland, 1993.

———. *Il Tesoretto (The Little Treasure).* Edited and translated by Julia Bolton Holloway. New York: Garland, 1981.

Christine de Pizan et al. *Debate of the "Romance of the Rose."* Edited and translated by David F. Hult. Chicago: University of Chicago Press, 2010.

Dante Alighieri. *Dante's "Il Convivio" ("The Banquet").* Edited by Richard Lansing. New York: Garland, 1990.

———. *Dante's "Monarchia."* Translated with a commentary by Richard Kay. Toronto: Pontifical Institute of Medieval Studies, 1998.

———. *De Vulgari eloquentia.* Edited by Steven Botterill. Cambridge: Cambridge University Press, 1996.

———. *The Divine Comedy of Dante Alighieri.* Translated by Allen Mandelbaum. Berkeley: California University Press, 1980 *Inferno;* 1981 *Purgatorio;* 1982 *Paradiso.*

———. *The Divine Comedy of Dante Alighieri.* Translated by Robert Durling. Oxford: Oxford University Press, 1996 *Inferno;* 2003 *Purgatorio;* 2010 *Paradiso.*

———. [Attributable to Dante] *The "Fiore" and the "Detto d'Amore": A Late 13th-Century Translation of the "Roman de la Rose."* Translated with introduction and notes by S. Casciani and C. Kleinhenz. Notre Dame, Ind.: University of Notre Dame Press, 2000.

———. *Il Convivio.* Edited by Maria Simonelli. Bologna: Prof. Riccardo Pàtron, 1966.

Domenico Cavalca. *Cinque vite di eremiti.* Edited by Carlo Delcorno. Venice: Marsilio, 1992.

———. *Il Pungilingua.* Edited by Giorgio Bottari. Milan, 1837.

———. *Vite dei Santi Padri.* Edited by Carlo Delcorno. Vol. 1. Florence: Galluzzo, 2009.

Étienne de Bourbon. *Anecdotes historiques, légendes et apologues tirés du recueil inédit d'Étienne de Bourbon, dominicain du XIIIe siècle.* Edited by Lecoy de la Marche. Paris, 1877.

Francesco da Buti. *Commento di Francesco da Buti sopra la "Divina Commedia."* Edited by C. Giannini. Pisa: Nistri, 1858–1862.

Gerson, Jean. *Œuvres complètes.* Edited by Palémon Glorieux. Vol. 7. Paris: Desclée and Cie, 1966.

———. *Œuvres complètes.* Edited by Palémon Glorieux. Vol. 9. Paris: Desclée and Cie, 1971.

Guillaume de Lorris and Jean de Meun. *Le Roman de la Rose.* Translated and edited by Armand Strubel. Paris: Librairie Générale Française, 1992.

———. *The Romance of the Rose.* Translated by Charles Dahlberg. 3rd ed. Princeton, N.J.: Princeton University Press, 1995.

Guillaume de St. Amour [William of St. Amour]. *De Periculis novissimorum temporum.* Edited by G. Geltner. Paris: Peeters, 2008.

———. *Opera omnia.* Constance, 1632.

Guglielmo Peraldo [William Peraldus, Guillaume Peyraut]. *Summa virtutum ac vitiorum.* Edited by Gulielmum Rovilium [Guillaume Rouillé]. Vol. 2. Lyon, 1585.

Hugh of St. Victor. *De Institutione novitiorum.* Patrologia Latina 176, cols. 925–52.

———. *The Didascalicon of Hugh of St. Victor: A Medieval Guide to the Arts.* Translated with an introduction and notes by Jerome Taylor. New York: Columbia University Press, 1961.

Iacopo Alighieri. *Chiose alla cantica dell'"Inferno" di Dante Alighieri scritte da Jacopo Alighieri.* Edited by G. Piccini. Florence: Bemporad, 1915.

Isidore of Seville. *Sententiarum libri.* Patrologia Latina 83, cols. 537–738.

"The Testament" of Jean de Meun: Vatican MS 367 (1291–1292). Edited and with an introduction by Aimé Céleste Bourneuf. New York: Ph.D. dissertation, Fordham University, 1956.

Le Testament maistre Jehan de Meun: un caso letterario. Edited and with an introduction by Silvia Buzzetti Gallarati. Turin: Edizioni dell'Orso, 1989.

John of Salisbury. *Policraticus: Of the Frivolities of Courtiers and the Footprints of Philosophers.* Edited by Cary J. Nederman. Cambridge: Cambridge University Press, 1990.

Justinian. *Corpus iuris civilis, III.* Edited by Rudolf Schoell and Wilhelm Kroll. Berlin, 1954.

———. *Corpus iuris civilis, III.* 12 April 2010. http://upmf-grenoble.fr/Haiti/Cours/Ak/Corpus/Nov77.htm.

Laurent of Orléans. *The Book of Vices and Virtues: A Fourteenth-Century English Translation of the "Somme le Roi" of Lorens d'Orléans.* Edited by N. Francis. London: Oxford University Press, 1942.

———. *Somme le Roi.* MS 2071. Bibliothèque de l'Arsenal, Paris.

Montaigne, Michel de. *Les Essays.* Edited by Pierre Villey. Paris: Presses Universitaires de France, 1992.

Ovid. *Metamorphoses.* Translated by A. D. Melville. Oxford: Oxford University Press, 1986.

Peter Cantor. *Verbum abbreviatum.* Patrologia Latina 205, cols. 9–528.

Pietro Alighieri. *Super Dantis ipsius genitoris Comoediam Commentarium.* Edited by V. Nannucci. Florence: Garinei, 1844.

Radulfus Ardens [Raoul Ardent]. *Speculum universale IX–XIV.* MS Lat. 3240. BnF, Paris.

Robert Grosseteste [attributable to]. *De Lingua.* MS 56, ff. 175v–306r. Lincoln College, Oxford.

Rutebeuf. *Œuvres complètes.* Edited by Michel Zinc. Paris: Librairie Générale Française, 2005.

Thomas Aquinas. *Summa Theologiae. Latin Text and English Translation.* Edited and translated by T. C. O'Brien. London: Blackfriars, 1974.

———. *Summa Theologica.* Translated by Fathers of the English Dominican Province. Vols. 1–4. Notre Dame, Ind.: Ave Maria Press, 1981.

SECONDARY SOURCES

Ahern, John. "Dante's Slyness: The Unnamed Sin of the Eighth Bolgia." *Romanic Review* 73, no. 3 (1982): 275–91.

Allen, Judson Boyce. *The Ethical Poetic of the Later Middle Ages: A Decorum of Convenient Distinctions.* Toronto: University of Toronto Press, 1982.

Allen, Valerie. *On Farting: Language and Laughter in the Middle Ages.* New York: Palgrave MacMillan, 2007.

Altmann, Barbara K., and Deborah L. McGrady. *Christine de Pizan. A Casebook.* Routledge: Taylor and Francis, 2003.

Arden, Heather. *The Romance of the Rose.* Boston: Twayne Publishers, 1987.

———. "Women as Readers, Women as Text in the *Romance of the Rose.*" In *Women, the Book and the Worldly.* Edited by Leslie Smith and Jane H. M. Taylor, 111–19. Cambridge: D. S. Brewer, 1995.

Ariès, Philippe, and Georges Duby. *A History of Private Life: Revelations of the Medieval World.* 2 vols. Cambridge, Mass.: Belknap Press of Harvard University Press, 1988.

Ascoli, Albert Russell. *Dante and the Making of a Modern Author.* Cambridge: Cambridge University Press, 2008.

Ashley, Benedict M., OP. *Dominic Cavalca and the Spirituality of the Word.* Web. 3 March 2004. http://www.op.org/domcentral/study/Ashley/Cavalca.html.

Auerbach, Eric. *Dante Poet of the Secular World.* Chicago: Chicago University Press, 1988.

Badel, Pierre Yves. *Le "Roman de la Rose" au XIVème siècle: Etude de la réception de l'œuvre.* Geneva: Droz, 1980.

Baird, Joseph, and John R. Kane. *"La Querelle de la Rose": Letters and Documents.* Chapel Hill: University of North Carolina Department of Romance Languages, 1978.

Baker, Denise N. "The Priesthood of Genius." *Speculum* 51 (1976): 277–91.

Bakhtin, M. M. *The Dialogic Imagination: Four Essays.* Austin: Texas University Press, 1987.

Bakker Mulder, Anneke B., and Renée Ni, T*he Prime of their Lives: Wise Old Women in Pre-Industrial Europe.* Leuven: Peeters, 2004.

Baldelli, Ignazio. "Le 'fiche' di Vanni Fucci." *Giornale storico della letteratura italiana* 114 (1997): 1–38.

Balducci, Marino. *Classicismo dantesco: Miti e simboli della morte e della vita nella "Divina Commedia."* Florence: Le Lettere, 2004.

Balfour, Mark. "Francesca da Rimini and Dante's Women Readers." In *Women, the Book and the Worldly.* Edited by Leslie Smith and Jane H. M. Taylor, 71–83. Cambridge: D. S. Brewer, 1995.

Barański, Zygmunt G. "Scatology and Obscenity in Dante." *Dante for the New Millennium.* Edited by Teodolinda Barolini and H. Wayne Storey, 259–72. New York: Fordham University Press, 2003.

Barański, Zygmunt G., and Patrick Boyde. *The "Fiore" in Context: Dante, France and Tuscany.* Notre Dame, Ind.: Notre Dame University Press, 1997.

Barbieri, Edoardo. "Domenico Cavalca volgarizzatore degli *Actus Apostolorum.*" In *La Bibbia in Italiano tra Medioevo e Rinascimento. Atti del Convegno Internazionale, Firenze, Certosa del Galluzzo, November 8–9 1996.* Edited by Lino Leonardi, 291–328. Florence: SISMEL, 1998.

Bardazzi, Giovanni. "Avari e prodighi, iracondiosi e accidiosi." *Studi Danteschi* 65 (2000): 1–39.

Bardsley, Sandy. *Venomous Tongues: Speech and Gender in Late Medieval England.* Philadelphia: University of Pennsylvania Press, 2006.

Barolini, Teodolinda. "Bertran de Born and Sordello: The Poetry of Politics in Dante's *Comedy.*" PMLA 94, no. 3 (1979): 395–405.

———. *Dante's Poets: Textuality and Truth in the "Divine Comedy."* Princeton, N.J.: Princeton University Press, 1984.

———. "True and False See-Ers in *Inferno* XX." *Lectura Dantis* 4 (1989): 42–55.

———. *The Undivine Comedy.* Princeton, N.J.: Princeton University Press, 1992.

———. "Medieval Multi-Culturalism and Dante's Theology of Hell." *Italiana* 9 (2000): 82–102.

Baron, Roger. "Hugues de St. Victor lexicographe." *Cultura Neolatina* 16 (1956): 109–45.

Bartuschat, Johannes, and Luciano Rossi. *Studi sul canone letterario del Trecento: Per Michelangelo Picone.* Ravenna: Longo, 2003.

Bastianetto, Sebastiano. "Cavalca, Domenico." In *Dizionario critico della letteratura italiana,* 561–63. Turin: Unione Tipografica-Editrice Torinese, 1986.

Batany, Georges. *Approches du "Roman de la Rose."* Paris: Bordas, 1973.

Bates, Richard, and Thomas Rendal. "Dante's Ulysses and the Epistle of St. James." *Dante Studies* 107 (1989): 33–44.

Bazán, B. Carlos, et al. *Les philosophies morales et politiques au Moyen Âge: Proceedings of the 9th International Congress of Medieval Philosophy.* New York: Legas, 1995.

Bel, Catherine, and Herman Braet, eds. *De la Rose: Texte, Image, Fortune.* Dudley, Mass.: Peeters, 2006.

Beltrami, Pietro G. "L'epica di Malebolge (Ancora su *Inferno* XXVIII)." *Studi Danteschi* (2000): 119–52.

Beltrán, Luis. "The Old Woman's Past." *Romanische Forschungen* 84 (1972): 77–96.

Bertoni, Giulio. "Il canto dei lenoni e degli adulatori (*Inferno,* C. XVIII)." *Archivum Romanicum* 12 (1928): 288–302.

Biard, Joël. "Signe monétaire et signe linguistique: La critique de la chrématistique dans l'école buridanienne." In *Les philosophies morales et politiques au Moyen Âge: Proceedings of the 9th International Congress of Medieval Philosophy.* Edited by B. Carlos Bazán et al., 1420–35. New York: Legas, 1995.

Bigi, Emilio. "Realismo e retorica nel canto XVII dell' *Inferno.*" *Studi Danteschi* 65 (2000): 87–99.

Bilotte, Dennis. *Le Vocabulaire de la traduction de Jean de Meun de la "Consolatio Philosophiae" de Boèce.* 2 vols. Paris: Champion, 2000.

Bisconti, Donatella. "Cordeliers et cordelières dans *La Divine commédie.*" *Actes du colloque "Dante poète et narrateur." Arzana: Cahiers de littérature italienne médiévale* 7 (2001): 271–304.

Bloch, R. Howard. *Medieval Misogyny and the Invention of Western Romantic Love.* Chicago: Chicago University Press, 1991.

Bloomfield, Morton W. *The Seven Deadly Sins: An Introduction to the History of a Religious Concept, with Special Reference to Medieval England Literature.* Ann Arbor: Michigan State University Press, 1967.

Blumenfeld-Kosinski, Renate. "Remarques sur songe/mensonge." *Romania* 101, no. 3 (1980): 387–90.

———. "Jean le Fèvre's *Livre de Leesce*: Praise or Blame of Women?" *Speculum* 69 (1994): 705–25.

———. *Reading Myth: Classical Mythology and Its Interpretations in Medieval French Literature.* Stanford, Calif.: Stanford University Press, 1997.

———. *The Selected Writings of Christine de Pizan: New Translations. Criticism.* New York: W. W. Norton, 1997.

———. "Jean Gerson and the Debate on the *Romance of the Rose.*" In *A Companion to Jean Gerson.* Edited by Brian P. McGuire, 317–55. Boston: Brill, 2006.

———. *Poets, Saints, and Visionaries of the Great Schism, 1378–1417.* University Park: Pennsylvania State University Press, 2006.

Bogner, Ralf G. *Die Bezahmung der Zunge: Literatur und Disziplinierung der Alltagskommunikation in der fruhen Neuzeit.* Tübingen: Niemeyer, 1997.

Boitani, Piero. "Beyond the Sunset: Dante's Ulysses in Another World." *Lectura Dantis* 9 (1991): 34–53.

Bordessoule, Nadine. "*Fine Words on Closed Ears:* Impertinent Women, Discordant Voices, Discourteous Words." In *Reassessing the Heroine in Medieval French Literature.* Edited by Kathy M. Krause, 123–32. Gainesville: University of Florida Press, 2001.

Botterill, Steven. "Dante's Poetics of the Sacred Word." *Philosophy and Literature* 20, no. 1 (1996): 154–62.

———. "Cavalca, Domenico." In *Medieval Italy: An Encyclopedia.* Edited by Christopher Kleinhenz et al. Vol. 1: *A–K,* 197–98. New York: Routledge, 2004.

Bouché, Thérèse. "L'obscène et le sacré ou l'utilisation paradoxale du rire dans le *Roman de la Rose* de Jean de Meun." In *Le Rire au Moyen Âge dans la littératures et dans les Arts: Actes du Colloque International des 17, 18 et 19 novembre 1988.* Edited by Thérèse Bouché and Hélène Charpentier, 83–93. Bordeaux: Presses Universitaires, 1990..

Bourneuf, Aimé Céleste. "The 'Testament' of Jean de Meun: Vatican MS 367 (1291–1292)." PhD diss., Fordham University, New York, 1956.

Boyde, Patrick. *Human Vices and Human Worth in Dante's "Comedy."* Cambridge: Cambridge University Press, 2000.

Brayer, Edith. "Contenu, structure et combinaison du *Miroir du monde* et de la *Somme le Roi.*" *Romania* 79 (1958): 1–38, 433–70.

Brinton, Crane. *A History of Western Morals.* New York: Harcourt, Brace, 1959.

Brook, Leslie C. "Malebouche dans le *Roman de la Rose* et le *Champion des dames.*" In *De la Rose: Texte, Image, Fortune.* Edited by Catherine Bel and Herman Braet, 421–34. Dudley, Mass.: Peeters, 2006.

Brown-Grant, Rosalind. *Christine Pizan and the Moral Defense of Woman: Reading beyond Gender.* Cambridge: Cambridge University Press, 1999.

Brownlee, Kevin. "Reflections in the *Miroer aus Amoureus:* The Inscribed Reader in Jean de Meun's *Roman de la Rose.*" In *Mimesis: From Mirror to Method, Augustine to Descartes.* Edited by John D. Lyons and Stephen G. Nichols, 60–70. Hanover, N.H.: New England University Press, 1982.

———. "The Problem of Faux Semblant: Language, History, and Truth in the *Roman de la Rose.*" In *The New Medievalism.* Edited by Kevin Brownlee and Marina Scordilis-Brownlee, 253–71. Baltimore: Johns Hopkins University Press, 1991.

———. "Pygmalion, Mimesis, and the Multiple Endings of the *Roman de la Rose.*" *Yale French Studies* 95 (1999): 193–211.

Brownlee, Kevin, and Sylvia Huot, eds. *Rethinking the "Romance of the Rose: Text, Image, Reception."* Philadelphia: University of Pennsylvania Press, 1992.

Brugnoli, Giorgio. *Dante Filologo: l'esempio di Ulisse.* Testi e studi di cultura classica 22. Pisa: Edizioni ETS, 1998.

Buzzetti Gallarati, Silvia. "Nota bibliografica sulla tradizione manoscritta del Testament di Jean de Meun." *Revue Romane* 13 (1978): 1–35.

———. *Le Testament maistre Jehan de Meun: un caso letterario.* Turin: Edizioni dell'Orso, 1989.

Cabantous, Alain. *Blasphemy: Impious Speech in the West from the Seventeenth to the Nineteenth Century.* New York: Columbia University Press, 2002.

Callay, Brigitte L. "Jean de Meun's *Romance of the Rose* and the Polemic of the Theological Meaning." In *De la Rose: Texte, Image, Fortune.* Edited by Catherine Bel and Herman Braet, 21–40. Dudley, Mass.: Peeters, 2006.

The Cambridge Companion to Aquinas. Edited by Norman Kretzmann and Eleonore Stump. New York: Cambridge University Press, 1993.

Capelli, Luigi Mario. "Ancora del *Tresor* nelle opere di Dante." *Giornale Dantesco* 5 (1898): 548–56.

Caretti, Lanfranco. "Canto XVIII." *Lectura Dantis Scaligera: "Inferno"* (1967): 583–617.

Carruthers, Leo M. *La "Somme le Roi" de Lorens d'Orléans et ses traductions anglaises: Etude comparée.* Paris: Association des médiévistes anglicistes de l'enseignement supérieur, 1986.

———. "Lorens of Orléans and the *Somme le Roi* or the *Book of Vices and Virtues.*" *Vox Benedictina: A Journal of Translations from Monastic Sources* 5, no. 2/3 (1998): 190–200.

Casagrande, Carla. "Motions of the Heart and Sins: The *Specchio dei peccati* by Domenico Cavalca, OP." In *In the Garden of Evil: The Vices and Culture in the Middle Ages.*

Edited by Richard Newhauser, 128–44. Toronto: Pontifical Institute of Medieval Studies, 2005.

Casagrande, Carla, and Silvana Vecchio. *I peccati della lingua: Disciplina ed etica della parola nella cultura medievale.* Rome: Istituto della Enciclopedia Italiana, 1987.

———. *I Sette vizi capitali: Storia dei peccati nel Medioevo.* Torino: Einaudi, 2000.

Cassell, Anthony. "*Ulisseana*: A Bibliography of Dante's Ulysses to 1981." *Italian Culture* 3 (1981): 23–45.

Centi, Tito S. *Domenico Cavalca. "Specchio della Croce": Testo originale e versione in italiano corrente.* Bologna: Edizioni Studio Domenicano, 1992.

Cervigni, Dino S. "Dante's Lucifer: The Denial of the Word." *Lectura Dantis* 3 (1988): 51–63.

Cherchi, Paolo. "Geryon's Canto." *Lectura Dantis* 2 (1988): 31–44.

Chiavacci Leonardi, Anna Maria. "La salvezza degli infedeli: Il Canto XX del *Paradiso.*" In *Regnum celorum violenza pate: Dante e la salvezza dell'umanità,* 193–203. Montella: Accademia Vivarium Novum, 2002.

Chiffouleau, Jacques. "Dire l'indicible: remarques sur la catégorie du *nefandum* du XIIIe au XVIe siècle." *Annales. Economie, Sociétés, Civilisations* (1990): 289–324.

Ciccuto, Marcello. "Tradizione delle opere di Domenico Cavalca: Gli esempi dei trattati morali." *Italianistica* 19, no. 1 (1990): 39–67.

Ciotti, Andrea. "Alano e Dante." *Convivium* 28 (1960): 257–88.

Clogan, Maurice Paul. "Dante and Statius: Revisited." *Medievalia et Humanistica* 35 (2009): 77–101.

Cogan, Marc. *Design in the Wax: The Structure of the "Divine Comedy" and Its Meaning.* Notre Dame, Ind.: Notre Dame University Press, 1999.

Colish, Marcia L. *The Mirror of Language: A Study in the Medieval Theory of Knowledge.* Lincoln: Nebraska University Press, 1983.

———. *Medieval Foundations of the Western Intellectual Tradition. 400–1400.* New Haven, Conn.: Yale University Press, 2005.

Conner, Wayne. "*Inferno* XVIII, 66 (*Femmine da Conio*) and 51 (*Pungenti Salse*)." *Italica* 32, no. 2 (1955): 95–103.

Connolly, James L. *Jean Gerson: Reformer and Mystic.* Louvain: Uystpruyst, 1928.

Contini, Gianfranco. "Sul XXX dell'*Inferno.*" *Varianti e altra linguistica; una raccolta di saggi (1938–1968).* Turin: Einaudi, 1970. 447–57.

———. "Un nodo della cultura medievale: La serie *Roman de la Rose-Fiore-Divina Commedia.*" *Lettere italiane* 25 (1973): 162–89.

———. *Un' Idea di Dante: Saggi Danteschi.* Turin: Einaudi, 2001.

Cook, William, and Ronald B. Herzman. "St. Eustace: A Note on *Inferno* XXVII." *Dante Studies* 94 (1976): 137–39.

Corti, Maria. "Le fonti del *Fiore di virtù* e la teoria della nobiltà nel Duecento." *Giornale storico della cultura medievale: La serie "Roman de la Rose"-"Fiore"-"Divina Commedia"* 136 (1959): 63–87.

———. "Le metafore della navigazione, del volo e della lingua di fuoco nell'episodio di Ulisses (*Inferno* XXVI)." In *Miscellanea di studi in onore di Aurelio Roncaglia.* 2:479–91. Modena: Mucchi, 1989.

Craun, Edwin. *Lies, Slander and Obscenity in Medieval English Literature.* Cambridge: Cambridge University Press, 1997.

———. *The Hands of the Tongue: Essays on Deviant Speech.* Kalamazoo, Mich.: Medieval Institute, 2007.

Crouzet-Pavan, Elisabeth, and Jacques Verger, eds. *La dérision au Moyen Âge: De la pratique sociale au rituel politique.* Paris: Presses de l'Université Paris-Sorbonne, 2007.

Curtius, Ernst R. "Dante und Alanus ab Insulis." *Romanische Forschungen* 62 (1950): 28–31.

Dallas, Denery G. "Biblical Liars and Thirteenth-Century Theologians." In *The Seven Deadly Sins: From Communities to Individuals,* edited by Richard Newhauser, 112–28. Leiden: Brill, 2007

Dante Encyclopedia. Edited by Richard Lansing. New York: Garland, 2000.

Davis, Charles T. "Brunetto Latini and Dante." *Studi Medievali* 3, no. 8 (1967): 421–50.

Dedeck-Héry, V. L. "Boethius' *De Consolatione* by Jean de Meun." *Mediaeval Studies* 14 (1952): 165–275.

Delcorno, Carlo. "Cavalca, Domenico." In *Dizionario biografico degli italiani,* 22:577–86. Rome: Istituto della Cultura Italiana, 1979.

———. "Dante e Peraldo." In *Exemplum e letteratura: Tra Medioevo e Rinascimento,* 195–227. Bologna: Il Mulino, 1989.

———. "Modelli aggiografici e modelli narrativi: Tra Cavalca e Boccaccio." In *La Novella italiana: Atti del Convegno di Caprarola, 19–24 settembre 1988,* 337–63. Rome: Salerno, 1989.

———. *La Tradizione delle Vite dei Santi Padri.* Venice: Istituto Veneto di Scienze, Lettere ed Arti, 2000.

Derby Chapin, D. L.. "Io and the Negative Apotheosis of Vanni Fucci." *Dante Studies* 89 (1971): 19–31.

Desmond, Marilynn. *Ovid's "Art" and the "Wife of Bath": The Ethics of Erotic Violence.* Ithaca, N.Y.: Cornell University Press, 2006.

Detienne, Marcel, and Jean-Pierre Vernant. *Cunning Intelligence in Greek Culture and Society.* Atlantic Highlands, N.J.: Humanities Press Inc., 1978.

Deyermond, Alan. "El Alejandro medieval, el Ulises de Dante y la busqueda de las Antipodas." In *Maravillas, peregrinaciones y utopias: Literatura de viajes en el mundo romanico,* 15–32. València: Universitat de València, 2002.

Dingjan, Francois. "*Discretio*": *Les Origines patristiques et monastiques de la doctrine sur la prudence chez Saint Thomas d'Aquin.* Arsen: Van Gorcum, 1967.

Dizionario critico della letteratura italiana. Turin: Unione Tipografica-Editrice Torinese, 1986.

Dolfi, Ana. "Il Canto di Ulisse: occasione per un discorso di esegesi dantesca." *Forum Italicum* 7–8 (1973–1974): 22–45.

Dondaine, Antoine. "Guillaume Peyraut, vie et œuvres." *Archivium Fratrum Predicatorum* 18 (1948): 162–236.

Donno, Daniel J. "Dante's Ulysses and Virgil's Prohibition: *Inferno* XXVI, 70–75." *Italica* 50 (1973): 26–37.

Dragonetti, Roger. "Specchi d'amore: Il *Romanzo della Rosa* e *Il Fiore*." *Paragone* 81 (1981): 3–22.

Driver, Martha W. "Romancing the Rose: the Reading of Chaucer and Christine." In *Writings on Love in the English Middle Ages.* Edited by Helen Cooney, 147–62. New York: Palgrave Macmillan, 2006.

Dronke, Peter. "Boethius, Alanus and Dante." *Romanische Forschungen* 78 (1966): 119–25.

———. *Dante and Medieval Latin Traditions.* Cambridge: Cambridge University Press, 1986.

Duby, Georges. *Age of the Cathedrals: Art and Society, 980–1420.* Chicago: Chicago University Press, 1981.

Dufournet, Jean. *Etudes sur le "Roman de la Rose" de Guillaume de Lorris.* Geneva: Slatkine, 1984.

Durling, Robert M. "Deceit and Digestion in the Belly of Hell." In *Allegory and Representation.* Selected Papers from the English Institute, 1979–1980. Edited by S. Greenblatt, 61–93. Baltimore: Johns Hopkins University Press, 1981.

———. "Dante among the Falsifiers." In *Lectura Dantis: Inferno,* edited by Allen Mandelbaum, Anthony Oldcorn, and Charles Ross, 393–406. Berkeley : University of California Press,1998.

Economou, George. "The Character Genius in Alain de Lille, Jean de Meun, and John Gower." *Chaucer Review* 4 (1970): 203–10.

———. *The Goddess Natura in Medieval Literature.* Cambridge, Mass.: Harvard University Press, 1972.

———. "*Inferno* XXIV." In *Lectura Dantis Virginiana, I. Dante's "Inferno": Introductory Readings.* Edited by Tibor Wlassics, 307–18. Supplement to *Lectura Dantis* 6 (1990). Special Issue. Charlottesville: University of Virginia, 1990.

Emmerson, Richard K., and Ronald B. Herzman. "The Apocalyptic Age of Hypocrisy: Faus Semblant and Amant in the *Roman de la Rose*." *Speculum* 62, no. 3 (1987): 612–34.

Enciclopedia Dantesca. 6 vols. Rome: Istituto della Enciclopedia Italiana, 1970–1984.

Evans, Gillian Rosemary. *Alain of Lille: The Frontiers of Theology in the Later Twelfth Century.* Cambridge: Cambridge University Press, 1983.

Eynde, Damien van Den. "Précisions chronologique sur quelques ouvrages théologiques du XIIe siècle." *Antonianum* 26 (1951): 241–43.

Falco, Francesco. *Domenico Cavalca moralista.* Lucca: Tipografia del Serchio, 1982.

Falvo, Jospeph D. "The Irony of Deception in Malebolge: *Inferno* XXI–XXII." *Lectura Dantis* 2 (1988): 55–72.

Fenster, Thelma, and Daniel Lord Smail, eds. *Fama: The Politics of Talk and Reputation in Medieval Europe.* Ithaca, N.Y.: Cornell University Press, 2003.

Ferrante, Joan M. "The Malebolge (*Inf.* XVIII–XXX) as the Key to the Structure of Dante's *Inferno.*" *Romance Philology* 20 (1967): 456–66.

———. "The Relation of Speech to Sin in the *Inferno.*" *Dante Studies* 87 (1969): 33–46.

———. *Woman as Image in Medieval Literature.* New York: Columbia University Press, 1975.

———. *The Political Vision of the "Divine Comedy."* Princeton, N.J.: Princeton University Press, 1984.

Ferrucci, Franco. *The Poetics of Disguise: The Autobiography of the Work in Homer, Dante, and Shakespeare.* Translated by Ann Dunnigan. Ithaca, N.Y.: Cornell University Press, 1980.

Fitzgerald, Allan D., ed. *Augustine through the Ages: An Encyclopedia.* Grand Rapids, Mich.: William B. Eerdmans, 1999.

Fleming, John V. *The "Roman de la Rose": A Study in Allegory and Iconography.* Princeton, N.J.: Princeton University Press, 1969.

———. *Reason and the Lover.* Princeton, N.J.: Princeton University Press, 1984.

Florescu, Vasile. *Conceptul de literatura veche.* Bucharest: Editura Stiintifica, 1968.

Forti, Fiorenzo. "Curiositas o fol hardement." In *Fra le carte dei poeti,* 41–77. Milan: Riccardo Ricciardi, 1965.

Freccero, John. *The Poetics of Conversion.* Cambridge, Mass.: Harvard University Press, 1986.

Freinkel, Lisa. "*Inferno* and the Poetics of *Usura.*" *MLN* 107 (1992): 1–17.

Friedman, Lionel J. "Jean de Meung, Antifeminism, and 'Bourgeois Realism.'" *Modern Philology* 57 (1959): 13–23.

———. "Jean de Meun and Ethelred of Rievaulx." *L'esprit créateur* 2, no. 3 (1962): 135–41.

Fubini, Mario. "Canto XXVIII." *Lectura Dantis Scaligera* 28 (1962): 997–1021.

———. *Il Peccato di Ulisse e altri scritti danteschi.* Milan: Riccardo Ricciardi, 1965.

Fyler, John M. *Language and the Declining World in Chaucer, Dante, and Jean de Meun.* Cambridge: Cambridge University Press, 2007.

Gambero, Luigi. *Mary in the Middle Ages: The Blessed Virgin Mary in the Thought of Medieval Latin Theologians.* San Francisco: Ignatius Press, 2005.

Gaunt, Simon. "Bel Accueil and the Improper Allegory of the *Roman de la Rose.*" In *New Medieval Literatures,* vol. 2, edited by R. Copeland, D. Lawton, and W. Scase, 65–93. Oxford: Clarendon Press, 1998.

Geltner, G. "Faux Semblants: Antifraternalism Reconsidered in Jean de Meun and Chaucer. " *Studies in Philology* 4, no. 101 (2004): 357–80.

Gentile, Giovanni. *I Problemi della Scolastica.* Bari: Laterza, 1923.

Gérard Paré. *Les idées et les lettres au XIIIe siècle: Le "Roman de la Rose."* Montreal: Centre de psychologie et de pdagogie, 1947.

Gilson, Etienne. *Moral Values and the Moral Life: The Ethical Theory of St. Thomas Aquinas.* Hamden, Conn.: Shoe String Press, 1961.

———. *Dante and Philosophy.* Translated by D. Moore. New York: Harper and Row, 1963.

Ginsberg, Warren. *Dante's Aesthetics of Being.* Ann Arbor: University of Michigan Press, 1999.

Glorieux, Palémon. *Répertoire des maîtres en théologie de Paris au XIIIe siècle.* 2 vols. Paris: Vrin, 1933–1934.

Goetz, Walter. "Dante und Brunetto Latini." *Deutsches Dante Jahrbuch* 20 (1938): 78–99.

Gründel, Johannes. "L'Œuvre encyclopédique de Raoul Ardent: Le *Speculum Universale.*" *Cahiers d'histoire mondiale* 9 (1966): 553–70.

———. *Die Lehre des Radulfus Ardens von den Verstandestugenden auf dem Hintergrund seiner Seelenlehre.* Munich: Schoning, 1976.

Gunn, Alan. *The Mirror of Love: A Reinterpretation of the "Romance of the Rose."* Lubbock: Texas Tech Press, 1952.

Güntert, Georges. "Canto XIV"; "Canto XVIII." In *Lectura Dantis Turicensis, I: "Inferno,"* 193–205; 245–59. Florence: Franco Cessati, 2000.

Hagedorn, Suzanne C. *Abandoned Women: Rewriting the Classics in Dante, Boccaccio and Chaucer.* Ann Arbor: Michigan University Press, 2004.

Harak, G. Simon, ed. *Aquinas and Empowerment: Classical Ethics for Ordinary Lives.* Washington, D.C.: Washington University Press, 1996.

Hatcher, Anna. "Dante's Ulysses and Guido da Montefeltro." *Dante Studies* 88 (1970): 109–17.

Heller-Roazen, Daniel. *Fortune's Faces: The "Roman de la Rose" and the Poetics of Contingency.* Baltimore: Johns Hopkins University Press, 2003.

Heywood, Melinda Marsh. "Lady Philosophy and La Vieille: Old Women, Aging Bodies, and Female Authority in Late Medieval French Literature." PhD diss., University of Pennsylvania, 1997.

Hicks, Eric. *Le débat sur le "Roman de la Rose."* Paris: Honoré Champion, 1977.

Hilder, Gisela. *Der scholastiche Wortschatz bei Jean de Meun: Die Artes Liberales.* Tübingen: Max Niemeyer, 1972.

Hill, Jillian M. L. *The Medieval Debate on Jean de Meung's "Roman de la Rose": Morality Versus Art.* Lewiston, N.Y.: Edwin Mellen, 1991.

Hobbins, Daniel. *Authorship and Publicity before Print: Jean Gerson and the Transformation of Late Medieval Learning.* Philadelphia: University of Pennsylvania Press, 2009.

Hollander, Robert. *Allegory in Dante's "Commedia."* Princeton, N.J.: Princeton University Press, 1969.

Holme, Timothy. *Vile Florentines: The Florence of Dante, Giotto and Boccaccio.* New York: St. Martin's Press, 1980.

Hult, David F. "Words and Deeds: Jean de Meun's *Romance of the Rose* and the Hermeneutics of Censorship." *New Literary History* 28, no. 2 (1991): 345–66.

———. "Language and Dismemberment: Abélard, Origen, and the *Romance of the Rose.*" In *Rethinking the "Romance of the Rose: Text, Image, Reception."* Edited by Kevin Brownlee and Sylvia Huot, 10–131. Philadelphia: University of Pennsylvania Press, 1992.

Huot, Sylvia. "Seduction and Sublimation: Christine de Pizan, Jean de Meun, and Dante." *Romance Notes* 25 (1985): 361–73.

———. *The "Romance of the Rose" and Its Medieval Readers.* Cambridge: Cambridge University Press, 1993.

Imbach, Ruedi. *Dante, la philosophie et les laïcs.* Fribourg: Editions Universitaires, 1996.

Ineichen, Gustav. "Le discours linguistique de Jean de Meun." *Romanistische Zeitschrift für Literaturgeschichte* 2 (1978): 245–53.

Jauss, Hans Robert. "La Transformation de la forme allégorique entre 1180–1240: d'Alain de Lille à Guillaume de Lorris." In *L'Humanisme médiéval dans les littératures romanes du XIIe au XIVe siècle.* Edited by Anthime Fourrier, 108–42. Paris: Librairie C. Klincksieck, 1964.

Jung, Marc René. "Jean de Meung et l'allégorie." *Cahiers de l'Association Internationale des Etudes Françaises* 28 (1976): 21–36.

Kay, Richard. *Dante's Swift and Strong: Essays in "Inferno" XV.* Lawrence: Regents Press of Kansas, 1978.

———. "The Sin(s) of Brunetto Latini." *Dante Studies* 112 (1994): 19–31.

Kay, Sarah. *The Romance of the Rose.* London: Grant & Cutler, 1995.

———. "Women's Body of Knowledge: Epistemology and Misogyny in the *Romance of the Rose.*" In *Framing Medieval Bodies.* Edited by Sarah Kay and Miri Rubin, 211–35. Manchester: Manchester University Press, 1996.

Kelly, Douglas. *Medieval Imagination.* Wisconsin: Wisconsin University Press, 1978.

———. *Internal Difference and Meanings in the Roman de la Rose.* Madison: University of Wisconsin Press, 1995.

Kiser, Lisa J. "Alain de Lille, Jean de Meun, and Chaucer: Ecofeminism and Some Medieval Lady Natures." *Mediaevalitas* 9 (1996): 1–14.

Kleinhenz, Christopher. "Deceivers Deceived: Devilish Doubletalk in *Inferno* 21–23." *Quaderni d'italianistica* 10, no. 1–2 (1989): 134–56.

Koritansky, Peter Karl. *Thomas Aquinas and the Philosophy of Punishment.* Washington, D.C.: The Catholic University of America Press, 2012.

Krause, Kathy M., ed. *Reassessing the Heroine in Medieval French Literature.* Gainesville: University of Florida Press, 2001.

Lage, Guy Raynaud de. *Alain de Lille, poète du XIIe siècle.* Montréal: Institut d'Etudes Médiévales, 1951.

Langlois, Charles V. *La Vie en France au Moyen Âge de la fin du XIIe au milieu du XIVe.* 2nd ed. 2 vols. Paris: Slatkine, 1984.

Langlois, Ernest. *Origines et sources du "Roman de la Rose."* Paris: E. Thorin, 1890.

Lanham, Richard A. *A Handlist of Rhetorical Terms.* 2nd ed. Berkeley: University of California Press, 2004.

Lanly, André. "La hardiesse de pensée de Jean de Meun." In *Linguistique et Philologie (applications aux textes médiévaux): Actes du colloque des 29 et 30 avril 1977,* Université de Picardie, Centre d'Etudes Médiévales. Edited by Danielle Buschinger, 345–58. Paris: Honoré Champion, 1977.

Le Goff, Jacques. *Pour un autre Moyen Âge: Temps, travail et culture en occident. 18 essays.* Paris: Gallimard, 1977.

———. *La Naissance du Purgatoire.* 2 vols. Paris: Gallimard, 1981.

———. *La Civilisation de l'Occident médiéval.* Paris: Flammarion, 1997.

———. *Les Intellectuelles au Moyen Âge.* Paris: Seuil, 2000.

Le Goff, Jacques, and Jean Claude Schmitt. "Au XIIIe siècle: Une parole nouvelle." In *Histoire vécue du peuple chrétien,* 257–79. Toulouse: Privat, 1979.

Lenfant, David, ed. *Concordantiae Augustinianae, Sive, Collectio Omnium Sententiarum Quae Sparsim Reperiuntur In Omnibus S. Augustini Operibus Ad Instar Concordantiarum Sacrae Scripturae.* Reprint of 1665 edition. 2 vols. Bruxelles: Culture et civilisation, 1982.

Leushuis, Reinier. "Fertilizing the French Vernacular: Procreation, Warfare, and Authorship in Jean de Meun, Lemaire de Belges, and Rabelais." In *Sexuality in the Middle Ages and Early Modern Times: New Approaches to a Fundamental Cultural-Historical and Literary-Anthropological Theme.* New York: Walter de Gruyter, 2008.

Leveleux, Corinne. *La Parole interdite. Le blasphème dans la France médiévale (XIIIe–XIVe siècles): Du péché au crime.* Paris: De Boccard, 2001.

Levy, Leonard W. *Treason against God: A History of the Offense of Blasphemy.* New York: Schocken Books, 1981.

Lewis, C. S. *The Allegory of Love.* New York: Oxford University Press, 1936.

Lindorfer, Bettina. "*Peccatum linguae* and the Punishment of Speech Violations in the Middle Ages and Early Modern Times." In *Speaking in the Medieval World.* Edited by Jean E. Godsall-Myers, 23–46. Leiden: Brill, 2003.

Looney, Dennis. "*Inferno* VII." In *Lectura Dantis Virginiana, I. Dante's "Inferno": Introductory Readings.* Edited by Tibor Wlassics, 82–93. Supplement to *Lectura Dantis* 6 (1990). Special Issue. Charlottesville: University of Virginia, 1990.

———. "The Purgation and Emendation of a Simile: *Purgatorio* VI and VII." *Lectura Dantis* 7 (1990): 133–41.

———. "Believing in the Poet: *Inferno* XIII." *Allegorica* 13 (1992): 39–52.

Lotti, Renzo. *Contributi su Domenico Cavalca (c. 1270–1342).* Amsterdam: Kaal Boek, 1987.

Lottin, Odon. *Psychologie et morale aux XIIe–XIIIe siècles.* Louvain: Abbaye du Mont César, 1954.

Louis, René. *Le "Roman de la Rose": essai d'interprétation de l'allégorisme érotique.* Paris: Honoré Champion, 1974.

Luca, G. de. *Prosatori minori del Trecento.* Milan: R. Ricciardi, 1954.

Lucken, Christopher. "Woman's Cry. Broken Language, Marital Disputes, and the Poetics of Medieval Farce." In *Reassessing the Heroine in Medieval French Literature.* Edited by Kathy M. Krause, 152–79. Gainesville: University of Florida Press, 2001.

MacDonald, Scott Charles. and Eleonore Stump, eds. *Aquinas's Moral Theory: Essays in Honor of Norman Kretzmann.* Ithaca, N.Y.: Cornell University Press, 1998.

Mancini, Franco. "Un' *Auctoritas* di Dante." *Studi Danteschi* 45 (1968): 95–119.

Mandonnet, Pierre. *Dante le théologien.* Paris: Desclée de Brouwert, 1935.

Masciandaro, Franco. "Notes on the Image of the Point in the *Divine Comedy.*" *Italica* 54, no. 2 (1977): 215–26.

Mastrobuono, Antonio C. *Dante's Journey toward Sanctification.* Washington, D.C: Regnery Gateway, 1990.

Mazzoni, Francesco. "Canto XI dell' *Inferno.*" *Lectura Dantis Neapolitana* (1986): 171–200.

Mazzotta, Giuseppe. *Dante, Poet of the Desert: History and Allegory in the "Divine Comedy."* Princeton, N.J.: Princeton University Press, 1979.

———. *Dante's Vision and the Circle of Knowledge.* Princeton, N.J.: Princeton University Press, 1993.

———. "Canto XXVI. Ulysses: Persuasion versus Prophecy." *Lectura Dantis* 23 (1998): 348–56.

———. "L'Esilio da Firenze: Il *De Vulgari Eloquenzia* e il cerchio della frode." In *Dante: Da Firenze all'aldilà.* Edited by Michelangelo Picone, 223–47. Florence: Cesati, 2001.

McGuire, Brian P., ed. *A Companion to Jean Gerson.* Boston: Brill, 2006.

McInerny, Ralph. *Ethics.* Edited by Norman Kretzmann and Eleonore Stump. Cambridge: Cambridge University Press, 1999.

McWebb, Christine, ed. *Debating the "Roman de la Rose": A Critical Anthology.* New York: Routledge, 2007.

Mercuri, Roberto. *Semantica di Gerione.* Rome: Bulzoni, 1984.

Michaud-Quantin, Pierre. *Sommes de casuistique et manuels de confession au Moyen Âge (XII–XVI siècles).* Louvain: Nauwelaerts, 1962.

Mieszkowski, Gretchen. "Old Age and Medieval Misogyny: The Old Woman." In *Old Age in the Middle Ages and the Renaissance.* Edited by Albert Classen, 299–321. New York: Walter de Gruyter, 2007.

Minnis, Alastair. *Magister amoris: The "Romance of the Rose" and Vernacular Hermeneutics.* Oxford: Oxford University Press, 2001.

———. "From 'coilles' to 'bel chose': Discourses of Obscenity in Jean de Meun and Chaucer." In *Medieval Obscenities.* Edited by Nicola McDonald, 156–78. York: Medieval Press/Boydell and Brewer, 2006.

———. *Fallible Authors: Chaucer's "Pardoner" and "Wife of Bath."* Philadelphia: University of Pennsylvania Press, 2007.

Montanari, Fausto. "La Piccarda di Dante." In *Miscellanea di studi danteschi in memoria di Silvio Pasquazi,* 2:589–93. Naples: Federico e Ardia, 1993.

Moore, Edward. *Studies in Dante: Scripture and Classical Authors in Dante.* New York: Greenwood Press, 1968.

Morrison, Susan Signe. *Excrement in the Late Middle Ages: Sacred Filth and Chaucer's Fecopoetics.* New York: Palgrave Macmillan, 2008.

Muresu, Gabriele. "La Rancura di Guido da Montefeltro (*Inferno* XXVII)." *Studi Danteschi* 70 (2005): 47–86.

Musa, Mark. "Virgil's Ulysses and Ulysses' Diomedes." *Dante Studies* 97 (1978): 187–93.

———. "Filling the Gap with *consiglio frodolente.*" *Italian Culture* 3 (1981): 11–21.

Musa, Mark, and Anna Hatcher. "The Kiss: *Inferno* V and the Old French Prose *Lancelot.*" *Comparative Literature* 20, no. 2 (1968): 97–109.

Muscatine, Charles. "The Fabliaux, Courtly Literature, and the (Re)Invention of Vulgarity." In *Obscenity: Social Control and Artistic Creation in the European Middle Ages.* Edited by Jan M. Ziolkowski, 281–308. Boston: Brill, 1998.

Nardi, Bruno. *Dal "Convivio" alla "Commedia."* Rome: Istituto Storico Italiano per il Medioevo, 1960.

———. *Saggi di filosofia dantesca.* Florence: La Nuova Italia Editrice, 1967.

———. *Dante e la cultura medievale.* Bari: Laterza, 1984.

Naselli, Carmelina. *Domenico Cavalca.* Città di Castello: Il Solco, 1925.

Nencioni, Giovanni. "Dante e la rettorica." In *Dante e Bologna nei tempi di Dante,* 91–112. Bologna: Commissione per Testi di Lingua, 1967.

Newhauser, Richard. *The Treatise on Vices and Virtues in Latin and the Vernacular.* Turnhout, Belgium: Brepols, 1993.

———, ed. *In the Garden of Evil: The Vices and Culture in the Middle Ages.* Toronto: Pontifical Institute of Medieval Studies, 2005.

———, ed. *The Seven Deadly Sins: From Communities to Individuals.* Leiden: Brill, 2007.

———, ed. *Sin: Essays in the Moral Tradition in the Western Middle Ages.* Ashgate: Variorum, 2007.

Newman, Barbara. *God and the Goddesses: Vision, Poetry, and Belief in the Middle Ages.* Philadelphia: University of Pennsylvania Press, 2003.

Nitzche, Jane Chance. *The Genius Figure in Antiquity and the Middle Ages.* New York: Columbia University Press, 1975.

Noakes, Susan. "The Double Misreading of Paolo and Francesca." *Philological Quarterly* 62 (1983): 221–39.

Padoan, Giorgio. "Il *Liber Esopi* e due episodi dell'*Inferno.*" *Studi Danteschi* (1964): 75–102.

———. *Il Pio Enea, l'empio Ulisse: Tradizione classica ed intendimento medioevale in Dante.* Ravenna: Longo, 1967.

Pagani, Ileana. *La Teoria linguistica di Dante.* Napoli: Liguore, 1982.

Pagliaro, Antonino. "Dialetto e lingue nell'oltretomba." In *Dante nella critica d'oggi: Risultati e prospettive.* Edited by Umberto Bosco, 254–70. Florence: Le Monnier, 1965.

Panaccio, Claude. "Augustin, le verbe mental e l'amour." In *Les philosophies morales et politiques au Moyen Âge: Proceedings of the 9th International Congress of Medieval Philosophy.* Edited by B. Carlos Bazán et al., 777–85. New York: Legas, 1995.

Papahagi, Marian. *Intelectualitate si poezie.* Bucharest: Cartea Romaneasca, 1986.

Paré, Gérard. *Les idées et les lettres au XIIIe siècle. Le "Roman de la Rose."* Montréal: Centre de Psychologie et de Pédagogie, 1947.

Paris, Gaston. *La Littérature française au Moyen Âge.* Paris: Hachette, 1914.

Patterson, Lee. "For the Wyves Love of Bathe: Feminine Rhetoric and Poetic Resolution in the *Roman de la Rose* and the *Canterburry Tales.*" *Speculum* 58, no. 3 (1983): 656–95.

———. "Feminine Rhetoric and the Politics of Subjectivity: The Old Woman and the Wife of Bath." In *Rethinking the "Romance of the Rose: Text, Image, Reception."* Edited by Kevin Brownlee and Sylvia Huot, 316–35. Philadelphia: University of Pennsylvania Press, 1992.

Patterson, Thomas. "Canto XXVIII: Scandal and Schism." In *Lectura Dantis: Inferno,* edited by Allen Mandelbaum, Anthony Oldcorn, and Charles Ross, 368–78. Berkeley : University of California Press,1998.

Payen, Jean Charles. "Le comique de l'énormité: goliardisme et provocation dans le *Roman de la Rose.*" *L'Esprit créateur* 16 (1976): 46–60.

———. "Eléments Idéologiques et revendications dans le *Roman de la Rose.*" In *Littérature et société au Moyen Âge: Actes du Colloque des 5 et 6 mai d'Amiens 1978.* Amiens: Université de Picardie, 1979. 285–304.

Pelen, Marc M. *Latin Poetic Irony in the "Roman de la Rose."* Liverpool: Cairns, 1987.

Pequigney, Joseph. "Sodomy in Dante's *Inferno* and *Purgatorio.*" *Representations* 36 (1991): 22–42.

Pertile, Lino. "*Inferno* XXVII: Il Peccato di Guido da Montefeltro." *Atti dell'Istituto Veneto di Scienze, Lettere ed Arti* 141 (1982–1983): 148–71.

———. "Canto XXIX: Such Outlandish Wounds." In *Lectura Dantis: Inferno,* edited by Allen Mandelbaum, Anthony Oldcorn, and Charles Ross, 378–91. Berkeley : University of California Press,1998.

———. "Ulisse, Guido e le sirene." *Studi Danteschi* 65 (2000): 101–18.

Pézard, André. *Dante sous la pluie de feu (Enfer, XV).* Paris: Vrin, 1950.

———. "Du *Policraticus* à la *Divine Comédie.*" *Romania* 70, no. 1–2 (1948): 1–36, 163–91.

Poggioli, Renato. "Tragedy or Romance? A Reading of the Paolo and Francesca Episode in Dante's *Inferno.*" *PMLA* 72, no. 3 (1957): 313–58.

Poirion, Daniel. "Les mots et les choses selon Jean de Meun." *L'Information littéraire* 26 (1974): 7–11.

———. "Alain de Lille et Jean de Meun." In *Alain de Lille, Gautier de Chatillon, Jakemart Giélée et leur temps,* 35–51. Lille: Presses Universitaires, 1978.

———. "De la signification chez Jean de Meun." *Recueils d'études médiévales* 3 (1983): 165–85.

Polet, Jean Claude et al., eds. *Patrimoine littéraire européen.* Vol. 5: *Premières mutations: de Petrarque à Chaucer (1304–1400).* Paris: Boeck University, 1995.

Porcelli, Bruno. "*Peccatum linguae,* modello mosaico, climax narrativo nel canto di Ulisse." *Critica letteraria* 19, no. 72 (1991): 423–43.

Pratt, Karen. "*De Vetula*: The Figure of Old Woman in Medieval French Literature." In *Old Age in the Middle Ages and the Renaissance.* Edited by Albert Classen, 321–43. New York: Walter de Gruyter, 2007.

Presberg, Charles. *Adventures in Paradox.* University Park: Pennsylvania State University Press, 2001.

Puttenham, George. *The Art of English Poesy: A Critical Edition.* Edited by Frank Whigham and Wayne A. Rebhorn. Ithaca, N.Y.: Cornell University Press, 2007.

Quilligan, Maureen. "Words and Sex: The Language of Allegory in the *De planctu naturae,* the *Roman de la Rose,* and Book III of the *Faerie Queene.*" *Allegorica* 2 (1977): 195–216.

———. "Allegory, Allegoresis and the Deallegorization of Language: The *Roman de la Rose,* the *De Planctu naturae,* and the *Parlement of Foules.*" In *Allegory, Myth and Symbol.* Edited by Morton W. Bloomfield, 163–86. Cambridge, Mass.: Harvard University Press, 1981.

Radhakrishnan, Manu. "Domenico Cavalca and the "Liber Vitaspatrum": Vernacular Hagiography in Late Medieval and Early Modern Italy." PhD diss., Princeton University, 2012. http://arks.princeton.edu/ark:/88435/dsp01sb397828g.

Reade, William H. V. *The Moral System of Dante's "Inferno."* 2nd ed. Port Washington, N.Y.: Kennikat Press, 1969.

Regalado, Nancy Freeman. "Villon's Legacy from Le Testament de Jean de Meun: Misquotation, Memory, and the Wisdom of Fools." In *Villon at Oxford: The Drama of the Text. Proceedings of the Conference Held at St. Hilda's College Oxford, March 1996,* 282–312. Atlanta: Rodopi, 1999.

Richards, Earl J. *Dante and the "Roman de la Rose": An Investigation into the Vernacular Narrative Context of the "Commedia."* Tübingen: Niemeyer, 1981.

———. "*Les contraires choses:* Irony in Jean de Meun's Part of the *Roman de la Rose* and the Problem of Truth and Intelligibility in Thomas Aquinas." In *Nouvelles de la Rose: Actualité et perspectives du Roman de la Rose.* Edited by Dulce Maria González-Doreste and Maria del Pilar Mendoza-Ramos, 383–398. La Laguna: Universidad de La Laguna, 2011.

Rice, Winthrop Huntington. *The European Ancestry of Villon's Satirical Testaments.* New York: Corporate Press, 1941 .

Rizzo, Stefano. "Il *De Vulgari Eloquentia* e l'unità del pensiero linguistico di Dante." *Dante Studies* 87 (1969): 69–88.

Rossi, Luciano. "Dante, la Rose e il Fiore." In *Studi sul Canone Letterario del Trecento: Per Michelangelo Picone,* 9–32. Edited by Johannes Bartuschat and Luciano Rossi. Ravenna: Longo, 2003.

———. "Alain de Lille, Jean de Meun e Dante, nodi poetici e d'esegesi." *Critica del testo* 7, no. 2 (2004): 851–75.

———. "De Jean Chopinel à Durante: La série *Roman de la Rose-Fiore.*" In *De la Rose: Texte, Image, Fortune.* Edited by Catherine Bel and Herman Braet, 273–98. Dudley, Mass.: Peeters, 2006.

Rossi, Olga A. "Questione del Cavalca: Further Findings." *PMLA* (1949): 829–63.

Ryan, Lawrence W. "Ulysses, Guido and the Betrayal of the Community." *Italica* 54, no. 2 (1977): 227–49.

Ryding, William W. "Faus Semblant: Hero or Hypocrite?" *Romanic Review* 60 (1960): 163–67.

Sanford Matthews, Eva. "The *Verbum Abbreviatum* of Petrus Cantor." In *Transactions and Proceedings of the American Philological Association* (1943), 33–48.

Sanguinetti, Edoardo. *Interpretazione di Malebolge.* Florence: Olschki, 1961.

Schibanoff, Susan. "Sodomy's Mark: Alan of Lille, Jean de Meun, and the Medieval Theory of Authorship." In *Queering the Middle Ages.* Edited by Glenn Burger and Steven F. Kruger, 28–56. Minneapolis: University of Minnesota Press, 2001.

Scipio, Giuseppe C. di. *The Symbolic Rose in Dante's "Paradiso."* Ravenna: Longo Editore, 1984.

———. "*Inferno* XIV." In *Lectura Dantis Virginiana, I. Dante's "Inferno": Introductory Readings.* Edited by Tibor Wlassics, 173–88. Supplement to *Lectura Dantis* 6 (1990). Special Issue. Charlottesville: University of Virginia, 1990.

Scott, John A. "L'Ulisse Dantesco." In *Dante magnanimo: Studi sulla "Commedia,"* 117–93. Florence: Olschki, 1977.

———. "Dante's Francesca and the Poet's Attitude toward Courtly Literature." *Reading Medieval Studies* 5 (1979): 4–20.

Seriacopi, Massimo. *All'estremo della "Prudentia": L'Ulisse di Dante.* Rome: Zauli, 1994.

Shanzer, Danuta. "The Punishment of Bertran de Born." *Yearbook of Italian Studies* 8 (1989): 95–97.

Shapiro, Marianne. "The Fictionalization of Bertran de Born (*Inf.* XXVIII)." *Dante Studies* 92 (1974): 107–16.

———. "On the Role of Rhetoric in the *Convivio.*" *Romance Philology* 40 (1986): 38–64.

Shoaf, Richard Allen. *Dante, Chaucer and the Currency of the Word: Money, Images and Reference in Late Medieval Poetry.* Norman, Ok.: Pilgrim Books, 1983.

———. "Dante and Peraldus: The 'acqua falsa' of Maestro Adamo (A Note on *Inferno* 30, 64–69)." *Quaderni d'italianistica* 10 (1989): 311–13.

Smith, Leslie, and Jane H. M. Taylor, eds. *Women, the Book and the Worldly.* Cambridge: D. S. Brewer, 1995.

Solterer, Helen. *The Master and Minerva: Disputing Women in French Medieval Culture.* Berkeley: University of California Press, 1995.

Spiegel, Gabrielle M. *Romancing the Past: The Rise of Vernacular Prose Historiography in Thirteenth-Century France.* Berkeley: University of California Press, 1993.

Spitzer, Leo. "Speech and Language in *Inferno* XIII." In *Dante: A Collection of Critical Essays.* Edited by John Freccero, 78–101. Englewood Cliffs, N.J.: Prentice-Hall, 1965.

Stakel, Susan. *False Roses: Structures of Duality and Deceit.* Saratoga, Calif.: Anma Libri, 1991.

Storey, H. Wayne. "*Inferno* XVIII." In *Lectura Dantis Virginiana, I. Dante's "Inferno": Introductory Readings.* Edited by Tibor Wlassics, 235–46. Supplement to *Lectura Dantis* 6 (1990). Special Issue. Charlottesville: University of Virginia, 1990.

Szabados, Béla, and Eldon Sofer. *Hypocrisy: Ethical Investigations.* Peterborough, Ontario: Broadview Press, 2004.

Szittya, Penn. *The Antifraternal Tradition in Medieval Literature.* Princeton, N.J.: Princeton University Press, 1986.

Taddei, Telio. "La Vita del Cavalca dai suoi scritti." *Memorie domenicane* 1 (1942).

Tartaro, Achille. "La questione dei voti (*Paradiso* V)." *Letteratura e società* 1 (1980): 21–37.

Thompson, David. "A Note on Fraudulent Counsel." *Dante Studies* 92 (1974): 149–52.

Took, John. *Dante Lyric Poet and Philosopher: An Introduction to the Minor Works.* Oxford: Clarendon Press, 1990.

Torrell, Jean-Pierre. *Saint Thomas Aquinas.* Vol. 1: *The Person and His Work.* Translated by RobertRoyal. Rev. ed. Washington D.C.: The Catholic University of America Press, 2005.

Triolo, Alfred A. "*Ira, Cupiditas, Libido:* The Dynamics of Human Passion in the *Inferno.*" *Dante Studies* 95 (1977): 1–37.

Troiano, Alfredo. "Un contributo alla tradizione manoscritta dello *Specchio di Croce* di Domenico Cavalca: il ms. 129 della Newberry Library di Chicago." *Lettere italiane* 2 (April–June 2008): 226–35.

Trovato, Mario. "Il Contrapasso nell'ottava bolgia." *Dante Studies* 94 (1976): 47–59.

———. "The Semantic Value of Ingegno and Dante's Ulysses in the Light of the *Metalogicon.*" *Modern Philology* 84, no. 3 (1987): 258–66.

Truscott, James G. "Ulysses and Guido: *Inferno* XXVI–XXVII." *Dante Studies* 91 (1974): 47–59.

Vallone, Aldo. "*Inferno* XIV." *Studi Danteschi* 65 (2000): 73–85.

Vanossi, Luigi. *Dante e il "Roman de la Rose": Saggio sul "Fiore."* Florence: Olschski, 1979.

Vauchez, André. *The Laity in the Middle Ages.* Translated by Margery J. Schneider. Notre Dame, Ind.: University of Notre Dame Press, 1993.

Walther, Helmut G. "Utopische Gesellschaftskritik oder Satirische Ironie: Jean de Meung und die Lehre des Aquinaten über die Entstehung menschlicher Herrschaft." *Soziale Ordnungen im Selbstverstaendnis des Mittelalters* 1 (1979): 84–105.

Welter, Jean-Thiébaut. *L'exemplum dans la littérature religieuse et didactique du Moyen Âge.* Paris: Occitania, 1927.

Wenzel, Siegfried. "Dante's Rationale for the Seven Deadly Sins (*Purgatorio* XVII)." *Modern Language Review* 60 (1965): 529–33.

———. "The Seven Deadly Sins: Some Problems of Research." *Speculum* 18 (1968): 1–22.

———. "The Continuing Life of William Peraldus's *Summa vitiorum.*" In *Ad litteram: Authoritative Texts and Their Medieval Readers,* 135–63. Notre Dame, Ind.: University of Notre Dame Press, 1992.

———. *The Peraldus Project.* Web. 12 August 2010. http://www.unc.edu/swenzel/peraldus.html.

Wetherbee, Winthrop. *Platonism and Poetry in the Twelfth Century: The Literary Influence of the School of Chartres.* Princeton, N.J.: Princeton University Press, 1972.

———. "The Literal and the Allegorical: Jean de Meun and the *De planctu naturae.*" *Mediaeval Studies* 33 (1971): 264–91.

White, Hugh. *Nature, Sex, and Goodness in a Medieval Literary Tradition.* Oxford: Oxford University Press, 2000.

Wicksteed, Philip H. *Dante and Aquinas.* New York: E. P. Dutton, 1913.

Wlassics, Tibor, ed. *Lectura Dantis Virginiana, I. Dante's "Inferno": Introductory Readings.* Supplement to *Lectura Dantis* 6 (1990). Special Issue. Charlottesville: University of Virginia, 1990.

Woodford, Christopher. "A Medieval Campaign against Blasphemy." *Downside Review* 55 (1973): 356–61.

Zanchetta, Mauro. "Il 'Pungilingua' di Domenico Cavalca (Edizione)." PhD diss., University of Studies of Padua, 2011.

Ziolkowski, Jan M. *Alan of Lille's Grammar of Sex: The Meaning of Grammar to a Twelfth-Century Intellectual.* Cambridge, Mass.: Medieval Academy of America, 1985.

Zumthor, Paul. "Narrative and Anti-Narrative: *Le Roman de la Rose.*" *Yale French Studies* 51 (1974): 185–204.

Zupan, Patricia. "Dante's Ulysses: Toward Recovering a Primordial Language." *Romance Languages Annual* 1 (1989): 222–26.

Index

The Rose and Geryon: The Poetics of Fraud and Violence in Jean de Meun and Dante was designed and composed in Garamond and Derivia by Kachergis Book Design of Pittsboro, North Carolina. It was printed on 60-pound Sebago Cream and bound by Maple Press of York, Pennsylvania.